THE
LAB

Also by Alice LaPlante

FICTION

Half Moon Bay

Coming of Age at the End of Days

Circle of Wives

Turn of Mind

NONFICTION

Write Yourself Out of a Corner

The Making of a Story: A Norton Guide to Creative Writing

Also by Matthew Clark Davison

FICTION

Doubting Thomas

THE LAB

Experiments in Writing
Across Genre

Matthew Clark Davison and
Alice LaPlante

W. W. NORTON & COMPANY
Independent Publishers Since 1923

For information about permission to reproduce selections from this book, write to
Permissions, W. W. Norton & Company, Inc., 500 Fifth Avenue, New York, NY 10110

For information about special discounts for bulk purchases, please contact
W. W. Norton Special Sales at specialsales@wwnorton.com or 800-233-4830

Manufacturing by Sheridan Chelsea
Book design by Beth Steidle
Production manager: Julia Druskin

Library of Congress Cataloging-in-Publication Data is available.

ISBN 978-0-393-86668-1

W. W. Norton & Company, Inc., 500 Fifth Avenue, New York, NY 10110
www.wwnorton.com

W. W. Norton & Company Ltd., 15 Carlisle Street, London W1D 3BS

1 2 3 4 5 6 7 8 9 0

Contents

THE
LAB

THE
LAB

Welcome to The Lab

In this book, we'll be helping you develop an artistic practice: you'll start by discovering or deepening what you most want to say by generating new material. Once you have something on the page, you'll study existing artistic works and the processes the artists used to realize them. You'll borrow their techniques to deepen your own work. Then you'll decide how you want to shape and revise your material into a final form. We will do this across a spectrum of genres: poetry, fiction, nonfiction, and prose poems, to name a few. We suspect that you will find studying these forms useful whether you have a preferred genre or not. You may even discover a not-yet-named hybrid form.

The goal isn't to force you to adopt a genre you don't feel comfortable with or suited to (although pushing you out of your comfort zone in other ways is one aim of this book). Rather, you will identify and learn techniques that writers in different genres routinely practice, make them your own, and see what wonderful things happen to your work in your chosen genre—whatever that happens to be.

Questions this book will explore:

What makes a poem a poem? How can we use poetic methods and apply them to prose and vice versa?

What is the line between fact and made-up things, and can we traverse it?

What do artists do—what steps do they take—to bring a project from impulse or idea to a finished form?

Encouraging Creativity

Creativity can't be taught, but it can be encouraged. It can be practiced. It can be inspired. It can be prompted. It can even be bullied if you like that teaching style (we don't). Creativity comes from within the individual—from what makes you uniquely *you*.

We have developed techniques to lure creativity to come forth from its shy, elusive place. We'll be applying those techniques in this book. The question we get from so many students is *Do you think I have it in me to be a writer?* The answer is *Of course!*

All would-be writers need tools—craft skills—to give shape to the observations they unlock from the elusive place. And craft can be taught. Those students who combine creativity techniques with the craft that they learn are eventually able to transform their initial noticings, impulses, and obsessions into art worthy of sharing with an audience.

A traditional textbook would first explain the theories behind various creativity or craft techniques and then encourage you to try to practice them. We'll often do the opposite. First, we may ask you to write. Don't worry—we won't force you to face the blank page without help. You will be given some very specific prompts, with very explicit directions. You will write. And then we'll look at what you've done and explain the theory behind it. We'll say, *Write Now* and you will, and you will surprise yourself with what you've done. We'll do some reading to deepen your understanding of what you've done. And we'll give you plenty of examples along the way to guide you. That's Part I.

By the time you reach Part II, you'll have a portfolio of work and a foundational understanding of how to productively gather more data (do more writing).

We'll then take you through three genres more systematically: fiction, creative nonfiction, and poetry. No one will be doodling in their notebook (unless those doodles help the writer's project) or staring at the clock. We'll examine techniques of craft and style that are unique to each genre. And we'll then experiment more—introduce condensed imagery of poetry into nonfiction, for example, or facts from nonfiction into fiction. And we'll see where it gets us. Again, the point isn't to force you in any one direction, but to open new possibilities for your own work.

Adopting the Scientific Method

Scientists analyze and replicate the processes used in others' experiments to arrive at something new. This replication, strictly adhered to at first, eventually gets modified—changes that, step by step, hopefully leads to new processes and insights.

The scientific method is a method of research in which a problem is identified through systematic observation, relevant data is gathered, a novel hypothesis is formulated from this data, and the hypothesis is empirically tested and honed to get the best result.

In scientific lingo, the word *novel* gets thrown around a lot. It's used more often in relation to results than techniques (although it certainly can be applied to new and exciting techniques). So what does the word *novel* mean in this context? *New and not resembling something formerly known or used*, according to Merriam-Webster.

We didn't call this book *The Lab* by accident. And we don't use the word *experiment* lightly. First, we ask you to experiment with processes inspired by the published work we examine. We try on the techniques and use the tools that other artists have used successfully, continually modifying to discover novel techniques as we go along.

Isn't all writing an experiment, then? We don't want to stretch the metaphor too far, but it holds firm for many aspects of writing.

Systematic observation: The word *observation* is defined as the act of noticing something or making a judgment or inference from something seen or experienced. For example, you notice an odd interaction between your loved ones. Not a fight, exactly, but body language and facial expressions that indicate something is happening between them. It puzzles you. It even worries you. What on earth is going on? There. You've observed. You have a mystery. You have the inspiration—you could call it the roots of an obsession.

Problem identified: We wouldn't call this a problem, per se, but the urge to create, to write something down, or perhaps to *re*-create a feeling or experience. Perhaps the so-called problem is simply the challenge: *I must write this down.* Or *can I do this?* Or *why did this happen?* Or *what does this mean?*

Data collected: We write down our observations, we try to re-create the experience for others, and we try to move others the way we are moved by our material—our observations.

Hypothesis formulated: Our hypothesis is that we will emotionally impact people with our selection and placement of words. We might even go so far as to plan and prescribe the emotional direction we hope to move people, although that is a little risky for reasons we will explain later in the book.

Testing (experiment): We test how effective the results are—on ourselves or, better, on readers. Do I get the reaction I want from my readers? Why or why not? What happens if I do something different? Take the barking dog out of the scene? Trigger a fight between the mother and son? Change the point of view to the neighbor? We modify and iterate. Over and over. This is called revising, and each "experiment" is thus a draft. It is not uncommon for writers to do many drafts before they feel satisfied with the results.

Authors known for their multiple drafts include Leo Tolstoy, who rewrote the whole of *War and Peace* seven times, and James Baldwin, who would rip things up and start over. Roald Dahl's *New York Times* obituary even mentions that he commonly spent six months on a story, his writing being "far from effortless."

Said James Baldwin:

> Sometimes it comes very quickly. Seems almost to come from the top of my head. But in fact, it's been gestating for a long, long time. Most of the time it's not like that. Usually it's a matter of writing, recognizing it ain't right or it won't move. You tear it up and do it again and again. And then one day something happens—it works.

Said Roald Dahl:

> By the time I am nearing the end of a story, the first part will have been reread and altered and corrected at least one hundred and fifty times. I am suspicious of both facility and speed. Good writing is essentially rewriting. I am positive of this.

Observing the Writer-Scientist at Work

Here's an example of the scientific method applied to writing:

Memoirist Mona Hanna-Attisha is a teacher and doctor, a professor at Michigan State University and a pediatrician at the Hurley Children's Hospital Pediatric Public Health Initiative. She had been taking care of kids in Michigan with lead poisoning for more than a decade, both from Flint and from Detroit, yet "I never knew, in all my training, that there was the possibility of lead in the water," she said.

Hanna-Attisha wrote *What the Eyes Don't See*, a memoir of her experiences. Here's how we saw her applying the scientific method to writing, as reflected in a Q&A in the magazine *American Scientist* conducted by Katie L. Burke.

Systematic observation: Children in her practice were suffering from a disproportionate number of complications due to lead poisoning. Blood samples from her patients contained elevated lead levels.

Problem identified: "If you haven't thought about something, you're not going to recognize it as a problem. That was my story," she said. Then she saw the connection between the poisoning she'd been treating in the children and the tap water they'd been drinking. That's when she knew she had to write a book.

Data collected: She worked with other scientists to prove the link between lead in the water and her patients' illness. She also compared the crisis in her community to other public health crises tied to systemic racism and poverty. She likely studied other nonfiction books written by doctors.

Hypothesis formulated: Dr. Hanna-Attisha figured if she could present the evidence and tell the story of Flint, she'd help improve Flint's conditions and prevent and ensure safety measures for its citizens—especially the children. She'd also expose those who knowingly allowed the problem to continue. She wanted justice for those who'd suffered.

Testing: Based on other interviews Hanna-Attisha gave, we can see that she first tried to write a medical-based, journalistic exposé—like those she likely studied. The early drafts focused on an extensive history of the city of Flint, the facts about the switch from Detroit to a Flint river for water, as well as systemic injustices elsewhere. But in the writing, her own family story kept coming up. She said, "I think it is a surprise to a lot of people when they read my book, because they expect that they're just going to read about Flint, and they say, 'What's all this weird family history stuff in here?' But my family was impossible to separate from the story, including the stories of my grandfather. When I started to write, I wanted the book to be only about

Flint, but with our current political climate and the anti-immigration movement, it became increasingly important for me to include that family history. To understand what I was doing and why I was doing it, you have to know who you are and where you came from."

Thus, in her *experiments*—using the techniques employed by other writers of such books—Hanna-Attisha discovered a limitation. Something wasn't working for her. She needed to expand her original plan to accommodate the unexpected thread of her family's story.

In this book, we call any "unexpected thread" the *nonconforming oddity*. It may be that section that a traditional writing workshop tells you to "cut" out of adherence to static ideas of form and consistency. But we will encourage you to identify those moments as possible gold among the straw—and then see if your piece, in its final draft, earns it. What do we mean by "earn"? You'll notice that it's a phrase we use throughout this book. We're asking, did the nonconforming oddity add to the richness of the world portrayed in the final draft? Did it move the story forward? Create atmosphere or sound that underscores or contrasts thematic concerns? These are a few ways writers "earn" their oddities in revision. (More on how nonconforming oddities are earned later.)

The title of Hanna-Attisha's book—*What the Eyes Don't See*—was even inspired by a literary source, a line from *Lady Chatterley's Lover* by D. H. Lawrence: "What the eye doesn't see and the mind doesn't know, doesn't exist."

Even though she was trained as a doctor, she didn't *see* the link between the tap water and lead poisoning—until she did. Once this fact became visible, her mind expanded and steered her toward other questions: about her family, her history as the daughter of Iraqi immigrants, the country her parents immigrated to, and herself. It's what she uncovered and shared after exploring this series of questions—this nonconforming oddity—that helped earn her praise for novel work.

Meara Sharma, who reviewed the book for *The Washington Post*, said that Hanna-Attisha's quest is "full of drama and suspense." She called the narrator "a breezy, charismatic raconteur," pointing out the author's "feisty character descriptions" by citing a spokesman for the Department of Environmental Quality as "a rabid pit bull" and a turn-of-the-century anti-lead activist as "a stubborn badass."

In the same article, Sharma reviewed another book that delves into the same subject matter (Flint's water) but did not compel her. She said that the other book "is meticulously researched. But in pursuit of comprehensiveness, the book can feel tedious and distant, missing a human element."

The first book allowed the nonconforming oddity. The second stayed true to an existing form.

We're not saying the second book failed because of one reviewer's comments. Scientists can't usually publish papers with such colorful language, and they don't interject their personal histories or weave in politics, either, because that's not the aim.

But it *is* the aim for creative writers. Creative writing makes people feel.

Avoiding Self-Congratulation

As we're doing our experiments—writing our drafts—we must be careful to avoid what scientists call "confirmation bias." This is the tendency to look for and see only evidence that confirms what we already believe. In our writing, this would be our own belief that we have, for example, successfully "earned" that nonconforming oddity when we haven't. If we need to explain or justify how a tangent or incongruent image is enriching, it may not be earned. It is the mistaken conviction that we have finished a piece and that it actually works—that it will emotionally move readers the way we ourselves were moved when inspired to write it.

Many times, we haven't experimented enough, or adequately collected—and presented—sufficient data. We have failed to connect the dots—be they logical or emotional—between the sentences we have written.

In an Instagram post, writer Yiyun Li wrote about seeing an exhibition at the Glyptoteket Museum in Copenhagen, a glass case full of dozens of "noses that lost their statues." Li wrote: "The orphaned noses are like the characters that got cut from novels (including a librarian in Buffalo, NY, with 150 pages of his story), from [her novel] *The Book of Goose*."

Sometimes, it takes work to tell what should be cut and what should stay. That's why we need time and space. Some of us also use readers. We must keep experimenting (revising) to ensure we've found the *mots justes*, the precisely right words, in exactly the right order, to bring the news of our world (as Raymond Carver would say) to others.

In this book, we talk about the "unit of satisfaction." This is what we aim for. Not necessarily change. Not necessarily even resolution. And especially not redemption.

These are effects we might legitimately strive for when writing. But they are not required to make a poem or piece of prose "finished."

It's a "sense of completeness" that is transmitted from the writer to the reader. It doesn't necessarily involve an epiphany. None of the other traditional litmus tests of whether a creative piece is "done" are involved. It's just the sense that the reader has been well served by reading—by experiencing—the work. We'll say more in upcoming chapters.

Trying a Simpler Approach

The scientific method we are proposing here is remarkably like what the poet Philip Larkin suggests poets do in his essay "The Pleasure Principle." Only in Larkin's opinion, writing a successful creative work has just three distinct steps to it.

1. A person becomes obsessed with something to the degree that they are "compelled to do something about it." This is what we have called "the problem."
2. The person writes down words (what Larkin calls "a verbal device") that attempt to capture the original experience in such a way that anyone who cares to read it will have the same experience reproduced for them.
3. Other people, from diverse backgrounds and cultures, can read the words and "set off" the device that then re-creates what the writer originally thought, felt, or experienced. In other words, the placement of words on a page triggers the *re-creation* of the obsession in the reader's mind (or, if you like, heart).

As Larkin says,

> If there has been no preliminary feeling, the device has nothing to reproduce and the reader will experience nothing. If the second stage has not been well done, the device will not deliver the goods, or will deliver only the goods to a few people, or will stop delivering them after an absurdly short while. And if there is no third stage, successful reading, the [creative work] can hardly be seen to exist in a practical sense at all.

Larkin got it right. We first feel something. We experience something. Then we have the urge to write it down.

Notice how carefully Larkin separates step 1 (the obsession) from step 2 (the "verbal device"). He's clear that without the obsession, it's a no go. Then, and only then, does craft knowledge help. Larkin stresses the need to close the loop with a reader. Yes, you can be your own reader. Yes, there is immense satisfaction in *naming* something we are feeling. But writing is, at its heart, communication. And for it to truly succeed, you need to communicate what you are trying to say—ideally to another human being.

Of course, this doesn't mean that you must experience something personally to write emotionally resonant stuff. If that were the case, we'd only be able to write nonfiction—only about things that were factual, or true. There are countless numbers of books of completely made-up things that move us deeply. That's because the imagination is enormously intoxicating. The human mind is complex. We can become as obsessed with things that are not true as with things that actually happened. It's like the false memories that scientists have discovered embed themselves in the brain so as to be physiologically indistinguishable from real memories. The human mind is very powerful and strange.

Did these things-that-didn't-really-happen come from your mind? They certainly did. Are they then not yours? They certainly are. As Gustave Flaubert famously said, "Madame Bovary, c'est moi." What could he have meant by that?

We guess that he "understood" Emma Bovary—that he entered her joys and sorrows personally—and that he, himself, accepted responsibility for her creation. Flaubert's "real" life as a cosmopolitan French writer stands in sharp contrast to Emma Bovery—a dissatisfied, bored suburban housewife. Still, the intensity of his experiences—lived through her—drove him to write his masterpiece.

Trusting That Your Weirdnesses Are Your Strengths

In her memoir *I Know Why the Caged Bird Sings*, Maya Angelou said, "Anything that worked against you, can work for you once you understand the principle of reverse."

You don't want to write down conventional wisdom—what everybody knows—but what you and only you know. And although this certainly includes facts (you may be an expert on giant tube worms who live deep in the Pacific Ocean), more often this will be the particular way you see the world. Perhaps the observations you draw from being an expert on giant tube worms gives you a keen insight into human behavior. Or perhaps you were just born with a singular point of view that you've learned to hide from others. Now—in your writing—is the time to let all that loose. In this book, we are going to encourage you to go deep inside yourself to discover your own weirdnesses and truths—and give you the tools to render them precisely on the page and to (again, Carver) carry news from your world to ours.

Staying Alert for Stories and Histories That Are Underrepresented or Portrayed Without Complexity

Writing allows the exploration of the inner life of the individual within a broader community. Toni Morrison famously said that she wrote *The Bluest Eye* because she wanted to read it. The journalist, writer, and cultural critic Hilton Als, in a piece called "Toni Morrison's Profound and Unrelenting Vision," published in *The New Yorker* on the fiftieth anniversary of *The Bluest Eye*, talked about Morrison's contributions to humanity with her writing and editing: "Like Morrison's writing, her editing had a very particular goal: to offer readers stories about blacks, women, and other marginalized characters which hadn't been told before."

Morrison demonstrated this repeatedly in her career, even though her professor at Howard University was "outraged" that she wanted to focus on the Black characters in Shakespeare's plays. Als went onto say:

> I knew that, in my small, working-class West Indian community in Brooklyn, my sexuality was considered ugly. My black world then (and, to be frank, it hasn't changed much) defined itself by the rules of heterosexuality, and one of the few things its inhabitants could agree on was how spiritually abhorrent gay people were—at best, objects of derision. I felt as trapped in Brooklyn as Pecola [the main character in Morrison's *The Bluest Eye*] did in [the novel's setting of] Lorain [Ohio].

For years, in his own writing, Als tried to overturn what *The Bluest Eye* predicted for him—and other under- or misrepresented peoples—a "type of madness" from trying to live happily in the existing society. "I didn't grow up at a time when you talked about the problem of not seeing yourself in books or of 'negative' portrayals," he wrote. *The Bluest Eye* changed that.

In an interview for *The New York Times*, Concepción de León asked C Pam Zhang about the inspiration for her book *How Much of These Hills Is Gold*:

> "I was so struck by the landscape of America...," [Zhang] said, recalling areas where they were pounded by torrential rain or in the plains of Oklahoma, where she could see weather patterns from miles away. "It's really beautiful but also, in many parts of the country, extremely bleak and kind of scary."
>
> Those lasting impressions informed her reading habits. A fan of Laura Ingalls Wilder and John Steinbeck, she said, "Eventually I realized that the people in these books that I loved were always white. I wanted to write a great American epic in which I saw myself reflected."

Like Morrison and Zhang, with each story you tell of an erased, misunderstood, or under- or non-represented person or community, you make way for multitudes of stories by others.

How to Use This Book

We wrote this book to mirror the way we teach. In Part I, we aim to inspire you to first observe what, from all that's around you, stirs something deep. Eventually, we encourage you to hone in on what moves you in another's work and, borrowing techniques, collect data in one place (write). Then you'll step back and look at what you've done: what's worth keeping, what's worth repeating. What's *novel*. We supplement this with readings—both creative works and works by writers about writing and craft.

You'll modify as necessary until you have a strong portfolio of "experiments" completed. In Part II, we really go to town on craft. We examine each of three genres—poetry, fiction, and nonfiction—and pull out what is unique from each. Then we give you exercises on applying these techniques even if you write *outside* of that chapter's genre. Stay alert, because fiction writers may find something applicable from the poetry section and vice versa. We'll also dedicate a chapter to cross-genre writing.

Speaking of the exercises, these are essential aspects of the book. You can't get a degree in chemistry without spending some hands-on time in the lab, and you can't learn to write (or learn to write better) without the same. These exercises have been carefully designed to push you in unexpected directions—so be prepared to be surprised by what you write. You are going to learn not just about craft and theory but about your own material—things that you might not have anticipated.

Here are three other things we'd like you to consider as you embark on your journey with this book.

Identifying Your First Language(s)

We'll encourage you to find your own voice (paradoxically, we'll sometimes recommend that you imitate others in pursuit of that), by which we mean eschewing formal or stilted prose or writing the way that was drilled into you by high school teachers who were seeking logically structured essays.

Try to find a voice that is genuine and unique to you. The caveat is, of course, unless you're writing in the voice of a character or a "persona" that is deliberately unlike you. That's a perfectly valid creative choice. But otherwise, seek that novel voice and sensibility that you and only you can write from.

The poet June Jordan encouraged her students to write in their "first languages," and it was up to them how they defined those languages. Her famous Poetry for the People classes were taught in English, a language each person in the class shared. But she encouraged students—if it was central to the vision of their piece—to use any other language. Students named quite a few languages they had access to, including "Black English," "Spanglish," "mixed Mandarin," and "gay English."

If you have access to a particular slang or a second or third or fourth language, mine it. If your grandparents pronounce words differently than your parents do or than you do and you see it as serving your project, use any and all of them. Above all, do not try to write in a way that someone else may have told you is "appropriate." Appropriate is for tea parties.

Honing Your Reading

Writers usually start by reading. But this can be tricky when searching for work that we personally find meaningful. Back in the day, to earn a college degree, we had to read a lot by writers we called "dead white guys." But if your beliefs or lived experiences are not validated by reading what's considered mainstream, you can become alienated rather than inspired. So it might take a little effort for you to find literary works that illuminate your lived experiences, the worldviews you want to explore (or challenge), or your own personal aesthetics. Our aesthetics (what we consider beautiful) are significantly influenced by who we are as individuals within the communities we belong to, how we identify ourselves both inside and outside those communities, and the geographies and cultures we and our ancestors came from. So, we encourage you to expand your reading (we'll try to help) to develop aesthetics that work for you as a writer—whether such works can be found in the public library or on a bestseller list or not.

Remember, Teaching Is (and Teachers Are) Highly Subjective

We hope it won't take you long to discover the subjectivity that informs creative writing books, programs, workshops, and teachers of all kinds. We are not asserting anything as objective fact—but giving you possible jumping-off places to experiment and find the "data" and processes and forms that work for you.

And as we will continue to say, take the suggestions we offer, use them however you want, break them open and modify them, and, if you see value in them, pass on your enhanced versions to others—and encourage them to do the same.

We hope you enjoy the experience.

Matthew Clark Davison and Alice LaPlante
Oakland, CA, and Mallorca, Spain
Winter 2025

PART I

Experiment

What Moves You

You've now heard from us. You know a bit about what we think. Now it's time to hear from you. So, let's jump right in. As we said in the Introduction, in Part I you will be experimenting: generating lots of material in responses to prompts. We'll then be building on—discovering and developing—the material you generate here in Parts II and III as we explore and experiment with the various genres: poetry, fiction, creative nonfiction, and hybrid work.

Chapter 1

Write Like a MF

> "You have to write the book that wants to be written. And if the book will be too difficult for grown-ups, then you write it for children."
> **—Madeleine L'Engle**

> "A writer is someone who has taught his mind to misbehave."
> **—Oscar Wilde**

These experiments can be done in any genre from any perspective. You can write a poem as yourself. Or you can write one from the point of view of a character, a persona who is most definitely *not* you. Or you can start out as you and later slide into fictionalizing (called autofiction). No matter what you do, it's all good. The goal we have in Part I? To write about what matters to you.

Write Now

We encourage you to dig deep, to get into that stuff full of mystery, contradiction, and ambiguity. Good writing often involves rendering what's mysterious and ambiguous through what can be seen, heard, smelled, tasted, and touched—not attempting to solve that mystery or resolve that ambiguity (that piece of advice is from Flannery O'Connor). The poet W. S. Merwin once told a workshop at Stanford that "poetry is the exact rendering of an ambiguity." We like that. Ambiguity, check. Exact, check. Rendering, check. Now you're going to try doing that.

1. Write a piece (any genre, any persona) beginning with the sentence "I have always wondered why . . ."
2. Pick something very specific, about a person, place, or situation you (or your persona) know well. Think of small things, not big philosophical ones. Not "I have always wondered why people can be so petty," but "I have always wondered why my father repeats the phrase *I'm tired, tired, tired* over and over after he gets home from work."

3. Render a description of the person, place, or situation precisely. Do not try to solve the mystery. Do not speculate about *why*. Concentrate on *what*. Write concretely so you put your readers *there* so they can experience the mystery for themselves.
4. Stuck? Need inspiration? Read what Joan Didion said about writing and check out the student example as well.

Writing Down the Details

Joan Didion wrote about her obsession with using details—real or made up—to bring memories to life in her essay "On Keeping a Notebook." Here are her thoughts on why writers feel compelled to write things down and why a traditional diary didn't work for her:

> In fact I have abandoned altogether that kind of pointless entry [a traditional diary]. Instead I tell what some would call lies. "That's simply not true," the members of my family frequently tell me when they come up against my memories of a shared event. "The party was not for you, the spider was not a black widow, it wasn't that way at all."
>
> Similarly, perhaps it never really did snow that August in Vermont; perhaps there never were flurries in the night wind, and maybe no one else felt the ground hardening and summer already dead even though we pretended to bask in it, *but that was how it felt to me, and it might as well have snowed, could have snowed, did snow. How it felt to me. This is getting closer to the truth.* [emphasis ours]

Note how interesting it is that Didion needs the details, even though they were (probably) false, to conjure up meaning from her memories.

> **STUDENT EXAMPLE (by Jeanette Russo)**
> I have always wondered why my father repeats the phrase *I'm tired, tired, tired* over and over after he gets home from work.
>
> My father always told everyone the story of how hard he had it. Times were rough. Jobs were hard to come by. When I was born he had two dollars in his pocket and a quart of milk in the fridge. When I was 10 he told

me that if he had it to do over again, he wouldn't have had any children. My mother, who'd had a sheltered upbringing, had to do piecework in a sewing factory with *vulgar women*. And she had three daughters in as many years.

Still, when I was a little girl, perhaps five or six, I was crazy about my dad. We lived in a small upstairs apartment and at five o'clock we could hear his work boots heavily climbing the stairs. I would throw myself on him, even though he was covered with his day dust—powdered cement, paint, tar— whatever he had been working on that day. It was hard graft, but he didn't have a full-time job, so he was grateful for what he could pick up.

When I was 16, we experienced a horrible tragedy. My middle sister died in a car accident. My father cried all the time. He started coming home later and later from work. His boots still sounded on the stairs, and woke me up. I would get up and kiss him. He always smelled of whiskey, an odor that is attractive to me to this day on men. He went out on weekends without us. He didn't seem to sleep much and still complained that he was so tired, tired, tired all of the time.

Now you've written your first piece, put it aside. Don't share it with anyone yet. It's just the first experiment, like a first reaction that a chemist achieves in a lab. You'll now move on to the next stage. In essence, you're gathering data so you can form your hypothesis at the end of Part I.

We encourage you to find your own notebook and start filling it with detailed observations, excerpts from books, and quotes from writers, artists, and thinkers that stir something unexpected in you.

Write Now

In this second experiment, you will explore your fears and desires as a writer.

1. You will make two lists. You will label the first list "FEARS" and the second list "DESIRES."
2. Under "FEARS," list all the things you are afraid will happen when you publicly share the piece you've just written with your class, writing group, or readers.

You might include all the ways you'll get it wrong. Be genuine. Don't worry—no one will ever see this list. It's for your data-gathering purposes only. For example:

- *I fear that as people read the piece, they will see my limitations as a human being.*
- *I fear that I will reveal things about myself that I'd rather keep hidden.*
- *I fear that as I read others' pieces, I will compare myself with them and feel envious.*
- *I fear that this piece will show my ineptitude, that I cannot write well or with intelligence.*
- *I fear that my piece won't move anyone emotionally.*
- *I fear my poem will be disregarded, mocked, and I will be laughed at.*

Now, under "DESIRES," write down all the things you'd like to achieve with this particular exercise you just completed. Again, be very, very specific. You might include the impact you hope your piece will have on your potential audiences, or perhaps what you hope to gain for yourself through writing it.

- *I want to capture the essence of my father. He died too young. I miss him.*
- *I want to write about my father. My father's story is one I can't live without telling.*
- *I want to understand my father.*
- *I want others to see my father, really see him, feel real empathy for him.*

3. Reread what you wrote. Underscore one entry on each of your two lists that you *least* expected to see.
4. Put your lists aside for now. We'll be doing something with them later.

Read Excerpts from "Dear Sugar"

Before the book *Wild* made Cheryl Strayed a *New York Times* best-selling memoirist, she'd been a working writer, a novelist, and a mom living in Portland, Oregon. She toiled away on *Wild*, which her website describes this way:

At twenty-two, Cheryl Strayed thought she had lost everything. In the wake of her mother's death, her family scattered and her own marriage was soon destroyed. Four years later, with nothing more to lose, she made the most impulsive decision of her life. With no experience or training, driven only by blind will, she would hike more than a thousand miles of the Pacific Crest Trail from the Mojave Desert through California and Oregon to Washington State—and she would do it alone.

Strayed wrote that memoir while dedicating herself to an unpaid gig as an anonymous advice columnist for a literary website called *The Rumpus*. The column became wildly popular, which increased the hype when she finally revealed her identity—and undoubtedly helped get word out about her memoir.

The following is a set of excerpts from a letter from a young writer named Elissa Bassist to "Sugar," Strayed's anonymous alter ego. Read it and read excerpts of Sugar's response. While you read, note any phrases that particularly resonate with you or inspire you—either in Elissa's letter or Sugar's response.

DEAR SUGAR, *The Rumpus* Advice Column #48: Write Like a Motherfucker

Dear Sugar,

I write like a girl. I write about my lady life experiences, and that usually comes out as unfiltered emotion, unrequited love, and eventual discussion of my vagina as metaphor. . . .

. . . Right now, I am a pathetic and confused young woman of 26, a writer who can't write. . . . David Foster Wallace called himself a failed writer at 28. Several months ago, when depression hooked its teeth into me, I complained to my then-boyfriend about how I'll never be as good as Wallace; he screamed at me on Guerrero Street in San Francisco, "STOP IT. HE KILLED HIMSELF, ELISSA. I HOPE TO GOD YOU ARE NEVER LIKE HIM." . . .

. . . my phobia that to be a writer/a woman/a woman writer means to suffer mercilessly and eventually collapse in a heap of "I could have been better than *this*." . . .

I want to jump out the window for what I've boiled down to is one reason: I can't write a book. . . . I know I'm not the first depressed writer. "Depressed writer"—because the latter is less accurate, the former is more acute. I've been clinically diagnosed with major depressive disorder and have an off-and-on relationship with prescription medication, which I confide so it doesn't seem I throw around the term "depression."

That said, I'm high-functioning—a high-functioning head-case, one who jokes enough that most people don't know the truth. The truth: I am sick with panic that I cannot—will not—override my limitations, insecurities, jealousies, and ineptitude, to write well, with intelligence and heart and lengthiness. And I fear that even if I do manage to write, that the stories I write—about my vagina, etc.—will be disregarded and mocked.

How do I reach the page when I can't lift my face off the bed? How does one go on, Sugar, when you realize you might not have it in you? How does a woman get up and become the writer she wishes she'd be?

Sincerely,

Elissa Bassist

* * *

Dear Elissa Bassist,

When I was 29 I had a chalkboard in my living room. It was one of those two-sided wooden A-frames that stand on their own and fold flat. On one side of the chalkboard I wrote, *"The first product of self-knowledge is humility,"* Flannery O'Connor and on the other side I wrote, *"She sat and thought of only one thing, of her mother holding and holding onto their hands,"* Eudora Welty.

I sat like that too. Thinking of only one thing. One thing that was actually two things pressed together, like the back-to-back quotes on my chalkboard: how much I missed my mother and how the only way I could bear to live without her was to write a book. *My* book. That I hadn't written the book by the time I was 29 was a sad shock to me. Of myself, I'd expected greater things. I was a bit like you then, Elissa Bassist. . . . I wrote stories in feverish, intermittent bursts, believing they'd miraculously form a novel without my having to suffer too much over it.

But I was wrong. As my 30th birthday approached, I realized that if I truly wanted to write the story I had to tell, I would have to gather everything within me to make it happen. I thought a lot of the same things about myself that you do, Elissa Bassist. That I was lazy and lame. That even though

I had the story in me, I didn't have it in me to see it to fruition . . . I'd finally reached a point where the prospect of not writing a book was more awful than the one of writing a book that sucked. And so at last, I got to serious work on the book.

To get to the point I had to get to write my first book, I had to do everything I did in my twenties. I had to waste time and grieve my mother and come to terms with my childhood and have stupid and sweet and scandalous sexual relationships and grow up. In short, I had to gain the self-knowledge that Flannery O'Connor mentions in that quote I wrote on my chalkboard. And once I got there I had to make a hard stop at self-knowledge's first product: humility.

Do you know what that is, sweet pea? To be humble? The word comes from the Latin words *humilis* and *humus*. To be *down low*. To be *of the earth*. To be *on the ground*. That's where I went when I wrote the last word of my first book. Straight onto the cool tile floor to weep. I'd stopped being grandiose. I'd lowered myself to the notion that the absolute only thing that mattered was getting that extra beating heart out of my chest. Which meant I had to write my book. My very possibly mediocre book. My very possibly never-going-to-be-published book. My absolutely no-where-in-league-with-the-writers-I'd-admired-so-much-that-I-practically-memorized-their-sentences book. It was only then, when I humbly surrendered, that I was able to do the work I needed to do.

I hope you'll think hard about that, honey bun. If you had a two-sided chalkboard in your living room I'd write *humility* on one side and *surrender* on the other for you. That's what I think you need to find and do to get yourself out of the funk you're in. The most fascinating thing to me about your letter is that buried beneath all the anxiety and sorrow and fear and self-loathing, there's arrogance at its core. It presumes you *should* be successful at 26, when really it takes most writers so much longer to get there. It laments that you'll never be as good as David Foster Wallace—a genius, a master of the craft—while at the same time describing how little you write. You loathe yourself, and yet you're consumed by the grandiose ideas you have about your own importance. You're up too high and down too low. Neither is the place where we get any work done.

We get the work done on the ground level. And the kindest thing I can do for you is to tell you to get your ass on the floor. I can tell you that you're not alone in your insecurities and fears; they're typical of writers, even those who don't have depression. Artists of all stripes reading this will understand your struggles. Including me.

Another layer of your anxiety seems rooted in your concern that as a woman your writing, which features "unfiltered emotion, unrequited love," and discussion of your "vagina as metaphor" will be taken less seriously than that of men. Yes, sweet pea, it probably will. Our culture has made significant progress when it comes to sexism and racism and homophobia, but we're not all the way there. It's still true that literary works by women, gays, and writers of color are often framed as specific rather than universal, small rather than big, personal or particular rather than socially significant. There are things you can do to shed light on and challenge those biases and bullshit moves. Organizations like Vida exist in order to connect women writers to do just that.

But the best possible thing you can do is get your ass down onto the floor.... How many women wrote beautiful novels and stories and poems and essays and plays and scripts and songs in spite of all the crap they endured. How many of them didn't collapse in a heap of "I could have been better than *this*" and instead went right ahead and became better than anyone would have predicted or allowed them to be. The unifying theme is resilience and faith. The unifying theme is being a warrior and a motherfucker. It is not fragility. It's strength. It's nerve. And "if your Nerve, deny you—," as Emily Dickinson wrote, "go above your Nerve." Writing is hard for every last one of us—straight white men included. Coal mining is harder. Do you think miners stand around all day talking about how hard it is to mine for coal? They do not. They simply *dig*.

You need to do the same, dear sweet arrogant beautiful crazy talented tortured rising star glowbug. That you're so bound up about writing tells me that writing is what you're here to do. And when people are here to do that they almost always tell us something we need to hear. I want to know what you have inside you. I want to see the contours of your second beating heart.

So write, Elissa Bassist. Not like a girl. Not like a boy. Like a motherfucker.

Yours,

Sugar

1. Which lines made you feel something when reading Elissa's letter? Which of her lines allowed you to align yourself with her? Which of them alienated you? Why?
2. Which lines made you feel something when reading Sugar's response? Which of her lines motivated you? Which of them discouraged you? Why?
3. Do you feel more or less inclined to write after reading this exchange of letters? Can you articulate why?

Looking and Doing

Now that you've both written something and read "Dear Sugar," let's hear what other artists of all types have to say about the creative process.

Charles D'Ambrosio was interviewed in *The New Yorker* by memoirist Leslie Jamison in a piece called "Instead of Sobbing You Write Sentences."

D'AMBROSIO: On a practical level, I'm just not an abstract thinker. Asked to consider a weighty ontological matter—why is there something rather than nothing?—I'll draw a blank. But if you give me a place to stand and some kind of plot, even the flimsiest situation, and a character, a line or two of dialogue, the ideas start to bubble up out of the context. It's like they get pressured into being.

JAMISON: I've known Charlie for nearly a decade: he has been a teacher, a mentor, and a friend. I'm grateful for what he's shown me about how writing can make a mess—and how this mess can move us deeper into the quivering nerve endings of a subject. In workshop, he was hard on our stories because he believed in what they could be. *In [his] essays he is hard on easy answers and false resolution because he believes in what lies beyond them.* [emphasis ours]

D'Ambrosio wants his students—wants us—to eschew being part of the crowd, to embrace our oddities and the oddities of others: "[You must] go around doing as Whitman says you should do, you stand up for the stupid and the crazy. You take ridiculous positions, you defend the indefensible, probably because you know you're ridiculous and indefensible too."

Nonconforming Oddities

We first saw the phrase "nonconforming oddities" (something we'll return to again and again) in the book *101 Things I Learned in Architecture School* by Matthew Frederick, an architect and urban designer. Frederick believes that "nonconforming oddities" can be the clues to what your artistic material is about—the truly rich, human aspects, we'd say—of what you need to write.

Examples of this are Joan Didion's August snowstorm and Elissa Bassist's vagina-as-metaphor. Frederick wants us to honor what Leslie Jamison called "the mess."

Keep this Matthew Frederick quote close as you write:

> Designers are often hampered by a well-intentioned but erroneous belief that a good design solution is perfectly systematic and encompasses all aspects of a design problem without exception. But nonconforming oddities can be enriching, humanizing aspects of your project. Indeed, exceptions to the rule are often more interesting than the rules themselves.

Look at how we would paraphrase what Frederick wrote for writers:

> Writers are often hampered by a well-intentioned but erroneous belief that a story or poem is systematic and encompasses all aspects of craft. But nonconforming oddities can be the most enriching and humanizing aspects of your story or poem.

So, what would a nonconforming oddity look like in writing? We've given you a couple of examples, but it could be any unexpected, seemingly incongruent image, an unconventional point-of-view shift, or even an unusual slip in language or diction. When you find yourself wanting to put something in that goes against the so-called rules, don't hesitate. Put it in. Or if your subconscious is in control of your draft, and suddenly your character is burying her father's gold watch in the tuna salad—for no apparent reason—leave it. At least for now. See what it tells you about your material.

In her novel *Mrs. Dalloway*, Virginia Woolf starts out by narrating the thoughts of middle-aged Clarissa Dalloway. Before long, she moves seamlessly into other characters' points of view to dramatize a full day in their intertwined lives. It begins with "Mrs. Dalloway said she would buy the flowers herself," referring to preparations for a party she is giving that evening.

> She had the oddest sense of being herself invisible; unseen; unknown; there being no more marrying, no more having of children now, but only this astonishing and rather solemn progress with the rest of them, up Bond Street, this being Mrs. Dalloway; not even Clarissa any more; this being Mrs. Richard Dalloway.
>
> Bond Street fascinated her; Bond Street early in the morning in the season; its flags flying; its shops; no splash; no glitter; one roll of tweed in the shop where her father had bought his suits for fifty years; a few pearls; salmon on an iceblock. "That is all," she said, looking at the fishmonger's. "That is all," she repeated, pausing for a moment at the window of a glove shop where, before the War, you could buy almost perfect gloves.

Although most of the book's narrative is from Clarissa's perspective, Woolf, from a "craft" standpoint, takes her readers on quite a few seemingly illogical detours through other characters' thoughts and experiences. One of the most prominent of these characters is Septimus Smith, a working-class man home from the war, likely suffering from post-traumatic stress.

> Septimus Warren Smith, aged about thirty, pale-faced, beak-nosed, wearing brown shoes and a shabby overcoat, with hazel eyes which had that look of apprehension in them which makes complete strangers apprehensive too. The world has raised its whip; where will it descend?
>
> "Let us go on, Septimus," said his wife, a little woman, with large eyes in a sallow pointed face; an Italian girl. "Come on," said Lucrezia. But her husband, for they had been married four, five years now, jumped, started, and said, "All right!" angrily, as if she had interrupted him.

Then we go into Lucrezia's perspective:

> People must notice; people must see. People, she thought, looking at the crowd staring at the motor car; the English people, with their children and their horses and their clothes, which she admired in a way; but they were "people" now, because Septimus had said, "I will kill myself"; an awful thing to say. Suppose they had heard him?
>
> She looked at the crowd. Help, help! she wanted to cry out to butchers' boys and women. Help! Only last autumn she and Septimus had stood on the Embankment wrapped in the same cloak and, Septimus reading a paper instead of talking, she had snatched it from him and laughed in the old man's face who saw them! "Now we will cross," she said.

And just seconds later, back to Septimus:

> She had a right to his arm, though it was without feeling. He would give her, who was so simple, so impulsive, only twenty-four, without friends in England, who had left Italy for his sake, a piece of bone.

Woolf concludes *Mrs. Dalloway* twelve hours later in narrative time, at Clarissa's party, by putting us in the mind of Peter, an early love of Clarissa's from thirty years prior, as he looks at her across the dance floor in the present-day scene:

> What is this terror? what is this ecstasy? he thought to himself. What is it that fills me with extraordinary excitement? It is Clarissa, he said. For there she was.

Woolf allowed her prose to bend the conventional rules of POV (point of view) in fiction. If she had presented the story in an MFA workshop, most likely she would have been told to "fix the POV" by sticking to one character's (Clarissa's) perspective. Instead, she gave herself the chance to earn the nonconforming POVs. Why would she do that? For one, the POV shifts highlight the intense range of emotions and experiences in the narrative. Perhaps this was even Woolf's attempt to deepen her thematic concerns: social class and privilege; mental health and trauma; gender and sexuality; as well as isolation and connection. Had she kept consistent and played by the "rules" of POV, she wouldn't have been able to portray how people perceive the same day so differently, depending on social status, cultural influences, life experience, and how they identified themselves compared with others. And the best reason? It works. During these nonconforming POV oddities, the novel gets enriched and goes deeper into the mysteries of the human condition.

Instead of banishing the nonconforming oddity because of a perceived rule, she let it ride, which is not always easy to do when workshopping drafts with others. In bad writing workshops, students look for anomalies like pigs hunting for truffles. When they spot something that doesn't quite fit, students suggest a correction or the chop. "You can't do that," conventional critics say, because it "violates craft rules."

But in art, a rule is a guide, not an absolute. With artists, so-called rules of craft exist within a community of people who are working with a form and trying to solve technical issues. And whether you're critiquing your own or someone else's draft, it's smart to be aware of these so-called rules. It's also smart to question if adherences or deviations add to or subtract from the magic of the work. Woolf's deviation adds to the pleasure of reading and deepens our ability to ponder the novel's themes.

Rules of science are different from those of creative writing. In science, rules are formed by the physical world and are tested, too, in the physical world. If rules are broken, there are physical consequences. That's why real labs are stocked with hazmat suits, goggles, gloves, and all sorts of other protective gear. It's natural law that peroxides, when mixed with combustible materials, barium, sodium, and potassium, form explosives that ignite easily.

Creative writing is a liminal space. It exists only in our minds and imaginations, where explosions are not deadly and are often wonderful. Rules are only valuable when they increase the capacity to transmit what exists in your imagination to the imagination of the reader.

In some classrooms and workshops, these guidelines are asserted as laws, and a lot of mediocre work is produced by those diligently following them. It's important to remember that rules are made of *average behaviors*. *We* don't see *average* as aspirational. We want you to amplify what makes you *not* average.

In many narratives, a shifting POV like Woolf's would confuse readers and bounce them out of the story. Had Woolf's shifts proved nonintegral—had they been discovered to serve no purpose and only highlighted an early draft's lack of attention to consistency—a master like Woolf would almost certainly have revised the draft and chosen to stick to conventional guidelines of maintaining consistency in POV.

How will you be able to tell whether or not to conform in your own work? Worry not. The more you read, the more you write, the better you'll get at determining if the nonconforming oddity needs to stay or go. Pause before hitting the delete key. See such things as possible signs of real life—of uniqueness—in your work, and explore what they might be telling you about your material.

Write Now

Now we're going to write again. Take your list of fears about writing. Did any surprise you? Good. Use them to do the following:

1. Create a persona based on you, but who is exaggerated, concentrated, more extreme. Think of a persona this way: the personality—distinct from the author—narrating your piece. The persona can be as close to you or as far away as you like.
2. Write a "Dear Sugar" letter from the point of view of this persona, in which you combine all the reasons you're drawn to writing and all your fears. Use your lists. Like Elissa Bassist, let it all hang out. Use (or make up) personal anecdotes to illustrate your fears.

Write Now

Now we're going to switch gears (and personas) and write some more.

1. Create a persona who would be good *to respond to* your character from the previous exercise and respond to it, just as Sugar did to Elissa Bassist.
2. Like Sugar, see if you can use a voice that's both sweet and tough. Respect the advice-seeking-letter-writer "you" in the response, but don't be afraid of tough love. Shine light into the advice seeker's blind spots. Most important of all, relate personal (or made-up) experiences that dramatize the advice you are giving. In other words, you must *earn* the right to give advice by relating your—or your persona's—personal experiences.

Dear Sugar,

I'm a twenty-two-year-old queer woman of color in an industry that's been dominated by cishet white men from beyond the grave. When I tell people I want to become a writer, I'm met with an uproar of infantilizing comments and jokes about how I intend to earn a living. Like most people in the city, I work two jobs, go to school, and spend a ridiculous amount of money on transportation. By the time I sit down to write, I'm already drained. How can I become a writer when I don't even feel like a person?

I want my writing to be taken seriously, but lately, the anxiety's gotten to me and I can barely get a sentence on the page. I've struggled with perfectionism my whole life and now I can't remember the last time I finished something that I was proud of. Sometimes I look back at my work to edit and end up crossing out each word. Now [because of COVID-19] that my routine has been put on hold, I thought I'd have the energy to get my story done, but I'm more exhausted and lost than I've ever been. Each time I can't help but think: Is there a place for me in the literary world? Of the seven billion people on the planet, what could I say that hasn't been done by someone with infinitely more wisdom, flair, and concision? Don't they deserve someone better, someone not like me?

Florence

* * *

Dear Florence,

The greatest mistake an artist could make is to conflate the quality of their work with their innate value as a person. The truth is, there's no certainty of a singular moment where you'll feel you've arrived. Even Toni Morrison believed herself a fraud throughout her literary career. The more you live, the more you understand that the parts of yourself you believe are broken or missing are the very things that make you human. It's the pursuit of your passions that makes the difference.

Some people are born into privilege, but there are no shortcuts to becoming a writer. Do you know what writers do? They write and then write again. They choose to put the hours into studying their craft. They read the writers who came before them. They know that they can never fully encapsulate the human experience, and still, they devote their lives to the art, hoping to capture a sliver of something in the ever-expanding universe. This doesn't mean that art and literature is futile, only that our capacity for creation and empathy grows with each day and each story. You've lived a unique configuration of experiences that only you can render, that I assure you are worthy of fiction.

Among all the things you cannot control, you have the choice to form meaningful relationships with others through words. Choose to finish that draft. Allow yourself the opportunity to be wrong. Have the humility to face rejection. Learn, read, and write again. Out of the billions of people, choose yourself.

Sugar

Discuss

Here are some things to think about or discuss in class or with your writing group:

1. Which was easier to write, the letter asking for advice or the writer giving advice? Why?
2. Would you take the advice you gave yourself? Why or why not?
3. Did you notice a natural tension—maybe call it drama—between the fears and desires?

Through Florence, Kirsten is addressing some very serious realities of who has and has not been published and taught. These realities aren't to be minimized and don't exist separately from the character's fears and desires. In fact, they give substance to the speaker's fears. Much of what causes tension and drama in creative writing is, in life, truly bad.

While the tensions in real life that inform drama in creative writing are often dehumanizing, stories and plays and memoirs are full of drama. Those of us who've been ignored by the publishing industry will have plenty to fuel our creative work after we succeed in opening the doors.

Don't let those fears and desires stop you. Let them propel you forward. Think of

Florence. Think of Elissa. Think of Cheryl Strayed, who, by the way, did not achieve instant success. Here's some inspiring advice she once posted on her Facebook page:

> Going through a drawer I found the submissions/applications log I've kept off and on over the years. Just in case you think it's all been roses I'd like to report that Yaddo rejected me (as recently as 2011). McDowell rejected me. Hedgebrook rejected me twice. The Georgia Review rejected me and Ploughshares rejected me and Tin House rejected me, as did about twenty other journals and magazines. Both The Sun and The Missouri Review rejected me before I appeared in their pages. Literary Arts declined to give me a fellowship three times before I won one. I've applied for an NEA five times and it's always been a no. Harper's magazine never even bothered to reply. I say it all the time but I'll say it again: keep on writing. Never give up.

The goal today is to get in touch with our fears and desires with writing and to use them to inspire us to *never give up*. Naming fears and insecurities often deflates them. Naming desires can unearth thematic concerns to pursue. They can remind us of what we find important.

So go ahead. Write like a MF.

Chapter 2

Beliefs and Everyday Magic

"The universe is full of magical things patiently waiting for our wits to grow sharper."
—Eden Phillpotts

"Those who don't believe in magic will never find it."
—Roald Dahl

Now that you've written a bit about your writing-related desires and fears, we'll attempt to minimize the fears (or actively engage and disarm them) and amplify the desires by continuing our conversation about what moves us to write. What, out of all that stirs us, is "worthy" of developing artistically?

At this point, we're also going to open our minds—just a little bit—to consider our (potential) audiences.

A note about what *we* mean when we say "audience" or "reader." This isn't a critic, nor the writer's conservative parent, nor the harsh teacher. It's *you* or some form of you. Perhaps it's your inner-Sugar, that wisest part of yourself. Or it's your younger self. Or it's the communities of people who make you feel most at home.

What are you—and your ideal reader—hungry for? What draws your attention? What expression on a face, what photograph, what words spoken in love or anger, what in nature? Why this and not that?

Seek out what moves you. Write it down. Capture it. If it sparks something for you, chances are good it will for someone else, too. A writer's job is to use words to illuminate something mysterious, *not* easily explained. Again, our job isn't to solve the mystery but illuminate it. Remember: At this point in the experimental process, we're simply collecting material and learning new ways to practice. We can decide later what's worth keeping, shaping, and perhaps finishing.

Read the following poem by the poet, scholar, and cultural advocate Elizabeth Alexander. Notice how concrete her examples of poetry are. By concrete we mean perceivable by one or more of the five senses (in our imaginations we feel as though we can see it, hear it, taste it, touch it, or smell it). Keep this in mind as you continue through the chapter. The difference between abstract and concrete is one of the most important points we will be making.

Ars Poetica #100: I Believe

Elizabeth Alexander

Poetry, I tell my students,
is idiosyncratic. Poetry

is where we are ourselves
(though Sterling Brown said

"Every 'I' is a dramatic 'I'"),
digging in the clam flats

for the shell that snaps,
emptying the proverbial pocketbook.

Poetry is what you find
in the dirt in the corner,

overhear on the bus, God
in the details, the only way

to get from here to there.
Poetry (and now my voice is rising)

is not all love, love, love,
and I'm sorry the dog died.

Poetry (here I hear myself loudest)
is the human voice,

and are we not of interest to each other?

What do you believe? What do you believe *in?* These are the biggies: questions that aren't easily answered, or easily answered well. But these (with some finagling) can be your lures.

Write a list of sentences, each of them starting with the words "I believe." Try to get at least ten. Don't think too hard. And don't be afraid to think grandly. Think of the big things you believe in. And try to be honest. If you surprise yourself with what you write, that's a good thing. Don't worry about exposing yourself by writing down your beliefs. You won't share them with anyone else (unless you want to, of course).

For inspiration, read what a student wrote in response to this exercise.

> **STUDENT EXAMPLE**
> - *I believe that unless we immediately address global warming, we're doomed.*
> - *I believe that blind consumerism is disgusting.*
> - *I believe in God's grace.*
> - *I believe art saves lives.*

We'll come back to these. For now, let's move on.

Read William Blake

Read (and reread) these two short poems. Think not only about what William Blake wrote in each of these but *how* he wrote it.

The Divine Image
William Blake

> To Mercy, Pity, Peace, and Love
> All pray in their distress;
> And to these virtues of delight
> Return their thankfulness.
>
> For Mercy, Pity, Peace, and Love
> Is God, our father dear,

And Mercy, Pity, Peace, and Love
Is Man, his child and care.

For Mercy has a human heart,
Pity a human face,
And Love, the human form divine,
And Peace, the human dress.

Then every man, of every clime,
That prays in his distress,
Prays to the human form divine,
Love, Mercy, Pity, Peace.

And all must love the human form,
In heathen, Turk, or Jew;
Where Mercy, Love, and Pity dwell
There God is dwelling too.

A Divine Image
William Blake

Cruelty has a Human Heart
And Jealousy a Human Face
Terror the Human Form Divine
And Secrecy, the Human Dress

The Human Dress, is forged Iron
The Human Form, a fiery Forge.
The Human Face, a Furnace seal'd
The Human Heart, its hungry Gorge.

We're not spotlighting Blake as a poet to imitate. We chose him for this chapter as one of many examples to look at because of how he followed his own beliefs and impulses.

Look at the Blake poems carefully. Do you get a strong feeling of what the poet (or the speaker in the poem) believes?

We don't.

In "The Divine Image," Blake first praises four abstract virtues—mercy, pity, peace, and love—then God, then finally humans. He does this by pointing out the similarities between God and humans. In fact, he's saying that these qualities, although belonging to God, take on human form. Thus, Blake's view of what humans are capable of is lofty and positive. At least that's one take. And it might tell you more about *us* than it does about Blake.

Why? Blake doesn't define or make *concrete* what he means by those terms, at least not within the poem. One person's act of mercy may seem to another an act of cruelty. He gives the reader a lot of leeway.

Abstract painters often say they want their audiences to feel and think whatever they choose in reaction to their paintings. When creating, the artists may have one set of ideas in mind, but they relinquish control when they turn it over to the viewer.

We know a lot of writers. Chief among their habits is *not* the practice of "completely relinquishing control." In fact, when it comes to their writing, it's often the opposite. Here we quote the writer Stephen Dunn:

> The good poem illuminates its subject so that we can see it as the poet wished, *and in ways he could not have anticipated*. It follows that such illumination is twofold: the light of the mind, which the poet employs like a miner's beam, and that other light which emanates from the words on the page in conduction with themselves, a radiance the poet caused but never can fully control. [emphasis ours]

When you read Blake's pair of poems, think more about what *you* imagine. The goal isn't to be *right* about what Blake may have believed but to form your own associations.

In "A Divine Image," Blake seems to be saying that cruelty, jealousy, terror, and secrecy are abstract ideas with no reality except for how they are manifested in humans. The attributes he lists are hardly benign. They seem to suggest that a comprehensive view of God reflects not only divine qualities, but terrible human ones, too. In other words, if we say that human beings are made in the image of God, then these negative abstract qualities must be related to God, too.

Questions come up for us. What *specific* ways do human beings enact cruelty in a manner that other animals in nature do not? This question gets our imagination stirring, but does the poem itself?

This seems to be an abstraction's limitation.

Very often, beginning writers have very specific scenes or images in their minds when writing. But instead of rendering those scenes or images, they turn them into abstractions and then are surprised when the reader isn't picking up what they had in mind.

Someone intent on writing abstractions may use abstract painting to defend their choices: "Look at those gorgeous images, they're abstract, and they work."

We might say: "Yes, they do, but they also have color, shapes, and decorative meaning that's harder to render in plain text on a blank page."

A painting's "unit of satisfaction" doesn't come from the transference of specific meaning from the artist to the viewer. It's delivered instead by the viewer's reactions.

Concreteness Versus Abstraction

What we see, in these two poems, is Blake playing with abstractions, which most creative writing teachers warn against. In the first poem, he veers to use the poetic device *personification* to make the abstractions more relatable (human faces and dress are paired with the conceptual terms). In the second poem, he uses imagery (a "fiery forge," a "hungry gorge"). In both cases, he starts with abstraction, then goes toward concreteness, perhaps to drive his points home.

While many think Blake is timeless, they also know he's Blake, and see him as part of a lineage that led to new poetic styles. For scholars and fans of his work, his poems succeed in delivering that unit of satisfaction in countless ways. Today's poets (and readers of all kinds) still glean meaning from Blake without imitating the style of this pair of poems.

Imagine finding these two poems apart from their William Blake-ness. Imagine if they were submitted to a poetry workshop. For many, they'd be too abstract.

Not all, but much contemporary poetry and prose finds its power by emphasizing concrete imagery and by weaving the more ephemeral aspects—the abstractions—in between portrayals of images that, in our imaginations, can be seen, felt, smelled, tasted, heard.

There are, of course, exceptions. A poem may be more like music, focusing purely on the sonic qualities of language, or like a painting, focusing on how letters and punctuation appear physically on the page.

Blake's poems seem, to us, to *want* to communicate something more specific.

What is an abstraction? At its most basic, it is a concept that is not attached to anything on this earth. It exists only in our minds. Take the four qualities that Blake extols in the first poem: mercy, pity, peace, and love. Okay, mercy. We may associate the word with things we have witnessed on this planet—manifestations of mercy, examples of it. But we can't see mercy itself. We can't hold it in our hand, examine it, squeeze it, or smell it. It is an abstraction. Same with pity, peace, and love.

Some poets want the reader to participate and interject themselves or their own experience or meaning or associations onto their poems. Those poems might lean toward the abstract rather than the concrete.

But other poets are trying to convey something about their unique worldviews—they want to immerse the audience into what they are feeling. Paraphrasing the writer Robert Stone, your job as a writer is to push your readers out of their space and occupy it as your own.

So, if your desire is to transmit to us, your readers, the specific situations in which you experienced the abstract concept of mercy, you'll have to work hard to replace your audience's individual associations with your own concrete examples.

What about love? Many beginning poets want to engage the lusty, romantic version of this subject, but find themselves frustrated.

Lucky you if you've felt love so intensely you want to write about it. We are delighted for you. But how can a poem hold or contain a fraction of the intensity of that experience? As the author of the poem, you may be moved to tears because of your own associative experiences, but can you get someone else to feel it?

We once attended an open-mic poetry reading. One young person was so moved by their own poem that the host of the show had to escort them off the stage as the aspiring poet wept copiously. The audience? Not a wet eye in the house. Everyone seemed to want, badly, to connect with the emotional intensity the writer displayed in their reading, but just couldn't—at least not because of the poem.

Does that mean love, as a subject, is off-limits for serious poets?

No. When it comes to writing, nothing is automatically off-limits. Later, in Chapter 4, we'll look at a poem by Bill Hicok with the word "love" in it nine times. It's a thin poem on a single page but has a real force to it.

One habit beginning writers work to break is remaining solely in the abstract, using abstract language that describes abstract feelings. The abstract concept of love means very little—and cannot be communicated effectively—without tying it to things of this earth. Look again at an excerpt of the poem we used to start this chapter:

> Poetry (and now my voice is rising)
> is not all love, love, love,
> and I'm sorry the dog died.

Flannery O'Connor cautioned, "We are made of dust, and if you scorn getting yourself dusty, then you shouldn't try to write fiction. It's not a grand enough job for you."

Instead of the abstract "he suddenly fell in love with her," listen to this sentence from the novel *Anna Karenina*:

> He stepped down, trying not to look long at her, as if she were the sun, yet he saw her, like the sun, even without looking.

This sentence happens to use a subset of imagery called *metaphor*—a comparison of two unlike things—in this case comparing Anna to the sun. To be even more precise, it is a *metaphorical statement* called a *simile*: a comparison of two unlike things that makes the comparison explicit by using words such as "like" or "as" or "than." In this case, Tolstoy makes concrete the abstraction of love by using a simile that tethers it to the sensual warmth and brightness of the sun.

And just as important, it takes away any personal imagery we might associate with "he suddenly fell in love with her" and replaces it with Tolstoy's.

What's wonderful about literature is the mysterious way a writer's specificity—a writer's preciseness—replaces our own associations temporarily and allows us to resee our own, later, after reading (or simultaneously while reading), with more nuance and clarity.

Why? Because it's *concrete*. In creative writing, concrete is the opposite of abstract. But how did writers come to agree on this term? Well, it's a good metaphor. Concrete, the substance, is made up of three things: water, ground stone, and cement. Mixed, it can be poured into molds and shaped into anything. The Roman Pantheon is made from concrete.

An especially powerful concrete image is one that uses language to create strong associations in the reader. (More on associations later.)

While concrete imagery uses words that provide a clear sensory experience, abstract words do not and therefore often fail to draw in the reader. Why? We're sensual beings. Pure abstractions are devoid of related sensory responses. They only represent intangible concepts and feelings.

More often than not, concrete imagery is better at communicating meaning—and especially emotion—to the reader than abstract language. However, abstractions can be very powerful if they are earned.

The famous Vietnam War story "The Things They Carried," by Tim O'Brien, starts with lists of the things that soldiers carried in the fields:

> The things they carried were largely determined by necessity. Among the necessities or near-necessities were P-38 can openers, pocket knives, heat tabs, wristwatches, dog tags, mosquito repellent, chewing gum, candy, cigarettes, salt tablets, packets of Kool-Aid, lighters, matches, sewing kits, Military Payment Certificates, C rations, and two or three canteens of water. Together, these items weighed between 15 and 20 pounds, depending upon a man's habits or rate of metabolism. Henry Dobbins, who was a big man, carried extra rations; he was especially fond of canned peaches in heavy syrup over pound cake.

Throughout the story, O'Brien continues these lists of concrete things. Then, suddenly, at a critical point in the story, he moves from the concrete to the abstract:

> They carried all the emotional baggage of men who might die. Grief, terror, love, longing—these were intangibles, but the intangibles had their own mass and specific gravity, they had tangible weight. They carried shameful memories. They carried the common secret of cowardice barely restrained, the instinct to run or freeze or hide, and in many respects this was the heaviest burden of all, for it could never be put down, it required perfect balance and perfect posture. They carried their reputations. They carried the soldier's greatest fear, which was the fear of blushing. Men killed, and died, because they were embarrassed not to. It was what had brought them to the war in the first place, nothing positive, no dreams of

glory or honor, just to avoid the blush of dishonor. They died so as not to die of embarrassment.

The question we like to ask our students is: What if O'Brien had started with the abstractions? Would the story have been as powerful? After all, the abstractions are beautifully written and evocative and would certainly be praised in any workshop. But certainly, the abstractions work better because the ground has been prepared for them.

Not every reader feels a sentimental tie to Kool-Aid (although it calls to mind childhood for some who do). Not every reader has owned or carried a pocketknife (but many may have their own associations with someone specific who did). Many readers have also chewed gum or used mosquito repellent. We could continue this down the line with each concrete, tangible object on the list. Each offers us—people of all gender expressions, generations, and backgrounds—an opportunity to connect. After, when the abstractions come in, the reader's connection to the concrete enables the reader to "see" and "feel" the writer's more abstract and philosophical concepts more deeply.

Perhaps it's a question of proportion. Imagine that a creative piece is a big, substantial sandwich, with layers and layers of meat and cheese to represent concrete imagery. Once you have that, a thin slice of crispy lettuce or tangy tomato represents the abstractions. They can provide texture and add flavor to the sandwich, but you probably don't want to switch the proportions. You ordered a sandwich, not a salad.

For those who are mathematically inclined, think of it as 95 percent concreteness to 5 percent abstraction. That's what we're about to try.

Fusing the Abstract with the Concrete

Return to your "I believe" list. We are going to ask you to put a stake in the ground and write a bit about your core beliefs. They're likely all abstract. But will they always be? Can you transform them?

Let's look at the very first entry from the student's "I believe" list from earlier in the chapter: "I believe that unless we immediately address global warming, we're doomed."

This is a clear belief but rendered in the abstract. We can't really see or feel or taste or hear or touch anything, can we? But let's imagine that the student was the writer Barbara Kingsolver. In an interview she gave with NPR, Kingsolver said:

> I had really wanted to write about . . . [global warming] . . . for a long time. I live in southern Appalachia. I am surrounded by neighbors and friends—people I respect very much—who don't really understand climate change or believe in it, even though, as farmers, they're getting socked by it. We've had unprecedented, disastrous weather time and again. So it's such a strange contradiction that the people in our continent who are first to feel the harm of a changing climate are the last to be able to talk about it.
>
> That was such a conundrum and such rich territory for a novel to tread, that I was just looking for the right way to get into the subject. And one morning, I just woke up with this vision in my eyes of millions of butterflies covering the forest behind my house. I just—I mean, I didn't actually see it. I imagined it. I woke up and there it was, and I knew that was it.

Here is a section of the novel *Flight Behavior*, in which Kingsolver took her abstract concern over the topic (global warming) and managed to find a way "into" it through fiction:

> After so much rain upon rain this was happening all over the county, she'd seen it in the paper, massive trees keeling over in the night to ravage a family's roofline or flatten the car in the drive. The ground took water until it was nothing but soft sponge, and the trees fell out of it. Near Great Lick a whole hillside of mature timber had plummeted together, making a landslide of splintered trunks, rock and rill. People were shocked, even men like her father-in-law who tended to meet any terrible news with "That's nothing," claiming already to have seen everything in creation. But they'd never seen this, and had come to confessing it. In such strange times, they may have thought God was taking a hand in things and would thus take note of a lie.

The interview portion engages our intellect, the novel excerpt our imagination, our emotion.

Let's return to our student's "I believe" list. She had also written, "I believe that blind consumerism is disgusting."

For inspiration, let's look at how writer Harmony Holiday successfully addresses this concern in her poem "Dear Babylon."

Dear Babylon,

Harmony Holiday

> In the constant lutte to not become that bougie housewife of an athlete taking too much oxy while the help cooks ethical fried chicken for my family and I'm also the help and the television sighs and wags in the back   some Wendy Williams   rerun and   this is acceptable and celebrating neon israel and soul   is so radio :   I walk alone.   I know myself. Or so I chant in the mirror right around discovering that trap music is all the new negro spiritual / righteous delirium try to defund the clown in the en   in negro   say it a little   less   enter the New Yorker in Desdemona's   scarf   and be this generative productive whistle   blower for the radicals / coal at the root of slow kill and not scream   at the Salvadorian man with the leaf blower   in my landscape and hide him and his hoes   when the ICE raid follows and swallow mister PCs   pcp   ,   in this constant   creaseless / as in iron willed / as in   willow weep for me /   effort to love my enemy I became him   The body of me. Its erotic   disbelief temporarily suspended .   alongside the American eagle   : temptation to define freedom   as consumerism, justice as my right to an object in a special whites only window : see that seedless eagle run the heavens so : suspended and   hovering over my own safe house and spraying it with liquid hog manure   literally. Check WikiLeaks.   Assange looks like a creep but he saves everybody but himself   so   he must be.   Negro do you wanna be that   creepy?

Notice how powerfully and effectively Holiday uses concrete imagery to capture the vulgarity and racism inherent in American consumerism.

Write Now

Now choose a belief from your list (perhaps the most surprising or interesting—or worthy of challenging), and think about it as you riff off the words below that have been borrowed from the poems we read by William Blake. Think (but not too hard) about how each of these words resonates with you and the belief you have chosen. What associations do they bring up? Memories? Images? Fictional incidents?

To do this exercise, you can free write (an informal, spontaneous writing exercise where you write continuously for a set period without worrying about grammar, structure, or editing), or you can take a piece (a poem, a bit of memoir, or fiction) that you're already working on.

Hint: You'll notice that most of the concrete images we've been reading are visual in nature: you can *see* them. But what about mixing it up a bit? Try including other senses as well. You'll be surprised at how alive your images will feel if you include two, three, or even more senses in your concrete descriptions.

1. Choose one of your beliefs from a list.
2. Write a paragraph in response to three of the words taken from Blake's poem as seen through the lens of your belief. Try to be as specific as possible.
3. Get past all the abstractions to the concrete, even if you only get a sentence or two for each.

Remember, keep your chosen belief in mind as you write. That will inform what comes out.

- *Mercy*
- *Pity*
- *Peace*
- *Love*
- *Cruelty*
- *Jealousy*
- *Terror*
- *Secrecy*

This student example is based on the statement: "I believe family love is the most complicated kind of love":

> Mercy: Despite her distaste for crawling things, she decided not to squash the spider, as her father certainly would have done, but to carefully carry

it out the door and place it on a leaf of the rosebush that was fragrant with yellow blooms.

Pity: The last time I lost a fight with my father, I sucked on my bloodied right knuckles where there would almost certainly be bruises, then held my head up and looked straight at his triumphant face. Pity was a sharp pain in my stomach. The waning king, oblivious to his fate.

Love: She watched as he reached behind him, took the bottle from the cabinet, and brought it around to the kitchen table to pour into a clean glass just for her. The sparkling liquid poured out, his face was intent on ministering to her the precisely right amount, and then, with a smile, he added an additional, generous splash.

See where this writer is headed? Did the student's work replace your notions of mercy, pity, and love? And did it supply more detail and texture to your associations? It certainly did for us. What's more, we may not *agree* with the writer's (or their characters') concrete notions of mercy, pity, and love. That can be very good news. It asks us to reconsider, broaden, or sharpen our own notions. Even better, it leaves little room for us to interject our own notions. The writer is pushing us into a space of her choosing.

Finding the Mystery and Magic in the Ordinary

Of course, beliefs don't have to involve God or anything spiritual at all. Many people have deep faith in things that are completely secular in nature. For an example of that, we turn to the writer/illustrator Maurice Sendak.

The Tate Museum in London had a show of William Blake's drawings and poems in 2019–20, and asked the late Maurice Sendak, the celebrated author of *Where the Wild Things Are* and many other books that are supposedly for children, to contribute to the exhibit.

In case you're one of the few people on the planet who hasn't heard of *Where the Wild Things Are*, the storybook follows Max, a very bad boy who is punished for various and sundry transgressions (the illustrations are whimsical and funny) by being sent to his room without dinner. Unabashed, Max simply grins as his room turns into a ship that takes him to the land where the wild things are, where he is crowned king. A series of pages are pure illustrations (no words needed) of the wild things and Max, their king, dancing exuberantly through the woods in sheer and utter joy. This continues until Max smells something good from over the seas. So he says goodbye to his (suddenly) deflated and sad subjects and sails home to find his hot supper waiting in his room.

What resonates in this book for so many people—adults and children alike—is Max's unbreakable spirit along with Sendak's skill of seamlessly immersing us in Max's pretend world—a world that is so vivid we believe in it more than in Max's ordinary home life. Max's wicked grin, the terror of the wild things, and the release Max feels in the land of the wild things are all captured in the sublime illustrations.

The Tate Museum interviewed Sendak. Here are some excerpts from the transcript:

> Herman Melville said that artists have to take a dive. Either you hit your head on a rock and you split your skull and you die, or that blow to the head is so inspiring that you come back up and do the best work you ever did. But you have to take the dive and you do not know what the result will be.
>
> . . . I'm much luckier than Herman Melville ever was, much luckier than William Blake ever was, but I still suffer from what they suffered from.

". . . artists have to take a dive." What does this phrase mean to you? To us, this means making a wholehearted commitment to explore something honestly, no matter how dark and painful the process might be. It's a willingness to see one's own work objectively enough to know when anything is rendered lazily, in a manner that's too obvious, or overly familiar. It's about the obligation that artists have not only to recognize what is surface level, but to honor it by getting underneath it—knowing in advance we might fail.

In your world, what's worth taking a dive into? What will you find out if you take that dive? Can you even know? In the video interview, Sendak seems to suggest that perhaps there are things only the subconscious can know:

> I'm reading an interesting book now on the life of William Blake. . . . I don't know what the hell he's talking about, but I love him.
>
> . . . He's an illustrator, I am an illustrator. He illustrates poems, his own

> poems. Mythical, dream poems. I guess it's the way his profound belief in something sounds kind of idiotic, but I believe him. I believe in his passion.

It sounds like Sendak feels similarly about Blake's poems as we do: there's something compelling, but it's *not* the imagery. It may be the unanswerable questions. Sendak's words to describe Blake? *Profound* and *idiotic*.

Sendak responds concretely to the concepts Blake explores abstractly. We're interested in this chain of events and have based this next set of experiments on this exact setup.

Sendak also talks about finding mystery and magic in his ordinary childhood in New York. We know that the most profound concepts are gleaned by the reader only after the writer portrays what may seem like the most mundane (to others) surroundings and circumstances:

> I just lived in Brooklyn where everything was *ordinary, and yet enticing and exciting and bewildering.* The magic of childhood is the strangeness of childhood. The uniqueness that makes us see things that other people don't see. [emphasis ours]

Can you remember or think of moments in your life or in the imaginative world of your piece that are "ordinary" and "exciting" and "bewildering" all at once? In the full interview, Sendak connects his childhood fascination with comics with what made him a writer and illustrator. Perhaps his beliefs were born out of this fascination with magic and "strangeness."

Sendak also alludes to having a view into things that others don't see. Seeing the world in a way most do not can feel like an isolating experience—but it can also be invigorating and exciting.

Once we find out that there are others out there like us—those with obsessions that they are willing to dive into—we can transform what used to isolate us into art, which connects us with an audience as well as other writers.

People have called all three of the writers we've mentioned (Melville, Blake, and Sendak) "crazy" or "weird" or "inappropriate." We don't call them any of those names. But we see how their visions were unique in ways that may or may not be attributable to life experience. Scholars assert that Blake and Melville were likely gay. Sendak was gay. But despite a long-term relationship with Eugene Glynn, his partner of fifty years, he didn't come out until a 2008 interview in *The New York Times* when he was eighty years old.

"All I wanted was to be straight so my parents could be happy," Sendak said at the time.

Sendak also worried about being a gay man writing children's books, likely because of the erroneous but common conflation of gayness and pedophilia in the collective imagination.

It's impossible to know, but it seems safe to say that the pressure to conceal important parts of themselves informed the beliefs and artistic visions of these and other writers.

Write Now

1. First, think of an ordinary place from your (or another persona's) past—perhaps childhood if that works for you.
2. Describe (or have your persona describe) something that might seem nondescript to someone else, but which was "enticing, exciting, bewildering" to you. Something with magic in it.
3. Make it as concrete as possible.

> **STUDENT EXAMPLE**
> My grandmother had this...thing...hanging on her living room wall. There, among the menorahs and bad paintings of drab Eastern European landscapes was a little three-dimensional carving within a small wooden box. About the size of a book, it portrayed a primitive kitchen, with a wood-burning stove (with a small fire painted inside it), a china cabinet, and a table and chairs, complete with tiny bowls and spoons on the table. It was painted in what had probably been bright colors, but which now had faded to drab browns and grays and maroons. I would stare at it for hours. To me, it was magical. What tiny beings lived here? Why could I never catch them sitting at the table eating their soup, or cooking at the stove? Where did they go when I was keeping guard? My grandmother died long ago, and so now the box is hanging above my desk. I look at it when I can't find the right words while writing. Now that I've traveled a bit, I know these little 3D dioramas are common throughout Lithuania, Bosnia, Georgia. But it

only deepens the mystery. My grandmother came over the ocean with just what she had on her back, her clothes and a small knapsack. Why bring this of all things? What did it mean to her? I will never know, but it helps to look at it as I struggle with language, trying to bring the unseen to life on the page.

On Belief and Magic—and Death

The following excerpt is from an interview by NPR host Terry Gross with Maurice Sendak close to the end of his life. He said many surprising things—especially for an avowed atheist:

I don't believe in an afterlife, but I still fully expect to see my brother again. And it's like a dream life. But, you know, there's something I'm finding out as I'm aging—that I am in love with the world.

And I look right now, as we speak together, out my window in my studio and I see my trees and my beautiful, beautiful maples that are hundreds of years old, they're beautiful. And you see I can see how beautiful they are. I can take time to see how beautiful they are. It is a blessing to get old. It is a blessing to find the time to do the things, to read the books, to listen to the music.

I cry a lot because I miss people. I cry a lot because they die and I can't stop them. They leave me and I love them more. . . . And so it's what I dread more than anything is the isolation. . . .

And I don't know whether I'll do another book or not. I might. It doesn't matter. I'm a happy old man. But I will cry my way all the way to the grave.

The full audio recording is well worth listening to. We hope you'll check it out.

If you read *Where the Wild Things Are* and Sendak's other works, you can see how his abstract ideas and beliefs (each containing contradictions) take the form of concrete details and are magically transformed into art.

If there were an easy recipe for how to make magic, it wouldn't be magic, but we've seen this again and again in the artists we admire: they have beliefs and opinions, and they pay attention and see and record particularities others might not. Then they explore.

The beliefs run in the background while the exploration of the concrete particulars takes place in the foreground. Still, both are running simultaneously.

In this process, something new is discovered by the artist about her or his own belief(s) and about the world—and the excitement of this newness somehow gets communicated to the reader. But always, always (well, almost always) through the *things* of this world. "No ideas but in things," wrote William Carlos Williams, and he's absolutely right.

Write Now

One last exercise in this chapter.

Sendak, in a quote from another part of the same interview, reaffirmed his atheism, but also said: "I am in love with the world . . . I have nothing but praise now for my life. . . . There are so many beautiful things in the world that I will have to leave when I die. . . . Thank God we're still around to do it."

1. Choose another one of your beliefs (one you haven't used before).
2. Write a piece (nonfiction, fiction, or poetry) in which you first state your belief.
3. Then immediately *contradict* it using concrete details. Start with the sentence: "I believe [whatever it is] BUT . . ."

> **STUDENT EXAMPLE**
> I believe the sun will come up tomorrow
> But at night I shake in my bed
> So many things to go wrong
> Trees fall, hearts stop, roofs cave
> Children cough blood, break bones, run into cars
> Some people count sheep
> I count catastrophes

We'll end this chapter with a few of our favorite quotes, the first two by Jyrki Vainonen, a Finnish writer and interpreter. He articulates what we believe about the creative act precisely and beautifully:

- *"Dive again and again into the river of uncertainty."*
- *"Create in the dark, only then can you recognize the light."*

Kurt Vonnegut captured the idea in a more humorous way:

- *"We have to continually be jumping off cliffs and developing our wings on the way down."*

Often, we see an early draft of a student's writing that doesn't yet work. The number one reason isn't craft related, it's bigger than that. There's no magic. Why? It's impossible to glean the failed draft's importance. We hope that this chapter helps you avoid that pitfall.

Maurice Sendak occasionally became infuriated by the combination of passion and confusion he saw in William Blake's work. That fury served as a lifelong inspiration for how Sendak engaged in his own work.

When you're reading and writing, keep this in mind. Each time you come across something that conceptually engages you, on a deep emotional or intellectual level, jot it down, then see if you can explore it in concrete ways. If you can't, if the abstraction must be said for the piece to gain its maximum impact, say it!

In this part of the book, we're focusing on generating material you may not have written on your own. Later, we'll talk about ways to shape the exercises. Meanwhile, and from now on, keep following your strong beliefs. Keep looking to find the magic in what seems mundane.

Chapter 3

Aesthetic Force

"Don't bend; don't water it down; don't try to make it logical; don't edit your own soul according to the fashion. Rather, follow your most intense obsessions mercilessly."
—Anne Rice

In Chapter 1, we explored our fears and desires about writing. In Chapter 2, we explored the magic that can happen when we align our desire to communicate with the unique vision each of us holds and a willingness to dive deeply into our beliefs. Now we want to think about beauty.

Beauty? Why beauty? Why not focus on any other quality that a person, place, object, or event can possess?

Because confronting beauty—true beauty—is an extreme experience. If you manage to render beauty on the page (real beauty, not a hackneyed, clichéd version of it), you've managed to transcend much that stands in the way of creating honest, raw poetry and prose that will surprise and delight readers.

In our combined years of teaching, we've noticed a trend. Those standout students of writing, those who show up ready to experiment—the ones who do the quiet hard work of facing their fears enough to get under and excavate what's most mysterious, most magical, most engaging about their material—tend to lean toward exploring the "darker" side of the spectrum.

There's nothing wrong with that. Much great writing has come from pain. But we'd like to offer a shortcut to writers that (we hope) will deepen and add complexity to even early drafts of their work—and that is, in the midst of darkness, to also focus on beauty. "Because the world is so full of death and horror, I try again and again to console my heart and pick the flowers that grow in the midst of hell." These are the words of Herman Hesse in *Narcissus and Goldmund*.

Now, we're not talking about sentimental, conventional notions of beauty, but about making connections in what you find beautiful even if readers, upon first look, disagree. In fact, thinking of beauty is also a way to deepen a practice we use almost like a religion: anticipating what would logically be thought of as "appropriate" when rendering images and dramatic events—and avoiding them by any means possible.

The philosopher Confucius wrote, "Everything has beauty but not everyone sees it." We'd argue that the most impactful poetry, memoir, and fiction is written to allow us to see what's beautiful, as well as its counterpoint, ugly, in what's generally asserted as their opposites.

We stress this because we've seen these talented students produce early drafts in which the language, syntax, and imagery—earnestly—match the subject matter. By this we mean that they write about beautiful things (like love) beautifully and ugly things (like violence) in an ugly manner. The result is that the overall effect can be quite flat. Or worse: it can leave the reader feeling manipulated, bounced out of the world, or annoyed.

Your writing will likely be more engaging if it is more complex than that. Beauty isn't (necessarily) about what's generally asserted as such. Neither is ugliness. Over the years we worked on this book, we kept in mind what Richard Pevear says in his introduction to his and Larissa Volokhonsky's translation of *The Brothers Karamazov*:

> *The Brothers Karamazov* is a joyful book. Readers who know what it is about may find this an intolerably whimsical statement. It does have moments of joy, but they are only moments; the rest is greed, lust, squalor, unredeemed suffering, and sometimes terrifying darkness. But the book is joyful in another sense: in its energy and curiosity, in its formal inventiveness, in the mastery of its writing. And therefore, finally, in its vision.

Here's the quote again. This time, to make our point, we've substituted the word *beautiful* for *joyful* and *beauty* for *joy*:

> . . . is a *beautiful* book. Readers who know what it is about may find this an intolerably whimsical statement. It does have moments of *beauty*, but they are only moments; the rest is greed, lust, squalor, unredeemed suffering, and sometimes terrifying darkness. But the book is *beautiful* in another sense: in its energy and curiosity, in its formal inventiveness, in the mastery of its writing. And therefore, finally, in its vision.

Now let's look at a poem about the beauty a mother sees in her own daughter and how touched this mother was to receive flowers from her adult child. Had this piece relied solely on standard notions of beauty, it might have failed. Imagine for a moment that the following (beautiful) lines had been the poem's only lines: "The tulips / arrived in a creamy box; your note / tucked in tissue paper. . . . The / tulips are white and iridescent purple. / Thank you for your brown eyes. I / believe they are still flecked with green. . . . Thank you / for the tulips. You sent so many I filled / three vases: one big, two small." At the end of the poem, speaking of the sweets at her grown daughter's wedding, she writes, "the donuts were / delicious. You were a delicious baby."

That would have been a perfectly "nice" poem. But this artist is after so much more. Let's read the actual poem. While reading, note where the poet positions the "beautiful" lines.

Thank You for the Tulips
Lisa Bellamy

During the pandemic, after I told you—
speaking up never easy—I was lonely
for you, your kids, and your husband,
you sent me tulips. Just like that, you
sent tulips. I wondered, though: did I
deserve them? I am sorry I was a drunk
when you were a kid. Thank you for not
hanging up when I call. The tulips
arrived in a creamy box; your note
tucked in tissue paper. I am sorry I could
not keep your father around or try very
hard to stop him when he said he was
leaving. I am sorry I did not love him
enough. Thank you for choosing such a
nice, funny guy for a husband. I am
sorry I pursued such a crazy boyfriend
after your father left—the shouting, the
slamming phones and slamming doors,
the walking out, the coming back. The

tulips are white and iridescent purple.
Thank you for your brown eyes. I
believe they are still flecked with green,
although sometimes, even now, I am
embarrassed to look you in the eye. I am
sorry I was so sick from drinking,
throwing up, and dizzy. Once, I could
not take you to your dentist appointment
because I felt shaky and kept falling.
You cried, you said nothing works,
nothing happens, everything falls apart.
Thank you for your clarity. Thank you
for your red face, your bursting, when
you were born. Thank you for your
anger when your stepfather and I
screwed up the car seat as we drove the
baby around the city, looking after her
while you were at your conference. Boy,
that woke us up! I am sorry you fell out
of your stroller when you were a toddler
because I was hungover and forgot to
buckle you in. I don't know if you
remember. Now you know. Thank you
for the tulips. You sent so many I filled
three vases: one big, two small. Thank
you for insisting you wanted hipster
vegan donuts at your wedding instead of
a white cake. That one threw me over
the handlebars—drama, etc. Your
stepfather was kind and calm throughout
and wrote the checks. He loves you. He
says, later you get all the money, no one
else. In the end, I was a good sport,
admit it; the donuts were
delicious. You were a delicious baby.

We quickly learn that the speaker, after receiving the flowers, is happy, but wonders if she deserves them. This darker inquiry gives way to compelling, concrete images of the speaker's actions while addicted. Let's look again at the lines about the daughter's eyes and the lines that follow:

> Thank you for your brown eyes. I
> believe they are still flecked with green,
> although sometimes, even now, I am
> embarrassed to look you in the eye. I am
> sorry I was so sick from drinking,
> throwing up, and dizzy. Once, I could
> not take you to your dentist appointment
> because I felt shaky and kept falling.
> You cried, you said nothing works,
> nothing happens, everything falls apart.

That author achieves a much more complex beauty through the contradictions portrayed in specific images throughout. The poet explores beauty and its opposite. The poem engages and transcends her readers' expectations to achieve power, blowing open one version of the sacred bond of mother and daughter.

Bellamy wants us (and we want you) to struggle (in that good, satisfying way) for truth, to allow in thrilling combinations of emotions like pleasure and regret, love and guilt. It seems she wants the reader to let go of any temptation to moralize.

Another poet, Sharon Olds, talked in an interview about art being the place where humans struggle with the truth. Olds also declared that "art is moral":

> Not that we're trying to be moralists, because then we won't write well, but
> it has something to do with why our species isn't dead yet. We've had art to
> scare ourselves with. And to have pleasure with.

By exploring beauty in its opposite, Bellamy's poem has the aesthetic force to scare us and give us aesthetic pleasure.

And here's a compelling example from *Demon Copperhead*, by Barbara Kingsolver, in which the protagonist, a young person addicted to oxycodone and fentanyl, comes home to find his girlfriend, whom he truly loved, finally (it had been coming for a long time) dead from an overdose:

It was April, not quite a year after Vester, and it happened the way I knew it would. I came home and found her. Early evening, not yet dark. Damn April to hell, I could be done with that one. November also. Birthdays, Christmas, dogwoods and redbuds, even football season. Live long enough, and all things you ever loved can turn around to scorch you blind. The wonder is that you could start life with nothing, end with nothing, and lose so much in between.

I almost didn't feel anything at first, cleaning her up like I'd done so many times, getting her decent. And then the house, cleaning up her mess and her kit. Hiding stuff, before I made any calls. There were few to make. Thelma had run out of reasons to know her. Like everybody else. I had no wish to see the aunt again, but the EMTs said they had to get hold of next of kin, so I turned over Dori's phone. Aunt Fred was in the contacts. I'd erased some other numbers first, but nobody cared to track down any mysteries. Another OD in Lee County. There'd been hundreds.

And just like that, I was "the boy that went in there and found her." People were saying I'd broken into the house, various things. Stories grow on the backs of others. Regardless my clothes and everything being all over the house. Aunt Fred didn't remember me at all. I watched her pick up a pair of my jeans off the floor like she's scrubbing a toilet, saying something to the mini-me daughter about Dori having a lot of men friends. I should have screamed the bitch to hell, but my throat had closed up. My baby girl. No words of mine were called for, because just like before, the aunt chose everything. Church, music, one funeral fits all. They buried her beside Vester and her mother. The only thing they got right.

I just felt like a rock through the service, or a hunk of ice. Not cold-hearted against the handful that came out to show respects, it wasn't their fault. Mostly they were the care nurses that had helped with Vester. Also Donnamarie and them, from the store, and a few girls that might have been friends with Dori in school before they got bored of her. Guilty, curious, who knows what brings people out to view the dead. The funeral was so wrong,

> I couldn't see how it mattered. I'd already done everything in the world I could do for Dori, and it added up to nothing.

We think this passage is achingly beautiful. While there is little that could be categorized as overtly so, there's something else: a tenderness in tone, and beauty in the narrator's exhaustion and patient resignation. For the reader, there's a sense that the narrator finds freedom from a love that, however pure it had been, had dragged him down as deep as anyone could go. There's beauty in that, too. Kingsolver also resists what would logically be thought of as "appropriate." There's none of the histrionics you'd expect in finding a loved one who has suddenly died, and not a hint of anything resembling an adolescent breakdown even if the narrator is only nineteen years old.

Readers can be convinced of the beauty (or ugliness) of anything when in the hands of a skilled writer.

From Lauren Groff's *Matrix*, here is a vision that the central character, Marie, experienced:

> Holding her hand was a woman of equal radiance, cloaked in the red of blood, with diamonds and silver upon her neck and wrists, and upon her brow was shining in rubies the wound made by the staff of the angel who had chased her from the first garden; for this was Eve, the first mother of all humankind. And she held in her other hand a rib made of crystal, for she herself had been molded from a rib, and so proved herself a refinement of the first mortal made of mere clay.

You can see how the vision is meant to be a thing of exceptional beauty, despite the references to blood, wounds, and ribs of clay. It's a complicated image, as fits a vision that a complicated character experienced.

We have two goals for you in this chapter:

1. To identify (or begin to discover) what *you*, personally, think of as beautiful (which also means defining its opposite, ugliness)
2. To be able to render those complex things precisely using surprising but convincing language and imagery

Beauty is tricky to discuss for several reasons. First, it's subjective. So many factors go into determining what makes each of us decide that something is or is not beautiful. Run an image search using "beautiful" as an adjective before a plural noun: hotel rooms, sweaters, neighborhoods, faces, cakes, birds, babies, or anything else you can think of.

There are bound to be images that you agree are beautiful, others that you think of as downright ugly. It's hard to discuss beauty without also discussing ugliness. So, we won't. We'll engage with both concepts.

Whether or not you would agree with our individual definitions of beauty when shopping for bar stools or picking flowers, we believe that a writer's attention to *aesthetics* can be a very powerful tool to capture their readers' imagination and keep them engaged.

What exactly is *aesthetics*? Aesthetics is the philosophy concerned with notions about the beautiful and the ugly.

A writer's aesthetics matter. That is, what the *writer* considers (or discovers in the process of writing as) beautiful or ugly is critical to each writer's particular take on the world. And your particular take on the world is going to be what makes your writing stand out among all the other writing being produced today.

So how does attention to aesthetics fit into your writing process?

That's what we're going to explore in this chapter—so let's get started.

Write Now

Do a free write for ten minutes or so.

1. Think of an incident that affected you deeply, for any reason: it was beautiful, it was ugly, it was horrifying, it was uplifting. Perhaps you witnessed a car crash. Or watched a father playing with his daughter in the park. Anything goes.
2. Write a piece in which you (or a character) begin by saying: "I can't explain the feeling, so I won't even try. Instead, I'll tell you what I saw that day that everything changed. There, in front of me, I saw . . ."

3. As concretely as possible, continue on after first writing those sentences. Avoid abstractions. Write down what can be seen, felt, tasted, touched, and smelled.
4. Do NOT try to interpret or explain. Instead, render the images so that the reader experiences it just as you did.

> **STUDENT EXAMPLE**
>
> I can't explain the feeling, so I won't even try. Instead, I'll tell you what I saw that day that everything changed. There, in front of me, in the classroom where my own teenager had attended first grade, I saw a child's arm, unattached. Its inner-side, pink, the pink of a cherry blossom. Not a new bloom, but the less girlie pink, more of a barely-pink, the color after the flower fades and is about to fall. My partner moved her flashlight, which illuminated the wrist holding a silver bracelet, so thin and delicate the glint and spark it cast didn't make sense. How could something so tiny capture all that light? The bracelet wrapped around to the sun-kissed side of the child's arm, more gold than pink. The hand rested, barely open, a flower just starting to unfurl, and the nail on each of the fingers held a dab of purple paint. The shooter, still a child himself, had already been taken into custody, all his arms and legs attached. We did our jobs: which, on this day, was to search for and catalog the bodies of his victims.

Now you'll analyze the student example. What's the *mood* of the piece? And how would you describe each individual image on a scale of beautiful to ugly?

It's important for the purpose of this exercise to analyze the images separately from one another—as if they're not connected—then consider the whole. Notice how you're being pulled into numerous (surprising) directions at once.

Experiencing Aesthetic Force

Now we're going to explore Sarah Lewis's concept of *aesthetic force*, which was introduced and explained in her brilliant book *The Rise: Creativity, the Gift of Failure, and the Search for Mastery.*

We will quote a portion of a discussion at the New York Public Library when Lewis talked with Anna Deavere Smith, the actor and playwright.

The part of the conversation we are focused on for this chapter involves the power of imagery and how an artist may be extraordinarily impactful when able to present beautiful imagery even in the midst of human ugliness.

> **SARAH LEWIS:** [The] importance of aesthetics is why Aristotle said... "Reason alone is not enough to make men good."... *[H]e understood that there's a force, there's a way that beauty kind of slips in the back door of our rational thought and gets us to see the world differently, but it does often— it's often accompanied by being off kilter.* [emphasis ours]

> **ANNA DEAVERE SMITH:** ... [You] say a lot about "aesthetic force" [in your book].... What does that mean to you?

> **SARAH LEWIS, READING FROM HER BOOK:** The words to describe aesthetic force suggest that it leaves us changed—stunned, dazzled, knocked out. *It can quicken the pulse, make us gape, even gasp with astonishment. Its importance is its animating trait.* Not what it is but what it does to those who behold it in all its forms.... Few experiences get us to this place more powerfully with a tender push past the praetorian-guarded doors of reason and logic than *the emotive power of aesthetic force.* [emphasis ours]

As writers, we want to experiment and then search our drafts for opportunities to revise away from reason and logic and toward "the emotive power of aesthetic force."

Lewis quotes Aristotle as saying, "Reason alone is not enough to make men good."

We say, "Reason alone is not enough to make *writing* good."

You can appeal to our minds all you want, but unless you appeal to our souls, you'll likely fail to convey what's most important.

There's an element in making creative work that must, on some level, dazzle, delight, and surprise—move the reader to feel something extraordinary.

These chapters are meant to work independently, but if you're reading them in order, you might see a through line here.

We spent all of Chapter 2 offering methods and experiments to mine what's most important to you. Chapter 1 helped you create the voice of a wise, higher self to counter any fears or doubts you have in your ability.

Our experiments in the previous chapters involve short-circuiting logical reasoning (we'll return to that part of the brain in the revision process) in favor of what's in your subconscious. But how do you get beyond reason to aesthetic force? We suggest (as we have elsewhere) that a key to creating powerful images is your level of emotional investment in the world you're exploring. Deavere Smith and Lewis discuss images created by artists who cared deeply for their subjects.

SARAH LEWIS:

[There are even] moments where [an image with] aesthetic force has gripped us so much that we have... inaugurated a movement, whether it's the environmental movement, and that occurred when people saw the image of the planet suspended in the environment that we know it inhabits but don't quite see as an environment and in 1968 realized that we needed to do something to honor the way that we care for ourselves collectively differently. [emphasis ours]

Apollo 8 astronaut Bill Anders's photograph of the first earthrise witnessed by humans. *NASA.*

"Oh my God, look at that picture over there! There's the Earth comin' up. Wow, is that pretty!"

Speaking here is astronaut Bill Anders, a crew member of the Apollo 8 mission and the first person ever to behold this view subsequently captured in the photo he took.

Sarah Lewis mentioned the photograph *Earthrise* because of its aesthetic force. It went on to become one of the most iconic images of the twentieth century and is often credited for propelling the environmental movement that led to the first Earth Day in 1970.

When something of great beauty is created and shared with the world, it can, depending on timing and luck, have an incredible impact. Bill Anders had no intention of changing the world with his photograph. In fact, he famously almost missed the shot when he struggled to get the color film loaded into his camera. But he knew it needed to be captured because of the effect it had on him.

People have since described the photograph as "lonely" and say the earth seems "fragile," but it's one of those rare images that people almost universally agree is beautiful. And something beautiful, according to Lewis, has the force to get us to see—really see.

ANNA DEAVERE SMITH:
Where would we have—where would the civil rights movement have been without the photograph . . . ?

On September 4, 1957, Will Counts took the iconic photograph of Elizabeth Eckford and Hazel Bryan, known as "Elizabeth and Hazel" and "The Scream" image. In the *New York Times* headline, it's called "The Photograph That Exposed Segregation."

Viewers are made to ponder the image's broader themes by seeing something particular, concrete: a girl being harassed by an angry mob on her first day of school. Its aesthetic force made people who hadn't experienced or witnessed such horrors sit up and take notice.

Hazel Bryan and Elizabeth Eckford, Little Rock, Arkansas, September 1957. *Will Counts Collection, Indiana University Archives.*

While the "ugliness" of what the image conjures is inarguable, it also contains beauty. Removed from the surroundings of those bullying and dehumanizing her, the image of Elizabeth Eckford herself—her posture, her clothing, her grooming, the books she holds close to her chest—effectively illuminates what many would see as a beautiful and promising young person.

This photograph's complex nature gives it its power—its aesthetic force.

What's beautiful and what's ugly is completely up to you. In fact, if you see beauty where others don't, or ugliness where others don't, you may have an advantage.

We'll look at two passages from Charles D'Ambrosio's short story "The Dead Fish Museum."

The piece features two characters, Ramage and Desiree, who are visitors to a small town while working on an adult film. Desiree is starring in the film as a performer, and Ramage is on the crew. They left the set together and wandered around town before settling into a cheap hotel.

In this first excerpt of the story, the characters wander through a decidedly unlovely landscape until they reach a spice factory, where workers are roasting and bottling oregano. Here the language becomes lyrical, the imagery almost magical.

As they drifted up from the beach and further from the ocean the damp cloying odor of kelp and sea lettuce was replaced by the arid and spacious scent of oregano cooking in the spice factory.

It was if they'd entered a new, fairer latitude. They walked through a back section of town where the sidewalks were cracked and slabs of concrete heaved up to make way for weeds and tree roots. A wooden boat listed in the dirt of a vacant lot; a cat with yellow eyes watched them from the glassless wheelhouse.

A brick building dominated by a high square clock tower was just across the street. The clock had a white face and roman numerals, and the black hands were stuck at the pleasant hour of seven o'clock, a time of beginnings, of a new day, a new night. They leaned their heads through a window, canted open with a pull-chain; blue smoke rose from the ovens and spread and was sucked away by a whirring exhaust fan.

Ramage shushed drunkenly with a warning finger to his lips. "Look," he whispered, "natives."

Two men and a woman stood in front of a large spinning machine; they were dressed in white smocks and paper hats and surgical masks; behind them glass bottles filled with spice and were shunted down a metal chute and conveyed up a rubber ramp into waiting boxes; the clinking bottles made a cool Latin-flavored jazz in the cavernous factory; particles of oregano rained down in a fine green dust that settled over the cement floor; a faint trail of footprints was visible, the tread of sneakers stamped into the green spice, and the men and the woman were coated in green dust too.

D'Ambrosio could have said, "The two walked through a coastal town that had seen better days." Instead, to imbue the setting with aesthetic force, he uses voice, specificity, syntax, and tone. A yellow-eyed cat, a weedy split in the sidewalk, and the whirring of a fan turns this "coastal town that had seen better days" into something beautiful. He's pointing the reader to all sorts of movement and life: tree roots, spinning machines, moving conveyor belts, and floating green dust. We can smell and taste the oregano, a spice often associated with comfort food. This allows the reader to see "beauty" in an "ugly" town. If his storytelling voice can portray the setting in this way, how might these same techniques be used to portray his characters?

In the second excerpt, Ramage and Desiree try unsuccessfully to have sex. If you've never met someone working in adult films, you might bring the stereotypes and expectations inherited from popular culture.

Ask yourself: What are the popular-media drop-down menu portrayals of working-class tough guys and porn-performing women? Then notice the difference between your drop-down menu and what D'Ambrosio delivers. The writer convincingly contradicts those stereotypes—or makes us forget, if only temporarily, that they exist. That's what gives this excerpt its aesthetic force:

> She slipped off her sandals and walked barefoot across the gold carpet. She poured rum into a plastic cup and sipped from her drink, then tipped out a little more rum and sat on the bed beside Ramage, her leg raised. Their knees touched. Ramage felt the faint pressure and in silence he ran his finger back and forth along her pants seam, tracing the outline of her leg as it rose and fell from her hip to her ankle. She primped the flat airless pillows beneath her head; she ran her tongue over her lips and her mouth settled into a pout as she stared at the ceiling. Ramage wished for ice but he was too tired to dress and search for some. Desiree balanced the plastic cup on her stomach, over her bellybutton. Ramage kissed her woodenly and touched her breasts; he faked the kiss a moment longer and slipped his hand under her shirt. Beneath her breasts, two faint surgical scars, like the twin curved lines of a cartoon bust, were clearly visible. He traced his finger along the pink welted tissue. The cakey foundation she had applied to cover the scars for the shoot came off on Ramage's finger in a kind of powdery dust the color of putty. He looked at his finger; he wiped it clean on the bedsheet. She reached for his crotch. His penis curled like a burnt match between his legs.

Here, the writer engages with familiar imagery while transcending it with beauty. His moment of contact with her breasts may be something a reader would expect. But tracing his finger along the "pink welted tissue"? This feels compelling. Surprising. And in its tenderness, beautiful. We also appreciate how the powdery dust of Desiree's foundation calls back the dust of the oregano factory. These images, juxtaposed against the characters' actions, show us two human beings attempting to connect and take comfort in each other.

And here's Jeanette Winterson's depiction of the observations of Villanelle, a gambling red-haired web-footed daughter of a Venetian boatman, whose husband has gambled away her heart. It's from the novel *The Passion*. Note how she takes a rather sordid subject—addiction to gambling—and manages to wring beauty from it:

> I have always been a gambler. It's a skill that comes naturally to me like thieving and loving. What I didn't know by instinct I picked up from working the Casino, from watching others play and learning what it is that people value and therefore what it is they will risk. I learned how to put a challenge in such a way as to make it irresistible. We gamble with the hope of winning. But it's the thought of what we might lose that excites us.
>
> How you play is a temperamental thing; cards, dice, dominoes, jacks, such preferences are frills merely. All gamblers sweat. I come from the city of chances, where everything is possible but where everything has a price. In this city great fortunes are won and lost overnight. It has always been so. Ships that carry silk and spices sink, the servant betrays the master, the secret is out and the bell tolls another accidental death. But penniless adventurers have always been welcome here too, they are good luck and very often their good luck rubs off on themselves. Some who come on foot leave on horseback and others who trumpeted their estate beg on the Rialto. It has always been so.
>
> The astute gambler always keeps something back, something to play with another time; a pocket watch, a hunting dog. But the Devil's gambler keeps back something precious, something to gamble with only once in a lifetime. Behind the secret panel he keeps it, the valuable, fabulous thing that no one suspects he has.
>
> I knew a man like that; not a drunkard sniffing after every wager nor an

> addict stripping the clothes off his back rather than go home. A thoughtful man who they say had trade with gold and death. He lost heavily, as gamblers do; he won surprisingly, as gamblers do, but he never showed much emotion, never led me to suspect that much important was at stake. A hobbyist, I thought, dismissing him. You see, I like passion, I like to be among the desperate.
>
> I was wrong to dismiss him. He was waiting for the wager that would seduce him into risking what he valued. He was a true gambler, he was prepared to risk the valuable, fabulous thing but not for a dog or a cock or the casual dice.
>
> On a quiet evening, when the tables were half empty and the domino sets lay in their boxes, he was there, wandering, fluttering, drinking and flirting.

Even in this small passage, we see how Winterson resists all that we anticipate and concretely and convincingly portrays beauty even in the midst of human vice.

Facing the Great Conundrum of Writing

Again and again, we'll stress the importance of being concrete, of being *particular*. But we've also tried to convey another essential aspect of good writing: that it tethers unique and personal interests of an individual (you) to something larger—something other people will either relate to or be affected by.

Sarah Lewis, with her concept of aesthetic force, wants us to go further—to think about those who inspired change, even global change, by the sheer power of their art.

It's important to note that the artists and thinkers she discusses didn't know in advance, nor did many of them plan or predict, the impact. In fact, most would have never guessed. We are not saying that to be a writer one must write something that leads to some big change.

No.

We all hope to write about things that matter. Big things. To say something of consequence about the world, about the human condition. And that's an utterly commendable intention. But it's also a lot of pressure and in creative writing may be counterproductive.

This conundrum is illuminated in this quote by poet Richard Hugo, from his book on writing poetry, *The Triggering Town*:

> A poem can be said to have two subjects, the initiating or triggering subject, which starts the poem or "causes" the poem to be written, and the real or generated subject, which the poem comes to say or mean, and which is generated or discovered in the poem during the writing. That's not quite right because it suggests that the poet recognizes the real subject. The poet may not be aware of what the real subject is but only have some instinctive feeling that the poem is done.

Hugo is adamant that thinking too large when trying to come up with a "triggering" subject can hurt the poem—or piece of prose—by paralyzing the writer's imagination. Again from Hugo:

> Often, if the triggering subject is big (love, death, faith) rather than localized and finite, the mind tends to shrink. Sir Alexander Fleming observed some mold, and a few years later we had a cure for gonorrhea. But what if the British government had told him to find a cure for gonorrhea? He might have worried so much he would not have noticed the mold. Think small. If you have a big mind, that will show itself. If you can't think small, try philosophy or social criticism.

It's hard enough to portray a scene or finish a stanza. Change the world with it, too? We get why Hugo said what he said.

Of course, philosophy, social criticism, and creative writing aren't 100 percent mutually exclusive. Some of our favorite creative works engage all three. Barbara Kingsolver is a master of this. She wrote *Demon Copperhead* because she was immensely distressed about the opioid epidemic in the part of the country where she lives, Appalachia.

As readers, we can all sense when a creative work is weighed down by its creator's conclusions about a "big" subject. For many of us, thinking of a big concept first, and the smaller details second, can backfire. In fact, many of us want to remain in what may seem like small details.

From a feminist perspective, women have been penalized for centuries for "writing small," for writing about domestic and household issues and interpersonal relationships that don't directly address matters of "larger" global concerns. Yet Jane Austen found depth in drawing room comedy dramas. George Eliot in the small-town lives of the residents of *Middlemarch*. Virginia Woolf when Mrs. Dalloway throws a party. By examining the people, relationships, and events within their own circles of experience, women writers have long conceived great works of art.

Toni Morrison said this about pressure on writers to produce "universal" works:

> I never asked Tolstoy to write for me, a little colored girl in Lorain, Ohio. I never asked [James] Joyce not to mention Catholicism or the world of Dublin. Never. And I don't know why I should be asked to explain your life to you. We have splendid writers to do that, but I am not one of them. *It is that business of being universal, a word hopelessly stripped of meaning* for me. Faulkner wrote what I suppose could be called regional literature and had it published all over the world. That's what I wish to do. *If I tried to write a universal novel, it would be water.* Behind this question is the suggestion that to write for black people is somehow to diminish the writing. From my perspective there are only black people. When I say "people," that's what I mean. [emphasis ours]

Lydia Davis, the acclaimed writer of very short stories, trains her eyes on things so microscopic as to be passed over by most others. Yet they resonate with readers of all kinds. Here's one of her stories, in its entirety.

Fear
Lydia Davis

Nearly every morning, a certain woman in our community comes running out of her house with her face white and her overcoat flapping wildly. She cries out, "Emergency, emergency," and one of us runs to her and holds her until her fears are calmed. We know she is making it up; nothing has really happened to her. But we understand, because there is hardly one of us who has not been moved at some time to do just what she has done, and every time, it has taken all our strength, and even the strength of our friends and families too, to quiet us.

Where does advice like that leave us? Lewis seems to say that we're supposed to write about big things that will cause the multitudes to tremble. But Hugo says a wise person once told him, "Never write a poem about anything that ought to have a poem written about it." Again, from *The Triggering Town*:

> Not bad advice but not quite right. The point is, *the triggering subject should not carry with it moral or social obligations to feel or claim you feel certain ways.* If you feel pressure to say what you know others want to hear and don't have enough devil in you to surprise them, shut up. [emphasis ours]

And as it turns out, the people Sarah Lewis describes in her book are, almost always, like Fleming, studying mold, not curing gonorrhea. They become obsessed with a unit of something that may have seemed small. Experimenting with their small obsession produces something unexpected.

But what do we do with all this seemingly conflicting advice?

It means we somehow have to balance three things when we write:

1. We should write about something we're personally interested in, preferably even obsessed by.
2. We should write about something that *may eventually* matter to the world outside our own head (but we don't worry about that when creating).
3. We should write about something that will surprise our readers by its beauty—and, in the best circumstances, move them through the power of its aesthetic force.

From time to time, look over your material (or have a trusted reader look it over) and search for possible connections with the larger world (including, and perhaps especially, those you didn't plan). See how you can subtly intensify and strengthen those connections, but by using aesthetic force, not reason. Look for those nonconforming oddities we've discussed—tangential, insignificant-seeming scenes or lines, and don't be too quick to cut.

We find wisdom in what Eudora Welty writes in an essay for *The Atlantic* titled "Must the Novelist Crusade?":

> [Great fiction] abounds in what makes for confusion; it generates it, being on a scale which copies life, which it confronts. It is very seldom neat, is given to sprawling and escaping from bounds, is capable of contradicting itself, and is not impervious to humor. There is absolutely everything in great fiction but a clear answer. Humanity itself seems to matter more to the novelist than what humanity thinks it can prove.

And here, Welty is talking about how novelists work, but we think it applies to all types of creative writing:

> *If one knows all about why and when and how something is important to them with zero hesitation or confusion or ambivalence it may be exactly the wrong thing.* . . . When people think they know they tend to be general rather than specific. [emphasis ours]

Above all, Welty stresses that generalities stand in the way of "any real, however modest, discovery of the writer's own heart." She goes on:

> This discovery is the best hope of the ordinary novelist, and to make it he begins not with a generality, but with the particular in front of his eyes, which he is able to examine.

George Saunders, in *A Swim in a Pond in the Rain*, talks about a story as being a room-sized black box. He says, "We want readers to go into that box in one state of mind and come out in another." And, most importantly, "What happens in there has to be *thrilling and non-trivial.*" [emphasis ours]

If you're able to do what Saunders suggests, we say you're well on your way, regardless of the particulars of your process.

Louise Erdrich's Pulitzer Prize–winning novel *The Night Watchman* is an aesthetic wonder, taking us on a wild ride of both the very beautiful and the very, *very* dark experiences in the lives of a Native American community in northern Minnesota. The author, in an afterword, explains that the book is based on a true story, about her grandfather's role in bringing together his tribe to fight unconscionable legislation that would have broken yet another land treaty. But even though she starts with this "large subject," Erdrich makes it small and particular enough to get past our reason into our hearts.

SEPTEMBER 1953

Turtle Mountain Jewel Bearing Plant

Thomas Wazhashk removed his thermos from his armpit and set it on the steel desk alongside his scuffed briefcase. His work jacket went on the chair, his lunch box on the cold windowsill. When he took off his padded tractor hat, a crab apple fell from the earflap. A gift from his daughter Fee. He caught the apple and put it out on the desktop to admire. Then punched his time card. Midnight. He picked up the key ring, a company flashlight, and walked the perimeter of the main floor.

In this quiet, always quiet expanse, Turtle Mountain women spent their days leaning into the hard light of their task lamps. The women pasted micro-thin slices of ruby, sapphire, or the lesser jewel, garnet, onto thin upright spindles in preparation for drilling. The jewel bearings would be used in Defense Department ordnance and in Bulova watches. This was the first time there had ever been manufacturing jobs near the reservation, and women filled most of these coveted positions. They had scored much higher on tests for manual dexterity.

The government attributed their focus to Indian blood and training in Indian beadwork. Thomas thought it was their sharp eyes—the women of his tribe could spear you with a glance. He'd been lucky to get his own job. He was smart and honest, but he wasn't young and skinny anymore. He got the job because he was reliable and he knocked himself out to do all that he did as perfectly as he could do it. He made his inspections with a rigid thoroughness.

As he moved along, he checked the drilling room, tested every lock, flipped the lights on and off. At one point, to keep his blood flowing, he did a short fancy dance, then threw in a Red River jig. Refreshed, he stepped through the reinforced doors of the acid washing room, with its rows of numbered beakers, pressure dial, hose, sink, and washing stations. He checked the offices, the green-and-white-tiled bathrooms, and ended up back at the machine shop. His desk pooled with light from the defective

> lamp that he had rescued and repaired for himself, so that he could read, write, cogitate, and from time to time slap himself awake.

Let's now do an experiment.

Write Now

For this exercise, we're going to talk about "termite art." An essay by art critic Manny Farber that originally appeared in *Film Culture* magazine, "White Elephant Art vs. Termite Art," was written as a diatribe against the idea of the masterpiece and works of art produced by "overripe technique shrieking with preciosity, fame, ambition," as Farber judged them. In other words, works of art made by artists who were thinking too big and with grandiosity.

Farber recommended art that was committed to detailed observation, deep attention, and what he called "the unique temporalities of the quotidian" (paraphrase: the unique moments of a daily routine).

In Farber's words, creating termite art is a process of "journeying in which the artist seems to be ingesting both the material of his art and the outside world" in tiny mouthfuls.

Exercise, Part 1

1. Think of a large issue that you care about, are perhaps even passionate about (human rights, the planet, abortion?).
2. With this issue in mind, write a piece of narrative or a scene (something happening at a specific place at a specific time) that directly touches on the issue.

STUDENT EXAMPLE
Big Topic: Climate Change

The storms are getting fiercer. They last longer, the volume of water pouring from the skies keeps increasing, neighbors no longer compare a heavy rain to taking a shower, but to being held upside down by the ankles with your head submerged in a bathtub. Marie and Billy had moved to the burbs outside St. Louis from the Bay Area precisely because it was in the middle of the country, insulated from the dangerous encroaching of oceans, unstable continental plates, tornadoes, hurricanes, and other extreme weather. They hadn't thought about rain. Simple rain.

Exercise, Part 2

1. Now take an image from the scene you just wrote (anything rendered with one or more of the senses). It can be a static description or a moving image. Focus on it deeply. What comes to mind? What do you know about it? What do you *not* know about it?

2. Do a free write in which you write "termite art"—nibbling around the edges of what's happening in that particular image—combining what's going on in your head with what's happening in the physical world of the image.

3. Try to write at least two pages and keep it moving—your termite mind should be continuously ingesting a detail and moving on to the next object.

4. Follow your interest wherever it goes, especially if it goes to odd, or unpredictable, places. Remember, always, those nonconforming oddities.

Hint: Keep the focus on the small, sensory details. Above all, avoid abstract ruminations or explanations.

STUDENT EXAMPLE

Image from Scene: Increasing Volumes of Water Pouring from the Skies
The rain came, and kept coming. The power went out around 11:30 at night while the rain was still pelting against our bedroom windows. My boyfriend sighed and put his book down. *The basement*, he said. Like most houses in the midwest, we were dependent on a gadget called a "sump pump" to prevent flooding. Don't ask me how a sump pump works, except that it looks like someone started to dig a well in the corner of your basement, and ceased before completing it. And if it isn't working properly, you spend a lot of time ankle deep in dirty, cold water bailing as though trying to keep a sinking ship afloat. It required electricity to function. This was the third major storm this month, and the second time we'd lost power. Why oh why had we moved to St. Louis? Because it was cheap, because it felt safe, smack in the middle of the country, padded on all sides by corn-fed states. No ocean to rise up, no shaking of the earth when the pressure on the underground plates drove the dogs and cats to run crazily through the streets. Here nature would

be our friend. I smoked a joint waiting for Billy to return from the disaster downstairs. I did not feel inclined to follow him down there. No one had a cellar in San Jose, just insect-filled crawl spaces where you never went. And the sump pump itself made me uneasy. The deep, dark, hole in the cement floor. The tangle of wires and pipes disappearing down into it, plunging into the black oily water. I knew that unspeakable things lived down there, this was their passage from the underworld to my new home, that I hadn't left my terrors behind when we packed the U-Haul at 3543 Hawthorne, because here they were waiting for me when we'd pulled up in front of our new rented space one month ago.

Before we close, let's return to these false ideas that (1) to write of something of importance means it will likely be "dark" and (2) "serious" or "dark" or "deep" subject matter can't also be beautiful. Intellectually, we just know these things aren't true. Still, many writers struggle, at every stage, to expand on and focus on notions of beauty after discovering what's most meaningful to them, and for good reasons.

Janet Burroway, in her seminal book *Writing Fiction: A Guide to Narrative Craft*, quotes poet and novelist Robert Morgan:

Almost all good stories are sad because it is the human struggle that engages us readers and listeners the most. To watch characters confront their hardships and uncertainties makes us feel better about our own conflicts and confusions and fears. We have a sense of community, of sympathy, a cleansing sympathy, as Aristotle said, and a relief that we are safe in our room only reading the story. A story of sadness, even tragedy, makes us feel, paradoxically, better, as though we are confronting our own conflicts and fears, and have endured.

Even if this is true, we still think sadness and beauty can coexist. Let's turn once again to science.

Associate professor of physics at West Texas A&M University Christopher Baird said the following when asked at what speed darkness travels:

Darkness travels at the speed of light. More accurately, darkness does not exist by itself as a unique physical entity, but is simply the absence of light.

In the liminal realm of art, darkness is completely subjective, but like the darkness in the universe, it only exists in its relation to light. And both travel at the same speed.

Keep this in mind as you generate new writing. The results are likely to be messy but exciting.

Chapter 4

Love and Other Paradoxes

> "I love America more than any other country in the world, and exactly for this reason, I insist on the right to criticize her perpetually."
> **—James Baldwin**

Matthew once led a twelve-week workshop at an LGBTQ youth center in San Francisco. Having never taught anyone younger than nineteen, and never to folks who weren't *already* interested in creative writing, Matthew asked one of his mentors, the writer Robert Glück, for advice. Without hesitation, Bob said, "Ask them to write about *what's not fair*. We all care about that."

Care about what's not fair? It turned out Bob was right. Participants filled pages responding to prompts. Then, about halfway into the residency, one of the brilliant young writers said, "I'm tired of writing only about my outrage. I also want to write about what I love."

Poet Stephen Dunn said, "I don't trust people until I know what they love. If they cannot admit to what they love, or in fact love nothing, I cannot take even their smartest criticisms seriously."

When students shared work *only* about what they felt unfair, others empathized, often agreed, and validated their sentiments—but the prose often sounded less like art and more like therapy. On the flip side, in other environments, when students wrote earnestly about love, it often sounded less like art and more like the sentiments on a Hallmark card.

The moment the young writer suggested we combine outrage and love, we all pivoted, instantly, and the group began to include the things their characters *passionately adored*. Yet whether or not they were consciously aware of it, "what isn't fair" continued to thread its way through their experiments.

By first naming what's not fair, then shifting away from those generalities toward experiments with the often tiny, always specific things they (or their characters) loved, the creative pieces gained more complexity, heft, and weight. Previously flat and earnest pieces were suddenly bursting with artistic paradox.

At the end of the twelve weeks, students staged a reading. One student—who uses they/them pronouns—brought down the house. They'd started the workshop journaling about their parents', religion's, and small hometown's homophobia. During that stage of their work, this particular student was their own worst critic. "But it's so boring," the student had complained. "It sounds like 'poor me.' I hate seeing myself as a victim, my mom some kind of villain. I love her. I just hate that she can't love me, too."

At the pivot point, after doing an exercise on things they loved, the student had an idea: switch from their own point of view to a voice-driven fictionalized letter they'd write from their mother's imagined point of view. Week by week, draft after draft, the writer worked to imbue the letter with more and more compassion, love, and understanding for a character based on a person who, in real life, had abandoned and rejected the writer.

At one point during the workshop, the student said, "It's not there yet. However awful she is about the gay and gender stuff, she's really funny, and this character isn't. You can't have funny, lovable homophobes."

Another student said, "You can't? I'm from Texas. That's three-quarters of the population."

The writer kept experimenting. By the evening of the reading, they were "almost happy with it" and received a standing ovation.

Like James Baldwin in his famous quote about America, this student loved their mom so much they insisted on the right to criticize her beliefs. The paradox? Prior to *portraying* the love and humor, the criticisms felt—to the writer—self-pitying and therefore flat, boring, and lacking in impact.

To paraphrase the Dunn quote, they couldn't take their own criticism seriously. Satisfaction for that writer only came after they took the emotional risk of showing love for the very person who'd withheld it.

Louise Erdrich said:

> Life will break you. Nobody can protect you from that, and living alone won't either, for solitude will also break you with its yearning. You have to love. You have to feel. It is the reason you are here on earth.

There we stood, in community, some of us broken, all of us cackling with laughter, most of us crying. Because of someone else's words on a page.

In this chapter we're going to continue to ask you to write about what you might not otherwise. We want this portion of the book to be generative—to get something on the page you may not have gotten on your own. To do this, we'll talk about love. Our goal is to move beyond the schmaltzy earnestness often associated with the subject into portraying moments imbued with the power of paradox.

Experimenting When Stuck in Love (or Hate)

A common self-criticism among students of writing is "I'm stuck. My draft feels stilted."

When they come to us, we ask *why*: Is it on one end of a spectrum? Lovey-dovey or angry? Assuming that the work is complex and meaningful enough to the writer, there's usually something that can be done. If the draft is too schmaltzy with love—say with a character who is grief-stricken over the pending loss of a loved one, and all of the reactions are maudlin because of the level of love—we encourage the student to try rewriting it, weaving in a thread of something mean or critical. If the draft is too flat because the character or narrative seems too critical, we ask the student to find a place in the text that can be infused with "love" or "humor."

Self-righteousness is also a tough one to earn. When students come to us because their scene is made flat by a "good" character upset about the behavior of a "bad" character, we sometimes suggest they write in the first person from the point of view of the "bad" character. We might say, "Make the bad character explain, convincingly, why you, the writer, misunderstood them. See if you can imagine them convincing you as to why they aren't, in fact, bad. Then take the new knowledge and weave it into the scene."

Our goal is to move beyond the schmaltzy earnestness often associated with the concept of love into portraying moments imbued with the power of paradox.

What Is a Paradox?

A literary paradox occurs when the author plays with words or concepts that appear contradictory at first glance. As readers delve deeper, they discover complexities that challenge their perspective, encouraging them to explore hidden layers of meaning within a text. Too often, writers of early drafts do not think of the opportunities to imbue the emotion of their work with paradox.

Let's see some writing rich with paradox.

First a poem, then some creative nonfiction. As you read each piece, look for how the writers play with words or concepts that appear contradictory at first glance.

The Thing Is
Ellen Bass

    to love life, to love it even
    when you have no stomach for it
    and everything you've held dear
    crumbles like burnt paper in your hands,
    your throat filled with the silt of it.
    When grief sits with you, its tropical heat
    thickening the air, heavy as water
    more fit for gills than lungs;
    when grief weights you down like your own flesh
    only more of it, an obesity of grief,
    you think, *How can a body withstand this?*
    Then you hold life like a face
    between your palms, a plain face,
    no charming smile, no violet eyes,
    and you say, yes, I will take you
    I will love you, again.

Loving a "plain face, / no charming smile, no violet eyes" engages clichéd images of love poems by conjuring and negating them. If we look closer, we see something decidedly emotional here, too. That love—the love of life itself—includes the "obesity of grief" "heavy as water."

When we're in the thick of grief (and our throats are "filled with the silt of it"), it's paradoxical to think of this experience as loving life.

Perhaps after encountering this poem, we, as readers, can look back on the griefs we've survived—and survival as a form of loving life. This idea stretches the notion of love, then reframes it so it can contain so much more than clichés.

Here are a few excerpts from a piece of creative nonfiction by Reginald Shepherd, from an essay about his poetry. In it, it's easy to glean some of what the speaker loves. Note how quickly paradox surfaces.

Why I Write (excerpt)

Reginald Shepherd

I write because I would like to live forever . . . I won't be there to witness that immortality, mine or my work's, that by definition I will never know whether my endeavor has been successful. . . .

My aim is to rescue some portion of the drowned and drowning, . . . an impulse to rescue my mother from . . . the wreckage of her life, out of which I emerged, . . . I escaped that wreckage, which she, by dying, did not. . . . Many of the poems in my first book, *Some Are Drowning*, centered around an absent, speechless other, an inaccessible beloved who frequently stood in for my mother, . . . her absence was always palpable, a ghostly presence haunting the text. My poems were an attempt to speak to her, to get her to speak back to me, and above all to redeem her suffering: that is, to redeem her life. . . .

The essay is the poet's reflection on his process of reading and writing. In it, the speaker understands he won't be able to witness his own immortality. Yet he desires to. "I would like to live forever."

It's powerful when a writer allows themself to desire the impossible.

Can words save lives? In a literal sense, of course not. But we frequently have students espousing that the memoirs, stories, poems, and novels they love altered their points of view. They name the authors whose work broke them open and allowed them to see some part of themselves or the world anew. Occasionally, a student will say, "That book saved my life."

If you were actually drowning, we're sure you'd choose a flotation device over a handful of sentences, but Shepherd is using metaphor and paradox to make his desire plain.

A question he asks in another part of the same essay: "When has impossibility ever deterred anyone from a cherished goal?" This question is great for two reasons. One, for the paradox it contains. Two, for the clue it gives us to what makes good writing.

The piece moves from the general "drowned and drowning" to the particular, the personal, "an impulse to rescue my mother from . . . the wreckage of her life, out of which I emerged." This, too, contains a paradox.

We normally don't associate wreckage as something vital. What happens when we pause to consider? This poet's loss of his mother, combined with his desire to communicate with her after her passing, created a collection of poetry.

Mother Teresa once said, "I have found the paradox that if I love until it hurts, then there is no hurt, but only more love." We see Mother Teresa's wisdom in Shepherd's essay.

Consider your early drafts. Do they feel too stiff? Too earnest? Perhaps you're too busy writing toward an *achievable* goal.

Let's continue looking at a few more excerpts from Shepherd's piece:

> Art reminds us of the uniqueness, particularity, and intrinsic value of things, including ourselves. I sometimes have little sense of myself as existing in the world in any significant way outside of my poetry. That's where my real life is, the only life that's actually mine.... I have a strong sense of things going out of existence at every second, fading away at the very moment of their coming into bloom: in the midst of life, we are in death, as the Book of Common Prayer puts it.
>
> In that sense everyone is drowning, everything is drowning, every moment of living is a moment of drowning. I have a strong sense of the fragility of the things we shore up against the ruin which is life: the fragility of natural beauty but also of artistic beauty, which is meant to arrest death but embodies death in that very arrest....
>
> What we take out of life is the luminous moment, which can be a bare branch against a morning sky so overcast it's in whiteface, seen through a window that warps the view because the glass has begun to melt with age. Or it can be the face of a beautiful man seen in passing on a crowded street, because beauty is always passing, and you see it, but it doesn't see you. It's the promise that beauty is possible and the threat that it's only momentary: if someone doesn't write it down it's gone....
>
> ...One is deluded if one believes that one can actually preserve the world in words, but one is just playing games if one doesn't try.
>
> ...But elements of the world can be and have been saved. Thus the history of art. Each artwork that has endured through time is a piece of the world that has survived, and carries with it other pieces of a world, of worlds, otherwise gone.... I seek to save the sensuous appearances, the particulate worldness of the world.

Nothing could be further from the literal truth than the assertion that a living writer exists nowhere but in their written work.

Yet so many writers feel exactly this way. There are variations on the theme: my real self is in my work; my true self is in my writing.

Narrative arts were, in part, born out of a need to portray our inner lives. These often contrast the public selves we perform in order keep jobs, relationships, peace. In varying degrees, we all conceal and hide things, and poetry and prose are places where these hidden things are often revealed. Perhaps this is why people who write feel more authentic "on the page" than they do "in real life."

Many say that portraying the significant details of their inner lives—a bare branch against a morning sky so overcast it's in whiteface, seen through a window that warps the view because the glass has begun to melt with age—is the lifeblood of good writing. Perhaps, then, an embrace of paradox is the soul.

Paradox, cognitive dissonance, real and meaningful contradiction and juxtaposition are powerful in creative writing because they offer deeper insights from the speaker or character. Strong emotions (such as love) add tension and surprise and delight for the writer (and perhaps, then, too, the reader).

Let's look at one last section of Shepherd's essay before we start to write:

> I would like each poem of mine to be as close to perfection as possible, and I think that good poems are much more rare than some believe them to be. I would also like my work to be more than just an accumulation of good poems, difficult as even a single good poem is to achieve. I would like the whole to add up to more than the sum of its parts.... To produce such a body of work is one of my goals as a writer.
>
> ... I won't live to know whether my work has outlived me. But one can't predict the future in general, and this doesn't prevent us from making decisions that influence, change, and often determine that future. The future isn't wholly unknowable, and the future doesn't just happen: in large part we make it. This works no differently in poetry than in any other field of endeavor. There is no guarantee that one will reach any of one's goals in this life. But not to struggle toward those goals is to guarantee that they won't be attained. I choose, in the words of Tennyson's Ulysses, "To strive, to seek, to find, and not to yield."
>
> ... And never to forget beauty, however strange or difficult.

This closing line reminds us that beauty, like love, when portrayed with layers of complexity, can be many things, including, paradoxically, strange and difficult.

Another paradox in this final section: artists seek perfection in their work knowing, in advance, it cannot be achieved. If an artist like Shepherd writes to bring his deceased mom back to life, he knows—before word one gets to the blank page—that he will, on a literal level, fail. But what's born out of this failure?

In the full version of his essay, Shepherd writes in detail about how these paradoxical ideas inform his poetry. The reader gets the sense that Shepherd could have analyzed his work only after he'd created—and perhaps published—it.

We do not believe he sat down to conjure paradoxes prior to his first drafts. Instead, it seems he turned to his obsessions, his desires.

With the following exercises we want to strengthen the muscle that may allow you to do the same.

Write Now

You can do this exercise as yourself or (as always) from the point of view of a fictionalized character in a story, or as the speaker in a poem, or any combination of the above. If you're using yourself as your character, see if you can access a higher self. Allow that higher self to reveal more than you'd usually reveal.

1. Answer each of these questions: What do you (or your character) love? What stands in your (or your character's) way of expressing love? What do you (or your character) think you "hate" but secretly "love" (or indulge in or revel in)?
2. See if you can write a full paragraph for each question.
3. Keep in mind the paradoxes discussed in the examples preceding this exercise.

Student Examples

These were written by Ryan Pittington, a student of The Lab, on a short story in progress titled "True Thoughts."

1 | *What do you (or your character) love?*
  He loves the fine arts, though he encounters them little in the story—he

expresses his love for the arts more than he exercises it, perhaps out of guilt for not being an artist, but instead working in tech, or maybe to counterbalance his drive for material possessions. He loves unconventional and transcendent moments, beautiful real-life images in an aesthetic life: like his boyfriend Gabe beside a window, or under a streetlamp, the city shimmering with light. And, of course, he loves Gabe, even if he objectifies him. It's too soon, but my character desperately wants to secure a relationship with Gabe. In some way, my character wants Gabe for selfish reasons that illuminate his insecurities. In other ways, it's out of his true love for who Gabe is as a person (as far as he can know).

2   *What stands in your (or your character's) way of experiencing love?*

My character is full of doubt. He struggles with loneliness because of his estrangement from his parents. He's sober, so drinking got in his way of experiencing love. Also, his fear of looking pathetic or desperate, of being abandoned or rated subpar. He's afraid of losing things he's accumulated, losing physical beauty. When he touches on what is true for him, it comes out in a confusing eruption. He can't express how much it means to him to talk on the bed, to hold hands beneath the ivy. This lack of ability to communicate, along with his draw to Marc (a guy he meets in an AA meeting while dating Gabe. Marc is still in rehab), who shows undiluted desire for him, keeps him from deepening his love with Gabe and finding something stable with him (though choosing Gabe was fraught to start, as his affections are divided and his situation unstable).

3   *What do you (or your character) think you "hate" but secretly "love" (or indulge in or revel in)?*

He thinks he hates drama, change, instability, non-monogamy. Yet, he seems to crave it all—he wants validation from the guy he should be helping, Marc, at the rehab, and stays on the line until the end. He wants to do it on the purple satin sheets of a house Gabe is house sitting, wants to mark his territory. At the same time, he thinks he hates the conventional, but he wants a relationship that looks stable and singular. Conventionality is a

> concept he doesn't fully grasp, he spends more time moving forward than looking around. He wants a purity of love, but is constantly complicating it—with Marc, with hiding his feelings, without speaking up (like in a moment with his sponsor, he disagrees, but just says OK). He seems to be holding his breath, propelling himself forward, with no real guide, only a mission to collect.

Now that you know a little more about what you (or your character) loves, write a short free write that creatively depicts that "thing that you/they hate but secretly love." In other words, not an analysis or explanation, but writing that evokes the emotion itself.

You can write this in the form of a scene (something happening at a certain place at a certain time) or as narrative or imagery, in any form you like: prose or poetry.

Student Example

Here's the opening of Ryan Pittington's story in progress, "True Thoughts," based on the questions he answered previously:

> On our third date, Gabe told me he was married to a man he met on Grindr. He sounded nervous at first, holding his breath before saying, "I have to tell you something." We were lying on my bed, beside the window. The moon was full and the steep streets between the Castro and Noe Valley glowed silver. I realized then that I had been asking for too much. I was thirty-one and Gabe was twenty-five, with big arms and a lean face. He had only been in the city a year after leaving Venezuela. At that time, I had no grasp of things like hyperinflation. I had trouble understanding macro social ideas; all my classes in college had focused on the particular: close readings, the composition of a photograph. In my work, I dealt with technical customer issues, debugging software glitches. I had no idea what it meant to leave a country. I had lived in California my whole life and I barely read the news. I knew the particulars of what Gabe had told me, that his sister had moved to the Bay Area and made space for him, that he took a six-month intensive English course and bussed tables at a restaurant that would pay him in cash. Back home, his father had waited twelve hours to buy soap with a backpack full of bolívars.

> "You don't wear a ring," I said. I sat up, suddenly aware that I must have been smothering him, lying on top of him with my full weight and my face so close to his that I could hear his eyelashes when he blinked.
>
> "It's in my pocket." He smiled and put it on, left it there.
>
> "Do you hang out with him a lot?" I asked.
>
> "The husband?" He laughed, apparently forgetting I was the wrong audience for that kind of joke. I knew it would be unkind to take it personally that he had married in order to work, but the way he relaxed so quickly, spread out the details, seemed to take pleasure in saying "I'm married" and waiting for my reaction, made me uneasy. The whole arrangement seemed to have some kind of fairy tale charm for Gabe, even if it was platonic. I remembered Gabe once said I looked like a Disney prince, by which I think he meant tall and broad. The husband's name was Chris. I wondered what Chris looked like and, though I was ashamed to admit it to myself, felt an urgent need to know I was more attractive.

Ryan's opening paragraphs are already infused with what are sure to become a set of complicated paradoxes as his narrator moves through the story. We don't yet see the character, Marc, that Ryan alludes to in the answers to his questions, but the careful reader can see the setup for the thing he "hates" but secretly "loves:" drama.

Sadness and Whimsy

Let's look at another poem to set up our next writing experiment. Here's "Getting By," by Bob Hicok. Keep your eyes peeled for paradoxes.

Getting By
Bob Hicok

> I love the idea of climbing a ladder
> carrying another ladder. Of climbing that ladder
> carrying a tree. Of climbing the tree
> to get closer to where rain
> doesn't fall, to touch the asceticism
> of the sky, the hem of drought.

As when the woman I love said,
I don't love you anymore, and I decided
to love her for not loving me.
Within a year, she loved me again
for loving her negations. In the same way,
I love the rain for killing itself
before it reaches the grass, I love the grass
for turning brown, I love brown
for being the color of my thirst, I love my thirst
for its willingness to kill me. But this is all
an idea, a man on a tree on a ladder
on a ladder on a planet in a solar system
in a poem that is fighting for its life,
like the city I see when I close my eyes,
or the night of my closed eyes
that falls upon the city, or the people
in the city who look up
and want moonlight, even a quarter moon,
even the word *moon* on a string will do.

The writer Karen Carlson wrote about Bob Hicok's poem. First, she quotes the opening line: "I love the idea of climbing a ladder carrying another ladder. Then she says:

> As whimsical as this poem starts out, there's a sadness underneath the whimsy that I find touching . . . the speaker of this poem is embracing that which is distressing, be it drought or rejection: he loved his wife for leaving him, and she came back; then he loves the drought: "I love my thirst / for its willingness to kill me."
>
> We don't find out if that quenches his thirst; throughout, desperation comes through:
>
> . . . the people
> in the city who look up

and want moonlight, even a quarter moon,
even the word *moon* on a string will do.

    I'm not sure what happens here; is this a warning? This lowering of standards is what happens when you embrace that which hurts you, when you start settling for less and less? Or simply a recognition that here is where we are, where we have always been, all of us, unable to get enough love, or water, or moonlight? Another poem that leaves me with more questions than answers. And that's just the way I like it.

Let's keep this analysis and these questions in mind as we jump into the next exercise.

Write Now

1. Reread your free write from the previous exercise.
2. Starting with the line "I love the idea of..." list five things, borrowing, if you wish, from the most muscular or compelling images you wrote in the free write.
3. Allow the speaker or narrator of your piece to list things that might be surprising, like "rain killing itself in the sky" and "the grass for turning brown."
4. Interrupt the succession of the list, like Hicok does, with a contradiction: "But...,
5. See what paradox emerges and surprises you with its truth. Keep on until you discover something about yourself (or your character) that's worth developing.

Student Example
I love the idea of the intelligence of this earth's creatures:
Of whales singing across oceans
Of cows remembering a kindness
Of pigs recognizing one pen mate from another.
I love the portrayal of nature as a benevolent mother, joyously sharing her
    bounty as she shields, protects.

> This is the same idea I have of my family, wanting intelligence and
>   goodness to be
> Our nature, but then an Orca drowns a baby dolphin, eats a Blue;
> A heifer attacks her calf with a back-kick to the snout;
> Adonis is impaled by the tusks of a boar.

Analyze

To cement the tone of this section, let's ponder a few opportunities to infuse work with paradox. Nineteenth-century philosopher Søren Kierkegaard said:

> One must not think slightingly of the paradoxical . . . for the paradox is the source of the thinker's passion, and the thinker without a paradox is like a lover without feeling: a paltry mediocrity.

Paradox in How One Thinks and Acts

One of our students loved the poem "Getting By," but said, "It's the first poem I've ever read (and liked) where the subject is a guy sulking."

Sulking? Isn't it paradoxical to enjoy someone's sulking? Novelist and contemporary philosopher Alain de Botton wrote on the subject of sulking:

> At the heart of a sulk lies a confusing mixture of intense anger and an equally intense desire not to communicate. The sulker both desperately needs the other person to understand and yet remains utterly committed to doing nothing to help them do so.

According to de Botton, sulking is a paradox, so it's a perfect subject for a poet. Paradoxes abound in George Orwell's *1984*:

> To know and not to know, to be conscious of complete truthfulness while telling carefully constructed lies, to hold simultaneously two opinions which cancelled out, knowing them to be contradictory and believing in

both of them, to use logic against logic, to repudiate morality while laying claim to it, to believe that democracy was impossible and that the Party was the guardian of democracy, to forget whatever it was necessary to forget, then to draw it back into memory again at the moment when it was needed, and then promptly to forget it again: and above all, to apply the same process to the process itself—that was the ultimate subtlety: consciously to induce unconsciousness, and then, once again, to become unconscious of the act of hypnosis you had just performed. Even to understand the word "doublethink" involved the use of doublethink.

Paradox in Settings/Place

What about exploring paradoxes where one lives? The poet Rickey Laurentiis, in an interview, was asked to speak about the South (and specifically New Orleans, where the poet grew up and then left). Laurentiis said:

Distance, I like to say, adds clarity. Distance, it also seems to me, can also lead to distortion—that is, of the details, of memory. So, there's a paradox there: leaving New Orleans, leaving the South, granted me the clarity with which I could better understand and certainly appreciate what it is I left. But, having left, I'm also prey to forgetting the specifics or, worse, exaggerating, inventing details in the gaps, dealing with fiction . . . Especially in a place like New Orleans—a city that continuously is and historically has been overwhelmed with various "fictions" about it, and a city that was more recently revised following Katrina—it seems important to me to regard both these impulses: to tell the truth and to lie, two things I think the South, in particular, and the U.S., in general, does very—if also dangerously—well.

Paradoxes in Imagined Places

Many religions attempt to comfort suffering practitioners with a distant reward, often after death. In a conversation with Elizabeth Farnsworth for *PBS NewsHour* on March 9, 1998, writer Toni Morrison pointed out this paradox: "All paradises, all utopias are designed by who is not there, by the people who are not allowed in."

Perhaps human beings want to believe that our individual lives have meaning and that we're also a part of something larger than our individual selves. Community is a vital part of many of our lives. Orson Welles's famous quote illuminates this paradox: "We're born alone, we live alone, we die alone. Only through our love and friendship can we create the illusion for the moment that we're not alone."

Now, for the final act of this chapter, let's write some more.

Write Now

1. Consider again this favorite Stephen Dunn quote:

   The good poem illuminates its subject so that we can see it as the poet wished, and in ways he could not have anticipated. It follows that such illumination is twofold: the light of the mind, which the poet employs like a miner's beam, and that other light which emanates from the words on the page in conduction with themselves, a radiance the poet caused but never can fully control.

   Now don't worry about "getting" it. Just let it sink in.

2. See if you can write an entire draft of a poem or scene (a scene has characters interacting in a particular place and time) from any of the material you've mined so far in this chapter.

3. The goal is to lose control. So write wherever your thoughts take you, no matter how illogical.

4. Write until a shift takes place. Perhaps that shift is something that your character thought they hated, but discovers, in fact, they loved. Or something or someone they thought was ugly, but now see as beautiful.

Chapter 5

The Unexpected

When Bad Things Happen to Good Characters

Investigating Opportunities for Surprises in Writing

Now we're going to focus on something that we hope will help you, whether you're generating material or working to shape it: surprise.

The first part of this book asks you to do a lot of what we call creative woolgathering. It's a process most artists go through in one form or another. They write and sketch in notebooks, record voices, take snapshots, bookmark and cut out articles, create collages or mind maps, doodle, send texts to themselves—all in hopes of capturing an image or an experience that they're passionate about or obsessed with.

The goal is to deepen and experiment with whatever sparks for you on your journey to find a form. In Part II, we'll start to get more specific about the craft choices writers make (often when revising), focusing on three genres: poetry, creative nonfiction, and fiction. Perhaps you'll be inspired to apply one or more of those craft choices to your gathered material—experimenting with knitting the wool into something more specific.

All along we've been inserting sneak peeks of craft and its vocabulary, just as we'll continue to woolgather and experiment in the genre-focused chapters.

The purpose of this chapter is to continue, deepen, and reinforce the practice of thinking outside of what's "expected." Creative writing isn't about retelling what happened to you or someone you know. Nor is it an intellectual exercise so abstract and private that a reader would require a decoder ring to decipher. It's an art form with many malleable genres, each containing its own set of tools to get your readers to listen to, hear, and share in the questions and mysteries of the things that are important to you.

As writers, we look everywhere for inspiration, for lures, for what leads us toward discovery. Reading others' writing is one obvious choice. One writer we know spent years working on a novel and then got stuck until two books he read—just for enjoyment—combined forces and unlocked a closed door to his imagination. The narrator of our friend's novel heard the voices of recently deceased loved ones, but the writer couldn't figure out how to convey that to the reader. When he looked, he didn't find solutions in classic ghost stories or supernatural fiction. He found a way back into the material only after he gave up on the search and started reading *Lincoln in the Bardo*, by George Saunders. With that novel, his imagination started stirring with possibilities for his own work. Then the second book, *The Friend*, by Sigrid Nunez, offered an entirely different take on how the deceased can occupy a character's mind, and the writer was able to learn from each and enter his own work with an idea and renewed energy.

Another writer we know is currently working on a piece in which she must capture exactly the right voice for the narrator. It was born (written in her first draft) as a plural first-person narration—a group of characters speaking as one—something that's not seen all the time because it's a challenge to maintain. She intentionally sought out Faulkner ("A Rose for Emily"), Jeffrey Eugenides (*The Virgin Suicides*), and, like the first writer, *Lincoln in the Bardo* as examples of how other writers took on voice-driven works with groups of characters. Through much trial and error, what she read helped her discover what she did and did not want in her own project.

Like scientists, each of our writer friends consulted other studies on their way to something new.

Reading great literature isn't the only solution—although we truly believe what comes out of our imagination is directly related to what we put in. We all indulge in our guilty pleasures for entertainment or comfort—and that's okay—but part of a writer's job is also developing a discipline to engage deeply in reading.

That said, we also recommend getting up and going outside. We asked the ghost story writer to talk about what fuels his work when he's not reading. He said he gets around the Bay Area on a motorcycle. While driving, he can't have or see a phone or computer. Surviving on a motorcycle means paying attention to the world around him. Many of the images that land in his fiction and essays are discovered on the motorcycle.

He said he sometimes feels compelled to pull over and make a voice note so as not to forget a particularly compelling scene, image, or tableau. Not too long ago, he'd been heading west on the south part of Martin Luther King Jr. Drive in San Francisco's Golden Gate Park when he noticed clusters of wild calla lilies. He'd never seen them there before, and there they were, silky white blooms surrounding the bright yellow pistils. They looked like they were vibrating in the green field surrounded by dense gray fog.

The writer with the voice-driven novel said she's less stimulated creatively by the outdoors, although she certainly appreciates it as she lives in the countryside. Although she characterizes her walks there as "lovely and calming," her writing is mostly concerned with character and relationships (which you don't find walking down rural nature paths). She gets more stimulated during discussions with friends and family, observing interactions at meetings or parties, and even through email exchanges.

In previous chapters, we showed you where else we look for inspiration: advice columnists, lectures by art historians, an interview with a children's book author. You'll also see quotes by visual artists, an acting coach, and philosophers. Help is everywhere! We want to enable you to tune your mind to it.

Today we're going to look at a hybrid form called a short-short, which combines the elements of a short story with the compression of a poem. We'll also look at a series of curated events as told to us by a brain scientist. All of this is aimed at the same target: to imbue your work with surprise.

Write Now

But before we get there, let's do a generative (free write) warm-up.

1. Make a list of three *concrete* external events in your (or your character's) life that significantly changed the way you (or they) saw the world, if only for a moment. This could be the first day of the COVID-19 lockdown; moving across town, country, or ocean; serving in the military; experiencing an earthquake, a fire, the illness or loss of a loved one; winning the lottery. The list goes on and on.
2. For each event, write a few sentences or a short paragraph that depicts a *precise* reaction perceivable with the senses. In other words, without *telling*

us how you or your character thought or felt, you're going to show how the emotional reaction is manifested in the physical world of the five senses.

Experiment with reactions that aren't what the reader might expect. See if you can earn something that seems truthful, but also surprising ("surprising but convincing," E. M. Forster's ever-helpful advice).

> **STUDENT EXAMPLE**
> Event: My son died.
> Reaction:
> The day I found out I lost my son, I took the phone call from his doctor while I was driving. I was listening to the Giants game on the car radio. I remember being irritated, and my skin prickled with sweat, even anger—not scared or sad, not yet—but pissed seeing the doctor's name on the display because she interrupted the game.

Now we're going to add yet another layer onto this event. Thinking from the point of view of your character ("I"), write ten statements beginning with the words "I am . . ." that show how the character sees themself in the world.

In other words, what are their *self-defining characteristics?* Try to get ten "I am" sentences for this exercise.

> **Example**
> Character: I am a husband. I am a father. I am an educator. I am a Californian. I am generous. I am a Democrat . . .

Now put the woolgathering aside. We're going to use it later.

Analyze

While reading the following short-short, ask yourself: What personal actions and reactions does the character manifest? When and how are external events portrayed? And, most importantly, is there a cause-and-effect relationship?

Grace Period

Will Baker

You notice first a difference in the quality of space.

The sunlight is still golden through the dust hanging in the driveway, where your wife pulled out a few minutes ago in the Celica on a run to the mailbox, and the sky is still a regular blue, but it feels as if for an instant everything stretched just slightly, a few millimeters, then contracted again.

You shut off the electric hedge trimmers, thinking maybe vibration is affecting your inner ear. Then you are aware that the dog is whining from under the porch. On the other hand you don't hear a single bird song. A semi shifts down with a long backrap of exhaust on the state highway a quarter mile away. A few inches above one horizon an invisible jet is drawing a thin white line across the sky.

You are about to turn the trimmers on again when you have the startling sense that the earth under your feet has taken on a charge. It is not quite a trembling, but something like the deep throb of a very large dynamo at a great distance. Simultaneously there is a fluctuation of light, a tiny pulse, coming from behind the hills. In a moment another, and then another. Again and more strongly you have the absurd sense that everything inflates for a moment, then shrinks.

Your heart strikes you in the chest then, and you think instantly *aneurysm*! You are 135 over 80, and should have had a checkup two months ago. But no, the dog is howling now, and he's not alone. The neighbors' black lab is also in full cry, and in the distance a dozen others have begun yammering.

You stride into the house, not hurrying but not dawdling either, and punch in the number of a friend who lives in the city on the other side of the hills, the county seat. After the tone dance a long pause, then a busy signal. You consider for a moment, then dial the local volunteer fire chief, whom you know. Also busy.

Stretching the twenty-foot cord, you peer out the window. This time the pulse is unmistakable, a definite brightening of the sky to the west, and along with it a timber somewhere in the house creaks. You punch the Sheriff. Busy. Highway Patrol. Busy. 911. Busy. A recorded voice erupts, strident and edged with static, telling you all circuits are busy.

You look outside again and now there is a faint shimmering in the air. On the windowsill outside, against the glass, a few flakes of ash have settled. KVTX. Busy. The *Courier*. Busy. On some inexplicable frantic whim you dial out of state, to your father-in-law. (Where is your wife, she should have the mail by now?), who happens to be a professor of geology on a distinguished faculty. The ringing signal this time. Once. Twice. Three times. A click.

"Physical plant."

Doctor Abendsachs, you babble, you wanted Doctor Abendsachs.

"This is physical plant, buddy. We can't connect you here."

What's going on, you shout, what is happening with the atmosphere—

He doesn't know. They are in a windowless basement. Everything fine there. It's lunchtime and they are making up the weekly football pool.

It is snowing lightly now outside, on the driveway and lawn and garage. You can see your clippers propped pathetically against the hedge. Once more, at top speed, you punch your father-in-law's number. Again a ringing. A click.

This time a recording tells you that all operators are busy and your call will be answered by the first available. The voice track ends and a burst of music begins. It is a large studio orchestra, heavy on violins, playing a version of "Hard Day's Night." At the point where the lyrics would be "sleeping like a log" the sound skips, wobbles, and skips again as if an old-fashioned needle has been bumped from a record groove.

You look out the window once more, as the house begins to shudder, and see that it is growing brighter and brighter and brighter.

We thought readers might enjoy remembering when phones were attached to walls by cords. Published in *Flash Fiction: 72 Very Short Stories* (W. W. Norton) in 1992, there are moments in this story that are anachronistic, but overall, it leaves the reader with a timeless feel—one that many of us know well by now—in capturing a moment just before one *feels* that everything—everything—is about to change.

This very short story does so many things skillfully: the title works to hint toward the story's thematic concerns; it engages all five of our senses; it uses poetic repetition (Busy. Busy. Busy.) to heighten tension; it resists paraphrasing; and it reverses a trope of the suburbs as "safe."

Beyond that, this piece shows unlikely—or *unexpected*—cause and effect between external events and personal actions and reactions. This narrator acts in ways that are fresh, believable, and surprising.

Let's read it once more. Notice which events are external and which are the narrator's personal actions and reactions. To help you out, we've underscored the personal responses.

You notice first a difference in the quality of space.

The sunlight is still golden through the dust hanging in the driveway, where your wife pulled out a few minutes ago in the Celica on a run to the mailbox, and the sky is still a regular blue, but it feels as if for an instant everything stretched just slightly, a few millimeters, then contracted again.

You shut off the electric hedge trimmers, thinking maybe vibration is affecting your inner ear. Then you are aware that the dog is whining from under the porch. On the other hand you don't hear a single bird song. A semi shifts down with a long backrap of exhaust on the state highway a quarter mile away. A few inches above one horizon an invisible jet is drawing a thin white line across the sky.

You are about to turn the trimmers on again when you have the startling sense that the earth under your feet has taken on a charge. It is not quite a trembling, but something like the deep throb of a very large dynamo at a great distance. Simultaneously there is a fluctuation of light, a tiny pulse, coming from behind the hills. In a moment another, and then another. Again and more strongly you have the absurd sense that everything inflates for a moment, then shrinks.

Your heart strikes you in the chest then, and you think instantly *aneurysm!* You are 135 over 80, and should have had a checkup two months ago. But no, the dog is howling now, and he's not alone. The neighbors' black lab is also in full cry, and in the distance a dozen others have begun yammering.

You stride into the house, not hurrying but not dawdling either, and punch in the number of a friend who lives in the city on the other side of the hills, the county seat. After the tone dance a long pause, then a busy signal. You consider for a moment, then dial the local volunteer fire chief, whom you know. Also busy.

Stretching the twenty-foot cord, you peer out the window. This time the pulse is unmistakable, a definite brightening of the sky to the west, and along with it a timber somewhere in the house creaks. You punch the Sheriff. Busy. Highway Patrol. Busy. 911. Busy. A recorded voice erupts, strident and edged with static, telling you all circuits are busy.

You look outside again and now there is a faint shimmering in the air. On the windowsill outside, against the glass, a few flakes of ash have settled. KVTX. Busy. The *Courier*. Busy. On some inexplicable frantic whim you dial out of state, to your father-in-law (Where is your wife, she should have the mail by now?), who happens to be a professor of geology on a distinguished faculty. The ringing signal this time. Once. Twice. Three times. A click.

"Physical plant."

Doctor Abendsachs, you babble, you wanted Doctor Abendsachs.

"This is physical plant, buddy. We can't connect you here."

What's going on, you shout, what is happening with the atmosphere—

He doesn't know. They are in a windowless basement. Everything fine there. It's lunchtime and they are making up the weekly football pool.

It is snowing lightly now outside, on the driveway and lawn and garage. You can see your clippers propped pathetically against the hedge. Once more, at top speed, you punch your father-in-law's number. Again a ringing. A click.

This time a recording tells you that all operators are busy and your call will be answered by the first available. The voice track ends and a burst of music begins. It is a large studio orchestra, heavy on violins, playing a version of "Hard Day's Night." At the point where the lyrics would be "sleeping like a log" the sound skips, wobbles, and skips again as if an old-fashioned needle has been bumped from a record groove.

You look out the window once more, as the house begins to shudder, and see that it is growing brighter and brighter and brighter.

Tell Don't Show?

Lisa Cron has worked as a literary agent, a television producer, and a story consultant for Warner Brothers and the William Morris Agency, among others. She advises writers on the art and craft of story. In an essay published in Literary Hub called

"Tell Don't Show? What Brain Imaging Reveals About Readers" (excerpted from her book *Story of Die*, published by Ten Speed Press), she writes:

> As counterintuitive as it may seem, a story isn't about what happens in the world. A story is about what happens in the mind of the protagonist—the person through whose eyes we're experiencing those events.
>
> That realization was a game-changer for me. It meant that we'd had it backward.
>
> Which brings us to the question: okay then, what *is* a story?
>
> A story is about how an unavoidable external problem forces the protagonist to change internally in order to solve it.

We don't agree with the absoluteness of this definition. We believe stories can be about many things, including the tiny stuff that happens in the world. But we think Cron has some interesting things to say, nevertheless:

> A story isn't about *how* someone solves a problem. It's about how the problem causes someone *to realize* something, internally—something that has been preventing them from solving said problem. It is that inner struggle that has us riveted, not the bombs bursting in air.
>
> And the *realization* that the protagonist's inner struggle leads to is what answers the question your audience is always tacitly asking: "Why does this matter to me?"

We'd like you to notice the ratio of external to personal actions/descriptions in "Grace Period" keeping Cron's quote in mind. You can see that external events rendered with the five senses seem to dominate. If we did a more careful analysis, we'd see that external observations or events come at about two times the frequency of the personal movements, thoughts, or actions.

Sometimes these ratios are reversed. Other times they're even. If you're rereading a draft of a scene and it feels stilted or slow, like not enough is happening, common workshop advice is that "there's not enough action."

Maybe. Or maybe not.

Everything is influenced by what happens—what we see outside of ourselves—so external action and internal change happen *in relation to each other*. In Baker's short-short, the reader sees how each of the *external* actions leads to a slight calibration in the *mind* of the narrator.

The narrator in this story doesn't resolve anything, but the external events—fluctuations of light, dog barking, ash settling on glass, snow starting to accumulate, and phone calls not connecting—force internal changes in the character and the reader. Even if the problem remains unsolved, changes are happening.

Examining the ratio (relationship) of external events to internal events can help a writer develop their piece. Compelling narratives often have double (or more) external actions that lead to internal change.

Write Now

1. Choose one of the three events that you wrote about in this chapter's last Write Now experiment. Try to pick the one that changed you (or your character) the most.
2. With as much sensory concreteness as you can manage, drop yourself (or your character) into the scene *as it's happening* (use present tense). Imitate the movement between external and personal events/reactions. Try to get the same proportion of personal to external as in Baker's piece.
3. If you'd like to use the second person ("you"), as Baker does, go ahead. If you want to change to the first person ("I"), that's fine.
4. Make your first line echo Baker's first line: "You notice first a difference in the . . . [something concrete from your external world] . . ."
5. Try to get 500 to 1,000 words out of this.

Analyze

Will Baker's "Grace Period" never reveals its inspiration—whether it comes from the author's lived experience or an imaginary experience. In either case, it captures something both ominous and beautiful and allows us, as readers, to ponder and reflect on our own lives—what is and is not out of our control and how much of life pushes us so far beyond what we expect.

Our next exercise switches forms, but we'll continue to look at ratios of external and internal events. We'll examine how external action often leads to internal change (or the opportunity for that change, even if not realized in the scene or story).

We humans are stubborn about our beliefs, and we're resistant to change. Therefore, we often need an uneven ratio, or *several* external events, to build up and accumulate before the character is able to update a belief.

Triggering Internal Reactions by External Events

Now we'll present you with excerpts from a talk given by brain scientist and author Jill Bolte Taylor. Continue to chart for yourself the back-and-forth, this dance between external events and then unexpected personal, individual actions and reactions.

A note before you begin reading: By the fourth paragraph, you'll learn that the speaker had a stroke. This happened *inside* her body and caused a hemorrhage "the size of a golf ball," but we think of this as an external event because strokes (like heart attacks and other forms of organ arrest) are often triggered (or at least preceded) by an event. More importantly, they are outside the control of the person experiencing the attack—the person has no choice, no control—and often experiences them as they might a tornado or fire.

My Stroke of Insight
Jill Bolte Taylor

I grew up to study the brain because I have a brother who has been diagnosed with a brain disorder, schizophrenia. And as a sister and as a scientist, I wanted to understand, why is it that I can take my dreams, I can connect them to my reality, and I can make my dreams come true—what is it about my brother's brain and his schizophrenia that he cannot connect his dreams to a common, shared reality, so they instead become delusions?

So I dedicated my career to research into the severe mental illnesses. And I moved from my home state of Indiana to Boston where I was working in the lab of Dr. Francine Benes, in the Harvard Department of Psychiatry. And in the lab, we were asking the question—What are the biological differences between the brains of individuals who would be diagnosed as normal control, as compared to the brains of individuals diagnosed with schizophrenia, schizoaffective, or bipolar disorder?

So we were essentially mapping the microcircuitry of the brain, which cells are communicating with which cells, with which chemicals, and then with what quantities of those chemicals. So there was a lot of meaning in my life because I was performing this kind of research during the day. But then in the evenings and on the weekends I traveled as an advocate for NAMI, the National Alliance on Mental Illness.

But on the morning of December 10 1996 I woke up to discover that I had a brain disorder of my own. A blood vessel exploded in the left half of my brain. And in the course of four hours I watched my brain completely deteriorate in its ability to process all information. On the morning of the hemorrhage I could not walk, talk, read, write or recall any of my life. I essentially became an infant in a woman's body.

If you've ever seen a human brain, it's obvious that the two hemispheres are completely separate from one another. And I have brought for you a real human brain. [At this point in her TedTalk, Dr. Bolte Taylor has an assistant bring out a real human brain on a tray. She puts on gloves and lifts it up.]

So, this is a real human brain. This is the front of the brain, the back of the brain with a spinal cord hanging down, and this is how it would be positioned inside of my head. And when you look at the brain, it's obvious that the two cerebral cortices are completely separate from one another. For those of you who understand computers, our right hemisphere functions like a parallel processor. While our left hemisphere functions like a serial processor. The two hemispheres do communicate with one another through the corpus callosum, which is made up of some 300 million axonal fibers. But other than that, the two hemispheres are completely separate. Because they process information differently, each hemisphere thinks about different things, they care about different things, and dare I say, they have very different personalities.

Our right hemisphere is all about this present moment. It's all about right here right now. Our right hemisphere, it thinks in pictures and it learns kinesthetically through the movement of our bodies. Information in the form of energy streams in simultaneously through all of our sensory systems. And then it explodes into this enormous collage of what this present moment looks like. What this present moment smells like and tastes like, what it feels like and what it sounds like. I am an energy being connected to the energy all around me through the consciousness of my right hemisphere. We are energy beings connected to one another through the consciousness of our right hemispheres as one human family. And right here, right now, all we are brothers and sisters on this planet, here to make the world a better place. And in this moment we are perfect. We are whole. And we are beautiful.

My left hemisphere is a very different place. Our left hemisphere thinks linearly and methodically. Our left hemisphere is all about the past, and it's all about the future. Our left hemisphere is designed to take that enormous collage of the present moment. And start picking details and more details and more details about those details. It then categorizes and organizes all that information. Associates it with everything in the past we've ever learned and projects into the future all of our possibilities.

And our left hemisphere thinks in language. It's that ongoing brain chatter that connects me and my internal world to my external world. It's that little voice that says to me, "Hey, you got to remember to pick up bananas on your way home, and eat them in the morning." It's that calculating intelligence that reminds me when I have to do my laundry. But perhaps most important, it's that little voice that says to me, "I am. I am." And as soon as my left hemisphere says to me "I am," I become separate. I become a single solid individual separate from the energy flow around me and separate from you.

And this was the portion of my brain that I lost on the morning of my stroke.

Okay, let's pause. Pretty fascinating stuff, right? We think Dr. Bolte Taylor is a great storyteller, but so far, she has given us backstory in a pretty straightforward college essay way: facts about herself and what the listener needs to know about the human brain. It's all interesting, as are the examples she notes to infuse life into the narrative information she's sharing, but she's not attempting to dazzle us with literary skills.

Pay attention to how things shift. The tone changes at this point in the story as the *emotion* picks up. Start tracking internal/external ratios now and how an internal calibration toward change is almost always preceded by one or more external actions. You'll notice that even Dr. Bolte Taylor talks about the pain as external. She says, "it just gripped me and then released me."

On the morning of the stroke, I woke up to a pounding pain behind my left eye. And it was the kind of pain, caustic pain, that you get when you bite into ice cream. And it just gripped me and then it released me. Then it just gripped me and then released me. And it was very unusual for me to experience any kind of pain, so I thought OK, I'll just start my normal routine.

So I got up and I jumped onto my cardio glider, which is a full-body exercise machine. And I'm jamming away on this thing, and I'm realizing that my hands looked like primitive claws grasping onto the bar. I thought "that's very peculiar" and I looked down at my body and I thought, "whoa, I'm a weird-looking thing." And it was as though my consciousness had shifted away from my normal perception of reality, where I'm the person on the machine having the experience, to some esoteric space where I'm witnessing myself having this experience.

And it was all very peculiar, and my headache was just getting worse, so I get off the machine, and I'm walking across my living room floor, and I realize that everything inside of my body has slowed way down. And every step is very rigid and very deliberate. There's no fluidity to my pace, and there's this constriction in my area of perceptions so I'm just focused on internal systems. And I'm standing in my bathroom getting ready to step into the shower and I could actually hear the dialogue inside of my body. I heard a little voice saying, "OK, you muscles, you got to contract, you muscles you relax."

And I lost my balance and I'm propped up against the wall. And I look down at my arm and I realize that I can no longer define the boundaries of my body. I can't define where I begin and where I end. Because the atoms and the molecules of my arm blended with the atoms and molecules of the wall. And all I could detect was this energy. Energy. And I'm asking myself, "What is wrong with me, what is going on?" And in that moment, my brain chatter, my left hemisphere brain chatter went totally silent. Just like someone took a remote control and pushed the mute button and—total silence.

And at first I was shocked to find myself inside of a silent mind. But then I was immediately captivated by the magnificence of energy around me. And because I could no longer identify the boundaries of my body, I felt enormous and expansive. I felt at one with all the energy that was, and it was beautiful there.

Then all of a sudden my left hemisphere comes back online and it says to me, "Hey! we got a problem, we got a problem, we got to get some help." So it's like, OK, OK, I got a problem, but then I immediately drifted right back out into the consciousness, and I affectionately referred to this space as La La Land. But it was beautiful there.

Imagine what it would be like to be totally disconnected from your brain chatter that connects you to the external world. So here I am in this space and any stress related to my, to my job, it was gone. And I felt lighter in my body. And imagine all of the relationships in the external world and the many stressors related to any of those, they were gone. I felt a sense of peacefulness.

And imagine what it would feel like to lose 37 years of emotional baggage! I felt euphoria. Euphoria was beautiful—and then my left hemisphere comes online and it says "Hey! You've got to pay attention, we've got to get help," and I'm thinking, "I got to get help, I got to focus." So I get out of the shower and I mechanically dress and I'm walking around my apartment, and I'm thinking, "I got to get to work, I got to get to work, can I drive? can I drive?"

And in that moment my right arm went totally paralyzed by my side. And I realized, "Oh my gosh! I'm having a stroke! I'm having a stroke!" And the next thing my brain says to me is, "Wow! This is so cool. This is so cool. How many brain scientists have the opportunity to study their own brain from the inside out?"

And then it crosses my mind: "But I'm a very busy woman. I don't have time for a stroke!" So I'm like, "OK, I can't stop the stroke from happening so I'll do this for a week or two, and then I'll get back to my routine, OK."

So I got to call help, I got to call work. I couldn't remember the number at work, so I remembered, in my office I had a business card with my number on it. So I go in my business room, I pull out a 3-inch stack of business cards. And I'm looking at the card on top, and even though I could see clearly in my mind's eye what my business card looked like, I couldn't tell if this was my card or not, because all I could see were pixels. And the pixels of the words blended with the pixels of the background and the pixels of the symbols, and I just couldn't tell. And I would wait for what I call a wave of clarity. And in that moment, I would be able to reattach to normal reality and I could tell, that's not the card, that's not the card, that's not the card. It took me 45 minutes to get one inch down inside of that stack of cards.

In the meantime, for 45 minutes the hemorrhage is getting bigger in my left hemisphere. I do not understand numbers, I do not understand the telephone, but it's the only plan I have. So I take the phone pad and I put it right here, I'd take the business card, I'd put it right here, and I'm matching the shape of the squiggles on the card to the shape of the squiggles on the phone pad. But then I would drift back out into La La Land, and not remember when I come back if I'd already dialed those numbers.

So I had to wield my paralyzed arm like a stump, and cover the numbers as I went along and pushed them, so that as I would come back to normal reality I'd be able to tell, yes, I've already dialed that number. Eventually the whole number gets dialed, and I'm listening to the phone, and my colleague picks up the phone and he says to me, "Whoo woo wooo woo woo." And I think to myself, "Oh my gosh, he sounds like a golden retriever!" And so I say to him, clear in my mind I say to him. "This is Jill! I need help!" And what comes out of my voice is, "Whoo woo wooo woo woo." I'm thinking, "Oh my gosh, I sound like a golden retriever." So I couldn't know, I didn't know that I couldn't speak or understand language until I tried.

So he recognizes that I need help, and he gets me help. And a little while later, I am riding in an ambulance from one hospital across Boston to Mass General Hospital. And I curl up into a little fetal ball. And just like a balloon with the last bit of air just, just right out of the balloon I felt my energy lift and I felt my spirit surrender. And in that moment I knew that I was no longer the choreographer of my life. And either the doctors rescue my body and give me a second chance at life or this was perhaps my moment of transition.

When I awoke later that afternoon I was shocked to discover that I was still alive. When I felt my spirit surrender, I said goodbye to my life, and my mind is now suspended between two very opposite planes of reality. Stimulation coming in through my sensory systems felt like pure pain. Light burned my brain like wildfire and sounds were so loud and chaotic that I could not pick a voice out from the background noise and I just wanted to escape. Because I could not identify the position of my body in space, I felt enormous and expansive, like a genie just liberated from her bottle. And my spirit soared free like a great whale gliding through the sea of silent euphoria. Harmonic. I remember thinking there's no way I would ever be able to squeeze the enormousness of myself back inside this tiny little body.

But I realized "But I'm still alive! I'm still alive and I have found Nirvana. And if I have found Nirvana and I'm still alive, then everyone who is alive can find Nirvana." I picture a world filled with beautiful, peaceful, compassionate, loving people who knew that they could come to this space at any time. And that they could purposely choose to step to the right of their left hemispheres and find this peace. And then I realized what a tremendous gift this experience could be, what a stroke of insight this could be to how we live our lives. And it motivated me to recover.

Two and a half weeks after the hemorrhage, the surgeons went in and they removed a blood clot the size of a golf ball that was pushing on my language centers. Here I am with my mama, who's a true angel in my life. It took me eight years to completely recover. [She shows the audience a photograph of herself with her mother.]

So who are we? We are the life force power of the universe, with manual dexterity and two cognitive minds. And we have the power to choose, moment by moment, who and how we want to be in the world. Right here right now, I can step into the consciousness of my right hemisphere where we are—I am—the life force power of the universe, and the life force power of the 50 trillion beautiful molecular geniuses that make up my form. At one with all that is.

Or I can choose to step into the consciousness of my left hemisphere where I become a single individual, a solid, separate from the flow, separate from you. I am Dr. Jill Bolte Taylor, intellectual, neuroanatomist. These are the "we" inside of me.

Which do you choose? And when? I believe that the more time we spend choosing to run the deep inner peace circuitry of our right hemispheres, the more peace we will project into the world and the more peaceful our planet will be. And I thought that was an idea worth spreading.

How do the ratios compare in Bolte Taylor's piece and in Baker's? Even though the pieces are different genres and much different lengths, the ratios are similar. Do you see a relationship between the way you experience each piece? We do.

As different as they are in the amount of time elapsed (the narrator in Baker's piece is experiencing the action "now," whereas Bolte Taylor is recounting what she's learned in the eight-plus years it has taken her to recover), a lot more can be realized in eight years than in a few moments. Yet each of the narrative voices allows us to *feel* the accumulation of events as if it were happening to us. In Bolte Taylor's case, we're told, in advance, that she had a stroke, so we don't expect that to be the big reveal. The surprise here is how this accumulation of external events changed her self-definition. Many believe that science and spirituality are incompatible. Bolte Taylor allows us to reconsider. What did "the character" of this Harvard scientist/intellectual want to learn by studying the brain? What did she end up learning instead—or in addition?

Do the following paragraphs sound like a brain scientist working at Harvard?

> I felt enormous and expansive, like a genie just liberated from her bottle. And my spirit soared free like a great whale gliding through the sea of silent euphoria. Harmonic. I remember thinking there's no way I would ever be able to squeeze the enormousness of myself back inside this tiny little body.
>
> . . . We are the life force power of the universe, with manual dexterity and two cognitive minds. And we have the power to choose, moment by moment, who and how we want to be in the world. Right here right now, I can step into the consciousness of my right hemisphere where we are—I am—the life force power of the universe, and the life force power of the 50 trillion beautiful molecular geniuses that make up my form. At one with all that is.

Taken out of context, these two paragraphs make Dr. Bolte Taylor sound more like a new-age spiritual type. How do we go from a Harvard scientist invested in her own credentials (which, in her case, is an investment at least partially born of the need to understand her brother—not just power or ego) to someone who sounds like she's recently finished yoga-teacher training?

From this:

> I was working in the lab of Dr. Francine Benes, in the Harvard Department of Psychiatry.... So we were essentially mapping the microcircuitry of the brain, which cells are communicating with which cells, with which chemicals, and then with what quantities of those chemicals.

To this:

> So who are we? We are the life force power of the universe, with manual dexterity and two cognitive minds. And we have the power to choose, moment by moment, who and how we want to be in the world. Right here right now, I can step into the consciousness of my right hemisphere where we are—I am—the life force power of the universe, and the life force power of the 50 trillion beautiful molecular geniuses that make up my form. At one with all that is.

And finally, to this:

> I can choose to step into the consciousness of my left hemisphere where I become a single individual, a solid, separate from the flow, separate from you. I am Dr. Jill Bolte Taylor, intellectual, neuroanatomist. These are the "we" inside of me.

Write Now

Stick with the same character that you used before. What might be the most ironic and unlikely thing that could happen to them, an equivalent of Dr. Jill Bolte Taylor, a brain scientist, having a stroke? Think of how Bolte Taylor renders this part of her talk to portray the life-changing moment. She starts in the past tense, but switches to the present ("I'm jamming away," "I'm realizing") as if it's happening now.

1. Reread your "I am" statements from the previous experiment. Choose one of them.
2. Write a scene in which your character questions their "I am" statement—and then acts differently than might be expected.

3. See if you can earn the surprise through an external event (or series of external events) that trigger believable but unexpected individual actions and reactions.

Before wrapping up, let's look at one more way to experiment with surprise, with the unexpected. It's an experiment based on the realizations Jill Bolte Taylor experienced eight years after the external events. This is a different kind of surprise, a different tone of unexpected turn.

Sometimes the external events of our lives are so shocking, so unexpected, we're unable to unpack the meaning they have to offer. A narrative time jump can help.

Jump in Time

So much of what we see in student drafts are sketches of characters who are static, who don't change at all (with most beginning and ending "angry" or "right" or "angsty").

In these student drafts, characters are angry with their jobs or their families or religions or hometowns and *they* decide enough is enough and make a change. Often the reason is their own inner strength. It's because they want to. This is great if you're a person who can do this in real life. But in creative writing it can be super exciting to see how external (or unplanned, uncontrollable) events can thrust a character, against their will, into discovering something new. We see this in Will Baker's piece and in Bolte Taylor's piece. Here are two more examples.

A writer and bioethicist named Margaret Battin spent her career fighting for the right of terminally ill patients and medically fragile people (like her mom, who had protracted suffering before she died) to end their own lives. She published books with the titles *The Least Worst Death: Essays in Bioethics on the End of Life* and *Ending Life: Ethics and the Way We Die.* Well into her writing and academic career, her husband had a serious cycling accident. This external event shifted her thinking, forcing her to question her previous assertions and identity.

In Ann Packer's novel *The Dive from Clausen's Pier*, a twenty-three-year-old Carrie Bell, as described by the publisher: "has spent her entire life in Wisconsin, with the same best friend and the same dependable, easygoing, high school sweetheart. Now to her dismay she has begun to find this life suffocating and is considering leaving it—and Mike—behind." She makes the difficult decision to break up with him. Almost immediately after that, Mike is paralyzed in a diving accident, forcing

Packer's protagonist to reevaluate everything about her life. (This is something the reader discovers at the beginning of the novel.)

Write Now

Back to the Future

1. Look through all the creative material you've generated in this chapter. Pick an event that resonates with you the most—that seems to have the most power, even if not fully developed.

2. Fast-forward your character to at least eight years after the event (the way Bolte Taylor narrated her stroke eight years after it happened).

3. Have your character, using first person ("I"), retell the story of what happened eight-plus years ago. The very point of this exercise is to reveal how the external events changed your character's self-definition over time.

4. Be as concrete and precise as possible, borrowing whenever you'd like from the wool you've gathered in any of the initial steps.

We subtitled this chapter "When Bad Things Happen to Good Characters." We aren't saying that the literary re-creations of real-life events like strokes or cycle accidents or apocalyptical vibrations are the only way to uncover "the unexpected" in your work. In fact, moments of tenderness or indifference or solitude can absolutely unearth the unexpected. We're asking you to look at how non-psychological events can lead to a change, however temporarily, in how a speaker or character sees themself in the world.

When a story, no matter how short, starts and ends with the character having the same list of beliefs about themself, it's just not as exciting, is it? And unearned change can feel even more distracting to a reader because it's difficult to believe.

So, as we continue to gather our wool and fill out notebooks, we want to encourage you to use what's going on in the external world to get you to write toward what's least expected.

PART II

Discovery

Exploring the Genres

"Immature poets imitate; mature poets steal."

—T. S. Eliot

Identifying Techniques to Beg, Borrow, and, Yes, Steal* from Other Forms of Writing

We hope that by now, our experiments have helped you gather enough material through the "woolgathering" we mentioned in Chapter 5 and that you're eager to apply techniques and transform your raw materials. You've exercised your imagination and experimented with language, images, and ideas that matter to you.

In Chapter 6, we'll explore a few features and techniques of poetry. We hope to give you sufficient insight into this genre so you can experiment with it and perhaps choose it as a "container"

---

* To err on the side of stating the obvious: we're not telling you to plagiarize other writers' work. But there is so much technique we can learn from the other genres that is worth analyzing, practicing, and making your own.

for your woolgathering. In Chapter 7, we're going to do that for fiction; in Chapter 8, for nonfiction. Finally, in Chapter 9, we'll look at how writers combine these elements of composition in hybrid forms.

Note that there is considerable overlap between the genres. Imagery, for example, is common to all three, although arguably used more compactly and precisely in poetry. We'll examine these nuances, show you examples of published works that display the various techniques, and give you exercises to try it yourself.

We will also switch up the format just a bit here. In the first five chapters, we asked you to "do" first and "think" later. In this section, since we're focusing on technique and strategy, we'll throw out a concept and then ask you to experiment with it. If you're more of a kinesthetic learner, you can always skip ahead to the Write Now sections and then afterward read about what you've done. If this is your path, try each creative experiment twice. Once before and once after. See what you learn.

Chapter 6

Poetry

"Use no superfluous word, no adjective, which does not reveal something. Don't use such an expression as 'dim lands *of peace.*' It dulls the image. It mixes an abstraction with the concrete. It comes from the writer's not realising that the natural object is always the *adequate* symbol. Go in fear of abstractions."
—Ezra Pound

"[Poetry is] based on a craving to get through the curtains of things as they appear, to things as they are, and then into the larger, wilder space of things as they are becoming. This ambition involves a paradox: an instinctive belief in the senses as exquisite tools for this investigation and, at the same time, a suspicion about their crudeness."
—May Swenson

"Rather than write about what you know . . . write about what you see. Assume that you know very little and that you'll never know much until you learn how to see."
—Sigrid Nunez

These things should sound familiar: *Go in fear of abstractions.* And *an instinctive belief in the senses as exquisite tools for this investigation.* That's how all creative work comes alive on the page: through sensory images. And although sometimes we can risk abstractions, we need to do so with great care.

Now, we'll ask the Big Question: What *is* poetry? What makes a collection of words a poem, and not something else?

Google this question and you'll see how many people have thrown up their hands over the centuries.

Some try to define along technical lines. They cite various poetic techniques that have been used through the ages. A poem, they say, must contain line breaks. That's what distinguishes it from prose. Or it must adhere to a scannable meter. It must have a certain form (sonnet, haiku, free verse), use rhyme, employ different kinds of metaphors, etc., etc.

Others define it based on the effect the poem has on a reader. They say it must produce illumination or induce a fresh intellectual or emotional state in the person reading or hearing the poem.

Still others say it's all about the writer's intent: If they intend to write a poem, then it is a poem. It might be a bad poem, but it is a poem, nonetheless.

(Sigh.)

Keep in mind that critics and academics might be in the business of defining things, but as artists, our job is to make the task difficult for them. We aren't writing to you as critics or academics. We're writing to you as artists. Our definitions are meant to make you want to write (not pull out your hair). In that vein:

Mark Yakich, in his book *Poetry: A Survivor's Guide*, writes:

> When I used to ask students what a poem is, I would get answers like "a painting in words," or "a medium for self-expression," or "a song that rhymes and displays beauty." None of these answers ever really satisfied me, or them, and so for a while I stopped asking the question.
>
> Then one time, I requested that my students bring into class something that had a personal meaning to them. With their objects on their desks, I gave them three prompts: first, to write a paragraph about why they brought in the item; second, to write a paragraph describing the item empirically, as a scientist might; and third, to write a paragraph in the first-person from the point of view of the item. The first two were warm-ups. Above the third paragraph I told them to write "Poem."
>
> Here is what one student wrote:
>
> > **Poem**
> > I might look weird or terrifying, but really I'm a device that helps people breathe. Under normal circumstances nobody needs me. I mean, I'm only used for emergencies and even then only for a limited time. If you're lucky, you'll never have to use me. Then again, I can see some future time when everybody will have to carry me around.
>
> The item he had brought to class? A gas mask.
>
> The point of this exercise wasn't only to illustrate the malleability of language or the playfulness of writing, but to present the idea that a poem is a strange thing that operates as nothing else in the world does.

Then there's Diane di Prima's lovely definition of poetry in "To a Student":

POEMS ARE ANGELS
come to bring you
the letter you wdn't
            sign for

earlier, when it was
            delivered
by yr life

Why Poetry?

We are both prose writers. So our minds tend to take compressed definitions and anecdotes and want to *expand them*, impose cause and effect and character motivation.

Poet friends say the opposite: often when they read a short story or novel or memoir, their minds (and pens) are eager to *compress*.

If reading in one genre makes us want to write in another, then the piece—whatever form it is in—is working. It's as great a reason to read widely as any other.

We hope this book inspires you to experiment in genres not your own. We've tried to dig deep into the essence of each genre in an effort to familiarize you with techniques you might not have known about—or perhaps were scared to try. As with all types of writing (and reading), the point is to ask: what (of any of these techniques) might be helpful to *me*?

In essence, that's what this book is about: locating a kernel of inspiration within an art form (or experience) and then using it in two ways—as a jumping-off place to generate new material and as a model of how you might organize your material.

When the poet Gregory Orr talks about poetry, he does so not in terms of craft or the aforementioned techniques, but in terms of the *temperaments* of the poet. In his essay "Four Temperaments and the Forms of Poetry," he says that each poet has varying inclinations for story, structure, music, and imagination that lead them to a certain style.

Story offers dramatic unity by providing a beginning, middle, and end to a narrative. Structure offers readers the pleasure of finding patterns in language and delivers a sense of balance and even beauty. Music offers rhythm and sound, with the poet controlling the poem's pitch, duration, and stress (think meter and rhyme). Imagination delivers a seamless flow of images that connect in ways that are not always obvious.

In Orr's opinion, a well-written poem is achieved through a skillful mix of these temperaments. Using them can help deliver that unit of satisfaction from writer to reader. Of course, no single poet is fully endowed with all these temperaments, but the peculiar mix of these qualities is what determines each poet's unique voice, according to Orr. We like this. We're going to (with gratitude) sprinkle some of his wisdom throughout this chapter.

What Defines Poetry?

A written poem is language, composed in strategically arranged lines on the page using compressed imagery, with attention paid to its rhythm and sound, which transports readers to a new, surprising space.

Why place these limits on poetry? Why not just let it be a free-for-all creative space? Because we want to put a stake in the ground to prepare us for talking about writing across genres. Of course, there are many subgenres of poetry, just as in fiction. Take spoken-word poems. They're essentially the same as written poems but may stress what Orr calls the "music"—the rhythms and sounds.

The boundaries between fiction and poetry and creative nonfiction are shifting every day. But in this chapter, we want to examine the techniques that poets, more than prose or memoir writers, use. The point isn't to teach you how to write poetry (there are tons of books out there and wonderful instructors to guide you) but to help you understand poetic techniques so you feel free to use them *whatever* you're writing.

For example, the Booker Prize–winning novel *Girl, Woman, Other*, by Bernardine Evaristo, is written in prose, but it has line breaks, the way a traditional poem would. Here's an excerpt:

> Amma
>   is walking along the promenade of the waterway that bisects her city,
> a few early morning barges cruise slowly by
>   to her left is the nautical-themed footbridge with its deck-like walkway
> and sailing mast pylons
>   to her right is the bend in the river as it heads east past Waterloo Bridge
> towards the dome of St Paul's

she feels the sun begin to rise, the air still breezy before the city clogs up
with heat and fumes
    a violinist plays something suitably uplifting further along the promenade
    Amma's play, *The Last Amazon of Dahomey*, opens at the National tonight
    she thinks back to when she started out in theatre
    when she and her running mate, Dominique, developed a reputation
for heckling shows that offended their political sensibilities
    their powerfully trained actors' voices projected from the back of the stalls
before they made a quick getaway
    they believed in protest that was public, disruptive and downright
annoying to those at the other end of it
    she remembers pouring a pint of beer over the head of a director
whose play featured semi-naked black women running around on
stage behaving like idiots
    before doing a runner into the backstreets of Hammersmith
    howling

What effect do these line breaks have on you as a reader? For us, it disrupts the flow of sentences and paragraphs in ways that force us to slow down and pause, reconnect with what's happening or what's being said or shown, and consider certain words or phrases more carefully.

In the chapter on hybrid forms, we'll look at many more examples like Evaristo's: works of art that defy or unify or mix forms.

We also love the novels of Michael Ondaatje, who is also a poet. They depend on rich imagery and vibrant metaphors to communicate Ondaatje's emotionally charged narratives. Here's a passage from the opening of his most famous novel (also a winner of the Booker Prize), *The English Patient*:

> Every four days she washes his black body, beginning at the destroyed feet. She wets a washcloth and holding it above his ankles squeezes the water onto him, looking up as he murmurs, seeing his smile. Above the shins the burns are worst. Beyond purple. Bone.
>
> She has nursed him for months and she knows the body well, the penis sleeping like a sea horse, the thin tight hips. Hipbones of Christ, she thinks. He is her despairing saint.

Shakespeare, of course, wove rhyme into the dialogue of his dramas. In *Othello*, Iago attempts to turn Othello against Desdemona. When Othello questions his motives, Iago pretends to be hurt, expressed in rhymed couplets:

> I thank you for this profit, and from hence
> I'll love no friend, since love breeds such offence.

Later, as things heat up, Iago uses a rhymed direct address of the audience, essentially asking them to be partners in his scheming:

> Will you go on, I pray? This is the night
> That either makes me, or fordoes me quite.

Shakespeare was a poet, too, of course, and this cross-hybridization of his creative work was probably calculated quite strategically. He *chose* these poetic techniques to have a desired effect on audiences of drama, a different genre altogether.

Do the exercises in this chapter in any genre you like. If you want to write poetry in response to the exercises in this chapter—whether that's because it's your preferred genre or because you'd like to give it a try—go ahead. Same with fiction and nonfiction. We'll provide lots of examples from which you can learn.

The first, the most basic, poetic technique to examine is imagery.

Fiction writers use imagery, of course. Nonfiction writers do too. So, what is different about the way that *poets* use imagery? What can we learn and use from their creative toolboxes?

Imagery is simply the use of language to evoke a sensory experience in the reader—in other words, to describe something of this earth, using one or more of the five senses. Not abstractions. Not theoretical thoughts or feelings. Physical things. We already talked about this in Chapter 2 (Beliefs and Everyday Magic), where we used the William Blake poems and Maurice Sendak interview to discuss the difference between concrete and abstract language and how varying the ratios of the two can be used strategically. Now we're giving you some more information about that concept.

When poets use sensory language well, they make magic. Writers in English use twenty-six letters, little shaped symbols, on paper or screen, and add a handful of other tiny symbols (punctuation) to *approximate* experience. These attempts play to the reader's senses, providing them with the illusion of sights, tastes, smells, sounds. When done well, this can feel as "real" as lived experience. When successful, sensory language rouses feelings and emotions. It's the sensory details that bring poems (and prose) truly to life—just by describing what the poets (or the speakers/personas in their poems) perceive.

Of course, a good image will transcend the actual physical description. In the mind of the reader, it will evoke emotions and feelings that resonate beyond what a tree or coffee machine would. The poet Mark Doty writes:

> It sounds like a simple thing, to say what you see. But try to find words for the shades of a mottled sassafras leaf, or the reflectivity of a bay on an August morning, or the very beginnings of desire stirring in the gaze of someone looking right into your eyes, and it immediately becomes clear that all we see is slippery, nuanced, elusive.

Here is a poem written by Jill Bialosky upon the death of her mother. Notice the concreteness of the images of snow—what it looks like, what it tastes like, what it feels like, how it lifts us beyond the actual experience of snow itself to something larger, more urgent.

> Snow of childhood,
> of dreams, of our poems
> & discontent, snow of our memories,
> some distorted,
> forgotten, trod upon, rendered
> to a whiteout, snow that dusts
> bridges, highways, roofs,
> that tastes of rust
> & weighs on the branches,
> *O don't forget them,*
> insufferable snow that falls
> on the pots that hold
> the pods of the dead
> in the brilliance
> of the outdoor gazebo

we see from the window
of the care home for the aged,
to praise our matriarch,
our boots wet, snow in our hair,
look how pale she is, look
what she has bore, those veins
in which flowed the blood
that flowed into us—

Bialosky's poem focuses on snow, not on the loss of her mother. Yet, the effect on the reader is as if it's the opposite. The final image is of the matriarch's adult children, alive with their mother's blood. While it may have appeared on the page from the writer's subconscious in an early draft, the writer eventually made a strategic choice to use snow as the unifying thread of the poem. This choice allows the poem's speaker to gently guide the reader from childhood to adulthood, the "distorted / forgotten, trod upon, rendered" memories of the past up until the present moment "from the window / of the care home for the aged."

That one syllable *snow* does all that work; it's enough to tether the speaker's specific situation (the loss of her mother) to broader thematic concerns of the poem (cycles of life and death; the subjectivity of the past; and, to use Mark Doty's word, the *slipperiness* of life).

Prose writers who deal with similar thematic concerns often write scenes that attempt to render abstract notions concretely by focusing on interactions between characters. If a character has a complicated history with an ailing parent, they might render a flashback of a fight and then contrast it with a present-day scene of a frail parent. How might those prose writers learn from Bialosky? Let's do an exercise to find out.

Write Now

1. Choose a tangible image or object (something that can be one or more of the following: seen, touched, held, smelled, tasted, or felt) that appears and reappears throughout the life of a character. As in the Bialosky poem, it could be snow. It could also be a family heirloom, such as a doll that was passed from grandparent to child to grandchild. Other examples: yearbooks

or other school memorabilia, travel souvenirs, gifts from loved ones, artwork or crafts, a musical instrument, sports equipment, clothing.

2. Now write five brief vignettes illustrating five incidents from a character's life. The first vignette should be the first time the character encountered the object. The other four vignettes can be at any point in their life as long as the object is also involved.

3. Reread Bialosky's poem and try to do your own take on her technique of weaving the image of snow to show how it shifts along with the speaker's phases in a life.

Remember the quote from Sigrid Nunez that this chapter opened with: "Rather than write about what you know . . . write about what you *see*. [emphasis ours] Assume that you know very little and that you'll never know much until you learn to see."

This is excellent advice, only we'd add the other senses: *write about what you see, feel, hear, taste, and smell.*

Figurative Versus Literal Imagery

Now we're going to talk about two distinct but related and extremely powerful language tools: literal and figurative imagery.

Literal language is a unit of language (words or phrases) that means exactly what it says. For example, when Ondaatje describes the "thin tight hips" of the English patient, we are meant to take that literally, a reflection of the reality of the scene.

Or in the following Mark Doty poem, "Esta Noche," the "gap in the center of her upper teeth" is a literal image.

Esta Noche
Mark Doty

In a dress with a black tulip's sheen
  la fabulosa Lola enters, late, mounts the stairs
to the plywood platform, and begs whoever runs
  the wobbling spot to turn the lights down

to something flattering. When they halo her
  with a petal-toned gel, she sets to haranguing,

shifting in and out of two languages like gowns
        or genders to *please* have a little respect

for the girls, flashing the one entrancing
        and unavoidable gap in the center of her upper teeth.
And when the cellophane drop goes black,
        a new spot coronas her in a wig

fit for the end of a century,
        and she tosses back her hair—risky gesture—
and raises her arms like a widow in a blood tragedy,
        all will and black lace, and lipsyncs "You and Me

against the World." She's a man
        you wouldn't look twice at in street clothes,
two hundred pounds of hard living, the gap in her smile
        sadly narrative—but she's a monument,

in the mysterious permission of the dress.
        This is Esta Noche, a Latin drag bar in the Mission,
its black door a gap in the face
        of a battered wall. All over the neighborhood

storefront windows show all night
        shrined hats and gloves, wedding dresses,
First Communion's frothing lace:
        gowns of perfection and commencement,

fixed promises glowing. In the dress
        the color of the spaces between streetlamps
Lola stands unassailable, the dress
        in which she is in the largest sense

fabulous: a lesson, a criticism and colossus
        of gender, all fire and irony. Her spine's

perfectly erect, only her fluid hands moving
    and her head turned slightly to one side.

She hosts the pageant, Wednesdays and Saturdays,
    and men come in from the streets, the trains,
and the repair shops, lean together to rank
    the artifice of the awkward or lovely

Lola welcomes onto the stage: Victoria, Elena,
    Francie, lamé pumps and stockings and always
the rippling night pulled down over broad shoulders
    and flounced around the hips, liquid,

the black silk of esta noche
    proving that perfection and beauty are so alien
they almost never touch. Tonight, she says,
    put it on. The costume is license

and calling. She says you could wear the whole damn
    black sky and all its spangles. It's the only night
we have to stand on. Put it on,
    it's the only thing we have to wear.

As a quick exercise, make note of all the literal images in Doty's poem. Read them aloud back-to-back. What effect do they have on you?

Unlike literal language, figurative language is a word or phrase that is not meant to reflect reality but to skew, interpret, distort, or compare something to something else. The goal of this "distortion," for lack of a better word, is, in "story"-leaning poems, to give readers insight into a situation or character. For nonnarrative poems, it's to evoke emotions—frequently complex ones.

Techniques for figurative language include similes, metaphors, hyperbole, personification . . . the list goes on and on. There are excellent resources both in print and online that define these techniques and how to use them.

In *The English Patient*, "penis sleeping like a seahorse" is clearly figurative imagery, in which we are asked to make a rather whimsical comparison of genitals to a nautical creature. "Raising her arms like a widow in a blood tragedy" is Mark Doty's figurative take on a drag queen performing a lip-sync at a bar in San Francisco's Mission District.

Learning to tell the difference between literal and figurative language isn't the important point. Using them both strategically is. Our goal is to create such evocative images that descriptions of things (people, objects, landscapes) carry more weight than they logically should.

It's important to stress at this point that literal language can be as powerful as figurative language. Some writers, when starting out, feel that something isn't "poetic" unless it contains a metaphor or some other kind of figurative image. That's simply not true (sounding too "poetic" can be a deterrent to an effective poem—more on this later). Some of the most affecting poems ever written—look at Bialosky's poem again—use plain, literal language to tell us quite simply what things *are*.

Remember what the writer Stephen Dunn says:

> The good poem illuminates its subject so that we can see it as the poet wished, *and in ways he could not have anticipated*. [emphasis ours] It follows that such illumination is twofold: the light of the mind, which the poet employs like a miner's beam, and that other light which emanates from the words on the page in conduction with themselves, a radiance the poet caused but never can fully control.

In other words, poets, through their use of imagery, push you toward insight. They must do the work of focusing your attention on the precise object at hand. This image should create a clear sensory picture in your mind but also drive you to *feel* something. But because you are you, and utterly unique, you might experience something *beyond* or *different from* what the poet intended—from what the poet could control by putting those precise words on the page.

The poet W. S. Merwin once said that *poetry is the exact rendering of an ambiguity*. Alice has always loved this definition.

The exact rendering of an ambiguity.

Let's break this down. An ambiguity is a situation or description with two or more possible meanings. And "the machinations of ambiguity are among the very roots of poetry," as William Empson famously wrote in *Seven Types of Ambiguity*.

So, an ambiguity is something that is difficult to pin down, difficult to *name*. And really, what are these poets trying to do but name things? Name thoughts, name emotions, name and put a voice to things that aren't yet—but deserve to be—described.

If we can render such things precisely on the page, we have achieved something worthwhile. By naming things, especially things that involve intense emotion, we can disrupt or delight—and perhaps provide solace to—others. How many times have you thought, "Thank god I'm not the only one," when hearing that someone else has had a certain experience or feeling?

Alternatively (or simultaneously), you can provide insight into circumstances that people might not experience personally, like what it means to live in a body or place or time different from your own.

On the humorous side, the writer Douglas Adams wrote the dictionary-like *The Meaning of Liff*, in which he made up words to describe situations or things that he felt the English language should contain. Here's a sampling:

> ahenny (adj.): The way people stand when examining other people's bookshelves.
> ampus (n.): A lurid bruise that you can't remember getting.
> bathel (vb.): To pretend to have read the book under discussion when in fact you've only seen the TV series.
> craboon (vb.): To shout boisterously from a cliff.
> huna (n.): The result of making the wrong decision.

These tickle us because they precisely describe ambiguous situations most of us have found ourselves in. That's akin to the magic that happens when we read a well-crafted poem.

Some poets deliberately put together images to disrupt our understanding of things and to infuse new meanings of language into our mind. Here's e. e. cummings's attempt to do this.

[anyone lived in a pretty how town]
e. e. cummings

anyone lived in a pretty how town
(with up so floating many bells down)
spring summer autumn winter
he sang his didn't he danced his did.

Women and men(both little and small)
cared for anyone not at all
they sowed their isn't they reaped their same
sun moon stars rain

children guessed(but only a few
and down they forgot as up they grew
autumn winter spring summer)
that noone loved him more by more

when by now and tree by leaf
she laughed his joy she cried his grief
bird by snow and stir by still
anyone's any was all to her

someones married their everyones
laughed their cryings and did their dance
(sleep wake hope and then)they
said their nevers they slept their dream

stars rain sun moon
(and only the snow can begin to explain
how children are apt to forget to remember
with up so floating many bells down)

one day anyone died i guess
(and noone stooped to kiss his face)
busy folk buried them side by side
little by little and was by was

all by all and deep by deep
and more by more they dream their sleep
noone and anyone earth by april
wish by spirit and if by yes.

Women and men(both dong and ding)
summer autumn winter spring
reaped their sowing and went their came
sun moon stars rain

"[anyone lived in a pretty how town]" describes a community in which a man called "anyone" resides. The community lives their lives in a familiar, socially acceptable way: maturing to adulthood, getting married, having children. Amidst what many would consider a boring existence, *anyone* finds true love with a woman named *noone*. By taking us through their story, the poem examines social mores and pressure to conform. It also stresses the power of relationships.

So, what's unique about the way imagery is used in poetry? How does it differ from the way imagery is used in fiction or nonfiction?

The difference, we argue, is that given the compression of poetry, the images must carry a great deal of weight—more weight than, say, in a novel, which uses thousands upon thousands of images to tell a story.

If a word in a poetic image is changed—say, swapped out for a less resonant synonym—the effect should be extremely significant *if the poet has done their work.* This is less the case, you could argue, for a work of prose. Of course, we're not saying to be sloppy with language when writing in prose. Finding *le mot juste* (the right word) is always our quest. But in poems you could argue that the stakes are higher.

So, when writing poetry, precise, evocative imagery is often key. Look at the word choices Toi Derricotte made in "The Peaches of August."

The long-awaited, here, at the local farm stand, are not as
comely as the ones at Whole Foods, but they are dollars
cheaper, and so we sweep them up like sweepstakes winners, and
stack them in our purposeful cloth bags. Tomorrow,
one of us, before the other awakens, will slice into Tupperware the 4 or 5 softest to the fingers (to test, press kindly
as a newborn's cheek), and stir them with brown sugar from
a box atop the refrigerator.

Let's just choose one image—the first one—of the long-awaited peaches that "are not as comely as the ones at Whole Foods." Just that one word—*comely*—draws our attention. An odd choice for peaches. "Comely" is a rarely used word, archaic, to be found in the works of long-dead writers. Tess Durbeyfield (from *Tess of the D'Urbervilles*, by Thomas Hardy) was described as "comely" in 1891.

Try substituting a different word. Attractive? No. Perfect? No. Delicious looking? Definitely not. The Cambridge Dictionary describes *comely* as "value-ridden," and indeed it is. Comely means gently attractive, something of beauty yet with modesty. It has all sorts of softly pleasing connotations—none of them related to peaches. And yet it works beautifully.

Like Bialosky, Derricotte puts an intense focus on a single literal object, the peaches of August. But it evokes a different but related (and equally complex) set of emotions as the snow poem, tenderly evoking a comparison between peaches and a newborn's cheek. This delicacy contrasts the sturdiness of brown sugar—another literal object—which, in this poem, is imbued with a different kind of power: the ability to maintain its sweetness, to last for months, from its perch.

Snow. Peaches. Both elusive. Both last only for a season. Both are difficult to keep. Let's do a prompt on literal and figurative language based on this concept.

Write Now

1. Write a list of three physical objects that can't be kept forever. Perhaps because they melt, like snow. Or rot, like fresh peaches.
2. Write an image for each object that is literal: you are trying to describe what it *is*. (That is, don't compare it to anything.) But still try to evoke emotion with your description.
3. Now write an image for each object that is figurative. You are trying to compare it to something else to evoke an emotion of how fleeting, even how precious, these difficult-to-hold-on-to things are.
4. Read through what you've written. Do any of these images carry more weight than they logically should?

In Shakespeare's *Romeo and Juliet*, Romeo describes his first sight of Juliet with rich visual imagery—most of it figurative. Torches, of course, do burn brightly (that's fairly literal), but the last two lines are clearly making comparisons that do not reflect reality but emotional truths that get to the heart of Romeo's feelings.

O, she doth teach the torches to burn bright!
Her beauty hangs upon the cheek of night
Like a rich jewel in an Ethiop's ear

Here's Mary Oliver's "At Black River," in which she uses a combination of literal and figurative language to write about, in a surprising twist, redemption. Note that she never names the animal that is the purported subject of her poem (an alligator). She only describes it. But she does so precisely in both literal and figurative imagery that we understand what she is talking about—and, even more so, what it means beyond the thing (the alligator) itself.

At Black River
Mary Oliver
All day
   its dark, slick bronze soaks
      in a mossy place,
         its teeth,

a multitude
   set
      for the comedy
         that never comes—

its tail
   knobbed and shiny,
      and with a heavy-weight's punch
         packed around the bone.

In beautiful Florida
   he is king
      of his own part
         of the black river,

and from his nap
   he will wake

into the warm darkness
    to boom, and thrust forward,

paralyzing
    the swift, thin-waisted fish,
      or the bird
        in its frilled, white gown,

that has dipped down
    from the heaven of leaves
      one last time,
        to drink.

Don't think
    I'm not afraid.
      There is such an unleashing
        of horror.

Then I remember:
    death comes before
      the rolling away
        of the stone.

Write Now

1. Think of something—a person, thing, place, or experience—that is so loaded with emotion for you that ordinary words fail. Like Douglas Adams, you wish the English language had a precise word for it.

   Could it be your childhood room? Your garden? The motorcycle ride along the Great Highway, Ocean Beach, at sunset? Is it Dolores, the ninety-year-old upstairs neighbor who has told you, for years, each time as if it were a confession, of her lover, Barbara, and the life they had as army nurses during World War II?

   The point is *not* to choose something that you could describe objectively (if true objectivity is even possible), but something that is so meaningful that even a perfect description might fall short of what the thing, place, person, or experience means to you.

2. Now describe that person, thing, or experience in a 20-line poem. Use both literal and figurative imagery. Don't worry for now if you don't know about poetic form or meter. Don't worry about rhyming. Just choose your words carefully, because each of them matters in such a brief piece of writing. And, for the sake of this exercise, use line breaks. As always, refrain from writing about abstractions like love or death. Write about something that can be perceived with the senses.

Often, poets who are masters of their craft will experiment and draft until their images do double (or triple) duty as both figurative and literal descriptions. In the following poem, for example, there is the hurricane that refers to Hurricane Katrina, but also to a ride in an amusement park dubbed the Hurricane, and, ultimately, the wild greater world into which a woman has to release and let go of her beloved maturing daughter.

Hurricane
Yona Harvey

Four tickets left, I let her go—
Firstborn into a hurricane.

I thought she escaped
The floodwaters. No—but her

Head is empty of the drowned
For now—though she took

Her first breath below sea level.
Ahhh   awe   &   aw
Mama, let me go—she speaks

What every smart child knows—
To get grown you unlatch

Your hands from the grown
& up & up & up & up
She turns—latched in the seat

Of a hurricane. You let
Your girl what? You let

Your girl what?
I did so she do I did
so she do so—

Girl, you can ride
A hurricane & she do
& she do & she do & she do

She do make my river
An ocean. Memorial,
Baptist, Protestant birth—my girl

Walked away from a hurricane.
& she do & she do & she do & she do
She do take my hand a while longer.

The haunts in my pocket
I'll keep to a hum: *Katrina was*
a woman I knew. When you were

an infant she rained on you & she

do & she do & she do & she do

Write Now

This exercise was created by poet Jennifer Burd, of Ann Arbor, Michigan. It is inspired by the following poem.

What My House Would Be Like If It Were a Person
Denise Levertov

This person would be an animal.
This animal would be large, at least as large
as a workhorse. It would chew cud, like cows,
having several stomachs.
No one could follow it
into the dense brush to witness
its mating habits. Hidden by fur,
its sex would be hard to determine.
Definitely it would discourage
investigation. But it would be, if not teased,
a kind, amiable animal,
confiding as a chickadee. Its intelligence
would be of a high order,
neither human nor animal, elvish.
And it would purr, though of course,
it being a house, you would sit in *its* lap,
not it in yours.

In this exercise, you'll write a poem, short prose paragraph, or mixed genre piece to portray a home. Doing this creates a type of metaphor known as personification—that is, describing nonhuman objects or animals as if they possess human characteristics. You'll also create an extended metaphor by developing the personification beyond a single instance.

1. Use the same title as Levertov: What My House Would Be Like If It Were a Person. (You can change the title later if you develop the piece. Or you can attribute your poem to being inspired by Levertov's.)
2. Describe where you live, giving your dwelling at least three human characteristics.
3. Allow yourself to explore this home-as-person without worrying about creating a polished piece.

Before we move on from metaphor and into the topic of line breaks (a choice poets use to make their metaphors sing), here is one more experiment you can try using metaphorical language.

Write Now

Here's another metaphor exercise from poet Burd involving synesthesia. In creative writing, synesthesia is a way to make a metaphor by describing something from one sensory realm through a different sensory realm. This often creates a fresh experience of something familiar. For example, you might describe the taste of your coffee as "loud." In this instance, you are mixing the sensory realms of taste and sound.

1. Describe what you last ate or drank in every sensory detail: what it looks like, smells like, tastes like, what its texture is like, and what it sounds like when you sip it or bite into it. Use literal, not figurative, imagery.
2. Now recast each of these descriptions using one of the other senses, as in the coffee example.
3. Order your images into lines of a poem or paragraph of creative prose in a way that is pleasing to you. Let yourself be as outrageous as your sensory comparison.

Line Breaks

Line breaks can imbue your image and metaphors with added power, as we saw with the novel excerpt *Girl, Woman, Other*. Let's start, contradictorily, with poets who choose *not* to use line breaks.

The only way to tell a prose poem from, say, flash fiction (very short fiction) is the author's stated preferred genre and the context. Is the piece without line breaks in a book of poetry? Is it by a poet? It's probably a prose poem.

Here's a prose poem "[Kills bugs dead.]" by Harryette Mullen:

> Kills bugs dead. Redundancy is syntactical overkill. A pin-prick of peace at the end of the tunnel of a nightmare night in a roach motel. Their noise infects the dream. In black kitchens they foul the food, walk on our bodies as we sleep over oceans of pirate flags. Skull and crossbones,

they crunch like candy. When we die they will eat us, unless we kill them first. Invest in better mousetraps. Take no prisoners on board ship, to rock the boat, to violate our beds with pestilence. We dream the dream of extirpation. Wipe out a species, with God at our side. Annihilate the insects. Sterilize the filthy vermin.

And here's the beginning of a prose poem by Sara Peters that won the 2015 Poetry Prize of *The Walrus,* a Canadian literary magazine. Note again the absence of line breaks. The piece was later published in a difficult-to-classify book, *I Become a Delight to My Enemies,* which was called "hybrid" by reviewers because of its unique mix of poetry and prose techniques:

One summer in my youth the young girl with the solar system tattooed on her face ruled the Town, and I spent all my nights wishing she would hitchhike to my parents' farmhouse, kick down the front door, and find me. Lying on top of my quilt I listened for the girl so hard I could hear the tomatoes from our garden drying out in the oven.

Perhaps the choice *not* to break lines comes from instinct. It's the opposite of Bernardine Evaristo's choice to use line breaks in her novel *Girl, Woman, Other.* Perhaps the prose poets experimented with breaks but found their pieces more able to deliver the unit of satisfaction with the strategic choice of a paragraph. In other words: line breaks would have *subtracted* from the power of the piece instead of *adding* to it.

Some writers see prose poems as *containing* line breaks: their often-rectangular shape and use of a traditional prose margins communicates *something,* just like white space and flush-left paragraphs in fiction and creative nonfiction cue prose readers, however quietly. It's possible to associate the justified paragraph with a suitcase or gift box. It makes some readers eager to open it and see what's there to unpack. Many poets allow the poem itself to determine the shape. But you don't need to be faithful to just one style. Do whatever you want.

So, what *is* a line break? It's the stopping of one line of poetry and the beginning of a new line. Unlike prose, in which sentences run into each other to form a paragraph and only break when a new paragraph (usually a new topic) is introduced, poem lines can be broken at any point.

Until the nineteenth century, the only conventionally approved way to break a line in formal verse was dictated by the poem's meter. (Meter is the pattern of stressed and unstressed syllables that create the rhythm of a poem.) But now? As far as line breaks are concerned, it's a free-for-all in the poetry world.

Sometimes the break comes after a certain number of syllables. A haiku is a succinct form of poetry originating from Japan, characterized by its adherence to strict syllabic and structural constraints. In English, it typically comprises three lines, with a total syllable count of seventeen, distributed in a 5-7-5 pattern. However, contemporary haiku practitioners often prioritize the essence of the form over rigid syllable counting, emphasizing brevity, simplicity, and a deep awareness of the present moment. Traditional haikus often incorporate *kigo* (seasonal words) and *kireji* (cutting words), enhancing their ability to evoke a profound emotional or philosophical response. Writers using the form often strive for precision in language, mastery of imagery, and an acute awareness of the interconnectedness between humanity and nature, seeking to distill complex experiences into moments of sublime insight.

Here is an English translation by Robert Haas of a haiku by Matsuo Basho, considered one of Japan's greatest haiku masters. Note that it doesn't adhere to the 5/7/5 syllable count:

> The old pond—
> a frog jumps in,
> sound of water.

Are poets who choose formal forms that include line breaks masochists? People who enjoy pain? We don't think so. Strict limitation is one of many choices a writer can make to narrow the focus, solve a puzzle, create surprise.

Here, a poet discusses how form (including free verse) and content have become "the very same thing." It's an excerpt from an interview with Randall Mann, who spoke to Tobias Wray for *The Adroit Journal* on the occasion of his publication of his collection *A Better Life*:

TOBIAS WRAY: I think of you as one of our most necessary practicing formalists for how your work breathes contemporary life into traditional forms, not to mention your cleverness for devising poetic constraints. Has your relationship to form evolved in these newer poems?

RANDALL MANN: I think what has been a constant is that each poem is asking for its own architecture; perhaps I am learning how to listen better to its demands. What has evolved is the following: I think when I started writing I would think of a formal choice—and even free verse is a formal choice—as a starting point, or an argument as one. I haven't thought like that for a while. Form and content are not merely complementary, they are the very same thing. The new book, like all my books—which I think of as one long conversation; even some of the titles recur, and that's no accident—has both strict forms and less strict ones, but in the new book, as in the last couple to a lesser extent, shorter lines with rhymes have been my main formal bent. In a time of logorrhea, I love the demands of the short line, and the way rhymes offer up content—if I listen to the poem.

TOBIAS WRAY: Although you pay homage to many kinds of poetic tradition, you especially honor queer lineages in your work. Many of your poems are in conversation with queer culture, but poets of a certain persuasion, Thom Gunn, David Trinidad, Hart Crane, to name a few, show up often. A queer poet myself, I sought out poems like yours (and theirs) to better understand the possibilities of queer experience in verse, what such a sensibility might look like on the page. Would you address the influence of that particular tradition, poetry that unabashedly addresses sexuality? And, what do you think is different about queer poetry today, publishing your fifth collection, than it was when *Complaint in the Garden* came out?

RANDALL MANN: I have learned who I am through the work of queer artists. I read Gunn in high school, and that did it, the early whiff of motorcycle uniforms and form. Then Auden and Cullen and Lorde and Ashbery and Lorca and Bishop, to name a few, very early in college, and I was struck by how large the queer universe was. (Bishop's colonialism and anti-feminism look more problematic by the day, but she'll always be my poetry mother.) I remember Merrill's notion of writing for "one perfect reader," and while I write to please myself, if I am writing to an audience, it's a combination of these writers and others, Bidart, Shepherd, Dixon, Dlugos, Trinidad, Doty, Brown. Marilyn Hacker taught me so much about order. D. A. Powell richly deserves a genius grant. When I write my short lines, I am always trying to get closer to James Schuyler, who might be my favorite poet, and May Swenson. My good friends Miguel Murphy and Aaron Smith, dangerous poets. Younger writers like Chen Chen, Cameron Awkward-Rich, Oliver Baez Bendorf, Omotara James, Ari Banias, Ricky Maldonado, and Emily Van Kley. I could go on and on; my artistic world is queer as fuck.

What's the point of a line break? Be aware that line breaks are about *pauses*—short breaks between the last word of the previous line and the first word of the next line. The pause will be even longer if a stanza break is involved.

Because of that, line breaks have to do with the rhythm of the language—how it sounds. And they emphasize certain words or phrases to add meaning.

Sometimes a line break comes at a logical point of grammar—the end of a phrase or clause or at the end of the sentence, a thought, or an image. This is called an *end-stopped* line break. But frequently poets will break lines at unexpected times. *Enjambment* is the running over of a sentence or phrase from one poetic line to the next, without terminal punctuation: the opposite of an end-stopped line break.

Alternatively, it might be the appearance of the poem on the page that the poet is after: long and thin, short and wide, something completely random, or even poetry that takes the shape of an object. A famous example of the latter is from *Alice in Wonderland*, by Lewis Carroll, in which the poem "The Mouse's Tale" is in the shape of, indeed, a mouse's tail.

Poet Rebecca Hazelton, in a piece written for the Poetry Foundation, says:

> The best way to approach the many ways poetic line breaks can operate is to first examine how poets actually use it. Let's start by reading Geoffrey Brock's "Homeland Security" aloud, emphasizing each line break with a distinct pause and each stanza break with a slightly longer pause. This is a clumsy way to read because you don't normally want to pause at the end of a line that doesn't have punctuation, but this exercise forces us to consider Brock's line-break decisions. When I read the poem aloud in this way, I notice how many of the lines are enjambed, meaning they don't end with punctuation or can't be understood independently on their own. Each time Brock enjambs a line, I face questions I can't answer without proceeding quickly to the next line. This withholding produces a subtle kind of mystery

or anxiety, as I'm not quite sure what each line means until I continue reading the next one. My thought process goes something like this: [Geoffrey Brock's poem is to the left; Rebecca Hazelton's reactions to each line after reading it aloud appear in parentheses.]

The four AM cries (Cries at four a.m., or is four a.m. itself crying?)
of my son worm (Ah, a baby or kid. Weird to end on worm. Is the son
    wormlike?)
through the double (Double what?)
foam of earplugs (Ah, earplugs! There must be two of them. OK, I'm
    feeling good here—wait, there's a big break.)
    and diazepam. (Oh. Huh. This is an anti-anxiety drug. That raises the
stakes a bit. And the diazepam is part of the double foam, isn't it? One
more barrier the cries must break through. The speaker is both physically
and mentally guarded.)

This line is worth repeating: "This withholding produces a subtle kind of mystery or anxiety." Isn't this what we're always after, regardless of genre?

Hazelton goes on:

Brock's use of enjambment allows him to dole out information bit by bit, heightening readers' curiosity and the drama hidden inside an otherwise common domestic scene. Look what happens if we reconfigure the poem to take away that enjambment and end-stop the lines, as below. This means each line terminates in a complete phrase or with end punctuation.

The four AM cries of my son
worm through the double foam
of earplugs and diazepam.

Far fewer questions propel me through the poem. The brief mysteries are clarified, and gone are some of the odder valences the enjambment produced, such as the interesting association between worm and son, which lumps the child in with other things to guard against, such as poisonous spiders. (Note, however, that the similar vowel sounds of son and foam are highlighted in this new arrangement, as are the em sounds closing off foam and diazepam—a hint of consonance. . . .) And if I take this experiment even further:

> The four AM cries of my son worm through the double foam of earplugs
>   and diazepam.

Well, now I'm just uninterested. Without the odd tones and questions the original enjambed lines produced, this scene seems ordinary and dull.

Some poets use line breaks to intentionally create an unusual cadence or phrasing in their poems. And using line breaks in these two different ways produces a very different effect. For example, consider the following two versions, which use the same words but employs line breaks in different places. (The first version has the line breaks of the original poem. In the second, we added line breaks deliberately to cause enjambment.) First, an excerpt of the original:

The Fetch (excerpt)
Ciaran Carson

I woke. You were lying beside me in the double bed,
prone, your long dark hair fanned out over the downy pillow.

I'd been dreaming we stood on a beach an ocean away
watching the waves purl into their troughs and tumble over.

Knit one, purl two, you said. Something in your voice made me think
of women knitting by the guillotine. Your eyes met mine.

Here's version 1:

I woke.
You were lying
Beside me
In the double bed,
Prone,

Your long dark hair fanned out
Over the downy pillow.
        I'd been dreaming
We stood on a beach
An ocean away
Watching the waves
Purl into their troughs
And tumble over.
        Knit one,
Purl two,
You said.
Something in your
voice
Made me
think
Of women
Knitting by
The guillotine.
Your eyes
Met
mine.

See how enjambed line breaks change the reading of the poem? It's now disjointed, interrupted. There's more mystery and anxiety there—perhaps too much? Certainly, Carson must have thought enjambment would be too much or perhaps inappropriate to this particular poem.

Let's now look at the opposite: taking out all the line breaks from the poem. What does that do?

Here's version 2:

I woke. You were lying beside me in the double bed, prone, your long dark hair fanned out over the downy pillow. I'd been dreaming we stood on a beach an ocean away watching the waves purl into their troughs and tumble over. Knit one, purl two, you said. Something in your voice made me think of women knitting by the guillotine. Your eyes met mine.

Now (in our opinion) the poem reads too quickly. Without the line breaks to slow it down and add the mystery and anxiety, the images come too fast and easily. The menace of the ending is diminished.

The poet e. e. cummings took line breaks as far as they could go—even breaking lines in the middle of words.

> dim
> i
> nu
> tiv
>
> e this park is e
> mpty(everyb
> ody's elsewher
> e except me 6 e

Lines of poetry are often aligned to the left side of the page, but poets sometimes indent lines (move them away from the left-hand margin) in order to complicate traditional line breaks.

Indentation does not mean that a line is not properly broken. Rather, the indentation, much like a line break itself, further informs the phrasing or rhythm of the poem. For example, a line that is indented more than others on the page might be read as having a slightly longer pause preceding it or a delayed beginning, as though the poet is catching their breath.

In the poem "summer, somewhere," poet Danez Smith breaks the lines at unlikely places. What is the effect?

> somewhere, a sun. below, boys brown
> as rye play the dozens & ball, jump
>
> in the air & stay there. boys become new
> moons, gum-dark on all sides, beg bruise
>
> -blue water to fly, at least tide, at least
> spit back a father or two. I won't get started.

history is what it is. it knows what it did.

Write Now

Now let's try a line-break exercise.

1. Find a prose piece, preferably your own, of about 500 words in length. If you haven't written one, do that as a first step. Or you can use a 500-word excerpt of your favorite story, book, or memoir.
2. Now go through and insert line breaks. Consider carefully where you place them: do you place them at natural points of pausing, or do you go for enjoyment—leaving fragments of sentences or phrases on their own?
3. Read through your piece without line breaks and then with them. Which is stronger, in your opinion? Why?
4. Do the line breaks prompt you to edit your text, either for reasons of brevity, rhythm, or meaning? What other changes can you make to your new poem that follow from the line breaks?

Paying Attention to the Music of Language

Poets also move readers by the sound—one could call it the music—of the language they choose to employ. They use *syntax* to produce a variety of sound devices to make their verses "sing" in such a way that the meaning is enhanced by the sound of the poem—whether read aloud or silently to oneself.

The Poetry Archive's "About Syntax" gives us this useful information:

> Syntax refers to word order and the way in which it works with grammatical structures. As we are used to hearing things in certain orders, the effect of breaking with normal syntax is to draw attention to what is being said and the way it is said. P J Kavanagh's "Beyond Decoration" has a speaker who says, rather than "I cannot go out", "Go out I cannot", which—by shifting its syntax—seems to make the impossibility in "cannot" stronger, as well as creating a reversed echo with the second half of that line. The opening of Dylan Thomas' "A Refusal to Mourn the Death, by Fire, of a Child in London" is hypnotic in part because of its rhythms and rhyming, but also in that

its syntax is designed to put such distance between "Never until . . ." and
". . . shall I".

Some poets will also deliberately fracture syntax beyond what is considered "grammatically correct." This choice aims to reveal what cannot be said within the habits of thought that rules of grammar maintain.

The syntax of Adrienne Rich's "For This" is stretched in the first two stanzas to hold off, in each case, what it is that depends on the "If" at the start of each stanza.

For This
Adrienne Rich

 If I've reached for your lines (I have)
   like letters from the dead that stir the nerves
 dowsed you for a springhead
   to water my thirst
 dug into my compost skeletons and petals
   you surely meant to catch the light:

 —at work in my wormeaten wormwood-raftered
  stateless underground
   have I a plea?

 If I've touched your finger
  with a ravenous tongue
   licked from your palm a rift of salt
 if I've dreamt or thought you
  a pack of blood fresh-drawn
   hanging darkred from a hook
 higher than my heart
  (you who understand transfusion)
   where else should I appeal?

 A pilot light lies low
  while the gas jets sleep

        (a cat getting toed from stove
into nocturnal ice)
      language uncommon and agile as truth
        melts down the most intractable silence

A lighthouse keeper's ethics:
    you tend for all or none
      for this you might set your furniture on fire
A *this* we have blundered over
    as if the lamp could be shut off at will
      rescue denied for some

and still a lighthouse be

Paying attention to the music in your writing, no matter what genre it is, is a marvelous thing to do. Again: this doesn't mean you have to use conventionally beautiful language to sound "poetic." In fact, that would be a mistake. Sometimes you want the sound of your work to be harsh, uncompromising. It all depends on the overall effect you are aiming for.

Rhyming is another way to employ syntax. It's not necessarily conventional, at the end of regularly spaced lines. You can also have what are called slant rhymes. A slant rhyme is a type of rhyme with words that have similar, but not identical, sounds. Most slant rhymes are formed by words with identical consonants and different vowels, or vice versa.

- *Beginnings / ascending*
- *Unionists / sponsor us*
- *Estate / days*
- *Good morning in / at 4 pm*

And, of course, rhythm (the beat) is an integral part of music. Indeed, at a very high level, this "music" that we want you to pay attention to can be divided into two categories: rhyme and rhythm. There are fine books on the music of poetry. Suffice it to say that there are many sound devices that poets use to hone their unique voices and to enhance the meaning of what they write. Let's look at those two broad categories and see how we can master the techniques and make them our own no matter what genre we choose to write in.

Reviewing: A (Brief) Primer on Rhyming Schemes

When words have the same or nearly identical sound, this similarity is heard as part of the music of the poem, and the words are said to rhyme. The most common and obvious rhymes have identical sounds. These are called "perfect" rhymes, such as "feather" and "weather" or "bet" and "wet."

End rhyme is of course the traditional way poets put language together. It occurs at the ends of the lines of verse, as it does in this first stanza of "1 January 1965," by Joseph Brodsky, translated by George L. Kline:

> The Wise Men will unlearn your name.
> Above your head no star will flame.
> One weary sound will be the same—
> the hoarse roar of the gale.
> The shadows fall from your tired eyes
> as your lone bedside candle dies,
> for here the calendar breeds nights
> till stores of candles fail.

An internal rhyme is more subtle than an end rhyme. Internal rhyme occurs in the middle, instead of at the end. A single line of poetry can contain internal rhyme (with multiple words in the same line rhyming), or the rhyming words can occur across multiple lines.

The subtlety of internal rhymes makes them a useful poetic tool for increasing the musicality of the language without being overtly "rhyme-y." Some modern poets don't use end rhymes at all but will intersperse internal rhymes throughout a poem, perhaps because it feels more nuanced and less obvious. Other poets use internal rhyme in addition to end rhyme—that is, they intersperse internal rhymes through-out a poem with an otherwise consistent use of end rhymes.

The sound repetition due to internal rhyme can add to a poem's uniformity. It stresses the meaning of words and enhances the musical effects of a poem. And the benefit of rhyming without creating a specific pattern can be used to surprise readers, to keep them on edge.

Let's talk about poet Kay Ryan's use of what some call "recombinant rhyme."

Turtle

Kay Ryan

Who would be a turtle who could help it?
A barely mobile hard roll, a four-oared helmet,
she can ill afford the chances she must take
in rowing toward the grasses that she eats.
Her track is graceless, like dragging
a packing-case places, and almost any slope
defeats her modest hopes. Even being practical,
she's often stuck up to the axle on her way
to something edible. With everything optimal,
she skirts the ditch which would convert
her shell into a serving dish. She lives
below luck-level, never imagining some lottery
will change her load of pottery to wings.
Her only levity is patience,
the sport of truly chastened things.

In an interview with *The Paris Review*, Kay Ryan says:

> When I started writing nobody rhymed—it was in utter disrepute. Yet rhyme was a siren to me. I had this condition of things rhyming in my mind without my permission. Still I couldn't take end-rhyme seriously, which meant I had to find other ways—I stashed my rhymes at the wrong ends of lines and in the middles—the front of one word would rhyme with the back of another one, or one word might be identical to three words.

Ryan, in the interview, cites "Turtle" as an example of internal rhyme, then says she also uses "recombinant rhyme" to get this effect:

> What's recombinant rhyme? It's like how they add a snip of the jellyfish's glow-in-the-dark gene to bunnies and make them glow green; by snipping up pieces of sound and redistributing them throughout a poem I found I could get the poem to go a little bit luminescent.

In addition to internal rhymes, nonperfect rhymes—the "slant rhymes" we referred to earlier—also can be effective. Emily Dickinson is particularly known for her slant rhymes. In the following poem, she uses a perfect rhyme with "Men" and "Ten" in the first stanza, then breaks expectations by using a slant rhyme (using a technique called consonance) with "Queen" and "Afternoon" in the second.

Not Any Higher Stands the Grave
Emily Dickinson

> Not any higher stands the Grave
> For Heroes than for Men—
> Not any nearer for the Child
> Than numb Three Score and Ten—
>
> This latest Leisure equal lulls
> The Beggar and his Queen
> Propitiate this Democrat
> A Summer's Afternoon—

According to broader definitions of slant rhyme, words (particularly last syllables) can have either similar consonant sounds (called consonance) or similar vowel sounds (called assonance). They are just two of the poetic sound devices that poets use to create unique voices and to enhance meaning in their work.

Why use slant rhymes? Repeating a sound—whether a vowel or a consonant, at the beginning or end of a word—can be very pleasing to readers. They might not even notice slant rhymes, as they aren't as apparent as perfect rhymes. Still, these rhymes can create a more enjoyable reading experience.

Slant rhymes can also confound expectations. In the Dickinson poem, for example, the "men"/"ten" pairing creates anticipation that we'll see the same rhyming scheme in the last three lines of the poem. But Dickinson surprises us. Finally, having to work with perfect rhymes can be creatively constraining. Sometimes constraints are good, but sometimes they are too limiting. Slant rhymes give you a bigger vocabulary of words to choose from.

Focusing on Rhythm

Another major contributor to your piece's particular syntax, rhythm can be described as the *pace* of a poem. Rhythm can help to strengthen the meaning of words and ideas in a poem.

In certain types of poems, such as syllabic verse, you may have a pattern that requires counting syllables, whether stressed or not. Lines can have equal numbers of syllables, or you can create a pattern based on different numbers of syllables.

In poetry based on meter, however, poets don't count the number of syllables; they count the number of "stresses," or beats. Meter is the pattern of beats and pauses that make up a poem.

The most common meter in English poetry is called iambic pentameter. Don't be scared by the term. All it means is that every other syllable in a line is stressed and that there are five stresses per line. Brain scientists probably have thrilling reasons why iambic pentameter seems to work best to get language to stick to our memories.

Here's an example from Shakespeare's *Romeo and Juliet*. Read it out loud to hear the beat of the language:

> But <u>soft</u>, what <u>light</u> through <u>yon</u>der <u>win</u>dow <u>breaks</u>?

(The syllables that receive a stress or a "beat" are underscored.)

Note the pacing, the rhythm, in the following poem by Randall Mann. Each couplet starts with a more expansive, sonically rich first line and then is undercut, as it were, by the subsequent one. The brevity and rhyme of the short lines both second-guess what has come before and simultaneously provide a sonic path forward. In other words, the ongoing contrast of each couplet creates a tension of movement, so that movement itself is a facet of argument.

Straight Razor
Randall Mann
> He slid the stiff blade up to my ear:
> Oh, fear,

this should have been thirst, a cheapening act.
But I lacked,

as usual, the crucial disbelief. Sticky, cold,
a billfold

wet in my mouth, wrists bound by his belt,
I felt

like the boy in a briny night pool, he who found
the drowned

body, yet still somehow swam with an unknown joy.
That boy.

Poets might even use a blank space in the line to create silence. Look at the opening of John Cage's "Lecture on Nothing" (opposite).

You can see the effect of syntax and space and line breaks in Cage's poem, but what else did you notice? What might you say about its form and what it does for your understanding of the meaning of his "lecture"?

Poetic Form (or Friendly Constraints)

Rhyme and rhythm are two of the patterns of language poets use, along with others, to create form. The form of a poem is how we describe the overarching structure or pattern of the poem. Certain forms of poetry—for example, sonnets, villanelles, and limericks—must stick to very specific rules about length, rhythm, and rhyme.

What are these rules but constraints that impose limits on what poets can do with language? And why do poets still embrace these (mostly) centuries-old constraints? Because they spur creativity.

The word "constraint" has certain negative connotations. And yet, constraints are immensely useful to artists (so much so that W. W. Norton published a book by Alice devoted to constraint-based exercises). But we're aware that the word might not work for you.

Hence, *friendly* constraints.

LECTURE ON NOTHING

```
I am here              ,              and there is nothing to say
                                                        If among you are
those who wish to get    somewhere          ,          let them leave at
any moment           .                      What we re–quire                    is
silence              ;              but what silence requires
          is              that I go on talking     .
                                                Give any one thought
                a push                    :          it falls down easily        .
;              but the pusher      and the pushed          pro–duce          that enter–
tainment              called              a dis–cussion                    .
                Shall we have one later  ?
                              𝕎
Or                    ,    we could simply de–cide                    not to have a dis–
cussion           .                                              But
now                              there are silences                    and the
words              make              help make                    the
silences          .
                                              I have nothing to say
          and I am saying it                                and that is
poetry                              as I need it                    .
                This space of time                              is organized
     .                      We need not fear these      silences, —
                              𝕎
```

Fun is often associated with friendship. We hope your experiments with constraints turn out to be fun, but doing so may not always be *easy*. Any friend worth their salt does two things simultaneously: enables us to be our true, authentic selves *and* challenges us when we're off. Parts of their personalities delight us, others annoy. Being friendly therefore isn't necessarily the same as being nice or easy. It's about adding substance and value.

The English adaptation of haiku (three sentences: 5 syllables, 7 syllables, and 5 syllables) forces poets to cut language to the bone. The Shakespearean sonnet (14 lines of iambic pentameter, with a rhyme pattern of abab/cdcd/efef/gg) compels poets to think within a rigid, almost mathematical formula.

Looking at the layout of a poem and listening for sound patterns—particularly rhyme and rhythm—help to identify the form. Here is a famous love sonnet by Shakespeare. Notice how he spends the first 12 lines saying things about his object of affection that normally wouldn't be considered praise (she "treads," she "reeks," her hair is "black wires"). Then, in the last two lines, he does the about-face that every true sonnet must do. "And yet," he begins . . . and explains how very much he loves her.

Sonnet 130

William Shakespeare

My mistress' eyes are nothing like the sun;
Coral is far more red than her lips' red;
If snow be white, why then her breasts are dun;
If hairs be wires, black wires grow on her head.
I have seen roses damasked, red and white,
But no such roses see I in her cheeks;
And in some perfumes is there more delight
Than in the breath that from my mistress reeks.
I love to hear her speak, yet well I know
That music hath a far more pleasing sound;
I grant I never saw a goddess go;
My mistress when she walks, treads on the ground.
    And yet, by heaven, I think my love as rare
    As any she belied with false compare.

Write Now

Let's try an exercise based on some of the attributes of a sonnet. If you want, you can use the sonnet rhyming scheme as well as iambic pentameter. (If ever in doubt about iambic pentameter, just think of these opening lines from Joyce Kilmer's 1915 poem "Trees." The stressed syllables are underscored.)

I think that I shall never see
A poem lovely as a tree.

1. Think of someone or something that you absolutely adore.
2. Write 12 lines in which you describe him/her/them/it in a way that wouldn't typically be considered positive. You can try to rhyme it according to a sonnet scheme or use iambic pentameter as the rhythm, but you don't have to.
3. In the last two lines, turn it around. Begin with "And yet" or "But still" and explain why your adoration is real and true.

We'll say it again: there's no way to exhaust all the tools poets use in a single chapter on poetry. We do hope that we've shown you the power and effect of a poet's bag of tricks. We hope that the poets among you will sense our appreciation for what you do. And we hope that the prose and hybrid writers among you will steal the techniques you've learned, imagine new ways to employ them to dazzle your readers, and get us to feel what's most at stake for you.

Chapter 7

Fiction

Inventing Reality

"Fiction is the lie that tells the truth."

Consider this quote, which has been attributed to a broad swath of artists over the centuries, including Camus, Picasso, Neil Gaiman, Dorothy Allison, and even Stephen King.

Let's try to analyze this quote to help us understand why so many intelligent, talented people throughout history would feel that this is an urgent lesson to pass on to writing posterity.

The main point is that "truth" is more than just the facts. Sometimes we, as fiction writers, must "lie," a little or a lot, to bring out the truth in the stories we tell. In the end, our allegiance is to the truth.

Facts? They can be changed to fit our truth-seeking narrative.

This is *not* the place where we'll talk about the increasingly gray area between fiction and creative nonfiction, autofiction, and the like. We're saving that discussion for Chapters 8 and 9. What we're asserting now is the importance of emotional force, authenticity, and honesty in a made-up work. You may have to tell more than a few little white lies and probably some whoppers as well. If you're writing fiction, it goes with the job.

Why Fiction?

This book encourages experiments in writing *across* genres. As in the poetry chapter and the nonfiction chapter to follow, the stakes put in the ground of this chapter are meant to be treated as trusted "markers." They should be used as ways to orient yourself within each genre, and obviously we can't cover everything. Once you get the lay of the land, the point is to ask yourself which of these techniques is potentially useful to *your* writing?

Chapter 9 will highlight hybrid works—pieces that blend aspects of different genres. But writing hybrid works isn't necessarily the goal here. The goal is to help you expand your creative options as you work to assemble the material you've gathered into something you'll eventually consider a cohesive whole.

Let's run through a few possible scenarios in which fiction—a short story or novel—might provide an apt "container" for your creative work. Fiction could be a great choice for your work if simply describing a "lived" (factual) experience doesn't have the impact you'd hoped.

Perhaps you've written an early draft of something important, and it's as true to life as possible, but once you see it written down, the impact on the page doesn't compare to the lived experience. You're tempted to invent or rearrange events to get to the capital-t Truth. So, you start to play with the "truth" by inventing, and the piece inches closer to revealing what's beneath the surface of the described experience.

Or, perhaps, the facts are *too outrageous*.

Author of middle-grade fiction Nicole M. Hewitt wrote this on her blog:

Have you ever read a book and felt like there was a bit of issue overload? Like it dealt with just too many topics, and you started to wonder if it was all maybe a bit too much for one story? I definitely have. But I've also read books that handled multiple issues incredibly well, and lately I've been thinking a lot about how, in real life, many of us deal with *a lot*. I mean, we don't really get to say, "No, sorry, I've already had my fill of 'issues'—it just isn't *believable* that I would have one more." Believable or not, life is what it is.

Take my family for instance: If I tried to write a book about my kids, people would read it and say, "This is so unrealistic. She just wanted to add in a bunch of diversity (or neurodiversity) for the sake of diversity." And I honestly wouldn't blame them. I don't think I'd attempt to write my family into a book because we do *not* fit the "average" mold and we would seem a little extreme. Let me give you a rundown:

- My youngest is a black internationally-adopted child with ADHD and a cognitive disability (due to the fact that he had encephalitis as an infant).
- My middle child suffers from anxiety. (Blessedly, it hasn't been nearly as bad in recent years—she went through a really difficult time when she was younger and still has a harder time than most kids in social situations and with certain fears, but she's doing *really* well these days.)

- My oldest is a transgender girl who is most likely on the spectrum. (She was diagnosed ADHD as a child and we were told that she's probably on the spectrum and definitely had social skills issues—but we never went back to get an actual diagnosis. (She would describe it as not *feeling* things the same way that others apparently do.) She's also amazingly gifted, especially in math—at 16, she's taking Calc 3 at our local community college.

  I was also on medication for ADHD once upon a time but didn't stick with it. Add to that the fact that we're (active and engaged) Christians, and you get an interesting mix, to say the least.

  And that's just my immediate family. (I also had a cousin who was blind and schizophrenic, another cousin who died of AIDS, an uncle who is Deaf, a brother with spina bifida, family members with addictions and depression, and more...) Let's just say a book about my family would be too packed with "issues" to feel reasonable.

This author isn't saying you can't write about multiple issues. In fact, she says she's read books where the author handles multiple issues well. We agree with her. You can write about multiple issues. She says she doesn't think *she'd* attempt to write about all the issues her family faces in one book. Perhaps for artists like Nicole, lying to tell the truth can be about subtracting rather than adding.

A Sunday Afternoon on the Island of La Grande Jatte (1886), by Georges Seurat.

Let's look at another reason to write fiction: You're interested in the compression of language, approaching things in a poetic way, but feel you have layers yet to uncover, corners to explore.

Let's expand on this thought by using an example from visual art.

Look at the iconic painting *A Sunday Afternoon on the Island of La Grande Jatte*, by Georges Seurat. Seurat used a technique called pointillism, creating an image out of tiny dots. Seurat worked on *A Sunday Afternoon* from 1884 to

1886, and it eventually became known as a founding work of the neo-impressionist movement.

Imagine that he started the painting with only two motivations in mind: (1) to practice a technique that seemed "new" (pointillism) and (2) to focus on his love for nature, specifically in the rendering of, say (we're just imagining this), leaves and grass.

But let's back up. In 1884, the painter had created another work titled *La Grande Jatte*, a fraction of the size of its more famous sibling. In it, he explored the differences in the renderings of leaves and grass in light versus shadow—like the techniques he used later in his much more famous piece.

While working on this smaller piece, perhaps he started to visualize the people in it. Something took hold of his imagination, which led to the expansion of the size of his canvas along with the ideas he explored.

La Grande Jatte (1884), by Georges Seurat.

His choice to *expand* does not, in any way, subtract from the time he spent focusing on trees and grass in his earlier piece, nor does it take away from the glorious rendering on the smaller canvas. Many viewers prefer the smaller 1884 work to the larger 1886 one.

To bring it back to writing: Certainly, there are poems that start and remain poems. A writer can also work on a single poem for a long time. There are book-length poems. A writer can explore similar themes and imagery in a variety of genres.

To work on a single painting for two years, Seurat had to be curious about something more: a broader field of inquiry; an obsession, perhaps; something other than wanting to render a pretty landscape using a cool technique.

The thing that makes this piece (housed at the Art Institute of Chicago) so compelling to viewers, apart from the scale (it's huge) and its formal mastery, is its *mystery*. The artist borrowed from several techniques and combined them in ways viewers hadn't seen before. The effect? The painting resists superficial interpretation.

Art writer Jeffrey Meyers describes the atmosphere of *La Grande Jatte* by quoting Baudelaire's lines from "Invitation to the Voyage": "there is nothing else but grace and measure, / Richness, quietness, and pleasure." In addition to the painting's grace, richness, and pleasure, Meyers suggests that the expressionless figures in Seurat's painting also convey their alienation and unease, as city dwellers, out of their natural element. The viewer may see more of one of these contrasting thematic concerns, but a deep study of the work reveals that the artist imbued the canvas with images that allow for a complicated experience: not just alienation or pleasure, but a sense of angst amid the leisure.

For the sake of this example, Meyers urges us to think of the smaller painting like a poem, focusing on Seurat's "tranquil mood" an "offering to the god of summer, Sunday, and plenitude" and his larger one as a short story or novel, incorporating what he discovered in the smaller, but adding "the alienation of modern man in a crowd" and "uneasiness, even angst," according to Meyers.

Perhaps, like Seurat, you started with an image, a particular mood, a moment of consciousness in a character. Your curiosity about the image, the mood, grew into imagining multiple situations, highlighting several points of view. Like Seurat with two paintings, you may end up with two works: a poem and a story.

Writer Terese Svoboda publishes poetry, fiction, and creative nonfiction as well as hybrid works. We interviewed her for this book. Let's look at the questions she answered about writing in both fiction and poetry genres:

> *(1) Have you ever started writing a poem or a series and decided it's a short story or a novel? And if so, what dictated that?*
>
> I have questioned when a poem isn't working whether it might be better in another genre. Sometimes my stories arrive very "poeticized" and have to be simplified. My novel *Tin God* began as a dream that I turned into a poem, then a story, then a novel. A sort of haunting, a persistent image that yielded more every time I recast it.
>
> *(2) What does the "container" of "fiction" offer the writer? What would make the poet use it?*
>
> Except for the triple space acting as a sort of stanza break, no structural

element holds the container of fiction other than the left and right margins. The fiction writer eschews all the rest of that lovely white space that the poet puts to work to extract meaning.

The sentence is fiction's primary structure—as opposed to the poet's line—and with it, the association between sentences and paragraphs are all that knit the narrative together. If the links suffer too little association, as is the case sometimes . . . the writing turns into poetry, relying heavily on the reader to intuit the associations.

The border difference between fiction and poetry is permeable, not as distinct as the difference between sculpture (3D) and painting (2D) since all writing is very one-dimensional, using the very same blocks, i.e., words, for effect. *Cannibal,* my first novel, could be considered a long prose poem. It's told in blocks, there's a first-person narrator, and no other characters speak. One could argue that too many things happen in it to be a poem, but there's plenty of incident in Anne Carson's poems.

The lure of fiction for a poet is the opportunity to seriously consider motive. Writers, when critiquing fiction, question very different things than the poets. *Why did she hit him over the head? I don't believe the narrator would say that.* Poets would not necessarily need to know why the protagonist in the poem was hit to make a subtle point about injury.

Poets rely mostly on tone for believability. The protagonist in a poem automatically accrues authenticity until otherwise contradicted. In fiction the protagonist has interior thought, which can contradict action. All genres, however, benefit from theft. My new book of poetry, *Theatrix: Poetry Plays,* steals many fictional attributes: interior thought, additional voices, associationally linked narrative—as well as the theatrical.

And of course, the final and perhaps most profound lure of fiction is that more people read it than poetry. A magnum of applause can be intoxicating.

Svoboda's answers offer a master class in the elements of composition that poets and prose writers use to communicate their concerns. She succinctly demonstrates the practice we're encouraging. Hers isn't meant to be *the* answer, but *an* answer, a way to push you to discover or articulate why *you* might choose *this* container, not *that one* or, as we said before, *both.*

Many writers consider themselves observers of the world. As in a painting, the meaning in a work of fiction can come from meditation on an object. Nature and human-made settings are also portrayed in fiction, usually as a means to illuminate the inner lives of the characters.

Curiosity about *people* often drives fiction. And characters in fiction are different from those in real life.

Depending on how the author uses point of view (a craft topic addressed in many of the books on fiction), sometimes the narrator knows more about the inner life of a character than the character knows about themself: In F. Scott Fitzgerald's *The Great Gatsby*, the narrator Nick tells us in the opening pages that "Everyone suspects himself of at least one of the cardinal virtues, and this is mine: I am one of the few honest people that I have ever known." By the end of the book, we see he's fooling himself—he is most definitely not honest in the way he proclaims.

Characters' thoughts can be revelatory, especially when compared with what they say: "I'd be happy to," I said. *Screw you, I thought.* More on this one later.

Other times, as in *Klara and the Sun*, by Kazuo Ishiguro, characters' thoughts can be opaque to the narrator. In this case, Klara is a robot companion for a teenage girl, and Ishiguro has interestingly made her the narrator—that is, put the story in her hands. Because Klara has no insight into her owner's thoughts, she must come up with theories of her own, some of which are startlingly accurate, some seemingly absurd.

This is equivalent to life, where people can guess what others are thinking but can't know. How could they? Knowing oneself is hard enough. Have you ever discovered you were wrong about a conclusion you've made about yourself? Some people are experts in reading body language, in anticipating what a friend or partner or family member might do or say. But even if they're right some of the time, they can't possibly inhabit another's inner life completely.

It's this *not knowing* combined with the *desire* to know that drives writers. What makes us tick? What are our secret or tender or vulnerable or sick or private thoughts? Why do humans do the strange and wonderful and awful things they do?

If you're interested in that, you might want to try fiction. Or, another reason to try fiction: Events seem linked. You're interested in cause and effect.

Let's expand upon the notion of *causality*.

E. M. Forster, in *Aspects of the Novel*, uses the example: "The king died and the queen died." The two facts lack causality, and for that reason, he thinks they're *not* suitable for a novel. But he then says that "The king died and then the queen died of grief" is most definitely a plot worthy of development.

In real life, stuff happens, often randomly. A child stubs her toe then grows up to be a tomato farmer. In between, she has an unrequited romantic crush on her best friend, who later goes to jail for insurance fraud. She loses her mom, meets a celebrity, and discovers she spent her five years in stomach pain due to undiagnosed celiac disease. Once she becomes a tomato farmer, she travels to Italy often to speak at conferences on heirloom varieties. Her friends envy her travel, but she hates it. She'd rather stay home. One day, she throws a load of laundry in the dryer and dies of a brain hemorrhage.

How can you make sense of this? It's chaos!

In life, there's chaos. So, we tell each other stories.

Finding the story can also involve chaos. In an article for Literary Hub, writer Stephanie Bishop says:

> A novel in progress is a cluttered, messy thing, at least in terms of how it exists in your head. And there are so many ways for that mess to be made, and it's much harder to make it tidy and organized. A novel in progress, is by definition, a disorganized system: one that seems to resist its own reorganizing, that clings to its own redundant parts, that is comprised of an almost infinite variability of patterns. The chaos stakes are high. In the drafting process one moves from higher chaos and lower complexity, to higher complexity with lower chaos. Expel, delete, expel, delete. There is only so much control one can assert: in the early stages the reigns [sic] are held tight: there is the false belief in the power of "making the decision"—playing the author.
>
> But once you are far enough inside the chaos, the energy of the work takes over. What cannot be there cannot be there. What must be there must be there. The only way towards this is through radical demolition.

In fiction, events are artfully and strategically arranged to communicate deeper meaning. Perhaps you're one who thinks there are no coincidences. If given the challenge, time, and access to interviews with the tomato farmer (from the absurd example above), you might be able to convincingly create a narrative portraying the character's farming as the unlikely outcome of something that happened during the toe-stubbing recovery period; how the celebrity encounter helped her remain close to her mother while she was ailing—and how her mother's suffering created a fear of doctors' offices that led to the undiagnosed gluten allergy. The finale? A brain hemorrhage in slowed-down time à la Tobias Woolf's "Bullet in the Brain" and recast the character's life events creatively and surprisingly and convincingly in a manner that leads to meaning for the reader. As a result, the reader would never think about fear and ambition and notions of home and tomatoes in the same way.

However, you'd need quite a few fictional techniques to pull it off.

Even if you have a highly associative imagination that gleans meaning from the tiniest (and most *un*expected) through lines of lived experiences, pulling it off is tricky. Meaning accumulates because of the *placement* of events, thoughts, behaviors, and images, the order in the telling, and the writer's mastery of technique. There's a causality to each scene that you, the writer, control.

However, here we'd like to issue a great big caveat. Put a big DON'T DO THIS sign in your path. Let's guard against simplistic causality.

Causality is not the easy, pop-psychology analyses that can sometimes happen in writing workshops. Well-meaning but not useful workshops can start with a legitimate "why" question. For example, why did the marriage fall apart? Or, why did he hurt the other boy when they were friends? Sometimes, in struggling to answer these questions, writers infuse early drafts with simplistic explanations that detract rather than enrich the narrative.

Flannery O'Connor was her usual stern self when admonishing against this. Don't solve your mysteries, she advised. "Render them." So perhaps it's best not to explain *why* a marriage failed; but portray *how* it happened. If a boy treats his friend badly, portray *how*.

If you do your job well as a writer, you'll achieve causality in a manner that's surprising and yet subtle and at a deeper level than if you consciously plotted out the "why."

Defining Fiction: So, What *Is* It?

We've covered four of the countless possible reasons *why* writers might choose fiction. But *what is* fiction?

Fiction is storytelling that relies as much (or more) on the creative imagination of the writer as on strict adherence to history, facts, or historical chronology.

Now, what's *compelling* fiction?

For fiction to be compelling, imaginary (made-up) people, places, or things must communicate meaning, illuminate important themes, or evoke emotional or intellectual reactions.

It's important to note that although the fiction writer's intentions and reader's experiences can match, often meaning unintended by the writer is perceived by the reader. This can make discussions between writers and readers very interesting!

Understanding Genres in Fiction

Almost inevitably, if you tell people you're a fiction writer, they'll ask, what kind? By this, they want to know what *genre* you work in.

Numerous genres exist under the fiction umbrella. Lengthwise, you can write everything from micro fiction (short-short fiction), to short stories, to novellas, to novels, to multibook series.

Other genres exist based on subject matter and style. These include speculative fiction, science fiction, fantasies, mysteries, romances, thrillers, and what's called "literary fiction."

And finally, there are age- and audience-based categories: children, preteens, young adult (YA), and adult, among others.

Some writers decide on a genre and target audience prior to beginning a draft. Others might use one of the many "formulas" for writing that are meant to help writers create successful commercial fiction in one of these categories.

We say: whatever gets the story written.

But the freshest and most surprising works seem to emerge, not from formulas, but from not knowing. In an interview, fiction writer Isaac Fitzsimmons said: "Yeah, I wrote that book [laughs]. But I wasn't planning on it. It just kind of came together that way."

We believe that the most inspiring fiction is composed by writers who allow the story itself to dictate how and for whom it's written. Perhaps your novel will, like Svoboda's, start out as a dream, then turn into a poem, then a short story, and finally be imagined into a novel.

Consider this excerpt from a short story by Lorrie Moore:

> To know the narrative in advance is to turn yourself into a machine. . . . What makes humans human is precisely that they do not know the future. That is why they do the fateful and amusing things they do; who can say how anything will turn out? Therein lies the only hope for redemption, discovery, and—let's be frank—fun, fun, fun! There might be things people will get away with. And not just motel towels. There might be great illicit loves, enduring joy—or faith-shaking accidents with farm machinery. But you have to *not* know in order to see what stories your life's efforts bring you. The mystery is all. [emphasis ours]

It's this mystery that adds to what's called "literary fiction," a genre that pays attention to the poetics and aesthetics of the individual sentence while exploring characters and situations resistant to easy answers or pat morality.

We also believe that this definition encompasses every other genre. Horror and dystopian stories can be literary. Speculative stories can be literary. YA can be literary.

Literary fiction may play with the ideas employed in more commercial fiction (villains who behave badly while heroes remain consistently noble; ideas like "goodness is rewarded" and "evil is punished"), but usually skews the proportions. Characters fluctuate between good and evil. Readers are often less sure whose side to be on and may see parts of their own humanity reflected in characters, even including so-called villains.

Literary fiction transports you from what can seem like an absurdly chaotic place (life) to a liminal place where the action (or images) adds up to meaning. However difficult it can be to unpack, in fiction the writer usually gives readers certain "units of satisfaction."

This book doesn't spend much time on the rules of craft. There are many excellent books to teach you how to write sonnets or dialogue or how to craft a scene in a novel. We're focused more on the artistic choices you make within the various forms and genres that exist—and even those that might not have been thought of yet. And we're also driving you to practice, practice, practice within those choices. (As in the punchline of that old joke: "How do you get to Carnegie Hall?")

Writer Mary McGarry Morris offers this advice:

> The mechanics of writing can be taught, the basic rules and tools and guidelines, but as in any ART, all the rest comes from DOING and DOING and

> DOING. The most important part of the process is learning to trust one's own vision, to work hard at developing one's own style and voice, and then having the confidence to follow where it goes.

And, finally, there's magic. There must always be magic. Here's what visual artist Marilyn Minter has to say:

> I want . . . magic to happen. I want surprise. I want the accident. I want to trust it. I trust the accident . . . It's where the process of discovery happens.

Much comes out of the *doing* and being content with the process, whether your creative work takes four or fourteen or forty drafts. Without *mystery*, without the big questions that are difficult to answer, and without *magic*, fiction might as well be yesterday's already-reported news.

The Elements of Fiction

Now, let's go a little deeper by experimenting with the tools that fiction writers use:

1. Plot
2. Characterization
3. Setting
4. Voice

Many additional elements of composition exist, of course, including point of view, dialogue, imagery, and all the other language-level elements we explored in the poetry chapter.

Write Now

1. Think of a story you would like to communicate. It should be real in essence. That is, not completely made up. Perhaps it is one of those stories that makes you say, "truth is stranger than fiction" to people who doubt it. And, most importantly, the impact of the event or events should be significant to you.

2. In this exercise, you will tell this story in a way that convinces others of its truth. You can change anything about the facts—the place, the people, the weather, the time of day, the food that was being eaten—anything you like so that the story has the same effect on other people as living through it had on you.

3. Do a free write for ten minutes in which you tell this story, but invent, exaggerate, embellish, or outright lie to tell it in a way that gets its truth across.

If it helps, start like this: "If I told you what I'm about to tell you is true, you wouldn't believe me. So, let's say it's a lie that tells the truth. Once upon a time . . ."

> **STUDENT EXAMPLE (by Zac Russi)**
>
> If I told you that what I'm about to describe is true, you wouldn't believe me. So, let's say it's a lie that tells the truth. Once, and this was a long time ago, but one day in early Autumn, the people running a corporation that had just hired me, told me to arrive at the warehouse at 9am, ready to fill out intake paperwork, and wearing closed-toed shoes. I thought, ok, typical first-day-on-the-job-type-shit, and I did as I was told.
>
> The warehouse was on a dead-end street, near the Goodwill bins, in deep SE, near what they now call the Woodstock neighborhood. When I arrived, there were three men and three women, standing on opposite sides of the large, drop-down, steel door entry way. Divided by gender. One of the men walked up to me, introduced himself, and had me fill out an NDA, along with the more standard I-9, payment info, etc. Afterward, one of the women asked me a series of questions that seemed to be designed to see how well I might work with potential demographics.
>
> Then she said, well, we're ready when you all are.
>
> There were no other potential new hires. The gate opened, and inside I saw more people, but this time divided into groups, with giant neon signs hanging from the ceiling, denoting categories. Signs said: Punk-rockers, women age 20-35, male athletes. . . .

Now that you have some work in front of you, let's continue with the experiment:

1. First, ask yourself: of these four elements (as you understand them right

now)—plot, characterization, setting, and voice—what are you most comfortable or proficient in? Rank from 1 to 4.

2. Find a thick paragraph of fiction prose you've written (this could be what you wrote in the first exercise of this chapter) that illuminates your number 1 attribute. You could find that setting is your strongest attribute. Or it could be plot. You decide.

3. Now, rewrite it three times, quickly, based on each of the three remaining elements.

Hint: Start with the element you are least comfortable with.

This is how Zac, who wrote the previous student example, ordered his strengths, from weakest to strongest:

4. Setting
3. Characterization
2. Plot
1. Voice

Zac figured that he was strongest at voice and weakest at setting, and so he rewrote the piece three times focusing on setting, characterization, and plot in sequential order.

ORIGINAL, WHICH HE THOUGHT CAPTURED VOICE

The warehouse was on a dead-end street, near the Goodwill bins, in deep SE, near what they now call the Woodstock neighborhood. When I arrived, there were three men and three women, standing on opposite sides of the large, drop-down, steel door entry way. Divided by gender. One of the men walked up to me, introduced himself, and had me fill out an NDA, along with the more standard I-9, payment info, etc. Afterword, one of the women asked me a series of questions, that seemed to be designed to see how well I might work with potential demographics.

SETTING

I arrived at the job site, a towering warehouse at the center of the dead-end of a poorly planned, drawn-out street in the deepest of the deep SE.

Past Woodstock, past the Bins, past the hipsters. The leaning, rusted metal building should be condemned, if it's still standing. Parts of the exterior were covered in wooden slats [how did the metal walls get holes in them?] and the solar panels that lined the roof hung off over the edges. A group of three men and three women stood in even rows on either side of the fifty-foot, retractable steel gate. As I approached, a man and a woman walked up, each holding a tablet. They asked me to fill out the standard new-hire packet and a series of non-standard demographic questions. It was Portland raining, light and consistent, but they didn't seem to care about the tablet.

CHARACTERIZATION

The job site itself, while being way out in the boonies of the SE, wasn't strange, didn't bother me—this wasn't my first rodeo, at that point, I would do pretty much whatever to make a buck. Now, the lines, with three women on one side, and three men on the other, I didn't know what to think about that. Why were they separated by gender? When two of them walked over with their apparently waterproof tablets, I tried to ask what the deal was, and the man said, "All in due time." The woman asked me a series of questions about my political affiliation, my race, my music taste, my sexual partners, the list goes on, and I answered as closely as I could. I asked the man what the reason for these questions was and he was cagey, the woman smiled and told me it had to do with genres. I asked, what like sci-fi and horror? She gave me a wishy-washy answer, she said sort-of, but with people.

PLOT

I arrived at the old warehouse in deep SE Portland at the scheduled time of 9:30 am. Sure, it was old and grimy, at very end of a closed off street, but that wasn't the weird part. Yea, yea, Keep Portland Weird, we get it, but here's the thing, this is why you need to think of it like I'm trying to scam you: the six employees at the gate were of varying positionality and stood divided by gender on either side of a massive retractable steel door. One of each gender, who I now know to be what they call the Filters, walked over with tablets, that for some reason weren't affected by the persistent drizzle. The man had me fill out the standard legal new-hire questions and the woman had me answer a thirty-minute-long string of questions regarding demographic information, what kinds of people I worked best with, who my friends and lovers had been, their corresponding demographic information, the interests that united me with larger groups, and so on. I didn't know it at the time, but she was doing what the Sorting calls "genreing."

Analyze

What did you discover? What does your wisest, most intelligent self tell you in answer to these questions?

1. Is your top proficiency how you define yourself as an artist?
2. Does it help you deliver the meaning you're attempting to convey? Or is it merely the one with which you've had the most practice?
3. Is it a crutch? (Think hard about this one. Do you resort to this element—say, setting—when you don't know what else to do?)
4. Perhaps number 1 is the aspect of your writing that garners the most praise from others?
5. What about the other three—the ones you judge yourself as being less proficient at? Would a honing of these elements enable you to get closer to your goals and help you communicate your vision more effectively?

Focusing When Everything's a Blur

Imagine a person with whom you regularly interact—a person you respect because of their combination of imagination, intelligence, sense of humor, perspective, and bullshit detector. You may love this person because they "get" you. Because you don't have to improve your communication skills. Because everything you want to express lands perfectly.

Now, go deeper. If you were able to improve a single aspect of your communication with that person, what would that be? If you wanted to get even closer, to communicate *everything* you had inside you in a crystal clear way—to get all your ideas, obsessions, fears, wants, and desires out on the table—what could you improve?

This is why we study craft—why writers practice and practice and do and do to achieve mastery of these fictional tools, or elements of composition.

Go through each of the four elements while asking: How can this help me *be known*?

Investigating Plot

Let's think of plot in two ways. One, plot is simply those things that happen, in a certain order, to bring about an effect or outcome. Two, plot is *a strategic ordering of events to maximize impact* and affect an outcome—both in the story and in the mind and body of the reader.

Body? Yes.

Let's dig a little deeper into the second definition, since it's a little more complicated than the first. When most of us first came to read and write, our desire to consume words on a page was neither intellectual nor philosophical. Kids are after stories. Later, when we're aspiring artists, we become interested in the theories of how things we want to make are made by the experts. But the original impulse that brings most of us to read and write is what's *felt*. Moreover, the word "strategic" is important to the second definition. Even if intuitive or unplanned and performed only in various stages of revision, the *strategic* ordering of events is critical.

There are many ways writers create plots. Run a search on Freytag's pyramid, and you'll find a tool developed by Gustav Freytag, a playwright and novelist, in the 1800s. It's a model that gets a lot of play in academic settings and follows a rather familiar formula: conflict, crisis, resolution.

A vast number of great stories use this structure.

But many compelling stories employ others.

Autobiography of My Mother, by Jamaica Kincaid, is narrated by a seventy-year-old woman, Zuela Claudette Richardson. A common trope heard in writing workshops (often good advice, actually) is start *in medias*

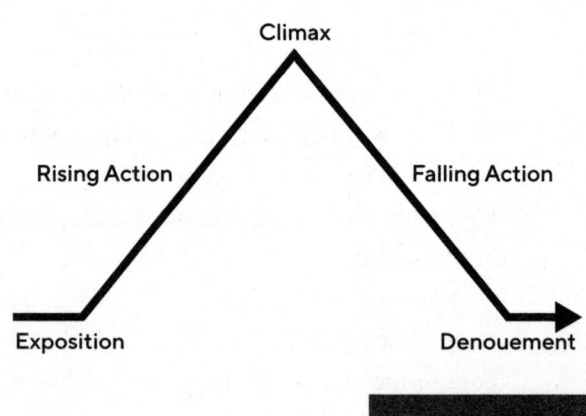

Freytag's pyramid.

res—in the middle of the action. Creative writing teachers have long been suggesting: "You don't need to start with the day the character was born. Begin with action!"

Kincaid seemingly decided to pass on this (often wise) suggestion by starting with Zuela's birth—an act that orphaned her. What's to be known in Kincaid's novel doesn't fit into any pyramid. It provides a different set of ways to be known—a different set of strategies to keep its reader's attention and curiosity.

Kincaid offers the reader something other than the thrill of rising action. Yes, she gives readers insight into the pleasures of sex, the body, and food, as well as an understanding of class divisions and the effects of colonialism and isolation (to name a mere few of Kincaid's themes).

In a *Boston Globe* interview by Kate Tuttle, Kincaid said:

> One of the things that young people need to know when they go into writing is that they ought to stop writing these stupid books that please people. They should write as if they might fail at it. To succeed at something mediocre is worse than to fail at something great.

Plot can also be arranged sequentially, or it can jump around. It can involve seemingly disjointed anecdotes positioned carefully next to each other. Virginia Woolf's *The Years* is one such story. Instead of easily mapped-out plot points, it follows various characters of an extended family from childhood to old age. Each chapter represents a year, seemingly randomly chosen. You never know, starting a new chapter, who is going to appear or what is going to happen. But by the end chapter (a brilliant party scene, rivaling the one in *Mrs. Dalloway*), you get many, many "units of satisfaction" for your reading pleasure.

There are whole books written about plot. But we want to share an extremely flexible approach to plot, one that can be used in limitless ways to get you writing. Your story will gain meaning through a series of connections and disconnections within the story that can be strategically arranged and rearranged for impact.

Write Now

1. Write a piece of fiction (or choose a draft you've already written) that has at least three scenes (three things that happen at three different places and at three different times).

2. Go through it, line by line.
3. Write "Connect" every time your character or characters are in some way connected (to the world, to others, to their own emotions) and "Disconnect" every time they are distant or disconnected. You can use physical or emotional connections or disconnections.
4. Try to rearrange the different parts of your story. Start with a connection.
5. Then alternate between *connect* and *disconnect* until one of the two gains traction.
6. See if you can "crescendo." Allow your story to rise in intensity like a musician playing their instrument, slowly increasing in volume and tempo.

Exploring Characterization

Defined simply, characterization is the set of techniques writers use to create fictional characters.

And characters are the *who* in the story's events.

These definitions may seem overly simple because when it comes to the "techniques" to create a character, there are endless options and no definitive rules. Even if an artist can articulate the techniques they used (and often the best writers cannot) to arrive at a particular rendering of character, can they repeat the process for the next story? Can someone else use that same approach to equal success? Each time someone nails down a theory that's seemingly definitive, a new artist emerges to dazzle us with the opposite.

And that's the *good* news. It's why we keep reading.

Characterization, along with every other craft topic, varies within the context. Different places, times, social and political contexts—as well as individual artists' visions and projects—create different impulses and artistic responses, which demand modification to techniques and strategies.

Most writers we've spoken to—including those with a variety of intersectional identities—want to read the characters *you* want to write, and most appreciate characters skillfully crafted to give the reader the *illusion* of complexity. Complexity is a good thing. When a reader you admire says, "Those characters are complex," it usually means you're on your way . . . that you've done your job.

Writer Hari Kunzru says:

> Good writers transgress without transgressing, in part because they are
> humble about what they do not know. They treat their own experience of
> the world as provisional. They do not presume. They respect people, not
> by leaving them alone in the inviolability of their cultural authenticity, but
> by becoming involved with them. They research. They engage in reciprocal
> relationships.

Art can transgress without the *writer* needing to transgress. Artists, often misunderstood as people who are bold about what they know, are often just the opposite. They're people whose boldness comes from dogged *curiosity, inquiry, investigation,* and *research.* They're able to explore ambiguity, contradiction.

Eudora Welty said, "Write about what you don't know about what you know."

Harkening back to our Chapter 2 discussion on aesthetic force, Welty also famously wrote in the *Atlantic* article:

> The writing of a novel is taking life as it already exists, not to report it but to
> make an object, toward the end that the finished work might contain this
> life inside it, and offer it to the reader. The essence will not be, of course, the
> same thing as the raw material: it is not even of the same family of things.
> The novel is something that never was before and will not be again. For the
> mind of one person, its writer, is in it too. *What distinguishes it above all from
> the raw material, and what distinguishes it from journalism, is that inherent
> in the novel is the possibility of a shared act of the imagination between its
> writer and its reader.* [emphasis ours]

In that same article, Welty distinguishes between the "novelist" and the "crusader" and said crusaders (those with a *fixed* moral stance) are necessary but might fare better as journalists.

If one knows all about why and when and how something is *important* with zero hesitation or confusion or ambivalence, it may be less effective as fiction. However, the crusader impulse can be very useful if it's the *force* of the pull to a subject or a set of events.

Certainty tends to be general rather than specific. According to Welty:

> [Generalities are] fatal to tenderness and are themselves non-conductors of any real, however modest, discovery of the writer's own heart. This discovery is the best hope of the ordinary novelist, and to make it he begins not with a generality, but with the particular in front of his eyes, which he is able to examine.

For these reasons, fiction writers often prioritize what they *don't* know over what they do and see their individual life and knowledge as limited—tethered to some larger community and set of truths—and they work hard to uncover these connections, especially the unexpected ones. This most happens through "the particular."

If you tend to be more concerned in early drafts with a character's internal life, now might be a good time to ask yourself some questions about what could happen next. We don't want to encourage students to write aimless expository prose. Shouldn't a character be confronted with something happening? Even if it's just that one of her shoes came untied and she tripped?

There. A plot point.

Perhaps by making that choice you discover that your character is always coming undone. Physically—shoelaces, belts, zippers, and so on. Perhaps emotionally, too. Or perhaps your character's emotional life is strong due to their focus and concentration. Perhaps their intense focus on keeping it together emotionally is what causes them to come undone physically.

Actions and reactions are there to experiment with, to explore, because plot, after all, is often just a series of actions and characters' reactions to them.

When it comes to this popular idea of "knowing" characters, so much seems to depend on the interpretation of the word "know."

Some might say it's a writer's job to know their characters before they start writing. But what do they really need to "know" in advance? Shouldn't at least some of it be discovered along the way? What if a writer doesn't discover their character's motivation until they've been writing for a while? Is that a problem?

No. For writers, not knowing is a gift—especially if, as Hari Kunzru says, they are "humble about what they do not know. They treat their own experience of the world as provisional. They do not presume."

Discovery is why we write—and why our readers want to read what we produce.

Failure to render a character with the illusion of a human being's full complexity can be a failure of craft. A writer simply doesn't have a strong enough grasp of language, of description, or of dialogue to render a fully realized character on the page.

Biases and blind spots inherited from a misogynist, racist, trans- and homophobic culture also show up in characterizations. Even writers who care sometimes unintentionally fail to provide necessary context or to give equal or adequate space or interiority to one character versus another. If that's the case, the revision process can help you earn the complexity that will keep your characters from reinforcing hurtful stereotypes.

A common criticism of stories and books with poor characterization is "the writer didn't do their homework." Research is vital, perhaps especially so when writing across differences. Stories (or drafts) can also be burdened by the highlighting of research that interrupts the narrative flow just to signal to the reader, as if to say, "This bad character is not *me*, the writer." There's no such thing as too much research, but there can be too little translation of that research into art.

Think of a character in a story or book that made you "feel seen." You are free to choose a character who you physically/psychologically/demographically/politically resemble—or from whom you differ. Perhaps the character of a British royal who lived in the 1700s makes you "feel seen" even if you were born in Chico, California, in 1990. Maybe the portrayed inner life of an enslaved character in Chattanooga, Tennessee, in the early 1800s pings a human bond of recognition, even though you're a retired autoworker from Detroit.

Whenever this happens, when you feel yourself relating to a character on multiple resonant levels, make a note of the strategic choices the writer made. Ask yourself: What's my version of that strategy? Or what version of that strategy is useful for my project?

A Few Strategies That Fiction Writers Use

Surprising Combinations of Characterization Techniques

Writers use various (and often contradictory) combinations of the modes for creating compelling characters. They portray what characters

1. look like
2. say
3. do (how they act and react)
4. think
5. feel

What if your characters *think* they look one way, but others may beg to differ? A character may see themselves as ugly and stupid because, as a kid, they heard those terms from a harsh and critical adult. Even if they directly say and do things that reinforce those self-beliefs, other characters (and readers) may notice something entirely different. A character's depiction can be made more compelling if there are surprising combinations of these other three modes:

1. How other characters within the world of your story react to your characters
2. Ways that the writer or narrator interpret the characters differently from the way the characters interpret themselves
3. Ways that the reader interprets the characters in ways that the writer, narrator, or characters themselves may not

Great characters are almost always inconsistent. Most have competing desires. They may need to win *and* want to be fair; to accept themselves *and* live in a world that's intolerant of some essential part of who they are; to remain faithful to the family they love *and* to seek out the life they want for themselves. Those are just for starters.

A comment often heard in workshops is "Cut that, it's out of character."

This is only useful when an action taken by a character is contradictory in a manner that feels, to your trusted readers, *unearned* within the world of a story. Blurting out a family secret over a plate of shared nachos might, in an early draft, seem unearned. A character shamed into keeping a family secret their entire life, who, after a set of interactions that chip away at their resolve, *finally* blurts out the truth over nachos? That may be the *perfect* setting, once earned.

The scene didn't need to be cut; the character-defining action leading up to the scene needed to be developed.

Let's go back to something mentioned earlier, a scene in which a character *says*, "I'd be happy to," and *thinks*, "Screw you!"

Often, it's much more interesting to hear what a character is *really* thinking when they're forced to behave well. If the flight attendant in your story is as pleased as he seems to be pouring a demanding passenger a second cup of cola, give that angel his wings. It might be more exciting to hear your flight attendant's thoughts that contradict his politeness while the cola fizzes in its cup.

Remember the *surprising* part and avoid contradictions for their own sake. Just because a writer is amused at the idea of a nun who moonlights as a sex worker, or a sailor who doesn't know how to swim, doesn't mean it's literary. Again, in fiction, consistencies and contradictions need to be earned.

But how?

Tether It

Think of the ball in the diagram as an individual character. The string is what's connecting it to a larger group of characters (symbolized as the top part of the pole). The base is the story's thematic concerns.

If your characters and their actions fail to *eventually* connect to a larger group of people, and if that larger group's situation isn't *eventually* connected to a larger human concern (the big philosophical questions about life), you're not tethered.

Let's return to a book of fiction mentioned earlier, *Autobiography of My Mother*, by Jamaica Kincaid. Here's how the book jacket describes it:

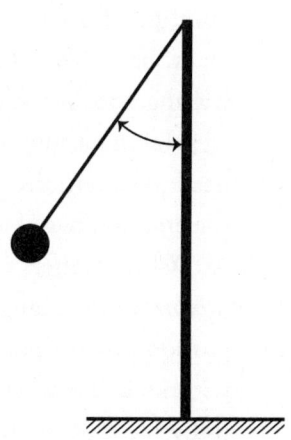

> Kincaid's third novel...is presented as the mesmerizing, harrowing, richly metaphorical autobiography of 70-year-old Xuela Claudette Richardson. Earthy, intractably antisocial, acridly introspective, morbidly obsessed with history and identity, conquest and colonialism, language and silence, Xuela recounts her life on the island of Dominica in the West Indies. In Kincaid's characteristically lucid, singsong prose, Xuela traces her evolution from a young girl to an old woman while interrogating the mysteries of her hybrid cultural origins and her parents, who failed to be parents: her mother died during childbirth; her often absent father, a cruel and

petty island official, cultivates a veneer of respectability ("another skin over his real skin"), rendering him unrecognizable to his daughter.

Based only on this description, let's ask what may "tether" the character of Xuela Claudette Richardson to others. First, her obsessions. Many readers may also be obsessed with "history and identity, conquest and colonialism, language and silence." Many of us are compelled by how present-day experience and the accumulated wisdom of age allows us to see or resee our pasts. A huge population of us come from "hybrid cultural origins."

All of these are possible points of tethering. Readers may see themselves as (or be curious about someone who, unlike them, is) "intractably antisocial" or "acridly introspective." Some readers may have parents who "failed to be parents" too. If not, they may reflect on their parents' plights or may have been failed by some other loved one or an institution meant to protect them.

Any or all of this is enough to tether the character to a larger group of people. This larger group of people is then connected to even larger concerns relevant to all humanity.

Without such tethering, scenes and stories might seem less like a story and more like a pop song. Breakup songs by divas are great whether or not their listeners have recently been dumped: "Stronger," by Kelly Clarkson; "Heartbreak Hotel," by Whitney Houston; "Not Gon' Cry," by Mary J. Blige; "Cry Me a River," by Justin Timberlake. Each of these has the same basic arc as early-draft student stories. But what unique ingredients (or elements of composition) make a song great?

Usually: a voice singing it, melody, instrumentation, a beat, and a maximum duration of five minutes. That's just for starters. Then there's tonal quality, arrangement, harmony, tempo, rhythm, and timbre. Some of these are present in creative writing, too, but others are impossible to have in a printed story.

Making a song is no easier than making a story, but a song doesn't *necessarily* need to be tethered to philosophical questions or complex characterization to yank the emotion out of its listeners.

Why? It offers other opportunities for engagement. One doesn't even need to *comprehend* the language of the lyrics to love a song. All around the world people are passionately fist pumping and screaming lyrics along with their favorite performers without a clue whether those sounds are a recipe for a blueberry pie or a scorching indictment of an unfaithful lover.

A ten-page short story asks something different of the audience than listening to a three-minute song. It also offers something different. As such, expectations of the characters are different.

Untethered characters can read like lyrics with no beat, no melody, no timbre, no voice.

Your Character Doesn't Need to Be Liked, but Your Reader Has to Care

Your story—somewhere—must contain the possibility that others can really care about it, too. Most people have that friend who loves to tell every detail of their dream. It seems like fun for the friend, but after a couple of minutes, the listener is praying for it to end. Unless the friend can provide the listener with a way to *care* about the dream, listening can quickly become an exercise in patience and tolerance. Why? A series of processes are usually needed before the stuff of our own imagination can be interesting and compelling to others.

Readers can only stay interested in fiction in relation to how words make them feel and think. Characters often play a huge part in this caring, but that doesn't mean the character or characters needs to be likable or "sympathetic"—another abused workshop word.

Do a search on *character likability* and you could spend the rest of your life reading the results. Writers are rightly infuriated by the idea that likable characters = good fiction, and unlikable characters = not publishable or bad. Why? The portrayal of a so-called horrible person (a subjective label) often *increases* (rather than decreases) the opportunity for a reader to care about important thematic concerns. Read *Animal Farm*. George Orwell didn't intend for readers to like Napoleon. He used him to artistically portray many of his concerns and obsessions, including the dangers of totalitarianism and dictatorship. Or read *Sula*. Toni Morrison, we'd guess, knew how most readers would feel about a title character having sex with her best friend's husband—and then, after getting caught in the act, refusing to apologize.

A deep reader, even one who doesn't approve of Sula, will see her as a lovable (or at least a compelling) character because the choices Morrison made in her novel offer readers much to reflect upon, including: the friendships between girls and women in a patriarchal society; an exploration far beyond simple notions of culpability; and the tragedy of a brilliant mind kept from opportunity because of racism and misogyny.

It's better for participants in a workshop to discuss what in the discussed story's draft is engaging them—*making them care*—even if (and likely *because*) they *don't* like or relate to the character.

Whether or not your character is likable, you can earn a compelling characterization by using unique, convincing, and surprising combinations of the modes of characterization. This is achieved through successive drafts. Tethering your character earns your readers' care.

Oh, and caring doesn't necessarily mean that a character gets your sympathy (you hear complaints about "unsympathetic" characters all the time as well). You can hate well-rounded characters. Despise them. Scorn them. Be afraid of them. But you're *interested*. You're *engaged*. You care about what's happening. Your terrorists needn't have hearts of gold, or your child molesters (I'm talking to you, Humbert Humbert) vulnerabilities that make readers feel sorry for them. Your characters can be bastards right through (although hopefully in complex ways). And you still must care about what happens in the story that they inhabit.

Deciding on the Number of Character Dimensions

In most literary fiction (there are exceptions, including literary farce, satire, and fables, just to name a few), it's best to work past flat characters and stereotypes—or, as is said in the biz, one-dimensional characters. We encourage you to practice eschewing the general in favor of the particular.

Either way, writers need to captivate readers with each character's catalog of behaviors. Most people have quite the catalog to showcase—even if, in real life, people try and even succeed at publicly showcasing only their most flattering character traits.

Think of a friend or family member who works hard to cross every I'm-in-complete-control *t* and dot every I'm-socially-acceptable *i*. You can see the cracks, can't you? And if you live with the person? Families, partners, and roommates witness much, much more.

Readers want to see those cracks.

What, out of that catalog of behaviors, is relevant for the story you're telling? And in what proportion? This is the good stuff.

Unrequited love and breakups suck. They create strong feelings. Strong feelings can be good for fiction. For this reason, many young creative writing students produce first-draft stories about an innocent character duped (and dumped) by a duplicitous one. They create a world in which the dumped gets all the pity they deserve, and the dumper is shown to be a true scoundrel. In the end, the dumpee comes out victorious, better, stronger without the dumper.

Even if there are compelling character details throughout these early drafts, the dumper and the dumpee's catalogs of behavior remain *too consistent* and therefore—like lyrics to a pop song without its beat—end up as too inert for final-draft fiction.

While these early drafts may be tethered to something that affects a wider group of people (we all struggle with relationships of one kind or another), there's usually no deeper exploration, nothing *surprising*.

Does that mean you can't write about breakups? No. In fact, "Reasons for and Advantages of Breathing," a short story by the brilliant Lydia Peelle, is all about a woman dealing with a breakup. You'll read it at the end of this chapter.

How Can I Deepen Character, Practically Speaking?

The process of continuously inventing and then reinventing is tricky. If you type "Character Questionnaire" into a search field, you'll find a bevy of them. These worksheets can help you clarify your character's appearance, personality, hobbies, political and ethical stances, spiritual or religious beliefs, superstitions, and whatever else. Others swear by Myers-Briggs or Enneagram or Zodiac charts to help deepen their understanding and propel their characters into action. These actions, when combined, can trigger ideas for their character's personality and contradictions.

They can also bog you down.

Why? Some writers assert that if your character's eye color, weight, or hairstyle isn't, in some tiny way, part of the overall mix vital to the story, it shouldn't be there. Fiction most often begins with a situation. A dilemma. Out of that dilemma the illusion of personality and characterization is crafted to serve the thematic concerns that arise through the writer's various drafts. A chicken-and-egg scenario.

An obsession with a certain person or personality type often serves as a starting point, and through that exploration a writer can find a dilemma worthy of fiction.

Personality questionnaires are most useful once a writer is already entrenched in a situation and is consciously or unconsciously exploring a thematic concern for which they care deeply. Otherwise, the writer stays in the realm of the exercise. We want the writer's satisfaction to come in the form of a compelling story of fiction, not in the completion of exercises and worksheets.

By now, you have gathered important-to-you material. Now that you have it, you can decide if fiction, including the strategies fiction writers use, is the best container to deliver it to readers.

Interweaving Plot and Character

Here are four ways characters and plot get interwoven:

1. The character can take an action (create a plot point by acting). Ayşegül Savaş's story "Future Selves" begins: "Some years after we moved to the city, my husband and I started looking for an apartment to buy."
2. The character can be acted upon (by others, by God, by nature, and so on) and create further plot points by reacting. *The Book of Form and Emptiness*, by Ruth Ozeki, follows a set of characters, including a teenage boy named Benny Oh, whose life takes a turn after the sudden death of his father, Yumi Oh. Benny starts hearing voices—the voices of everyday objects. Benny's mom also reacts, both to her husband's death and to her son's struggles.
3. The character can remember things (flashbacks). In *Their Eyes Were Watching God*, by Zora Neale Hurston, Janie Crawford recounts her life to her best friend, Pheoby Watson. By relaying the remembered stories of her three marriages (and much more), the reader can glean the contrast between how Janie is perceived by others and who she really is.
4. The character can imagine things (fantasize). Joseph Cassara's novel *The House of Impossible Beauties* is full of young characters imagining their futures, sharing their dreams. This strategic choice works double time by giving readers nuanced, layered characterization and by setting up the series of joys and sorrows, connections and disconnections that happen when dreams are made and broken.

Keep in mind: The four examples of how character and plot are interwoven are not mutually exclusive. Sure, you can talk about the qualities of flour or water or salt or (in some cases) yeast, but it's the magic of their combination and the addition of air and fire that makes bread. To get truly good at baking, a baker must practice using each of the individual ingredients. It's only after all the ingredients are combined and put in the oven that the baker knows if they have bread. Same is true in a story.

Lincoln Michel's essay "On the Many Different Engines That Power a Short Story: It's Not Just Plot or Character That Drives Fiction" (published by Literary Hub) encourages students to rethink plot and character as the sole means of engagement:

> The hard thing about writing—or one of the hard things in the endless series of hard things about writing—is that there's no one way to do it. Instead, there are infinite paths in the dark woods of fiction leading to infinite types of stories. It's hard, a little scary, yet ultimately thrilling.
>
> Despite this, there are countless articles that insist that there are in fact only two methods of storytelling: plot driven and character driven. It's understandable that writing guides and craft classes are reductive. Who would pay for a writing guide that said "lol who knows ¯_(ツ)_/¯" followed by 200 blank pages? Still, the plot-driven vs. character-driven binary has always made me wonder why those two aspects of fiction are the only ones allowed in the driver's seat. Couldn't a story be driven by voice? Couldn't setting have a turn at the wheel?

Our answer? Indeed, they can.

Lincoln Michel also says:

> My interest, as a writer and creative writing professor, is less in how we can analyze stories than in how writers can generate work. I'm interested in what devices—engines let's call them, since surely the author is always the driver (even when they're crashing their story into a ditch)—can supply power to the rest of story.

Michel talks about plot and character as "external" engines but in his article draws attention to "internal" engines, too. Examples are "form" and "language." These engines are put to incredible use in poetry—and if you're interested in experimenting across genres (and we assume you are because you have this book)—this theory might prove extremely practical. Of "form," he says:

The form engine is probably easier to recognize. You can look at Carmen Maria Machado's brilliant "Especially Heinous," a short story told in the form of 272 capsule reviews of (fictional) SVU episodes, or Alejandro Zambra's amazing novel *Multiple Choice* that has no real characters or plot, but unfolds entirely in the form of a standardized test. Each chapter takes the form of standardized test questions, such as multiple choice or reader comprehension questions, while using this constraint to create meaning and feeling. If you are writing with a character or plot engine, you might impose a form later—shaping your story in the revision process—but with a form engine the form comes first.

To his list of form-driven stories, add Lydia Peelle's "Reasons for and Advantages of Breathing" (for reasons you'll see later in this book) and Tobias Woolf's story "Bullet in the Brain," which experiments with matching form to the human experience of time—how it seems to speed up and slow down, depending on the intensity of the situation.

Leveraging Language

For an experiment, we created a "found poem" using words found in the first two paragraphs of a published short story. Found poems use one text to create another and must always give credit to the original source text. This is from "Tiny, Meaningless Things," by Marisa Silver.

Tiny Meaningless Things

Wednesday is ironing,
a day of smoothness, smell of
wet heat, satisfactions of erasure.

Work the tip into
wrinkled underarms and
Transformation, fresh and untried.

She is seventy-four,
skin elasticity
like a head of wilted lettuce

She tried
to impart:
the proper way

    to store vegetables,
to fold clothing,
to wash faces

    They hadn't listened,
They couldn't imagine decay
understand the value of preservation

    the grownup pleasures of responsibility

    The doctor told her
it would be safe to
take those days off from

    her vigil, that Frank
had a while
yet.

    It had been up to Paula to
keep tabs on her
Father

    All Paula had to
do was peek into the
bedroom once or twice before

    she went to bed, just to make sure
that her father
was sleeping.

We chose the lines from the story, in the order they were written, then broke them and added white space. Before you read ahead, jot down some quick answers to these questions:

1. What are the found poem's thematic concerns?
2. What are the most arresting images?
3. What's the mood of the piece?
4. What choices did the arranger make, using the elements of composition of poetry (line breaks, white space, syntax, and so on), that enabled you to answer questions 1 to 3?

Now let's read the opening two paragraphs from Marisa Silver's "Tiny, Meaningless Things," the short story we used to create the poem:

Wednesday is ironing day, a day of smoothness, the pleasing, embryonic smell of wet heat, and the satisfactions of erasure. How rewarding it is, Evelyn thinks, to work the tip of the iron into the wrinkled underarms of her favorite blouses and watch their instant transformation into material that is fresh and untried. Now that she is seventy-four, and her skin has lost its elasticity, this trick of reversing time is no longer available to her.

It's like a head of wilted lettuce, she thinks, as she mists a blouse with water. All you have to do is put it in ice water and it springs back to life. These were lessons she'd tried to impart to her daughters: the proper way to store vegetables, to fold clothing, to wash their faces (never soap, only water). They hadn't listened, of course. They couldn't imagine decay. Her daughters' bored or frankly antagonistic responses to her attempts to make them understand the value of preservation had agitated her, and she'd repeated her warnings two or maybe three times until they screamed or slammed doors. They were young. How could they know the disaster of carelessness? She knew. She'd been at her cousin's wedding in Tulsa when her husband died so long ago. The doctor had told her that it would be safe to take those days off from her vigil, that Frank had a while yet. Naomi and Ruth were away at school, Naomi in Lincoln, Ruth all the way east at a private college that had given her a scholarship to insure her sharp and critical company. It had been up to Paula to keep tabs on her father that weekend. Evelyn paid for a nurse to come in during the day. All Paula had to do was peek into the bedroom once or twice before she went to bed, just to make sure that her father was sleeping easily. It wasn't a lot to ask of a sixteen-year-old who stayed awake late into the night, whispering on the phone to boys. Evelyn had been surprised that

Paula hadn't complained. That had touched her, and she'd thought that perhaps now that Paula's sisters were gone, and she was no longer the youngest, alternately teased or ignored, she was beginning to feel the grownup pleasures of responsibility. Evelyn had left phone numbers for people Paula could call should anything be amiss—Dr. Barnes and Vivian Branch next door. She'd left the number of the house where she'd be staying. But Paula hadn't called anyone. She hadn't even checked on her father when she came home from the party she'd promised to forgo. The next morning, when the nurse called Evelyn, she said that Frank had been gone for "some time." Evelyn hadn't asked how long. She didn't want to know if the nurse had found him with his mouth agape, didn't want to imagine that he'd been that way for hours, his final call unheard. Paula was still asleep, the nurse said. Should she wake her?

Now ask yourself:

1. What thematic concerns can you see in the story's opening paragraphs?
2. What are the most arresting images from the story's excerpt?
3. What's the mood of the excerpt?
4. What choices did the writer make, using the elements of composition in fiction (voice, characterization, detail, setting, and so on) to help you answer questions 1 to 3?
5. What are the similarities in your observations between the found poem and the author's short story opening? Differences?

By borrowing a poet's techniques to reimagine a short story's opening paragraphs as a poem, we learned a lot. To leverage language as an engine to power a story, we had to slow our reading. We thought about which lines to choose and why.

We wanted lines (or portions of lines) with syntactic impact (meaning they sound great when read aloud). We wanted the lines to be aesthetically pleasing, or visually stunning to our imagination's eye. We found the vast majority fit these criteria. Most importantly, we chose each line for how it illuminated the story's important thematic concerns. Having read the entire story, we were curious how many of the story's broader themes are present from the get-go.

Once we chose the lines, we started experimenting with their placement. We kept them in chronological order (how they appear in the story), eventually arranging them into tercets (three-line stanzas), hoping each one would work almost like chapters in a novel, revealing new information while building tension.

In doing so, we can now see how Marisa Silver has fooled us in the most gratifying way. By using the prose writer's tools of characterization and setting, she imagined concrete details to illuminate the circumstances of Evelyn's life. We became so immersed in the task at hand, ironing, we didn't notice how cleverly and strategically she was providing backstory and setting the stage for the rest of the scenes.

The activity, ironing, is portrayed as "real" within the "world of the story" (we believe that Evelyn is ironing, not thinking about ironing as a metaphor for reversing time). The narrative intelligence (or third-person storytelling voice) is direct in explaining why ironing is *also* a metaphor:

> Now that she is seventy-four, and her skin has lost its elasticity, this trick of reversing time is no longer available to her.

We find out that Evelyn has three daughters. The details about her family and their past—their names, the towns, the schools—work like a magician's cloud of dust, allowing the writer a sleight of hand to sneak in deeper, more layered thematic concerns around issues of culpability, resentment, grief, guilt, anger, and loss. These are details that are relevant and pertinent to the story and are also thematic concerns that deepen and develop as subsequent scenes unfold.

After we borrowed a poet's tools to "write" the material into a new form, it became plain to us (in a way we hadn't yet seen) that the important themes start in the title. In fact, they're expertly woven throughout both opening paragraphs.

The poet's set of tools sharpens the prose writer's set, and vice versa.

Going back to your own prose, you are now able to ask yourself the following questions:

1. Are my sentences impactful on the level of syntax and image?
2. Is the main character or narrator involved in an activity? Or are they merely thinking?
3. Are the metaphors, if any, "working" first in the "real world" of the story?
4. Are the story's thematic concerns somehow illuminated in the title and opening paragraphs? Are there too many? Too few?

5. Are the images concrete, constantly pulling the reader deeper into the world of the story?
6. Does my opening introduce the major players (characters)?
7. Is a pivotal action revealed that tells the reader why the story is being told "now"?

The experiment of creating a poem from your opening paragraphs may provide clues for how to best revise your chapters or short stories.

Even if Marisa Silver had not consciously borrowed from the poet's toolbox, we see the technical choices that she shares with poets. If applied, these same choices could make your own stories better.

Leveraging Setting

Whole books should be written on setting. Why? It offers endless possibilities to engage the imagination of the reader.

Setting is the "where" of fiction, the place the action is set. If your scene takes place in a restaurant or a beach or the supermarket, those places should drive the plot or reveal character or explore voice. The setting must be so integral to a piece of fiction that the fiction couldn't stand without it. The feeling should be that it could never have happened anywhere else.

People often note, usually with surprise, when they see this on the page: "The setting is a character too!" Exactly. Yes. The setting *is* a character too.

We trust that if writers engage with material that's deeply meaningful to them, a huge number of the setting details come organically—that is, without strategic forethought. Too much strategizing in early, generative drafts can result in wooden portrayals stifled by the writer's desire to solve issues in advance.

Filmmakers obsess over "the location" and how it works to tell the story. They purposely manipulate the viewer with color choice, weather, music, lighting, and so on.

Take the movie *Moonlight*, directed by Barry Jenkins, who also wrote the screenplay based on a story by Tarell Alvin McCraney. In the act of making the film, Jenkins noticed that each time the character Little entered a setting, by the time he left the setting he was in some way changed, even *transformed* by the setting.

Consider these questions about your setting:

1. What challenge is your character facing when your character walks into the scene/particular setting?
2. What's at stake?
3. How is your setting working to raise the stakes?
4. How is your character different/transformed by the end of the scene? What external factors facilitate that change? How does the setting look/seem different to the character at the end? And how does your character react differently to the setting at the end of the scene?

Write Now

1. Write a scene with a distinct setting (or choose an existing scene with a distinct setting). This could be a dressing room at a bridal gown store or a meat processing plant's assembly line or a tree fort or an exam room at a doctor's office. The point is it should take place *someplace,* not just in the narrator's mind.
2. Answer the previous set of setting questions about your setting.
3. Now reenter your scene. See if you can make your character interact *deeply* with the setting.
4. Work toward a change in character that's tied to the setting.
5. Try to make it so that this scene couldn't possibly have taken place anywhere but in the setting you chose.

These experiments show us just how alive setting can seem, serving as an active environment to push your characters toward discovery. Characters may leave a setting having made a self-discovery. They may discover something about another character. They may discover something about the setting itself. In all cases, the writer has worked to tether the character to the setting and the setting to the wider concerns of the story. As with your character choices, these settings can also tether the reader to your story. Even if readers have never been to Chicago or Mumbai or Freetown or Seoul (or the entirely imaginary places as invented by writers such as Octavia Butler, Italo Calvino, and Chen Qiufan), they have likely experienced hot and cold, dry air and humidity, the smell of garlic, the sound of a screaming baby, a gray or blue or pink-red sky.

Writers frequently revise scenes to push their settings to the point where they are fully dramatized and portray important moments of discovery. As a result, such scenes increase the chances that their readers will feel emotions that are essential to the story.

Finding Your Voice

The goal is to find *your* voice, the voice that isn't like everyone else's. And this is a very difficult thing to do.

For some, the difficulty is an internal challenge caused by a desire to fit in, be appropriate, and gain the approval of those around us.

There are also external challenges. Too often writers who'd naturally include multilingual, regional, and perhaps even queer forms of arranging language have been told not to—either explicitly or implicitly. We say write the book you have in you, no matter how many or few languages, how regional or colloquial or cosmopolitan or international.

Often people come to write creatively after they've developed an academic or professional writing style—say, lawyers or philosophy students or folks who work for corporations. The very point of these styles is to limit or even eliminate the individual voice. A former director of communications for a huge tech company told us that even seemingly simple emails sent to customers and stakeholders went through thirty or more drafts to ensure the message stayed "on brand."

Learned habits that prove effective in one place can stump a writer and keep them from finding their voice in another.

Students in MFA programs sometimes struggle to let go of the stylistic choices of writers they admire. Denis Johnson's *Jesus' Son* was a popular favorite in graduate writing programs decades ago. Toni Morrison's *Beloved*, too. Both are worthy of every bit of their praise. Still, something happened back then, and the equivalent still happens today. A few books each year earn their accolades in a collective imagination, then writers in workshops imitate them, sometimes successfully, sometimes not.

Writer Joe Okonkwo, author of the short story collection *Kiss the Scars on the Back of My Neck* and the novel *Jazz Moon*, was asked, on Twitter, "What do you wish you could tell yourself about writing, back when you started?" He replied, "Don't try and write like Toni Morrison."

There are a lot of things writers could do that are much worse than imitating Denis Johnson or Toni Morrison (or whomever else is worthy of your admiration).

Still, a time comes when an apprentice writer needs to let go of the writer's voice they're imitating and lean more into discovering their own.

Some of the most useful writerly advice for fiction writers comes from memoirist Mary Karr. In *The Art of Memoir*, Karr says:

> As I've detailed elsewhere, it took me fifteen years of scribbling—first in poetry, then in fiction—to dredge up nerve to tell my childhood story in a voice that fit my face. Before then, I hid from readers on pages that sugar-coated any emotional truths about us all, part of an overall effort to sanitize our past and remold myself into somebody smarter, faster, funnier than harsh reality had afforded me to become.
>
> Literature, when I was growing up, had been the stuff of cool, diffident, hypereducated white guys. And I was solidly blue-collar, crown princess of the crap job—crayfish trucker, waitress, T-shirt factory seamstress—a drop-out with an itinerant past.

About voice:

> Each great memoir lives or dies based 100 percent on voice. It's the delivery system for the author's experience—the big bandwidth cable that carries in lustrous clarity every pixel of someone's inner and outer experiences. Each voice is cleverly fashioned to highlight a writer's individual talent or way of viewing the world. A memoirist starts off fumbling—jotting down facts, recounting anecdotes. It may take a writer hundreds of rough trial pages for a way of speaking to start to emerge unique to himself and his experience, but when he does, both carnal and interior experiences come back with clarity, and the work gains an electrical charge. For the reader, the voice has to exist from the first sentence.

Substitute "work of fiction" for "memoir" and it works. In fiction, "voice" is talked about in several different ways:

- *Voice of the author*
- *Voice of the piece*
- *Voice of the character(s) or narrator(s) within the piece*

Each is distinct. The author's voice is something a reader or reviewer might describe of all the writer's published work. Great reviewers often read the writer's full catalog of published work to arrive at how a particular work fits into the oeuvre. The reviewer might make observations about the themes the author takes on and how, stylistically, they address them across their career.

Each story in a collection or each book written over a novelist's career will have its own distinct voice—perhaps recognizable enough to attribute to the author, but with something about it that stands alone within the individual project. Finally, there's the voice of the narrator and characters within the story itself—and these can vary and strike readers as being very different from the overall piece or the author.

Write Now

1. Write or choose a paragraph of your work you feel is so alive that it's appropriate for the opening scene of a short story or novel chapter.
2. Rewrite it in a voice completely different from your current draft. Rewrite it in an exaggerated voice that's not authentic to you or your story.
3. The point here is to be silly, have fun. Limit yourself to 300 words. (Don't think of it as a scene yet, but the opening page of the story you're working on.) It often helps to start in a scene or situation at a particular place and time with characters who are acting and reacting.

Mary Gaitskill's story "The Other Place" starts like this:

> Douglass and I were sitting together in the living room last week, half watching the TV and checking e-mail, when an advertisement for a movie flashed across the screen: it was called "Captivity" and the ad showed a terrified blond girl in a cage, a tear running down her face.

Think about this quote from Mary Karr:

> For me, say, a penchant for gloom has to be confessed to throughout any book I write. Bleak humor right at the edge of being wrong has kept me alive, so it's wound up in my work. Asked by my sister why I was sexually assaulted as a kid but she wasn't, I quipped, "Maybe you're not cute enough"—which

takes one of the darkest events in my life and tries to turn it into a putdown for somebody else. Talk about grim. To chirp my story like some bouncy cheerleader would be a lie. That grimness has to make it in.

4. Now, rewrite the exaggerated opening scene you previously wrote to see what you can do to deepen the emotion, sharpen the focus, tune the sound of the voice toward authenticity/truth. Allow it all in, even the grimness (or whatever you might not ordinarily include for whatever reason). Push more. Exaggerate more.

Voice was saved for last because it's the most elusive. If we were to return to the metaphor of bread, it's perhaps the bread's aroma and taste. You can't get it to be good unless you get all the other ingredients to work together proportionally.

These four elements of composition are just as relevant to many of the poems and nonfiction pieces you may want to write, so use them liberally and across genres.

As you read "Reasons for and Advantages of Breathing," ask yourself how you'd describe the overall voice of the piece. How did the writer achieve it? Did it seem character driven? Plot driven? Setting-heavy? And how did all those elements work together?

Fiction Chapter Supplement: Patterns of Connection and Disconnection

Scientists rely on the study of patterns in various ways across different scientific disciplines. Patterns are essential for making observations, formulating hypotheses, conducting experiments, and drawing conclusions. Here are some ways in which scientists use patterns:

Astronomers study the patterns of celestial objects in the night sky to identify stars, planets, and galaxies. In statistics and data science, scientists use patterns in data to draw conclusions and make predictions. They identify trends, correlations, and anomalies. Biologists rely on patterns in the characteristics of organisms to classify and categorize them. Geologists analyze rock layers, fossils, and landforms to discern patterns in the earth's history, such as the history of climate change, earthquakes, and volcanic activity.

In essence, the study of patterns is fundamental to the scientific method and serves as a critical tool for making sense of the natural world, formulating theories, and advancing knowledge across various scientific disciplines.

How Will This Apply to Writing?

There are creative writing teachers who tell their students not to write breakup stories. We wonder if they say why. Perhaps it's because self-pity is often a writer's and character's main motivation for first-draft breakup stories (and many other types of stories). Readers don't want to identify with self-pitying characters.

Writer Molly Giles, author of *Wife with Knife*, says this:

> Anger is fuel for a writer. Most "bad" feelings are. Jealousy, hatred, lust: terrific. The only bad feeling that's truly *bad* for a writer is, sadly, the most common: self-pity. Self-pity just doesn't work. Sigh.

More than that, stories rely on *variance* and *surprise*. Imagine a breakup story with six scenes. If all six are a character feeling sad for the loss, there's no *variance*. If one or more of the scenes portray an enraged character, but that rage is expressed by the dumped partner enacting revenge on (say, by slashing the car tires of) their cheating partner, there's no *surprise*.

So how do we, as writers, strategically deal with characters who have every right to feel sorry for themselves?

"Reasons for and Advantages of Breathing" could be categorized as a breakup story. The character feels bad. She's also arguably enraged. Just not *always*. Sometimes she's also connecting. It could be argued that her state of mind *allows for* the connections she experiences.

Pay attention not only to the pattern we ask you to track, but the imagery, the white space, the surprising metaphors, the dialogue, and the contrast between action and thought. Although full of surprises, aspects of this story are consistent: its tone and the narrator's measured voice. It also follows a kind of pattern of connections and disconnections we find compelling.

What Do We Mean by Connect and Disconnect?

Think of the worst social event you've ever attended. Or the best. What made it "the worst"? Usually, it's a disparity between expectations and outcomes. People interact expecting all kinds of connections, including those with friends, family, business associates, and potential romantic partners (just to name a few). What makes a social event "the best"? The same gap in expectation versus outcome.

Think of one of your characters. Imagine the scenario that would land in the worst category. Did they expect something good (a tender reunion, a great conversation, a bond formed from a shared interest), only to be disappointed? This is an example of a disconnect.

Maybe your character dreads going to a boring conference, but they're required to attend to keep their job. The third day of it, on a dinner break, picking at a dry chicken breast and soggy broccoli florets from the awful buffet, they spot a beloved friend they haven't seen in decades. This is a connect.

Peelle's piece shows its protagonist making unexpected connections (and suffering from attempted connections that result in a series of unexpected disconnects) in quite a few situations. She interacts with her coworkers at a Christmas party, with her ex at her place, and with a herpetologist she meets on the bus. There are also moments where she connects, deeply, to animals: first, with a turtle; later a snake, a crow, anoles. She feels connected to and disconnected from nature, the weather, and herself.

The connections and disconnections are dramatic, both glorious and cringeworthy.

When charting each of the story's small sections in terms of connection and disconnection, a pattern emerges. The *variance*—the way the writer bounces from connection and disconnection—creates an *effect* like Freitag's pyramid, but without having to think in terms of rising action, climax, and falling action. What's that effect? Stated simply: the impulse as a reader to keep reading.

The old upside-down checkmark often works for stories. Thinking in terms of creating a pattern of connects and disconnects expands our choices to produce the effect.

First, let's look at Peelle's story. Later, once you've generated an entire beginning-to-end draft of your own work, after you've worked on all other aspects of the story, ask yourself, scene by scene: Is my main character making a connection in the scene? Is there a disconnect? If the answer to both questions is no, perhaps you need to up the stakes in revision, creating more of a gap between expectations and outcome.

If you reach the stage where your scenes are ripe with these sorts of connections and disconnection, and you find that some aspect of your story is stilted, it could be because of the number of connects versus the number of disconnects. Or vice versa. Or the dramatic ordering of them.

Applying this method of inquiry, you'll then be able to make dramatic choices in the number and arrangement of the connections and disconnections in your piece. Strategically. Afterward, you can ask: Do I have too many or too few scenes that accomplish the same thing? How might the rearranging of the scenes bring about a more powerful effect?

Note: Several of the sections in Peelle's story are difficult to label as either connects or disconnects because both happen in the same scene. Nothing in art fits neatly into any system—we're analyzing Peelle's story to determine a useful pattern.

The whole story will be included again, uninterrupted by commentary, at the end.

Reasons for and Advantages of Breathing
Lydia Peelle

SHELL

I meet the herpetologist on the bus. Rush hour is in its deepest throes, a snow storm has clamped down on the city, and the bus is packed with people in bulky coats, impatient and aggressive at the end of the day. Trapped at the center of the crush, I am starting to doubt that I will be able to hold it together all the way to my stop. Then a surge from behind sends me sliding into the man in front of me, and the flaps of a cardboard box he is holding pop open. I find myself looking down at a turtle, its shell mapped with orange and yellow and green. *A turtle*, I say as he gently folds the flaps back down. Then, shocked to hear myself unlock a door to conversation, *Do you mind if I see it again?* He opens the box just enough for me to see inside. *Are you particularly interested in reptiles?* he says kindly. *Absolutely*, I say, though it isn't true. I just want to keep looking at the turtle, which has drawn its head inside its shell, so utterly still and complacent in the midst of the chaos of the bus. *It's rare to meet young people with an interest*, he says. *Oh yes*, I say quickly, thrilled to be considered young. Then I look up at his face and realize how old he must be himself—gray beard, eyes big and watery behind thick glasses. *I'm a professor*, he says, *at the university. I've written a book you might find interesting.* He pulls a card from his pocket and points to the address with a shaky finger. *Drop by any time.*

The narrator seems to be in a state of general disconnect. See how, as the small scene starts, the snowstorm has "clamped down" on the city. People are "impatient" and "aggressive." She's "trapped." She tells us that she's "starting to doubt" if she'll "hold it together all the way to her stop." But just as the narrator edges toward self-pity, something shifts. She sees the turtle (something she likely didn't expect by getting on the city bus) and meets the herpetologist. He calls her "young," gives her his card, and tells her to drop by the university. She's "thrilled." What starts as a disconnection with the world (and, perhaps, the self) ends in a connection with a turtle and an older man.

CLASSIFICATION

Most nights, I don't sleep. Instead, I lie in bed and page through my list of dread and regret, starting with my childhood and ending with the polar ice caps. Everything in between I file into something like schoolroom cubbies, marked with labels like Disaster and Desire. When my husband left, he told me he hadn't been happy in years. *Happy?* I thought. *We're supposed to be happy?* I was under the impression that no one was truly happy, given the raw materials we have to work with in this life. Since he's been gone, I keep the lamp on all night. I'd rather lie awake in the light and keep an eye on his absence than reach out in the dark, thinking he's there. The fact that I may do this for the rest of my life is unclassifiable, too much to bear. When the list comes to this I get up and sit at the kitchen table and watch the snow, the snow which seems always to be falling.

So far, the pattern we see from the first section to the second is connect (with the herpetologist)/disconnect (as a general state caused by anxiety and abandonment). The character's control of language—and her ability to use it to describe her inner life—adds complexity to the section's overall disconnect. Although she's struggling, the narrator is not playing the victim.

This section could've worked as the opening scene because it provides the story's situation: an unhappy person has been left by her partner and she's having a rough go of it. The section raises questions. Will she get out from under it? Will she ever be happy? Often this kind of information, provided up front, helps ground readers in the world of the story.

Instead, the writer offers her readers an opening scene full of possibility, creating a question in their minds: Will the narrator meet the herpetologist again? Let's keep going.

NAVIGATION

After looming for weeks, the day of my office Christmas party arrives. Every year it is the same. We all bring our husbands and wives to a third-rate steak house and get drunk and have a gift swap. The husbands and wives stand around making awkward small talk, and we all compliment one another on how nice we look out of our office clothes, drinking swiftly and heavily, sick to death of one another. At the center of all this sits an enormous, blood-rare roast. Last year my husband stole a bottle of vodka off the bar and we snuck out to the back alley, where we wrapped up in his coat and tried to name the constellations we could see between rooftops. The thing I was most grateful for: he could look at any situation, no matter how dire, and instantly know the best way to navigate through. If I was lucky, I'd be pulled along with him. At five o'clock someone comes by my cubicle and reminds me brightly, for the third time today, about the gift swap. I can see those gifts—the scented candles, the plush toys in Santa hats—already tossed in the garbage and on their way to the landfill. I reach into my bag for an aspirin and find the herpetologist's card. *I just remembered,* I say to no one in particular. *I have plans this afternoon.* I pull on my coat and hat and go, stumbling through the exhaust-stained snow, the wind slicing through my clothes. The university looms on a distant hill. When I finally arrive, it seems deserted, nothing but an expanse of iced-over parking lots. It takes a while to find the building whose name is printed on the herpetologist's card, and just as I am about to give up I see it, a low industrial structure that sits on the edge of the campus like an afterthought. Inside, the halls are ill-lit and empty. I follow the signs to the herpetology department. Down one flight of stairs, then another, then another. With each flight I grow warmer, strip off a layer—coat, hat, sweater, scarf. By the time I have found the herpetologist's office, deep in the basement, I am breathless and damp with sweat.

Let's keep thinking of how the writer strategically arranged the scenes—or plot—to affect the reader. The overall tone of the story shifts, however slightly, with the change in setting. The narrator leaves her day-to-day job, goes underground. As she does, the winter chill (and the clothing she's wearing to protect herself from it) peels away. She's "breathless." Like in the first section, the character starts in a state of disconnection from her surroundings but lands in a connection. Once again: a gap has been created between expectation and outcome.

Let's also look at a few other tools Peelle has put to good use. First, particular details of past office Christmas parties: a blood-rare roast, a bottle of vodka, a back alley, scented candles, plush toys in Santa hats (tossed in the garbage and on their way to the landfill), exhaust-stained snow, wind slicing through clothes, expanse of iced-over parking lots.

These details add to the overall tone and voice of the piece. It's somber! But as we've said, it's also darkly funny.

And remember what we previously said about setting. So far, we've ridden the horrible, crowded bus, lingered in the lonely apartment, sat in the cubicle where she works, and we've "gone" to a memory of a Christmas party. All the settings so far have revealed variations of the narrator's depression, grief. But then?

> ... just as I am about to give up I see it ... I follow the signs to the herpetology department. Down one flight of stairs, then another, then another. With each flight I grow warmer, strip off a layer—coat, hat, sweater, scarf. By the time I have found the herpetologist's office, deep in the basement, I am breathless and damp with sweat.

A *connection.*

> ### ANTICIPATION
> When I knock, the herpetologist flings open his door and beams at me, ushering me in. The tiny room is tropically warm, one wall lined with aquariums that glow with ultra-violet light. *This is my office,* he says proudly, *and those are my anoles.* He is wearing battered khakis and sandals with socks, as if he has just come from a jungle expedition. The anoles give the room frantic energy. They puff and posture, do push-ups, circle one another warily. Their bodies are sharp and lizard-like, the dulled green and brown of sea glass, and fans of brightly colored skin hang from their chins: red, purple, blue. *Do you want to hold one?* the herpetologist asks, eyes sparkling. When I step closer, their faces seem wise and irascible, and as they swivel their eyes I

get the sense that they are sizing me up. But the herpetologist has already pulled the mesh cover off one of the tanks and is watching me, expectant. I reach in and make a halfhearted show of trying to catch one, my hand sending streaks of panic through the tank. I look at him and shrug. *Like this*, he says, and I see his hand slip in like a stealthy animal. Suddenly, an anole is clasped in his fingers, its head between his thumb and forefinger, tongue flickering, as startling as a bright scarf conjured in a magic trick. I gasp, my lungs blooming with the warm air, and find I've been holding my breath. *You've got to anticipate*, he says, grinning.

So far, the author of this "breakup" story has written three out of four opening scenes with unexpected connections. This demonstrates the power of surprise and contrast in fiction.

Let's start analyzing this section by looking at the verbs. The verbs used in a first-person narrative can clue us in to the mental state of the character. In this section, Peelle uses "flings," "beaming at," "ushering . . . in," "puff," "posture," "do push-ups." Later she "gasps" and "grins." While the tone of the piece and the overarching struggles of our narrator remain consistent, the word choice and syntax change in this section, adding variation and altering the current mood.

It's not just the syntax that leaves us feeling as if this section can be labeled a connection.

The tiny room is tropically warm (a stark contrast from the weather described in previous sections); brightly colored skin . . . red, purple, blue. The herpetologist asks a question with eyes sparkling. Our favorite? After the herpetologist grabs the anole, "its tongue is as startling as a bright scarf conjured in a magic trick." This metaphor delights us because it's as vivid as it is unexpected—a crucial combination in the earning of metaphors.

The delight our narrator experiences doesn't eliminate the grief. She's still struggling to figure out if she can go on, and yet in the midst of it all, she makes a connection.

Pattern: Scene 1: Connect, 2: Disconnect, 3: Connect, 4: Connect. So: C-D-C-C.

RAFT

I come home to a red light flashing in the dark of the living room: a message on the machine from my husband. I have to play it twice—his voice is slurred and halting. This is how it has been for several months: when he gets drunk, he wants to work it out. I call him back and tell him to come over, willing to take him any way I can get him. He arrives already bristling with defenses, a cape of snow on his shoulders. As we stand there in the living room, hashing it all out, I try to keep it together by fixing my eyes on the snow, watching the flakes turn to drops of water and then disappear into the fabric of his coat. A brand-new coat, I notice, and I am side-swiped by an image of his new apartment, where I've never been, all the furniture I know he has treated himself to—top of the line, paid on credit, same-day delivery, as if he can buy his way back to a beginning. Exhausted, I collapse into him, and he pilots me towards the bed, but when we make love I feel as if I am struggling for a grip on a slippery raft, trying in vain to pull myself up. Afterwards, we are lying side by side, not touching, when he turns to me and flexes the mattress with his fingers. *I know why you can't sleep*, he says. *It's obvious. What you need are individually wrapped coils.* When he falls asleep I turn on the light and watch his eyes flutter in a dream. I imagine all his women, in there with him. I close my eyes and picture them, one by one, lingering on the torturous details: their optimism, their young skin, their white teeth flashing as they smile at him across his expensive new bed. But in between, I find I keep seeing the herpetologist's office. Familiar, like an ill-used back room of my mind: the glow of the lamps, the dust-cloaked bookshelves, the anoles—a many-colored bouquet.

The ex leaves a voicemail that is basically a booty call. Given what the narrator has taught us about her ex in prior sections, we're surprised by the contrast between what we expect and what happens: our narrator reveals her vulnerability and desperation. In life, many people try to conceal and avoid what makes them appear vulnerable and desperate. Here, the narrator tells us she's "willing to take him any way I can get him."

Lovemaking is a situation most might associate with connection—but this is not how Peelle presents it: "when we make love I feel as if I am struggling for a grip on a slippery raft, trying in vain to pull myself up."

Of all the ways a person could describe consensual sex with someone they care about, this author chooses "struggling for a grip on a slippery raft."

To us, this is an even bigger *disconnect* than the first. It's less general, more particular, and therefore more biting. It zooms in and gets personal. But then it's also tempered by the last image, one harkening back to earlier, more hopeful sections with the herpetologist. This offers contrast in emotion and tone: "I keep seeing the herpetologist's office. Familiar, like an ill-used back room of my mind: the glow of the lamps, the dust-cloaked bookshelves, the anoles—a many-colored bouquet."

Pattern: C-D-C-C-D.

Imagine we made the final D a bit bigger here. Why? The stakes were raised. Is it a coincidence that the intensity of the disconnect is increased after two concurrent scenes of connection? Let's see.

ADAPTATION

On the coldest day of December, the heat goes out at work. I sit hunched at my desk, freezing, my hands pulled up into my sleeves, dreaming about the tropical warmth of the lamps in the herpetologist's office. I get up, switch off the computer, and go. Outside, a thick sleet is falling, turning the city the color of asphalt. The cold air slices through my clothes. When I arrive I try to think up a reason for why I've returned, but the herpetologist takes my coat without question and in fact seems overjoyed to see me. *Let me show you the lab,* he says, clasping my arm. *Is it as warm as your office?* I ask sheepishly. *Warmer!* he says. *Come on.* Our shoes squeak on the linoleum as we walk down the long hall. No one else seems to be around. He opens the door of the lab with a key on his crowded ring. At first, the room seems full of empty aquariums. Then, slowly, as the herpetologist leads me from one to the next, the animals reveal themselves. There is a sidewinder and a hellbender. There is a chuckwalla from Texas that, when it sees us, rushes between two rocks in its habitat and puffs itself up until it is wedged tightly in. There is a nightmarish creature from Australia called a thorny devil, with spines that have spines. Its Latin name, typed on a card taped to its aquarium, is *Moloch horridus*. In the next cage, a giant Gila monster sleeps under a heat lamp, its sides pooled out around it, POISONOUS! written in red on its card. A brilliant green gecko uses its tongue to wipe its eyes. The herpetologist's face is shining. *All these diverse adaptations, with one common goal,* he says. *To live to see tomorrow.* He turns abruptly towards the back of the room, tripping over a cardboard box full of crickets. *Come here,* he says, motioning, and I go to him and watch a barking tree frog, an impossible, unnatural yellow, delicately eat a fly out of his hand.

This story is about survival. While a herpetologist shares about the survival of various species, the story also asks, more subtly, if the narrator will survive the winter and a depressive episode complicated by the unexpected departure of her husband.

It's only upon rereading that we discover what clever choices Peelle made. Depression and despair can, in early drafts of fiction, feel too static. These states of mind can be hard to earn as they can come across as the author's own self-pity. But here, Peelle propels her character forward by shifts in what she's obsessed with and thinking about.

This scene would not be as powerful had we not seen the turtle on the bus first and then, later, the brilliant anoles at the herpetologist's office. Let's think about why.

For starters, a turtle is in a shell. When the story begins, the narrator is in a shell of grief. When she first encounters the herpetologist's office, the anoles are perhaps too bright, too filled with theatrics and color. They may symbolize the gap between the narrator's current mindset and the beauty available in the world. After this series of connections and disconnections, we see that even the ugly and poisonous among the population show us their beautiful qualities and their capacities to adapt and survive.

The story gains forward momentum, causality, and variance as the writer portrays the narrator a bit like Goldilocks. Instead of trying beds or porridge, she's looking into the world to where she can find herself reflected in nature and others. She's trying to classify and make sense of this phase of her life. The past is sometimes triggered by her present state. Each timeframe informs the other. With the help of the herpetologist (and his creatures), she begins to imagine a future.

This section is a big "connect."

Pattern: C-D-C-C-D-C.

NATURAL HISTORY

My husband and I sit side by side on the couch in the light of one lamp. We say the same things we always do, slicing back through the scar tissue in one another's heart. *I've always felt*, he says, *that you never had any hope for us.* I stare at the puddle of melted snow around his boots by the front door, no idea where to begin. My hopelessness extends to include the entire human race. We've mortgaged our lives, ruined the planet, and with modern technology rendered ourselves nearly obsolete. What is there to hope for? Who

> is equipped to take on what's to come? I saw our love as a fallout shelter
> for the future, and thought he did too. But all along he'd been with other
> women, with whom, he told me, he could have fun. Fun. When we make
> love I stare up at the ceiling, already imagining him pulling his pants back
> on, sliding into those boots, sneaking out soundlessly in the morning while I
> squeeze my eyes shut, feigning sleep.

What might initially be seen as an opportunity for connection (sharing space on a couch and then later making love) turns out to be a big old disconnect. The narrator's sense is so different from her husband's. She thinks, "I saw our love as a fallout shelter for the future."

During the sexual encounter, she stares up at the ceiling, thinking of him sneaking out in the morning.

It's another disconnect.

Pattern: C-D-C-C-D-C-D.

The writer has written us seven sections so far. Four of them show connections. Those took up three of the first four sections of the story. What does the author accomplish that she would not have if the ratio had been reversed? If you aim to cast a darker tone and voice in your work, it's worth considering peppering the beginning of your story with various types of connections. Peelle shows us that those connections do not need to be cheery, only meaningful.

NIGHT VISION

> I come home the next evening to find a dark snake draped across the foot
> of the bed. Motionless, waiting for my next move. I freeze, thrilled to the
> sheer shock of it. My pulse rips with terror and delight. Fingers quivering, I
> switch on the light. But it is only my husband's limp black sock, left from last
> night. Caught where it landed when we pulled off our clothes once words
> had failed us, as they always have.

This tiny section subverts expectations. What would you expect from someone who finds a snake draped across her bed? Depression is not a state of negative emotion, but a lack of feeling altogether. It's a state that renders the daily tasks of living meaningless.

Peelle engages our snake expectations first with "I freeze" and "shock" and

"My pulse rips with terror" but subverts the expectation by adding "thrilled" and "delight."

To this person, a potentially deadly situation becomes a welcome source of joy.

As it turns out that the "snake" is her husband's black sock, left from the previous night, the author effectively evokes a phallic symbol. "Limp," here, is an especially illuminating adjective.

After the unexpected jolt of emotion, the narrator makes a realization. In her relationship, words have always failed. This is a subtle, but important, update from the section that precedes it: she no longer is convinced that her husband ever shared her beliefs.

While it's a disconnect, it's a complex one, utterly alive with the possibility that the narrator will connect with a deeper truth in herself, but she isn't quite there yet. It shows a shift away from her worldview (represented by the ex), toward an exciting future (represented by her new friend and the new world of animals).

C-D-C-C-D-C-D-D.

So far, the writer has given us an equal number of disconnects and connects.

Let's keep moving.

SPADEFOOT TOAD

Walking home from work, I go far out of my way to pass the university. I descend the steps to the herpetologist's office with as much sense of purpose as if I have been given my own key. He is at his desk when I arrive, and he looks up from his papers and tells me about the spadefoot toad. *You're lucky to see one in the wild*, he says. *They burrow deep, deep in the ground. They've been found, unharmed, among the embers of brushfires. And*, he says, dropping his voice, leaning in close, *they freeze solid in winter. Solid. Like an ice cube. You could actually pick one up and throw it against a wall, and it would shatter.* As he says this, he makes the motion one would make to dash a frog against a wall, as if sidearming a tennis ball. His glasses slip off with the effort, and he fumbles for them with both hands. The silence that follows is intimate and close. Startled by this, I search his face, wondering if he notices it too. His gray beard is etched in red, annals of his younger self. Suddenly I want to tell him everything, things I have been afraid even to tell my husband. *I tried to kill myself once*, I say. *When I was young. I jumped off a bridge into a half-frozen river.* The herpetologist is quiet for so long that

> I wonder if I shouldn't have said it, then wish I could take it back. Finally he says, *And were you shivering, when they pulled you out? Of course I was shivering,* I say, confused. He nods. *Trust the body, not the mind,* he says, smiling. *The body loves itself.*

The author portrays shattered frogs and an admission of a suicide attempt—and yet?—somehow, when they're combined, in the hands of this writer, it's a connect!

Let's look at the pattern: C-D-C-C-D-C-D-D-C.

Our narrator, who we'd say is guarded (as illuminated by her pessimism), is moved by the herpetologist's fascination with the wild creature. This fascination contrasts her dissatisfaction with the world and people in it.

The narrator reads the silence between her and the herpetologist as "intimate and close." When compared with the portrayal of the lovemaking sessions with her ex, the reader feels the intimacy, the closeness. As a result of being "startled by this," she makes herself vulnerable, engaging and subverting expectations.

Within the world Peelle has created, we find it's 100 percent believable. But without the scenes that led to it, the herpetologist's unexpected response would have seemed downright bizarre and would likely have been too much of a stretch for readers, who might dismiss the herpetologist as too antisocial or not empathetic enough. Instead, we see how his unique manner of being in the world (through the subjective lens of our narrator) makes him the perfect person for her story.

This scene is timed perfectly—placed only after the author portrays several disconnects.

HABITAT

> On Christmas Eve, I end up at another party. Every instinct says not to go, but it's no time to be alone, I keep telling myself, and there's a possibility my husband may be there. I manage to get myself into a dress and a pair of panty hose and go. By the time I arrive, tight packs of people are already impenetrably formed around the room, plates expertly balanced, voices tinkling. I find a drink and arrange myself near the hors d'oeuvres, where I keep an eye on the door and stab my drink with its tiny straw. As time wears on, my panty hose sag around my thighs, hobbling me there. I watch the faces around the room, wondering how everyone can be having such a good time, given the devastating stories I'm sure that they too all saw

on the six o'clock news. The only thing keeping me going is the Christmas tree, which smells like bracing outdoor work, well-being, and fulfillment. The hostess comes over and offers me another drink. *The tree smells lovely,* I say, motioning to it across the room. *Oh!* she says gaily. *It's a spray!* and sweeps away to fill my drink. I carry myself like a broken glass to the dark of the corner, where at least I can yank up my sagging panty hose. Sliding behind the tree, I see the holes in the plastic trunk where the wire branches screw in. A new low, to be failed by a tree. I grasp a bough between my thumb and forefinger for balance and find that I am nonetheless searching its needles for any sign of life, hoping for anything, the blink of an eye, a flash of a disappearing tail.

Humor charges this disconnect and shifts the tone. Those of us with a darker sense of humor may have also seen the limp sock as funny (or clever), but the tree spray in this scene is both tragic and hilarious, especially when paired with sagging panty hose.

Our narrator is, at least, still comforted by nature: "The only thing keeping me going is the Christmas tree." In a moment of needing comfort, she finds out that the thing she's clinging to is also manufactured. The line "A new low, to be failed by a tree" is funnier because of what we've learned.

It reinforces her shift toward taking action (versus going through the motions) and undermines it.

Beginning fiction writers may be too rigidly delineated in their portrayal of fear versus instinct. Here we find a small thrill, a unit of complete satisfaction in our character's misreading of the situation.

Within the course of the story, our narrator has gained experience. Connecting with the herpetologist has been portrayed as if it were less instinct and more desperation. What if it were both? What if her wires, once crossed, are getting a bit less tangled every time she takes a risk? Were that true, it's a type of progression. Meeting the herpetologist is a recent reward for leaving her comfort zone. Add to that the power of nostalgia (previous Christmases with her husband) and social pressure to conform, and she's bound to get confused.

Pattern: C-D-C-C-D-C-D-D-C-D.

Keep asking yourself: Why here? Would the impact have been different if this scene were positioned differently in the emerging pattern?

> **A GIFT**
>
> On Christmas morning I step out onto the stoop and find the herpetolo-
> gist's book, laid carefully on a patch of white ice. A bright green chameleon
> is staring up at me from the dust jacket, its eye following my every move.
> When I pick it up I open to a mimeographed list of errata pasted to the fly-
> leaf. The copyright date is thirty years ago. I turn to the back flap, hoping to
> see a photograph of the herpetologist as a young man, but there is only a list
> of his degrees and credentials. On the inside front cover, there is an inscrip-
> tion made out to me: With warmest regards. Only then do I wonder how he
> found my apartment. I stay home all day and read it cover to cover. I read
> that, at six weeks, a human embryo is nearly identical to a salamander's—gill
> slits, webbed hands, tail bud. I read that snakes have two hundred pairs of
> ribs and tiny, vestigial leg bones. I read all about hibernation and estivation.
> In the section on evolution, I find a chapter titled "Reasons for and Advan-
> tages of Breathing."

Remember when we said that literary fiction pays attention to the poetics and
aesthetics of the individual line? Remember when we quoted Lincoln Michel, who
said that language can be one of the internal engines that power a story?

Peelle shows us how it's done. Word nerds delight: "mimeographed," "errata,"
and "flyleaf"; the imagery is popping: "white ice," "bright green chameleon," "gill
slits, webbed hands, tail bud," "two hundred pairs of ribs and tiny, vestigial leg
bones." These gorgeous images are part of what's fueling the momentum of the story.

Then, on a plot level, Peelle makes compelling choices. She could have had the
herpetologist show up at her place—used dialogue and interaction to convey the
plot points in this section. Instead, she uses the herpetologist's book. Why? It shows
us her desire to see a picture of "the herpetologist as a young man," which may be a
hint of a future type of "connect" we haven't seen yet: a romantic one.

Engaging and subverting: the herpetologist's book acts as a time machine back to
when he was a much younger man, closer in age to our protagonist. Readers wonder
with the narrator how the book arrived at her apartment, which increases their intimacy with her as it deepens the narrator's longing to connect (which is underscored
by her reading the book from "cover to cover" in one day). This movement away from
her solitude and toward connection is what's most important here.

The object, the herpetologist's book, successfully works to earn the heightened poetic language of the piece. We learn that the story's brilliant title comes from a chapter (and we can infer that the section titles do too).

The last sentence of this section (and title of the story) is a chapter within the fictive book written by the herpetologist in a section on evolution. And we're left with the optimistic feeling that our narrator, who started the story as completely bereft, is evolving, "breathing." She's slowly inching closer to satisfaction. This section is a connect.

Pattern: C-D-C-C-D-C-D-D-C-D-C.

PERPETUATION

A bullfrog in a corner aquarium has laid her eggs. They float in a raft of jelly on the surface of the water, knocking against the glass. The big green frog courses around, kicking her thick thighs, oblivious to them. *In the wild, she'd be long gone by now,* the herpetologist says. *Her existence is a perpetual struggle. She can't be burdened by babies. But still, she must replace herself.* I think of all of us, people racing around trying to leave something to the world as we put the world itself at stake in the process. *What's the point?* I don't realize I've said it aloud. *Who knows?* the herpetologist says. He taps the glass. *Ask her.* I turn towards him. *Did you ever have children?* He shakes his head. *Always been married to my work. We never did,* I say. *My husband wanted to. But I just couldn't bring a child into this world. I don't know. Do you think I should have?* He shakes his head. *Should have, should have,* he says. *Look at her.* He taps the glass again. *She knows no such word as "should." She knows only "can" and "do."* I look down at the eggs. There must be thousands of them, each with a dark spot at the center like the pupil of an eye, and I am suddenly dismayed by the thought of the mother kicking away from them without leaving behind so much as a promise. *How many will make it?* I ask. The herpetologist ticks off the hazards that would face the eggs in the wild: flood, drought, pollution, construction, snakes, fish, turtles, toads, raccoons, other frogs. *The tadpole stage is even chancier,* he says, *and you can just about forget it when you're a froglet.* Then he says, *But at least one.* One? I think, looking at the mass of eggs with a sinking sense of despair. Which one? The lucky one?

If you see her ex as the antagonist and the herpetologist as the narrator's ally, it's important to note that Peelle is careful not to make either of them 100 percent consistent in how they fulfill their roles.

The section before this one, when the narrator looks through the herpetologist's book, left us with a sense of connection even though the narrator was alone. Here our narrator once again finds herself in the herpetologist's company, but the information he delivers unsettles her this time. The "sinking sense of despair" made us label this one a disconnect.

Pattern: C-D-C-C-D-C-D-D-C-D-C-D.

LOCOMOTION

On a day with little else to justify my getting out of bed in the morning, the herpetologist gives me a turtle skeleton. *A turtle's backbone is fused to its carapace,* he chants, *an arching armature for its armor.* The neck and leg bones are impossibly frail, fine as pebbles. They seem far too delicate to support the heavy awning of the shell. *Yes,* the herpetologist says, seeing me looking, *poorly designed for locomotion on land. No lateral possibility, with those bones.* He takes the skeleton from me and shows me how a turtle moves: lifting two legs, deliberately throwing itself off balance until it falls forward. Lifting the other two legs and falling forward again. Falling, picking itself up, falling. *Like this, the turtle has lurched its way through two hundred million years. Through all kinds of weather.* This strikes me as the most remarkable thing I've heard in months. *Humbling,* I say. *Yes! But think of your own skeleton,* he tells me. *The bipedal frame is a triumph of design. Thirty-three articulated vertebrae, all in a line. And at the tip, the unparalleled mass of electricity that is your mind. And you didn't even have to ask for it.*

This is a connect.

Notice how the back-and-forth from connect to disconnect continues, establishing a kind of rhythm. When this happens, the reader is unsure (in a good way) which way things will go and will need to keep reading to find out. If the pattern is earned, it's likely slightly unnerving.

The reader will then become destabilized and subconsciously propelled to continue with the story to find where it will land.

Pattern: C-D-C-C-D-C-D-D-C-D-C-D-C.

As I walk through the frozen city, I do think of it, my skeleton hanging in perfect balance. The bones of my toes and feet, flexing inside my shoes. I trace them up my shinbones, the long bones of my thighs, up the ladder of my spine. All the way up to the thought that I could walk for miles, hundreds of miles if I so chose, clear out of the city to a warmer place.

In class discussions of this story, several students have reported that they may have missed the large number of connections Peelle portrayed because of how much her narrator suffers. "It's weird," one student wrote in her notes on the story. "We're rooting for her, maybe because she's honest about her struggles but doesn't feel sorry for herself. She's striving, curious. I might have missed how difficult this must have been for Peelle to keep my attention because, honestly, reading about a depressed lady in a breakup doesn't seem like a good time. Instead, I was transfixed."

This section is a continuation of the last: another connection, not only with the herpetologist but with other living beings (turtles) and perhaps, most importantly, a connection between the narrator and herself.

The back-and-forth pattern is slightly broken here, giving us two connections in a row.

Pattern: C-D-C-C-D-C-D-D-C-D-C-D-C-C.

COMPANY

On New Year's Eve I go out for a walk, surprised by a sudden desire to breathe the sharp night air. People scurry through the street two by two, heads bent against the cold, wearing their best clothes. The men check their watches as if there is a train to catch, headed for a fabulous destination. A man and a woman are leaning close to a shop window, their voices filled with delight. It is my husband with a much younger woman, both dressed for a party. When he looks up and sees me, a strangled noise escapes his throat. *I don't want to see you anymore*, I say, because it's all I've got. *Okay*, he says, *all right*, not even pretending to put up a fight. As they walk away and join the throng on the street, I get the sense that the train is departing imminently, and that there's no chance that I will be on it. I look in the window at what they had been examining. It is a glittering diamond and emerald brooch, something I myself have admired in the past. But now it seems gaudy and crude, and I realize I was expecting something infinitely more beguiling to be crouched behind the glass. I hear a noise behind me and wheel around, thinking that maybe he's come back, but it is just a lone crow, picking delicately through an overturned trash can. It feels as if we're the last two creatures left in the abandoned city, just me and this crow. Grateful for the company, I raise my hand. *Oh, hello,* I say.

No one wants to get dumped, then run into an ex with someone "much younger" looking not just at jewelry, but an exact piece of jewelry that the dumped one had herself coveted.

This "setup" alone causes half of any room to insist it's a disconnect. However, through the lens of literary fiction writing, this is a connect. Why?

Our narrator has finally made a definitive choice. Instead of limp-sock sleepovers, she tells him, "I don't want to see you anymore." Even if she thinks, "it's all I've got," it's still definitive.

Also, the diamond and emerald brooch that she once admired now seems in poor taste. This, too, shows a shift away from her past selves and toward a newer version. Finally, the writer uses the word "grateful" to find herself in "company" and on equal footing with a crow: "the last two creatures left."

Pattern: C-D-C-C-D-C-D-D-C-D-C-D-C-C-C.

LAS VEGAS LEOPARD FROG

There is a grainy black-and-white photograph of a frog taped above the herpetologist's desk. It is an ordinary-looking frog. Beneath the photo hangs a narrow page torn from a field guide. I read it so many times I am able to repeat it from memory, or almost. It reassembles itself in my mind as a sort of a poem:

Last seen in 1942, long before worry
about endangered species
Probably extinct
As the city of Las Vegas grew
groundwater pumped out,
springs capped
hope for *Rana fisheri* was filled in with
cement

> Discovery of a remnant population
> would be a herpetological event

This, too, is a connect. It's subtle, but we learn that the narrator has been to the herpetologist's office often enough to memorize a page torn from a field guide taped above his desk. This is another of many sections that uses language as an engine to power the story. The lines she's memorized are filled with juxtaposing imagery: extinction and hope of discovery. The combination of our narrator's repeat visits to her new friend's office and the lingering optimism in the last lines led us to our choice.

Pattern: C-D-C-C-D-C-D-D-C-D-C-D-C-C-C-C.

Note: That's four connections in a row.

You've heard the expressions "I was on the edge of my seat" and "I'm waiting for the other shoe to drop." People use these phrases to describe good storytelling. As a reader, the sensation that brings us to the edge comes from many things, including waiting for the other shoe.

DEFICIENCY

The herpetologist needs my help. *I wouldn't ask*, he says on the phone, *except that no one else is here.* A snake has just been brought in, a confiscated reticulated python that someone has been keeping as a pet. When I arrive, the herpetologist is standing in front of its tank, dwarfed by it. *I'm afraid it must be destroyed*, he tells me sadly. *It has an irreversible and degenerative vitamin deficiency, resulting from an inadequate diet. Nothing can be done.* I watch it slowly map the terrain of its tank, staggered with disbelief that someone would keep such a massive, commanding thing in the house and not take pains to see that it has everything it needs. *Ready to shed, too*, the herpetologist says, pointing to its milk-white eyes. *Dull all over. Would be brilliant in a week or two. I've seen them tie themselves in knots in an effort to shed the old skin. What a shame*, I say, and feel a shiver of grief as the loss suddenly multiplies—the snake, and the newness the snake won't have the chance to inhabit. *People*, the herpetologist sighs. I help him hold the snake as he makes the injection, and in my hands I feel a change in the taut muscles, the exact moment that life leaves them. We hold vigil over the enormous body. The herpetologist looks stricken, drawn

> and old. *I don't know,* he says over and over. *I just don't know.* I shove my
> hands in my pockets, wishing I could give him something. We stand there
> together for a long time, bewildered as two night travelers with a map they
> can't make out in the dark.

Shared grief creates bonds. Shared pain, too. As sad as it is, the section portrays action that adds momentum. If it's true that a story's plot relies on momentum, and momentum in stories relies on contrasts—trial and error, failures as much as breakthroughs—what is the reader, consciously or unconsciously, preparing to read next?

We see the herpetologist now has the narrator's phone number. He trusts her enough to make a call, however hesitantly. The two are both physically and emotionally connected by this enormous snake.

Remember the first time a snake was evoked in the story? It was in the section Night Vision. Our narrator was terrified, even though it turned out to be a sock.

The second time, the narrator is reading about the number of the animal's ribs. Her terror turned to curiosity.

Now? A real snake she cares about.

The herpetologist and narrator share a lack of faith in humans—a lack that gets validated by the neglectfulness of the snake's previous owner. So, a connect.

Pattern: C-D-C-C-D-C-D-D-C-D-C-D-C-C-C-C-C-C.

> **BLOOM**
>
> All night, I lie awake in the light of the bedside lamp, studying my hands.
> What was it, exactly, that I felt pass out of the snake? The one thing I know
> for certain: I've witnessed a slight parting of the curtain that hangs over the
> unknown. By morning I feel a bloom of gratitude for this, which I wear, a
> bright badge, pinned to my chest for days.

The death of the snake and shared grief causes yet another connection. Ask yourself: What are you anticipating after all these connections?

Pattern: C-D-C-C-D-C-D-D-C-D-C-D-C-C-C-C-C-C.

HERALDS OF SPRING

I leave my apartment at five to help the herpetologist with his morning feedings. So this is what it feels like, I think, to be out at dawn, meeting the world head on. Salt trucks are rumbling by, preparing the icy streets for the coming day. The sky is a color I've never seen before. It is as if a corner of the city's gray overcoat has blown back to reveal an orange satin lining. We drink Postum out of Styrofoam cups. He apologizes that there is no real coffee. I tell him I don't drink it anymore, a last attempt to reclaim sleep. *Good girl*, he says, *good girl*. He pulls a record off the bookshelf and puts it on the turntable. Through the scratchiness I hear a high-pitched, insistent whistle, like crickets, only the notes are rounder, wetter, like water dropping from a leaf into a pond. *The dawn song of the peeper*, he says, *the herald of spring*. He beams. *I don't think spring is ever coming*, I say. *Nonsense*, he says. *And in a week or so, the students will come back. I must say, as much as I enjoy the quiet, it does get lonely around here when they're gone*. The students! The fact of them has never occurred to me. Now I see their bright, eager faces, I see them shaking snow off their boots and talking excitedly, listening raptly to the herpetologist in a lecture room, notebooks open, carrying him away in a wave down the hall. The record switches to the call of a bullfrog, mournful. I have the sudden urge to reach behind me and lock the door.

This section starts with an inarguable connect! "The sky is a color I've never seen before. It is as if a corner of the city's gray overcoat has blown back to reveal an orange satin lining." When combined with her actions to go out at dawn to meet the world "head on," this language portrays the intimacy established between the narrator and the herpetologist as well as a turning point in how the narrator sees the world (at the top of the story, nothing blew the gray overcoat to reveal anything at all).

Peelle reveals the herpetologist's humanity (beyond his expertise) and broader life experience (beyond his bond with our narrator). He admits that it "gets lonely" without the students.

Note, too, the soundtrack in this section: a recording of animal noises. The narrator, at first, describes what she's hearing—"like water dropping from a leaf into a pond"—but after hearing about the students' imminent return, it switches to "mournful."

These details allow us to glean that the narrator, starting the scene with new-found confidence, ends it feeling apprehensive, insecure about her new relationship.

The overall sense of this scene is one big connect, but we're paying attention to how it ends on a note of disconnect.

Pattern: C-D-C-C-D-C-D-D-C-D-C-D-C-C-C-C-C-C-C-C.

> ## SECRET
>
> *I want you to see something,* the herpetologist says. *A secret.* He leads me to a door at the back of the lab that I haven't noticed before. He selects a large key from his ring and unlocks it. We step into a tiny antechamber, and when he closes the door behind us, we stand together for a moment in the utter darkness. Then I hear the click of a key in another lock, and we step through to another room, even darker than the first. He switches on a dim red light. As my eyes adjust I see a chest-high tank of water in the center of the room. We step to its edge. In the red light I can just make out something swimming around in the water, tiny ghost creatures with red ruffs of gills. *The Georgia blind salamander,* he whispers. *It exists only in the deep wells and subterranean waters of one particular farm in south-east Georgia. You're maybe the tenth person in the world to see one alive.* The salamanders seem to give off a light of their own, dark eye buds showing through the clear skin of their faces, their red gills waving like feathers as they weave through the water. For a heartbeat I forget myself completely. Then I catch my breath and say, *They don't even know we're here.* The herpetologist moves closer. I slip my hand in his. *I think I love you,* I say. He shakes his head firmly, as if it's the wrong answer to a question. *No, you don't.*

Being human is messy! Wires get crossed! Feelings go haywire! So common is the phenomenon of intense feelings of love for a mentor or caretaker there's a psychological word for it: *transference.* And hasn't the herpetologist been so kind to the narrator to earn such an intense emotion?

Let's return to the pattern. For a story with an overall tone that communicates the narrator's grief and despondency with humans, there's a whole lot of *connection* happening with the herpetologist.

Two steps forward, one step back. Two steps back and one step forward.

So often beginning drafts lack this rhythm. The writer has an idea in mind and then writes scene after scene hammering the same point.

We know our narrator has had a troubled past. She's learned that she's not so unique. That she's among many species that are faced with seemingly impossible odds. She's gained perspective and a measure of independence (from her ex).

The herpetologist brings our narrator into the fold of maybe ten people to see this kind of salamander. She has a tiny realization: "They don't even know we're here," and after the herpetologist moves closer, well . . . you know the rest.

A lesser writer might have chosen to have the herpetologist act in a way that would establish a romantic connection. Yet not a single aspect of his portrayal up to this point indicates that his attraction to the narrator is physical. Also, wouldn't that be cheesy? Didn't the narrator just untangle herself from a dependency on some other man?

Intimacy is awkward. Missed cues and mistakes, embarrassment, shame, and regret: they are all part of the mix. Many beginning writers avoid putting their characters in situations that would embarrass or humiliate them, and that's a shame. A certain amount of cringe works for readers. They recognize the truth in what causes the cringe, and they don't have to experience it personally because it is happening to someone else.

Because of the setup, we feel this is a disconnect, at least for now, and a big one. Pattern: C-D-C-C-D-C-D-D-C-D-C-D-C-C-C-C-C-C-C-C-D.

A HERPETOLOGICAL EVENT

I stay late at work, in no state to face my dark apartment, overcome by a new sort of loneliness, one that seems as if it will outlive me. By the time I get on the bus, late in the evening, it is hushed and mostly empty, and I collapse into a seat near the back. As we rattle down the street I close my eyes and think of the blind salamanders, down there in their well in Georgia, far from the city, far from me. When I open my eyes I have long since missed my stop. I sit up in a panic, recognizing nothing outside. But then, as the bus voyages through unfamiliar streets, the salamanders come back like a dream. The darkness deep in the earth where they've been all along. Arcing, looping, somersaulting through the water, somehow finding one another in the dark. Without any thought, care, or need for me. And for an instant, just before the bus turns on its loop, I catch a glimpse of the infinite. There I am inside of it, for one suspended moment—tiny, inconsequential, and utterly free.

We noted the slight note of disconnect within the connection in "Heralds of Spring." "A Herpetological Event" is its mirror opposite: a section that starts out in a clear disconnect but ends in a smaller connect.

Once a pattern is established, variations are not only possible, but enjoyable insofar as they add to the unexpected believability of complex situations.

Pattern: C-D-C-C-D-C-D-D-C-D-C-D-C-C-C-C-C-C-C-C-D-D.

DAWN SONG

Late in the night a storm settles on the city, throwing snow against the windows and rattling them in their frames. My husband calls to tell me his power has gone out and asks if he can come over. *Just this one night*, he says. *I don't have anywhere else to go.* I sit at the kitchen table waiting for him, listening to the silence of the streets, the weather too bad for even the plows to be out. Things are so still that I am startled to look down and see the collar of my robe is quivering steadily with my pulse. He comes in with a red wind-burned face and cold clinging to his clothes. We sit side by side at the table, no words left for one another. Soon my power goes out as well and there is nothing for us to do but get into bed and huddle beneath the blankets, press tight together to conserve warmth. We make love, a matter of survival, our bodies desperate to generate heat. My heart pounds against his chest with the insistence of self-preservation, tenacious and bright. It is still beating hard, determined, by the time he has fallen asleep. I sit up and try to make out his sleeping face in the dark, left with the unshakable feeling that there is a stranger in my bed. Sometime before dawn I get up in the cold room to look out the window. The snow is slackening, but down the block, all the street lights are still off. In the darkness, the shine of the deep, white drifts is the only thing I can make out. It seems to conceal a great mystery, the snow. I stand there watching, struck by the possibility of what might be hidden beneath. I watch for as long as I can stand the cold, knowing that by morning the trucks will have come to clear it all away.

Pattern: C-D-C-C-D-C-D-D-C-D-C-D-C-C-C-C-C-C-C-C-D-D-?

That's the end.

What is the "unit of satisfaction" in this story? And how did the writer use this pattern to achieve it?

Peelle uses a series of connections and disconnections in a strategic pattern. Turns out, a little disconnect can go a long way. Look at all the Cs! It's true what Molly Giles said: "Anger is fuel for a writer. Most 'bad' feelings are. Jealousy, hatred, lust: terrific."

Beginning students are often drawn to the page because they feel these strong emotions. Anger at the world. Perhaps at the family. The self. In the case of breakup stories, an ex. It's logical to think a story's dramatic potential is reached by scenes that increase the intensity of those bad feelings.

What this story's pattern demonstrates, however, is the importance of portraying a character attempting to connect. Sometimes that attempt will succeed, sometimes it will fail—but they're committed to trying.

Peelle has not cracked any code, nor are we recommending simply copying this story's particular pattern. It's the variation we're after. It's the disparity between expectation and outcome.

The character begins the story bereft. By the end, there's hope that she'll be able to move on in a positive direction. Given the overall feeling, simple logic could've been: start and end it with a connection. And perhaps that's what the writer did. She may have written these sections in an entirely different order, then, once having written them, rearranged them strategically for dramatic impact and effect.

In the final section, we see that our narrator has relapsed a bit into old behavior. She's allowed her ex back into her place and into her bed. The two make love again. Prior to that scene, the writer resists what may have been a temptation: to portray a makeup conversation between the herpetologist and the narrator. Instead, she allows the awkward encounter to linger, which may have propelled our narrator into old habits. A less imaginative writer may have forced an epiphany.

Remember, our job isn't to rescue all the characters that come under our care. Perhaps our job is simply to render what their predicament is, rather than solving their problems for them.

What's portrayed is a complex character who makes and breaks deals with herself. Curiosity drives her, as does a desire to know herself and how she fits into the grander scheme of life. The fact that she sees her ex as a stranger in the bed leads us to believe that she's facing life with fewer illusions. The ideas we have about ourselves and each other might be a bit like the snow, there "to conceal a great mystery." What happens if we let go of old notions, even if we can't shake all our old behaviors? Perhaps we'd also be struck by opportunities for growth or change that could be hidden beneath.

And here again is Lydia Peelle's complete story—this time without all the interruptions.

Reasons for and Advantages of Breathing
Lydia Peelle

SHELL

I meet the herpetologist on the bus. Rush hour is in its deepest throes, a snow storm has clamped down on the city, and the bus is packed with people in bulky coats, impatient and aggressive at the end of the day. Trapped at the center of the crush, I am starting to doubt that I will be able to hold it together all the way to my stop. Then a surge from behind sends me sliding into the man in front of me, and the flaps of a cardboard box he is holding pop open. I find myself looking down at a turtle, its shell mapped with orange and yellow and green. *A turtle,* I say as he gently folds the flaps back down. Then, shocked to hear myself unlock a door to conversation, *Do you mind if I see it again?* He opens the box just enough for me to see inside. *Are you particularly interested in reptiles?* he says kindly. *Absolutely,* I say, though it isn't true. I just want to keep looking at the turtle, which has drawn its head inside its shell, so utterly still and complacent in the midst of the chaos of the bus. *It's rare to meet young people with an interest,* he says. *Oh yes,* I say quickly, thrilled to be considered young. Then I look up at his face and realize how old he must be himself—gray beard, eyes big and watery behind thick glasses. *I'm a professor,* he says, *at the university. I've written a book you might find interesting.* He pulls a card from his pocket and points to the address with a shaky finger. *Drop by any time.*

CLASSIFICATION

Most nights, I don't sleep. Instead, I lie in bed and page through my list of dread and regret, starting with my childhood and ending with the polar ice caps. Everything in between I file into something like schoolroom cubbies, marked with labels like Disaster and Desire. When my husband left, he told me he hadn't been happy in years. *Happy?* I thought. *We're supposed to be happy?* I was under the impression that no one was truly happy, given the raw materials we have to work with in this life. Since he's been gone, I keep the lamp on all night. I'd rather lie awake in the light and keep an eye on his absence than reach out in the dark, thinking he's there. The fact that I may do this for the rest of my life is unclassifiable, too much to bear. When the list comes to this I get up and sit at the kitchen table and watch the snow, the snow which seems always to be falling.

NAVIGATION

After looming for weeks, the day of my office Christmas party arrives. Every year it is the same. We all bring our husbands and wives to a third-rate steak house and get drunk and have a gift swap. The husbands and wives stand around making awkward small talk, and we all compliment one another on how nice we look out of our office clothes, drinking swiftly and heavily, sick to death of one another. At the center of all this sits an enormous, blood-rare roast. Last year my husband stole a bottle of vodka off the bar and we snuck out to the back alley, where we wrapped up in his coat and tried to name the constellations we could see between rooftops. The thing I was most grateful for: he could look at any situation, no matter how dire, and instantly know the best way to navigate through. If I was lucky, I'd be pulled along with him. At five o'clock someone comes by my cubicle and reminds me brightly, for the third time today, about the gift swap. I can see those gifts—the scented candles, the plush toys in Santa hats—already tossed in the garbage and on their way to the landfill. I reach into my bag for an aspirin and find the herpetologist's card. *I just remembered,* I say to no one in particular. *I have plans this afternoon.* I pull on my coat and hat and go, stumbling through the exhaust-stained snow, the wind slicing through my clothes. The university looms on a distant hill. When I finally arrive, it seems deserted, nothing but an expanse of iced-over parking lots. It takes a while to find the building whose name is printed on the herpetologist's card, and just as I am about to give up I see it, a low industrial structure that sits on the edge of the campus like an afterthought. Inside, the halls are ill-lit and empty. I follow the signs to the herpetology department. Down one flight of stairs, then another, then another. With each flight I grow warmer, strip off a layer—coat, hat, sweater, scarf. By the time I have found the herpetologist's office, deep in the basement, I am breathless and damp with sweat

ANTICIPATION

When I knock, the herpetologist flings open his door and beams at me, ushering me in. The tiny room is tropically warm, one wall lined with aquariums that glow with ultra-violet light. *This is my office,* he says proudly, *and those are my anoles.* He is wearing battered khakis and sandals with socks, as if he has just come from a jungle expedition. The anoles give the room a frantic energy. They puff and posture, do push-ups, circle one another warily. Their bodies are sharp and lizard-like, the dulled green and brown of sea glass, and fans of brightly colored skin hang from their chins: red, purple, blue. *Do you want to hold one?* the herpetologist asks, eyes sparkling. When I step closer, their faces seem wise and irascible, and as they swivel their eyes I get the sense that they are sizing me up. But the herpetologist has already pulled the mesh cover off one of the tanks and is watching me, expectant. I reach in and make a halfhearted show of trying to catch one, my hand sending streaks of panic through the tank. I look at him and shrug. *Like this,* he says, and I see his hand slip in like a stealthy animal. Suddenly, an anole is clasped in his fingers, its head between his thumb and forefinger, tongue flickering, as startling as a bright scarf conjured in a magic trick. I gasp, my lungs blooming with the warm air, and find I've been holding my breath. *You've got to anticipate,* he says, grinning.

RAFT

I come home to a red light flashing in the dark of the living room: a message on the machine from my husband. I have to play it twice—his voice is slurred and halting. This is how it has been for several months: when he gets drunk, he wants to work it out. I call him back and tell him to come over, willing to take him any way I can get him. He arrives already bristling with defenses, a cape of snow on his shoulders. As we stand there in the living room, hashing it all out, I try to keep it together by fixing my eyes on the snow, watching the flakes turn to drops of water and then disappear into the fabric of his coat. A brand-new coat, I notice, and I am side-swiped by an image of his new apartment, where I've never been, all the furniture I know he has treated himself to—top of the line, paid on credit, same-day delivery, as if he can buy his way back to a beginning. Exhausted, I collapse into him, and he pilots me towards the bed, but when we make love I feel as if I am struggling for a grip on a slippery raft, trying in vain to pull myself up. Afterwards, we are lying side by side, not touching, when he turns to me and flexes the mattress with his fingers. *I know why you can't sleep*, he says. *It's obvious. What you need are individually wrapped coils.* When he falls asleep I turn on the light and watch his eyes flutter in a dream. I imagine all his women, in there with him. I close my eyes and picture them, one by one, lingering on the torturous details: their optimism, their young skin, their white teeth flashing as they smile at him across his expensive new bed. But in between, I find I keep seeing the herpetologist's office. Familiar, like an ill-used back room of my mind: the glow of the lamps, the dust-cloaked bookshelves, the anoles—a many-colored bouquet.

ADAPTATION

On the coldest day of December, the heat goes out at work. I sit hunched at my desk, freezing, my hands pulled up into my sleeves, dreaming about the tropical warmth of the lamps in the herpetologist's office. I get up, switch off the computer, and go. Outside, a thick sleet is falling, turning the city the color of asphalt. The cold air slices through my clothes. When I arrive I try to think up a reason for why I've returned, but the herpetologist takes my coat without question and in fact seems overjoyed to see me. *Let me show you the lab*, he says, clasping my arm. *Is it as warm as your office?* I ask sheepishly. *Warmer!* he says. *Come on.* Our shoes squeak on the linoleum as we walk down the long hall. No one else seems to be around. He opens the door of the lab with a key on his crowded ring. At first, the room seems full of empty aquariums. Then, slowly, as the herpetologist leads me from one to the next, the animals reveal themselves. There is a sidewinder and a hellbender. There is a chuckwalla from Texas that, when it sees us, rushes between two rocks in its habitat and puffs itself up until it is wedged tightly in. There is a nightmarish creature from Australia called a thorny devil, with spines that have spines. Its Latin name, typed on a card taped to its aquarium, is *Moloch horridus*. In the next cage, a giant Gila monster sleeps under a heat lamp, its sides pooled out around it, POISONOUS! written in red on its card. A brilliant green gecko uses its tongue to wipe its eyes. The herpetologist's face is shining. *All these diverse adaptations, with one common goal*, he says. *To live to see tomorrow.* He turns abruptly towards the back of the room, tripping over a cardboard box full of crickets. *Come here*, he says, motioning, and I go to him and watch a barking tree frog, an impossible, unnatural yellow, delicately eat a fly out of his hand.

NATURAL HISTORY

My husband and I sit side by side on the couch in the light of one lamp. We say the same things we always do, slicing back through the scar tissue in one another's heart. *I've always felt*, he says, *that you never had any hope for us.* I stare at the puddle of melted snow around his boots by the front door, no idea where to begin. My hopelessness extends to include the entire human race. We've mortgaged our lives, ruined the planet, and with modern technology rendered ourselves nearly obsolete. What is there to hope for? Who is equipped to take on what's to come? I saw our love as a fallout shelter for the future, and thought he did too. But all along he'd been with other women, with whom, he told me, he could have fun. Fun. When we make love I stare up at the ceiling, already imagining him pulling his pants back on, sliding into those boots, sneaking out soundlessly in the morning while I squeeze my eyes shut, feigning sleep.

NIGHT VISION

I come home the next evening to find a dark snake draped across the foot of the bed. Motionless, waiting for my next move. I freeze, thrilled to the sheer shock of it. My pulse rips with terror and delight. Fingers quivering, I switch on the light. But it is only my husband's limp black sock, left from last night. Caught where it landed when we pulled off our clothes once words had failed us, as they always have.

SPADEFOOT TOAD

Walking home from work, I go far out of my way to pass the university. I descend the steps to the herpetologist's office with as much sense of purpose as if I have been given my own key. He is at his desk when I arrive, and he looks up from his papers and tells me about the spadefoot toad. *You're lucky to see one in the wild,* he says. *They burrow deep, deep in the ground. They've been found, unharmed, among the embers of brush fires. And,* he says, dropping his voice, leaning in close, *they freeze solid in winter. Solid. Like an ice cube. You could actually pick one up and throw it against a wall, and it would shatter.* As he says this, he makes the motion one would make to dash a frog against a wall, as if sidearming a tennis ball. His glasses slip off with the effort, and he fumbles for them with both hands. The silence that follows is intimate and close. Startled by this, I search his face, wondering if he notices it too. His gray beard is etched in red, annals of his younger self. Suddenly I want to tell him everything, things I have been afraid even to tell my husband. *I tried to kill myself once,* I say. *When I was young. I jumped off a bridge into a half-frozen river.* The herpetologist is quiet for so long that I wonder if I shouldn't have said it, then wish I could take it back. Finally he says, *And were you shivering, when they pulled you out? Of course I was shivering,* I say, confused. He nods. *Trust the body, not the mind,* he says, smiling. *The body loves itself.*

HABITAT

On Christmas Eve, I end up at another party. Every instinct says not to go, but it's no time to be alone, I keep telling myself, and there's a possibility my husband may be there. I manage to get myself into a dress and a pair of panty hose and go. By the time I arrive, tight packs of people are already impenetrably formed around the room, plates expertly balanced, voices tinkling. I find a drink and arrange myself near the hors d'oeuvres, where I keep an eye on the door and stab my drink with its tiny straw. As time wears on, my panty hose sags around my thighs, hobbling me there. I watch the faces around the room, wondering how everyone can be having such a good time, given the devastating stories I'm sure that they too all saw on the six o'clock news. The only thing keeping me going is the Christmas tree, which smells like bracing outdoor work, well-being, and fulfillment. The hostess comes over and offers me another drink. *The tree smells lovely,* I say, motioning to it across the room. *Oh!* she says gaily. *It's a spray!* and sweeps away to fill my drink. I carry myself like a broken glass to the dark of the corner, where at least I can yank up my sagging panty hose. Sliding behind the tree, I see the holes in the plastic trunk where the wire branches screw in. A new low, to be failed by a tree. I grasp a bough between my thumb and forefinger for balance and find that I am nonetheless searching its needles for any sign of life, hoping for anything, the blink of an eye, a flash of a disappearing tail.

A GIFT

On Christmas morning I step out onto the stoop and find the herpetologist's book, laid carefully on a patch of white ice. A bright green chameleon is staring up at me from the dust jacket, its eye following my every move. When I pick it up I open a mimeographed list of errata pasted to the flyleaf. The copyright date is thirty years ago. I turn to the back flap, hoping to see a photograph of the herpetologist as a young man, but there is only a list of his degrees and credentials. On the inside front cover, there is an inscription made out to me: *With warmest regards.* Only then do I wonder how he found my apartment. I stay home all day and read it cover to cover. I read that, at six weeks, a human embryo is nearly identical to a salamander's—gill slits, webbed hands, tail bud. I read that snakes have two hundred pairs of ribs and tiny, vestigial leg bones. I read all about hibernation and estivation. In the section on evolution, I find a chapter titled "Reasons for and Advantages of Breathing."

PERPETUATION

A bullfrog in a corner aquarium has laid her eggs. They float in a raft of jelly on the surface of the water, knocking against the glass. The big green frog courses around, kicking her thick thighs, oblivious to them. *In the wild, she'd be long gone by now,* the herpetologist says. *Her existence is a perpetual struggle. She can't be burdened by babies. But still, she must replace herself.* I think of all of us, people racing around trying to leave something to the world as we put the world itself at stake in the process. *What's the point?* I don't realize I've said it aloud. *Who knows?* the herpetologist says. He taps the glass. *Ask her.* I turn towards him. *Did you ever have children?* He shakes his head. *Always been married to my work. We never did,* I say. *My husband wanted to. But I just couldn't bring a child into this world. I don't know. Do you think I should have?* He shakes his head. *Should have, should have,* he says. *Look at her.* He taps the glass again. *She knows no such word as "should." She knows only "can" and "do."* I look down at the eggs. There must be thousands of them, each with a dark spot at the center like the pupil of an eye, and I am suddenly dismayed by the thought of the mother kicking away from them without leaving behind so much as a promise. *How many will make it?* I ask. The herpetologist ticks off the hazards that would face the eggs in the wild: flood, drought, pollution, construction, snakes, fish, turtles, toads, raccoons, other frogs. *The tadpole stage is even chancier,* he says, *and you can just about forget it when you're a froglet.* Then he says, *But at least one.* One? I think, looking at the mass of eggs with a sinking sense of despair. Which one? The lucky one?

LOCOMOTION

On a day with little else to justify my getting out of bed in the morning, the herpetologist gives me a turtle skeleton. *A turtle's backbone is fused to its carapace,* he chants, *an arching armature for its armor.* The neck and leg bones are impossibly frail, fine as pebbles. They seem far too delicate to support the heavy awning of the shell. *Yes,* the herpetologist says, seeing me looking, *poorly designed for locomotion on land. No lateral possibility, with those bones.* He takes the skeleton from me and shows me how a turtle moves: lifting two legs, deliberately throwing itself off balance until it falls forward. Lifting the other two legs and falling forward again. Falling, picking itself up, falling. *Like this, the turtle has lurched its way through two hundred million years. Through all kinds of weather.* This strikes me as the most remarkable thing I've heard in months. Humbling, I say. *Yes! But think of your own skeleton,* he tells me. *The bipedal frame is a triumph of design. Thirty-three articulated vertebrae, all in a line. And at the tip, the unparalleled mass of electricity that is your mind. And you didn't even have to ask for it.*

RANGE

As I walk through the frozen city, I do think of it, my skeleton hanging in perfect balance. The bones of my toes and feet, flexing inside my shoes. I trace them up my shinbones, the long bones of my thighs, up the ladder of my spine. All the way up to the thought that I could walk for miles, hundreds of miles if I so chose, clear out of the city to a warmer place.

COMPANY

On New Year's Eve I go out for a walk, surprised by a sudden desire to breathe the sharp night air. People scurry through the street two by two, heads bent against the cold, wearing their best clothes. The men check their watches as if there is a train to catch, headed for a fabulous destination. A man and a woman are leaning close to a shop window, their voices filled with delight. It is my husband with a much younger woman, both dressed for a party. When he looks up and sees me, a strangled noise escapes his throat. *I don't want to see you anymore,* I say, because it's all I've got. *Okay,* he says, *all right,* not even pretending to put up a fight. As they walk away and join the throng on the street, I get the sense that the train is departing imminently, and that there's no chance that I will be on it. I look in the window at what they had been examining. It is a glittering diamond and emerald brooch, something I myself have admired in the past. But now it seems gaudy and crude, and I realize I was expecting something infinitely more beguiling to be crouched behind the glass. I hear a noise behind me and wheel around, thinking that maybe he's come back, but it is just a lone crow, picking delicately through an overturned trash can. It feels as if we're the last two creatures left in the abandoned city, just me and this crow. Grateful for the company, I raise my hand. *Oh, hello,* I say.

LAS VEGAS LEOPARD FROG

There is a grainy black-and-white photograph of a frog taped above the herpetologist's desk. It is an ordinary-looking frog. Beneath the photo hangs a narrow page torn from a field guide. I read it so many times I am able to repeat it from memory, or almost. It reassembles itself in my mind as a sort of a poem:

Last seen in 1942, long before worry
about endangered species
Probably extinct
As the city of Las Vegas grew
groundwater pumped out,
springs capped
hope for *Rana fisheri* was filled in with

cement
Discovery of a remnant population
would be a herpetological event

DEFICIENCY

The herpetologist needs my help. *I wouldn't ask*, he says on the phone, *except that no one else is here*. A snake has just been brought in, a confiscated reticulated python that someone has been keeping as a pet. When I arrive, the herpetologist is standing in front of its tank, dwarfed by it. *I'm afraid it must be destroyed*, he tells me sadly. *It has an irreversible and degenerative vitamin deficiency, resulting from an inadequate diet. Nothing can be done.* I watch it slowly map the terrain of its tank, staggered with disbelief that someone would keep such a massive, commanding thing in the house and not take pains to see that it has everything it needs. *Ready to shed, too*, the herpetologist says, pointing to its milk-white eyes. *Dull all over. Would be brilliant in a week or two. I've seen them tie themselves in knots in an effort to shed the old skin. What a shame*, I say, and feel a shiver of grief as the loss suddenly multiplies—the snake, and the newness the snake won't have the chance to inhabit. *People*, the herpetologist sighs. I help him hold the snake as he makes the injection, and in my hands I feel a change in the taut muscles, the exact moment that life leaves them. We hold vigil over the enormous body. The herpetologist looks stricken, drawn and old. *I don't know*, he says over and over. *I just don't know.* I shove my hands in my pockets, wishing I could give him something. We stand there together for a long time, bewildered as two night travelers with a map they can't make out in the dark.

BLOOM

All night, I lie awake in the light of the bedside lamp, studying my hands. What was it, exactly, that I felt pass out of the snake? The one thing I know for certain: I've witnessed a slight parting of the curtain that hangs over the unknown. By morning I feel a bloom of gratitude for this, which I wear, a bright badge, pinned to my chest for days.

HERALDS OF SPRING

I leave my apartment at five to help the herpetologist with his morning feedings. So this is what it feels like, I think, to be out at dawn, meeting the world head on. Salt trucks are rumbling by, preparing the icy streets for the coming day. The sky is a color I've never seen before. It is as if a corner of the city's gray overcoat has blown back to reveal an orange satin lining. We drink Postum out of Styrofoam cups. He apologizes that there is no real coffee. I tell him I don't drink it anymore, a last attempt to reclaim sleep. *Good girl*, he says, *good girl*. He pulls a record off the bookshelf and puts it on the turntable. Through the scratchiness I hear a high-pitched, insistent whistle, like crickets, only the notes are rounder, wetter, like water dropping from a leaf into a pond. *The dawn song of the peeper*, he says, *the herald of spring*. He beams. *I don't think spring is ever coming*, I say. *Nonsense*, he says. *And in a week or so, the students will come back. I must say, as much as I enjoy the quiet, it does get lonely around here when they're gone.* The students! The fact of them has never occurred to me. Now I see their bright, eager faces, I see them shaking snow off their boots and talking excitedly, listening raptly to the herpetologist in a lecture room, notebooks open, carrying him away in a wave down the hall. The record switches to the call of a bullfrog, mournful. I have the sudden urge to reach behind me and lock the door.

SECRET

I want you to see something, the herpetologist says. *A secret.* He leads me to a door at the back of the lab that I haven't noticed before. He selects a large key from his ring and unlocks it. We step into a tiny antechamber, and when he closes the door behind us, we stand together for a moment in the utter darkness. Then I hear the click of a key in another lock, and we step through to another room, even darker than the first. He switches on a dim red light. As my eyes adjust I see a chest-high tank of water in the center of the room. We step to its edge. In the red light I can just make out something swimming around in the water, tiny ghost creatures with red ruffs of gills. *The Georgia blind salamander*, he whispers. *It exists only in the deep wells and subterranean waters of one particular farm in southeast Georgia. You're maybe the tenth person in the world to see one alive.* The salamanders seem to give off a light of their own, dark eye buds showing through the clear skin of their faces, their red gills waving like feathers as they weave through the water. For a heartbeat I forget myself completely. Then I catch my breath and say, *They don't even know we're here.* The herpetologist moves closer. I slip my hand in his. *I think I love you,* I say. He shakes his head firmly, as if it's the wrong answer to a question. *No, you don't.*

A HERPETOLOGICAL EVENT

I stay late at work, in no state to face my dark apartment, overcome by a new sort of loneliness, one that seems as if it will outlive me. By the time I get on the bus, late in the evening, it is hushed and mostly empty, and I collapse into a seat near the back. As we rattle down the street I close my eyes and think of the blind salamanders, down there in their well in Georgia, far from the city, far from me. When I open my eyes I have long since missed my stop. I sit up in a panic, recognizing nothing outside. But then, as the bus voyages through unfamiliar streets, the salamanders come back like a dream. The darkness deep in the earth where they've been all along. Arcing, looping, somersaulting through the water, somehow finding one another in the dark. Without any thought, care, or need for me. And for a instant, just before the bus turns on its loop, I catch a glimpse of the infinite. There I am inside of it, for one suspended moment—tiny, inconsequential, and utterly free.

DAWN SONG

Late in the night a storm settles on the city, throwing snow against the windows and rattling them in their frames. My husband calls to tell me his power has gone out and asks if he can come over. *Just this one night,* he says. I don't have anywhere else to go. I sit at the kitchen table waiting for him, listening to the silence of the streets, the weather too bad for even the plows to be out. Things are so still that I am startled to look down and see the collar of my robe is quivering steadily with my pulse. He comes in with a red wind-burned face and cold clinging to his clothes. We sit side by side at the table, no words left for one another. Soon my power goes out as well and there is nothing for us to do but get into bed and huddle beneath the blankets, press tight together to conserve warmth. We make love, a matter of survival, our bodies desperate to generate heat. My heart pounds against his chest with the insistence of self-preservation, tenacious and bright. It is still beating hard, determined, by the time he has fallen asleep. I sit up and try to make out his sleeping face in the dark, left with the unshakable feeling that there is a stranger in my bed. Sometime before dawn I get up in the cold room to look out the window. The snow is slackening, but down the block, all the street lights are still off. In the darkness, the shine of the deep, white drifts is the only thing I can make out. It seems to conceal a great mystery, the snow. I stand there watching, struck by the possibility of what might be hidden beneath. I watch for as long as I can stand the cold, knowing that by morning the trucks will have come to clear it all away.

Chapter 8

Creative Nonfiction

Your Wildly Personal Interpretation of Reality

"Write a nonfiction book, and be prepared for the legion of readers who are going to doubt your facts. But write a novel, and get ready for the world to assume every word is true."
—Barbara Kingsolver

Creative nonfiction is the mirror image of fiction. In fiction, you don't worry about facts. Facts are malleable, changeable, disposable, make-up-able. If we are going to go lofty, we will say (again) that as fiction writers, we are after truth, not facts.

In creative nonfiction, facts are foundational. Sticking to them is a part of the deal. Facts are both this genre's most powerful resource and its greatest challenge. Powerful because they're real. They can strike readers with awe because of their improbability, even impossibility. Or they can resonate with readers' souls because of their small but intimate familiarity. But deviate from facts even one iota without informing your readers, and you risk losing their trust. They may even cry foul. To paraphrase what we say about fiction, when writing creative nonfiction, we are after truth *through* facts.

Of course, facts only account for the "nonfiction" half of the equation. Then comes the "creative" part.

Interpreting these facts, shaping them into a narrative that somehow delivers a "unit of satisfaction," is where creative nonfiction gets very interesting indeed. Humans, whether reading truths derived from facts or the writer's imagination, are still interested in narrative, and in story. It's just that the plot (what "happens") seems like it has been handed to you by experience or history or current events. The challenge is making it meaningful.

Whether you're writing fiction or creative nonfiction, you still must *select* and *portray* the events in a way that holds your smartest, most-engaged readers' attention. Just because, in real life, it took you five days in a Renault Alliance to drive cross-country on I-80 from Massachusetts to California does not mean that portraying each hour of those days is compelling to the central concerns of your nonfiction piece.

Some say, "all art is selection." You select the most meaningful moments—the ones that deepen and illuminate and contradict the concerns of your piece. Others—even if they actually happened—you dismiss, rearrange, cut, leave out.

To return to the lab metaphor, consider this quote in a book edited by Adrian P. Mouritz called *Introduction to Aerospace Materials*. The book digs into the science and selection of material to realize design in aircrafts:

> Materials selection is an ordered process by which engineers can systematically and rapidly eliminate unsuitable materials and identify the one or a small number of materials which are the most suitable.

The stakes aren't quite as high in creative nonfiction, but the metaphor is a good one. Aircraft designers can imagine the shape of an aircraft, but if their material disintegrates at a certain velocity, it needs to be eliminated and replaced with something that will get the passenger safely from the ground to the sky and back to the ground.

The writer of creative nonfiction is both the designer and the engineer. Before we dig in, let's experiment.

Write Now

1. Think of an incident—it can even be an impression of an interaction or event—that you experienced that has stuck in your mind over the months or years. Make it an external incident—that is, something that happened in the physical world, not an internal thought or realization. There doesn't have to be any resolution or obvious meaning to this incident. You just have to remember it vividly.

2. Write down five of the most important facts of the incident. For example: "It was July." "The temperature was more than 100 degrees, so we went to the beach." "Evelyn nearly fainted from heat exhaustion." "Our mother drew a heart in the sand with unfamiliar initials in it." "I had a terrible stomachache that turned out to be the start of my first menstrual period."

3. If there's inherent drama in the facts (as in our examples), good. If not, don't worry. That will come naturally as you write. After all, you remember this incident for a reason.

4. Write a short piece (perhaps 500 words) in which you layer observations, reactions, emotions, and thoughts on top of these (and other) facts. First state a fact in the following way: "The fact is, it was July." Then write an interpretation of that fact *that is true.* "I was hating that summer. My best friend had betrayed me. Our beloved dog had died." You are not making things up. You are making connections.

5. Don't be afraid to go wild with your "connective tissue" between the facts. You are turning dry facts into truth by allowing associations to take you to surprising places.

6. After you are done, highlight all your observations, interpretations, or explanations of the facts—all the "subjective" things you wrote. See how much more interesting they are than just the dry facts? There. You've put the *creative* in *creative nonfiction.*

Let's look at examples from the pros.

Writing About What Haunts Us

Peter Orner

I've been trying to lie about this story for years. As a fiction writer, I feel an almost righteous obligation to the untruth. Fabrication is my livelihood, and so telling something straight, for me, is the mark of failure. Yet in many attempts over the years, I've not been able to make out of this tiny—but weirdly soul-defining—episode in my life anything more than a plain recounting of the facts, as best as I can remember them. Dressing them up into fiction, in this case, wrecked what is essentially a long overdue confession.

Here's the nonfiction version.

I watched my father in the front hall putting on his new, lambskin leather gloves. It was a sort of private ceremony. This was in early November, 1982, in Highland Park, Ill., a town north of Chicago along Lake Michigan. My father had just returned from a business trip to Paris. He'd bought the gloves at a place called Hermès, a mythical wonderland of a store. He pulled one on slowly, then the other, and held them up in the mirror to see how his hands looked in such gloves.

A week later, I stole them.

I remember the day. I was home from school. Nobody else was around. I opened the left-hand drawer of the front hall table and there they were. I learned for the first time how easy it is to just grab something. I stuffed the gloves in my pants and sprinted upstairs to my room. I hid them in the back of my closet under the wicker basket that held my license plate collection. Then I braced myself, for days. It was a warm November.

When we finally left that house—my mother, my brother and me—I took the gloves with me to our new place. I took them with me to college. To Boston, to Cincinnati, to North Carolina, to California. I even took them with me to Namibia for two years. I have them now, on my desk, 30 years later.

I've never worn them, not once, although my father and I have the same small hands. I didn't want the gloves. I never wanted the gloves. I only wanted my father not to have them.

Now that he is older and far milder, it is hard to believe how scared I used to be of my father. Back then he was so full of anger. Was he unhappy in his marriage? No doubt. He and my mother never had much in common. But his anger—sometimes it was rage—went beyond this not so unusual disappointment. My own totally unscientific, armchair diagnosis is that like other chronically unsatisfied people, the daily business of living caused my father to despair. At no time did this manifest itself more powerfully than when he came home from work. A rug askew, a jacket not hung up, a window left open—all could set off a fury. My brother once spilled a pot of ink on the snowy white carpet of my parents' bedroom: Armageddon.

His unpredictability is what made his explosions so potent. Sometimes the bomb wouldn't go off, and he'd act like my idea of a normal dad. When he finally noticed those precious gloves were missing, he seemed only confused.

"Maybe they're in the glove compartment," my mother said.

"Impossible. I never put gloves in the glove compartment. The glove compartment is for maps."

"Oh, well," my mother said.

He kept searching the front hall table, as if he had somehow overlooked them amid all the cheap imitation leather gloves, mismatched mittens and tasseled Bears hats. I am certain the notion that one of us had taken the gloves never crossed his mind.

Haunted by my guilt, a frequent motivation for my fiction in general, I've tried to contort my theft into a story, a made-up story.

In my failed attempts, the thief is always trying to give the gloves back. In one abandoned version, the son character (sometimes he's a daughter) mails the gloves back to the father, along with a forged letter, purportedly written by a long-dead friend of the father, a man the father had once betrayed. I liked the idea of a package arriving, out of the blue, from an aggrieved ghost. I'm returning your gloves, Phil. Now at least one of us may be absolved.

The problem was that it palmed off responsibility on a third party. And it muddied the story by pulling the thief out of the center of what little action there was.

In a simpler but equally bad version, the son character, home for Thanksgiving, slips the gloves back in the top left-hand drawer of the front hall table of the house he grew up in, the house where the father still lives. This attempt was marred not only by cooked-up dialogue but also by a dead end.

"Dad! How about we take a walk by the lake?"

"It's been years, Son, since we've taken a walk."

"Pretty brisk out. Maybe you need your gloves?"

The moment arrives: the father slides open the drawer. Voilà! (Note the French.) Cut to the father's face. Describe his bewilderment. I must have checked this drawer a hundred thousand times. Decades drop from the father's eyes, and both father and son face each other as they never faced each other when both were years younger. The son stammers out a confession I could somehow never get right. He tries to explain himself, but can't. Why did he take the gloves? My character could never express it in words and the story kept collapsing.

This is where the truth of this always derails the fiction. I can't give the gloves back, in fiction or in this thing we call reality. If I did, I'd have to confront something I've known all along but have never wanted to express, even to myself alone. My father would have given me his gloves. All I had to do was ask. He would have been so pleased that for once we shared a common interest. This happened so few times in our lives. All the years I've been trying to write this, maybe I've always known that this essential fact would stick me in the heart.

Our imaginations sometimes fail us for a reason. Not because it is cathartic to tell the truth (I finally told my father last year) but because coming clean may also be a better, if smaller, story. A scared (and angry) kid rips off his father's gloves, carries them around for decades. Sometimes he takes them out and feels them but never puts them on. When I see my father these days, we graze each other's cheeks, a form of kissing in my family. I love my father. I suppose I did even then, in the worst moments of fear.

Well-made things eventually deteriorate. The Hermès gloves are no longer baby-soft. All the handless years have dried them up.

In 1982, my father wasn't much older than I am at this moment. I think of him now, standing in the front hall. He's holding his hands up in the mirror, pulling on his beautiful gloves, a rare stillness on his face, a kind of hopeful calm. Was this what I wanted to steal?

Can you see how the writer is grappling with the facts? We chose this piece because the narrator's fiction writing informs his struggle. He's grappling, in real time, with his choice to bring this material from that genre (which couldn't hold it) to this one.

The writer is obsessed, he keeps coming back to these *facts*: his father went to France, bought Hermès gloves, admires the gloves in the mirror, then the narrator steals the gloves.

In her book *The Situation and the Story: The Art of Personal Narrative*, Vivian Gornick explores the idea that a compelling story is one in which the situation is filtered through the writer's unique voice and perspective, allowing readers to connect with the narrative's emotional truths and complexities.

Gornick emphasizes that as important as the facts is the narrator's perspective and emotional engagement. She has argued that the way a writer interprets and presents a situation is equally as important as the situation itself. We also believe that well-crafted creative nonfiction is not just a factual account of events but a narrative shaped by the writer's perspective, emotions, and personal insights.

Undoubtedly, Orner could have portrayed any number of his and his father's interactions that led to his choice to steal the gloves. Notice what the writer *doesn't* tell you: he could have started with his first memory of his father; the first time he felt alienated in his presence; the first time he realized that he and his father don't share common interests. Instead, he focuses on portraying the *situations* that best illuminate central thematic concerns.

Discuss

In Peter Orner's piece, the situation is the father returning from France with gloves that the narrator later steals. But what's the *story*?

Within the piece itself, Orner is haunted (the title is "Writing About What Haunts Us") by a "tiny—but weirdly soul-defining—episode," both great categories for *a list of things from your life worth exploring in nonfiction.* Within the situation, a story starts forming immediately, with personal insights. He writes, "I learned for the first time how easy it is to just grab something." The reader ponders this on two levels. First, how does this newly gained knowledge inform the narrator's life? (What else has he taken since "the first time"?) Second, readers might reflect on whether or not it's easy to "grab something" and what, if anything, we, the readers, have stolen. Another personal insight: "I've never worn [the gloves] . . . , not once, although my father and I have the same small hands. I didn't want the gloves. I never wanted the gloves. I only wanted my father not to have them."

In life, it's easier for us to reconcile what makes logical sense, what's easily explained with clear motivations. If the temperature is low and a person's hands are cold, it makes sense why they'd steal gloves. Or if they're broke, in need of cash, and know how much they can get on the resale market for Hermès, that, too, would add up. Hatred would make sense. Jealousy. But if a person steals gloves and doesn't ever wear them, just hauls them from country to country and state to state without ever using them, we, along with the writer, must wonder.

He writes:

> My father would have given me his gloves. All I had to do was ask. He would have been so pleased that for once we shared a common interest. This happened so few times in our lives. All the years I've been trying to write this, maybe I've always known that this essential fact would stick me in the heart.

Often, it's not what the writer of nonfiction says about themselves in a personal essay that's most satisfying, but what the reader gleans about the narrator—even if the narrator doesn't see it, wouldn't agree, or couldn't name it.

For discussion (or pondering), think about your own insights that Orner does not mention. Do you have your own opinions of Orner's narrator because of the situation and the story? Try not to veer too far away from the piece itself. Find as much evidence in the text as you can to validate your opinion.

Write Now

1. Reread Orner's "Writing About What Haunts Us."
2. Make a list of five things that "haunt" you.
3. Use one of them as the subject matter in a scene that starts with the sentence "I learned for the first time how easy it is to . . ."

Why Creative Nonfiction?

We've covered poetry and fiction and discussed some of the reasons you might want to choose those genres—or techniques from those genres—for your creative work.

So: Why would you choose to create nonfiction over other genres? After all, being tethered to facts, it might seem like you have a lot less freedom than you would otherwise. When writing personal essays, memoirs, historical biographies, journalism, or even when producing podcasts, you can't blithely introduce made-up characters, put false words into the mouths of real people, or change circumstances to fit your narrative arc. If you do so without acknowledgment while publishing your work as nonfiction, you risk public disgrace along with other unpleasantries—because you will have broken what is the foundational rule of nonfiction: stick to the facts.

Of course, facts can sometimes depend on subjective experience. It's the glass half empty or half full conundrum. Two people can see the same glass, same amount of water, yet take away different "facts."

To effectively deliver the units of satisfaction, nonfiction writers use all the tools you've studied in the other genres. Those tools will help you craft your account of the "facts." You can portray brilliant, funny, powerful, and dramatic effects through the use of imagery and vivid descriptions of thoughts and emotions—the "connective tissue" of creative nonfiction.

Think of the facts as the bones of a human being, and the connective tissue as everything else that makes that person whole—the muscles, the tendons, the veins that carry blood, the brain cells, the synapses. The bones alone—dry and colorless—are essential, of course. But it's everything else that sparks life.

So, *who* would choose to write creative nonfiction, and why? We rather think that temperament has a lot to do with it. Of course, some writers do both fiction and creative nonfiction with equal skill. But it takes special talent and craft skills to adhere to facts while making the connections that add up to something dramatic, memorable, and true.

Some writers, even when attempting to work with nonfiction, find themselves sneaking little lies into the real-life narrative, and before long, they get blown so far off course that little is left of what really happened. It's just not in their toolboxes, sticking to facts. Those writers need the freedom to manipulate—even fracture—the bones.

Other writers want to write the truth, even if their emphasis *isn't* on the facts. Facts provide a structure, points of departure and return, and a home base. This makes it easier for some temperaments to explore what's unwieldy and chaotic about *emotional truths*.

Back to that idea of temperament. Perhaps you have a real-life story, and part of the story's power is that it actually happened. Or your reaction to it was unique, or startling, or off the scale. Perhaps it resonated with you because of other events in your life.

Lidia Yuknavitch is a multigenre writer. What makes her decide what's fiction and what's memoir? Her nonfiction *The Chronology of Water* is startling and mesmerizing, yet her fictional *The Book of Joan* is equally compelling, with many of the same themes and *emotional truths*.

Yuknavitch published an essay in *Guernica* in 2015. We've included it here because she speaks to some of our observations through the lens of her storytelling experience. We'll interject after three of the essay's starting sections. Afterward, we ask you to continue your own analysis. At the end, we'll comment some more.

Woven

Lidia Yuknavitch

I can't remember the name of the bar, but I remember I was twenty-two, and I was having the time of my life on Halloween night with my then-girlfriend in Greenwich Village. At twenty-two we could drink like beautiful androgynous unafraid fish. Young badass women in love in the bohemian capital of the world. That's how it felt to me, anyway. She was a student at New York University. I wasn't anything, having flunked out of college. We had plans that spanned continents. Youth foreshortens everything—faces, lives.

Partway through a shit-ton of cheap vodka shots she got up on our rickety little wooden bar table and danced. When I say "danced" I mean punched the air like a boxer. So I climbed up on my chair and "danced" just underneath her, and she started laughing uncontrollably, pointing, pointing at my midsection, because my skirt was tucked up into my neon-blue tights enough that my neon-blue butt was showing. I guess I'd made a miscalculation the last time I'd used the bathroom. We laughed that kind of deep-throated about-to-be-women laugh. The laugh of girls before their voices thin out and tighten from the exhaustion of womanhood.

In fact—and it's only because I'm old and no longer give a crap that I can tell you this—I laughed so hard I made a little unstoppable poop in those neon-blue tights. Like a perfectly round deer turd.

It was a night I wanted never to end.

Or, I wish with all my heart that the story ended there.

Mythic youth.

But that's not where the story ended.

Look at the very first words of this piece. It starts with "I can't remember...." It's memoir. Nonfiction. By acknowledging in the very first line what the narrator cannot remember, she's indicating something to readers. While based on events that happened, this piece is less about the specific facts and chronology and more about a particular time.

The narrator also positions herself in the future by saying "it's only because I'm old and no longer give a crap that I can tell you this," which indicates why she's telling it. She must have, in the time that has passed, learned something about her life that required distance. Add this (I can only tell you because I'm too old and no longer give a crap) to the categories of things from your life worth exploring in nonfiction.

Let's continue with the essay:

When I was four years old my Lithuanian grandmother told me a folktale about the water spirit Laume. I'd accidentally locked myself in my grandparents' bathroom and gone into hysterics when I couldn't get out. My father was furious at my ineptitude. His yelling nearly broke the door down. This is the story she told me once I was liberated.

Laume came from transcendental waters, and her spirit lives in all waters, even in baths and showers, in rivers, streams, oceans, the rain, and in toilets. She is the guardian of all children, the not yet born, the newly born, the orphaned, the forgotten, even the dead children. If there is a child coming into the world, she can foresee it. If a child is mistreated, she will sometimes take him and raise him herself. If a child is lost, she protects him, while gathering information about the usefulness of the parents. If parents are mishandling a child, she will transform him into whatever lesson they need to learn.

Above all she values sincerity, and next industriousness on the part of mothers, particularly the women's work of weaving.

Laume rewards those who work hard; she also punishes severely those who seek reward without an attention to hard work, and those in pursuit of self-aggrandizement.

Go look underneath your pillow to see if she has left you treasure.

I walked upstairs to the bedroom.

My whole body shook. I stood in the bedroom a long minute with my eyes closed, waiting for hands on my shoulders. I looked around for my father there in the dark, because that's the life I had, a father there in the dark, but he wasn't anywhere.

I looked underneath my pillow.

There was a star woven from straw.

∗

Laume takes many forms and inhabits many tales. One of the most famous Laumes was a fisherman's daughter, Egle, queen of the serpents. One day Egle finds a large eel in her clothes after swimming in the Baltic Sea. The eel takes her clothing and only returns it when she promises to marry him. When she accepts, the eel becomes a handsome young man named Zilvinas. They live underwater together and have three children, two sons and a daughter. After a time, Egle longs to visit her parents and siblings on land.

Zilvinas is terrified that Egle's former family will reject her. But though he

> is worried, he agrees to let her go and bring their children. Zilvinas instructs Egle to call to him: "If you are alive and well, come back to me in a milky wave; if you are dead, in a bloody wave."
>
> When she arrives to visit her earthly family, Egle's brothers, jealous of her freedom, torture her sons to death; her daughter, smitten with one of the earth brothers, betrays the secret call and lures Zilvinas to shore, where he is murdered. When Egle returns to the lip of the water, she sees a bloody wave and learns that her earth brothers have betrayed her. She curses herself and her daughter, turning them into trees forever.
>
> Many infant girls in Lithuania have the names of trees.

Notice that Yuknavitch starts moving backward in her chronology, away from the bar where the narrator, on the brink of womanhood, dances under her girlfriend with her skirt tucked into her tights. This time she's a little girl locking herself in a bathroom, which incites anger in her father. The narrator's grandmother is also portrayed, comforting our narrator by introducing her to a folktale character. We learn certain "facts" about the "situation" in the second section: the narrator's dad is volatile; the family is Lithuanian; the grandmother is a source of comfort, as are her folktales. In the third section, the writer gives us less about her own life and more about Laumes. This is when the story starts to emerge for us. We're asking, how are these folktale spirits relevant to the narrator's life?

Let's read some more:

> In the ninth year of our eleven-year marriage, my second husband emerged from our kitchen pointing a gun at me. I haven't written much about this, at least not literally. I don't ever talk about it. It's a bit like a little malformed myth still lodged between my heart and my rib cage.
>
> In America, it's tricky to describe violence without it turning into entertainment.
>
> A Sig Sauer P229 9mm handgun. Statistically, the most popular handgun in the United States.
>
> I'd just entered the house after work. The kitchen light was on, but not the living room light, so he was backlit. The whole house smelled like Jameson. I stood in the dark. My car keys were still in my hand. He crossed the space between us. When he was maybe three feet away, he stopped.

> The gun was pointed at my chest. The air in my lungs concrete. I walked the rest of the distance between us, until the gun was between my breasts. That's how I know he was crying.
>
> I stared at my second husband.
>
> Nothing moved in the house except our breathing.
>
> "Stop loving me," he finally said, the gun heavy enough for me to feel my sternum ache.
>
> As if love was killing him.
>
> Stop loving me.
>
> "No," I said, and I closed my eyes and put my arms around him and pressed in. I waited for the possible death moment between a man and a woman.
>
> Walking straight into violence was nothing new to me. I'd learned how to walk deliberately and unflinchingly into violence from my father, like so many other children do in this country.
>
> In fact, in this country we raise all of our children on one form of violence or another. And so my question is not, "Why did you walk into that violence?"
>
> My question is, "Where does my love come from that I walk through male violence to find it?"

The writer has created a pattern with these sections. She tells something from her life, then something of the Laumes. Concerns about men and violence (starting with her father, moving to her second husband) and the spirits that protect women and children are recurring, each building their own thread of the "story." As the piece takes on thematic weight, she's asking herself questions. If you read enough creative nonfiction and memoir, you'll see that, like in fiction, the narrator almost always posits more questions than answers. The reader's unit of satisfaction is rarely a pat answer to a complicated question, but a simple question with many complicated possibilities. As the exploration continues, the reader learns more about the consciousness of the narrator and forms questions of their own.

We won't interrupt your reading of the piece again. We encourage you to think analytically about the strategic choices Yuknavitch made and how you might want to experiment with similar choices.

> Laumes are the oldest spirits of Lithuanian mythology. The images of these spirits may have developed during the historical Mesolithic period, just after

the Ice Age. Laume first appeared in the form of animals, like goats, bears, or mares. Later she took on a half-human appearance, usually bird claws for feet, the lower body of a she-goat, and large stone nipples. Later still she was represented as a beautiful and supernatural water woman-creature, with fair hair and skin the color of the moon. Laumes were both benevolent and dangerous. They could tickle men to death and then eat their bodies. They could protect women and children or punish them brutally.

Laumes lived near lakes, abandoned bathhouses, rivers, swamps, or other waterways. Laumes liked to gather near water under the New Moon at night and dance. They could cause rain and storms and hail by singing and dancing and swimming.

Anyone who knows me knows why I am attracted to Laumes. I am a child of the waters. But then so are all of us, before the breach.

✷

I had a recurring dream for twenty years that I would have three sons.

I did not have three sons, and I'm fifty-two, so it's not looking likely. What I did have was a daughter, who died, and one son, sun of my life. But I did have three husbands.

Maybe dreams don't mean a goddamned thing.

Or maybe they mean everything.

They say you marry a man who is like your father. My father, the artist-turned-architect, molested and abused us. He was big. Angry. Loud-fisted. Marked us forever—three little women, making for their lives.

My first husband was gentle as a swan. A painter with long fingers and eyelashes. You can see what I was shooting for. I almost self-immolated next to his passivity.

My second husband, another painter, used harsh lashing strokes on the canvas. He was big and loud, but made softer by alcohol and art. Except when he wasn't. The gun of him. Sig Sauer.

My third husband, father of my son, is big and loud and a filmmaker. But there is the gentleness of a cellist in his hands and eyes.

So sometimes I wonder if my dream was meant to show me not three sons, but three husbands. Take my second husband, for instance—the one who pressed the gun of him to me—he was a lot like a child. I wonder if Laume came and took my baby daughter, who died right before I met him, and replaced her with a man-child. This is kind of how we get through our lives: we tell ourselves stories so that what's happening becomes something we can live with. Necessary fictions.

Maybe I had some hard lessons to learn about the difference between doing good work and trying too hard to be a woman.

Woman. Like anyone even knows what that is still.

Or violence. Maybe this is a story about violence.

Or maybe I'm still looking for a way to forgive myself for that failure of womanhood. Two marriages gone busto. Jesus, woman. I keep waiting to feel like a failure.

I wonder what would happen if I didn't know what this story was about.

I think this might be a children's story.

✳

It is said that Laume was a silken-haired sky goddess who lived in the clouds. One myth claims that she fell in love with a beautiful young man down on earth, and that they had a son. Laume descended to earth from the sky to feed her son with her breasts. But when the highest god found out about the son and the sacrilegious love, he killed the boy and scattered his remains between the stars in the sky, and he cut Laume's breasts. Stone pieces of them can still be found on earth in the form of sea-creature fossils.

You would not believe how many sea-creature fossils I've collected over the years. Tons of them. I don't know why. Crustaceans and sea spiders. Conglomerate rocks with pieces of hermit crab fossilized in them. Fish from the desert hills. Ammonites. It's a wonder to see something so clearly meant for movement in water captured swirling in stone. Like a petrified snapshot. Or like history's motion arrested.

✳

I'm going to try it again.

When I was twenty-two I spent Halloween night in Greenwich Village. I drank vodka in a Russian bar with my girlfriend at the time. A huge middle-aged Russian man and his male friends said drunk fat Russian things to us all night, not a word of which we understood, and we laughed, they laughed, and we toasted, and things seemed strangely OK, like when you are young. I kept yelling, "I'm Lithuanian!" to the Russian men, like that was something. Later in life I'd learn what an idiotic thing that was to be yelling. But at the time it seemed everyone, even the moon, was laughing and drunk.

At midnight a giant parade of costumed people passed the bar, and so we joined them, and walked for miles together. There were animals: goats, bears, horses, unicorns, centaurs. There were bird claws for feet, the lower bodies of she-goats, large, extended tin foil breasts and exaggerated codpieces, and all sorts of witches, fairies, and mermaids. It was one of the happiest nights of my life. We were two girl-women in love, we were walking with an army of people in Halloween costumes more vivid and outrageous than reality would ever be. Fear was not anything about us.

Later on, we found ourselves a few alleys away from her crappy dorm room. We were stumble-walking, arm in arm. We kissed and teetered along and laughed. I put my hand up her shirt. Then I saw her head lurch forward in a not-right way, and she made a sound—or something did—like someone smashing a pumpkin with a bat. Something hard at my back, and then my side imploding.

Two men had come up behind us. One hit her in the skull with a baseball bat, another stabbed me in the lower back and side with a knife. My girlfriend dropped to her knees, her head hitting the pavement. I saw her body perfectly balanced, head and knees keeping her perched upright, blood everywhere. I saw the two men laughing and yelling. I saw their shaved heads. I saw stars before I passed out. The last thought I remember thinking was: *Skinheads.*

There is language enough to describe it, but going there is beyond language, so mostly I don't. I don't know how to belong to the story in a way that doesn't betray it. I don't even want to be in the story, the one in which a woman I loved was left partially paralyzed.

But mostly I don't tell the story because I didn't stay with her happily ever after forever and ever.

I've noticed the scar at my back and side has softened over the years. It's so tiny you can barely see it. Receding with age and fat, I suppose. Or the guilt of wanting more life.

*

A woman was harvesting a flowerbed and had taken her child with her. She was so busy with her work that the child slept through the day.

The woman went home in the evening to milk the cows and make dinner. She served her husband, who asked her, "Where's my son?" With terror she whispered, "I have forgotten him!" She ran as fast as she could to the place where she had left her son, and she heard Laume speak: "Hush, forgotten child." The mother asked Laume for her child back. The fairy said, "Come, come, dear woman, take your child, we have done nothing to him. We know that you work very hard, at many jobs, and that you didn't want to leave your child behind."

The Laumes went on to shower the babe with treasures, enough gifts to raise several children on. The mother went home with her precious baby and with her gifts; she was greeted with great joy.

Another woman, hearing of this good fortune, was taken over by jealousy. She thought, "I shall do the same as her, and also be showered in gifts." The next evening, at dusk, she took her child, left him in the fields, and went home. When, after dinner, she returned to the field, she heard the Laumes: "Hush, you left your child in greed." And the child screamed with great pain, for he was being pinched mercilessly. The Laumes continued their torture until the mother approached. Then they tossed the child at her feet. The babe was dead.

✳

When my infant daughter died, spilling out with our shared waters, the story breached. Every story I have ever told has a kind of breach to it, I think. You could say that my writing isn't quite right. That all the beginnings have endings in them.

✳

Violence doesn't only exist in men.

Think of mother violence, for example. When my son was in grade school I had hysterically violent thoughts. I was afraid he'd be bullied. I actually pictured the moment—I saw myself stride across the school grounds, pick a bully child up by his ankles, hold him upside down, shake the shit out of him, and fling him in a dumpster. I thought all the way through "Mamma has to go to jail."

My Lithuanian grandmother cut the tip off my father's tongue as a boy.

After I became a mother and married for the third time, I had a skinhead in my writing class. I know he was a skinhead not from the way he looked, though that's exactly what he looked like: the '90s version of a London skinhead. I know he was a skinhead because he came to my office and told me. He asked not to have to do group work. I'm embarrassed to say that made me laugh. I also remember thinking: *You are a brutal abomination* and *Not long ago this guy was just a boy, just his mother's son—what happened?*

His writing was impeccable. He completed every assignment. His theses were not Hitleresque. He was oddly polite and courteous. I gave him a C, only because I could, whether or not I should have. If he'd challenged the grade, he'd have won. In many ways he was the best writer in the class.

What is a teacher? A mother?

＊

Another Laume is a goddess of the home and a warm hearth. If you do not tend to your family and fire well, she burns your house down. With everyone inside. The word for "fireplace" in Lithuanian has come to be understood as "family relations."

＊

In my twenty-third year of teaching college, on a day we were discussing violence as a theme, something repressed inside me lurched, and I told my Halloween-night story to the class. I mean it shot out of my mouth before I could stop it.

Sig Sauer-like.

I lifted up my shirt and showed them my scar. It was one of the more unprofessional teaching moments of my career, though it would certainly not be the last. So much shame came out of my mouth. The shame of a daughter whose body was written by her father. The shame of leaving a woman I loved. The shame of failed marriages and motherhoods.

At the end of the story I also told them what I'd learned about our attackers. They weren't skinheads. They'd been Marines. My then-girlfriend would be neurologically damaged and partially paralyzed for the rest of her life. The marines spent three months—ninety whole days—in jail. One was dishonorably discharged.

Everyone got quiet. I thought maybe the story was over, and my intention was to get us all writing and out of the well of overly personal pathos I'd let us fall into, but then a Latino man in the class, his neck covered in tattoos, stood up. All I knew from his writing was that he'd been a gang member. That he'd made mistakes and gone to jail. That he was writing A+ ideas with C+ skills. That his parents were undocumented workers. That he had four sisters. But I learned that day that he'd also been on three tours of duty for our country before he'd turned twenty-two. I also learned that the military had begun relaxing tattoo restrictions in 2004. He stood up and said, "I apologize on behalf of Marines." His sentence was perfect. The air in the room vacuumed.

He walked the length of the room, straight at me. I braced myself for the moment—I wasn't sure how much longer I could keep from crying. Briefly it occurred to me that I might die if he got any closer, closer than three feet away. Then he did a regular human thing. He hugged me. He said it again. This time in my ear, and his breath made the hairs on my neck shoot up. "I apologize on behalf of Marines."

But that's not what I heard. I heard, "You don't have to punish yourself for love."

I didn't die like I thought I might. From his random compassion, I mean. I wasn't a very good teacher. I don't know what I was. I gave him an A in the class, in the end. That day we wrote stories about the small violences in our daily lives.

*

In one story, Laume takes all the children away from their parents in a particular village, because they sent their eldest boys to war. The mothers become barren and the fathers can no longer hold any food down, and thus they die. The village fades from history because the parents did not take care of their children.

*

You know, stories change, just like the lives we've lived and selves we've inhabited. Nobody's been the same person twice. I mean really. It's the people walking around acting and sounding especially self-assured and whole who worry me the most.

I like hearing the world's stories about itself. That's partly why I teach world literature. It helps me feel less incarcerated by the world, or my past, or my mistakes and confusions. It helps me remember I'm not just American.

> I'm not just a woman. A mother. A teacher. A wife. I find value in thinking in stories. Aren't we all woven through with stories? Isn't that how we think of our lives, how we survive them? Now, when someone hurts me, I remember that they are only living the terms of their own fictions—sometimes desperately—so their selves don't unravel.
>
> I like that idea. A woven person.

Yuknavitch writes: "This is kind of how we get through our lives: we tell ourselves stories so that what's happening becomes something we can live with. Necessary fictions." Creative nonfiction can serve as a wonderful container in which we can open up and get "truthful" about "necessary fictions," or the events that our subconscious mind, at an earlier point in our lives, altered.

Yuknavitch also offers several possibilities before deciding she likes the idea of herself as not one thing, but as "a woven person." She says:

> Maybe I had some hard lessons to learn about the difference between doing good work and trying too hard to be a woman.
>
> Woman. Like anyone even knows what that is still.
>
> Or violence. Maybe this is a story about violence.
>
> Or maybe I'm still looking for a way to forgive myself for that failure of womanhood. Two marriages gone busto. Jesus, woman. I keep waiting to feel like a failure.
>
> I wonder what would happen if I didn't know what this story was about.
>
> I think this might be a children's story.

Here we see a nonfiction author using and expanding the elements of nonfiction to illuminate what's most mysterious, what's most at stake for her.

Write Now

1. Reread "Woven."
2. Make a list of "necessary fictions" in your personal or family history: things that you (or your family) may have subconsciously modified, lied about, exaggerated, changed, or distorted. Choose only those things you're ready to get "truthful" about.

3. Make a list of children's' stories or folktales that you love. Without thinking about how they connect, write as much specific detail as you remember about those stories and who told you about them.
4. Experiment with "weaving" the children's story or folktale throughout your piece as you update the "necessary fiction" with the more truthful one.

What Is Creative Nonfiction?

For all the reasons we've discussed, defining creative nonfiction is challenging. Like fiction, it must have a story. Like poetry, it uses imagery and association to make the most of the facts at hand. And, we would venture to say, it is extremely personal. In a way, that's the whole point of creative nonfiction: to push facts through a personal filter so they come out transformed and illuminated.

So, the definition really comes down to the subtitle of this chapter: creative nonfiction is a writer's wildly personal interpretation of reality. Now, let's be clear: "personal" doesn't have to mean that the writer bares their soul. It just means that the filter being used is unique to the writer's intelligence, knowledge, experiences, and moral code. And it is that uniqueness that will distinguish one creative nonfiction rendering of a particular event from another and make it worth reading for its insight.

We see the writers' points of view powerfully threaded through the preceding examples, which are lyrical, vividly portrayed, and voice driven. You can chart their scenes, just like we did in "Reasons for and Advantages of Breathing" in the fiction chapter. If you do, you'll see tension building through moments of connection and disconnection. You'll see struggle punctured by breakthroughs.

Are we suggesting that an event or incident must be hugely dramatic to be worthy of creative nonfiction? No. A son who stole his dad's gloves, in the scheme of things, is no big deal, at least on the surface. There's an enormous continuum of choices.

As with other writing (and other art forms) we've put into this book, wonderful creative nonfiction can be written about the most minuscule of subjects, so long as you're invested, so long as you care, so long as whatever you're writing about is vital to you, urgent.

Memoirist Catherine Raven could hardly be surprised when she encountered a fox in the mountain valley where she lived in rural Montana. More foxes than people live in the area.

Raven, a biologist, studied animal life and had been trained to avoid anthropomorphizing (assigning human characteristics to nonhuman animals). Yet, the decidedly human endeavor of a "friendship" inspired her memoir *Fox & I: An Uncommon Friendship*.

Like Yuknavitch, Raven survived a violent childhood—but Yuknavitch's short piece may give more childhood details than Raven's whole book. Raven portrays some particulars, but also hints at the reasons that led to a preference for nature and nonhuman animals. The not-about-the-fox material she weaves in is less about her personal past and more about her work as a scientist. Her training and the demands of her career are portrayed not only because they're *true*, but because they underscore what's most *unlikely*: that she came to consider a fox a friend. Good memoir is often about leaving out the likely bits and really working to earn what's *most unlikely*.

In doing so, Raven allows her readers to ponder the bigger questions about the limits of intellect, training, and how we define ourselves. She teases out questions about the boundaries between the human and natural worlds, the ethics of intervention in wildlife, and our role as stewards of the environment.

All of this by describing a friendship with a fox? Yes.

Raven is a gifted writer. She's witty, at times acerbic, straightforward to a fault, and funny. In other words, she has a unique point of view.

Like Orner's and Yuknavitch's pieces, Raven's book touches on universal themes such as loneliness, connection, and the search for meaning in difficult relationships.

In much popular storytelling, the question of whether the main character will survive harrowing experiences is at stake, either literally or metaphorically. While some work is published posthumously, with most autobiographical work we know the protagonist survived because they're writing it.

So, the stakes shift from the question of whether they'll survive to *how* they survived or what they learned along the way. Yuknavitch, Raven, and Orner all seem (in varying degrees) less interested in portraying the most tormented moments of their younger lives and more interested in how their lived experiences set them on a journey.

It's entirely up to you which path you take. Plenty of creative nonfiction writers find and transmit meaning out of the direct exploration of their experience. One of the paradoxes of writing creative nonfiction is that you can get away with writing more outrageous things than in fiction. We can't tell you how often in workshops students have doubted a story (fiction) because it didn't ring true, and the writer cried, in defense, "But it really happened!" Facts count for pretty much nothing in fiction if they don't come across as authentic and organic to the narrative. As the saying goes, truth is often stranger than fiction. Or rather, than believable fiction.

Write Now

1. At the top of the page, underscore these words: The Least Likely and Most Difficult to Believe Fact About Me.
2. Imagine Catherine Raven starting with "I'm a scientist with decades of training to resist anthropomorphizing and yet one of my best friends was a fox."
3. Write a scene that captures and portrays the moment you acquired that "least likely" fact.

Borrowing from the Elements of Creative Nonfiction

What's unique about creative nonfiction?

1. Basing the Narrative on Facts

Facts can be powerful. The world is full of astonishing things. Choosing your facts—deciding what events or people or objects or geographies or just stuff to write about—is your first step.

Of course, what many creative nonfiction writers say is that they don't choose their subjects, the subjects choose them. Keep an eye out for obsessions, even tiny ones. That's where the richest material lies.

In her incredible book, *Let the Record Show: A Political History of ACT UP New York, 1987–1993*, Sarah Schulman writes, "AIDS activist history has been mistakenly placed in the trajectory of gay male history."

Shulman, in her imagination of the book, used *facts* (the situation) to correct the erroneous mythology of AIDS activism in New York. In doing so, she attempts not only to give credit where it's due, but to show readers how political activism can change the course of history.

The story that emerges from the situation is just how effective the movement was, even with the challenges of racism, sexism, and infighting. For a long time, the group was able to stay focused on their primary purpose and effect change that has benefited everyone. Women and people of color whose stories are often erased from the activism are given their due in Shulman's book, and a much more compelling story arises.

2. Digging Deeper with Research

This is related to facts and involves hard work. Writers of historical nonfiction, including biographies and even memoirs, can spend years on research.

Take the book *Salt: A World History*, by historian Mark Kurlansky. Yes, a 494-page book about salt. And it's riveting. Here's just a few paragraphs from the opening:

A MANDATE OF SALT

Once I stood on the bank of a rice paddy in rural Sichuan Province, and a lean and aging Chinese peasant, wearing a faded forty-year-old blue jacket issued by the Mao government in the early years of the Revolution, stood knee deep in water and apropos of absolutely nothing shouted defiantly at me, "We Chinese invented many things!"

The Chinese are proud of their inventions. All Chinese leaders, including Mao Zedong, sooner or later give a speech listing the many Chinese firsts. Though rural China these days seems in need of a new round of inventions, it is irrefutably true that the Chinese originated many of the pivotal creations of history, including papermaking, printing, gunpowder, and the compass.

China is the oldest literate society still in existence, and its 4,000 years of written history begin as a history of inventions. It is no longer clear when legends were made into men and when living historic figures were turned into legends. Chinese history starts in the same manner as Old Testament history. In the Book of Genesis, first come the legends, the story of the Creation, mythical figures such as Adam and Eve and Noah, generations of people who may or may not have lived, and gradually the generations are followed to Abraham, the beginning of documented Hebrew history.

In Chinese history, first was Pangu, the creator, who made humans from parasites on his body. He died but was followed by wise rulers, who invented the things that made China the first civilization. Fuxi was first to domesticate animals. Apparently an enthusiast for domesticity, he is also credited with inventing marriage. Next came Shennong, who invented medicine, agriculture, and trade. He is credited with the plow and the hoe. Then came Huangdi, the Yellow Emperor, who invented writing, the bow and arrow, the cart, and ceramics.

You can tell just from this small excerpt how much research the author has done, and we haven't even gotten to his main subject yet: salt. The narrative intelligence of the piece, the "I," standing on the bank of a rice paddy in rural Sichuan Province, will undoubtedly develop more, as will his subject, but the reader's attention in this small section is held by what's being revealed about Chinese history.

3. Revealing Deeply Personal Connections with the Subject Matter

Remember: The writing must reflect your own unique perspective on the world. Otherwise, why write (or read) it? We can all go to Wikipedia in search of dry facts. To be called "creative nonfiction," the facts must be run through the filters of your consciousness.

Here we have a short piece of deeply personal creative nonfiction from writer Valerie Geary, who weaves in facts about solar eclipses and our atmosphere.

The Stories We'll Tell: Getting Ready for a Total Eclipse of the Sun
Valerie Geary

I have a faint memory of watching a total solar eclipse as a child. My sister says she remembers being there with me. But this isn't possible. The last total eclipse to occur in the contiguous United States was in 1979—two years prior to my sister's birth and four years prior to mine. Most likely, we witnessed the partial solar eclipse that occurred in 1993. Yet somehow, over time and through retelling, our collective memory shaped a bigger story.

This happens all the time. Memories are malleable. Details slip away from us so easily. After a while, or after no time at all, pieces of our life get forgotten. And the things we do remember are usually some hybrid form of truth and fiction, new layers added with each retelling. I remember standing with my sister and looking up at the sun. No one told us not to. I remember feeling that something important was happening but not really understanding the hows or whys or what would come next, only that in that moment, anything seemed possible.

The summer after I graduated high school, I worked at a summer camp in Oakhurst, California. I wasn't doing something cool like counseling or life-guarding. I was kitchen staff. I washed dishes and tended to the salad bar. It was my first time living apart from my parents, my first time on my own—as much as one can be on her own when sharing a double wide with eight other young women—and I was miserable.

I'm shy. I always have been. It's difficult for me to just go up to people and start a conversation. But that summer especially, homesick and lonely and completely out of my comfort zone, I struggled to make friends.

One night, the summer nearly over, a dozen of us piled into several cars and drove out of camp and the town of Oakhurst, away from lights and into the mountains. We parked at a trailhead and hiked up and up, what seemed like forever, to the top of a ridge. By the time we got there, the sun was starting to set. We settled down on a rocky promontory, stretched out on our backs, and lifted our faces to the sky. First one star appeared, then another and another, until the whole sky was splattered with pinhole lights. After a while, the distant lights began to dance.

＊

Every August, Earth passes through a stream of debris left by the Swift-Tuttle comet. These bits of space debris burn up in Earth's atmosphere, causing a dazzling display known as the Perseid meteor shower. The sky fills with streaks of light, sometimes long and brilliant, sometimes little more than a flash, blink and you'll miss it. We call them shooting stars and send our wishes after them into the dark.

That night, sitting atop some mountain whose name I can't remember with trees stretched below and stars stretched above, I witnessed my first meteor shower. With each new illumination came gasps of delight and wonder. With each meteor, a feeling of soaring.

The group hiked back in the dark. In my memory, we were silent, contemplating what it means to be human, floating on this blue planet, captured in a net of stars. We had experienced beauty, witnessed mystery and power and felt the pull of the infinite. Together we stepped out of ourselves and our individual loneliness and became part of something bigger.

＊

Humans are story creatures. From ancient cave art to the internet, stories are the way in which we communicate and make sense of the world. I see stories everywhere, maybe because I write them. My brain is trained to recognize their patterns. But I think it might be more than that. I think stories allow us to be vulnerable in ways we might otherwise avoid. Stories open us up to a richer human experience by connecting us. I write to understand and be understood. I read for the same reasons.

Before cell phones, before the internet, before television, before radio, before books and words, there were stars. We used them to navigate, to grow crops, to hunt, to pray, to explain our existence on this planet. We don't see them the way we used to anymore. We walk with our heads lowered, bent over cell phones. We spend our days inside, eyes fixated on screens. Even if we do pause to look up, we can't see very much anyway. So many of us live in large cities now, densely populated areas, our skies choked by light and air pollution, nothing at all like the expanse our ancestors witnessed. There is a disconnect now. The mystery, the wonder, the stories we told are all fading.

Today, the moon will pass between the sun and the Earth, blocking all or part of the sun for several hours. Everyone in North America, as well as some in South America, Africa, and Europe, will experience a partial eclipse. In the United States, the path of totality will cross through portions of 14 states, including the state where I live, Oregon. People who have witnessed a total solar eclipse before say it is a once in a lifetime event, that it changes you. They say it is something you must experience if given the opportunity. So my family has made plans to be there when it happens. We have eclipse glasses and camping chairs and a place picked out in the path of totality to sit and watch this extraordinary event take place. We've invited friends. There will be food and drinks. We're turning it into a party. It certainly feels like something worth celebrating.

During a total eclipse, many strange things happen, or so I've heard. Temperatures drop. The horizon is dappled with sunset colors. Birds stop singing. Nocturnal animals start to prowl. In the two to three minutes that this eclipse's totality will last, the veil will be peeled back, our reality will shift, and we'll have no choice but to notice, to look up at the stars we so often ignore, to see them looking back at us.

It will certainly be a powerful moment, a narrow thread of time where

> millions of us across the country will step out of our houses, set down our
> phones, and turn our gazes skyward. It will provide a chance to feel the
> stretch of infinity, the expansion of possibility, the expectation of hope. And
> when it's over, when the moon continues its orbit and the sun reappears, we
> will still have this story to tell, a story that connects us to one another, but
> also to the people who came before us, and the people who will come after.

For the sake of an exercise, make note of everything in Geary's piece that you might find out about the sky, stars, and solar eclipses on Wikipedia. Then make note of everything you learn about the narrator. Compare the ratio. Compare the impact. How does "the personal" buff and shine "the facts" of the author's chosen subject and vice versa?

Write Now

1. Make a list under the category "Subjects I Have a Deeply Personal Connection To." Examples: astronomy, taxidermy, knitting, beach shells, criminal pathology, ancient Rome, Sufism, entomology, the history of sex work in Amsterdam, color theory, Eastern Thailand's modern cuisine, 1980s fashion.
2. Write a scene that weaves facts about your subject with facts about you. Forget connecting the dots, forget "logical sense." Instead, experiment by first finding a ratio similar to what you observed in Geary's piece.
3. In revision, find your own ratio.

4. Arriving at Insightful Conclusions

Another possible difference between nonfiction and other genres is that nonfiction writers can (and often do) draw conclusions from the stories they write. It can be blatant or subtle. An example of the more subtle, in Geary's piece, is the phrase "set down our phones." Offering definitive conclusions in fiction tends to sound preachy, and many writers as well as readers are uncomfortable with it, feeling that it detracts from the power of the narrative. Not so in creative nonfiction.

In fact, much of the suspense and drama of nonfiction can be in following the writer as they try to derive meaning from the facts at their disposal and sharing their "unit of satisfaction" when they succeed.

You can read an example of this in Joan Didion's classic essay "On Keeping a

Notebook." Indeed, many of Didion's personal essays follow this pattern of discovery-while-musing-over-facts. That it feels spontaneous, as if Didion is thinking out loud and drawing these conclusions in real time, is part of the Didion magic of drawing us in.

In this essay, Didion explores all the possible reasons she might have been, since childhood, obsessed with writing things down. In the end she concludes what you wouldn't necessarily have expected when you started reading the essay.

Beginning of essay:

"'That woman Estelle,'" the note reads, "'is partly the reason why George Sharp and I are separated today.' Dirty crepe-de-Chine wrapper, hotel bar, Wilmington RR, 9:45 a.m. August Monday morning."

Since the note is in my notebook, it presumably has some meaning to me. I study it for a long while. At first, I have only the most general notion of what I was doing on an August Monday morning in the bar of the hotel across from the Pennsylvania Railroad station in Wilmington, Delaware (waiting for a train? missing one? 1960? 1961? why Wilmington?), but I do remember being there. The woman in the dirty crepe-de-Chine wrapper had come down from her room for a beer, and the bartender had heard before the reason why George Sharp and she were separated today. "Sure," he said, and went on mopping the floor. "You told me." At the other end of the bar is a girl. She is talking, pointedly, not to the man beside her but to a cat lying in the triangle of sunlight cast through the open door.

Insight revealed (toward the end of the essay):

It all comes back. Perhaps it is difficult to see the value in having one's self back in that kind of mood, but I do see it; *I think we are well advised to keep on nodding terms with the people we used to be* whether we find them attractive company or not. [emphasis ours] Otherwise they turn up unannounced and surprise us, come hammering on the mind's door at 4 a.m. of a bad night and demand to know who deserted them, who betrayed them, who is going to make amends. We forget all too soon the things we thought we could never forget. We forget the loves and the betrayals alike, forget

> what we whispered and what we screamed, forget who we were.... It is a
> good idea, then, to keep in touch, and I suppose that keeping in touch is
> what notebooks are all about.

We don't know Didion's process, so we can't say whether this essay came to her gift wrapped in one draft or took months (or more) of labor. Readers experience her insight along with the narrator in real time, drawing conclusions at the end that they didn't know in the beginning. Not incidentally, revealing insights in this natural-seeming way can make creative nonfiction much more raw—and genuine.

The more unusual or surprising the insight, the better. It's difficult to pull off a successful piece of creative nonfiction about an obvious discovery. No one would be shocked to find out you burnt your fingers by touching a hot stove.

However, if you've convinced us that it's important to keep a notebook by remembering a time in a Delaware bar when a woman in a silky robe comes down for a beer while a girl talks to a sunlit cat, you may be on to something.

Write Now

1. Make a list under the category "Things I Know Now but Didn't Know Then." Examples: "It's better to get Cs and Bs rather than As in school. The difference is a lot of life, a lot of fun." "Even if I were bullied, it was bad for me to bully others." "Forgiving others is overrated." "After years of prioritizing chosen family over biological, I now know blood is thicker than water."

2. Focus on the most compelling entry in your list. Write a scene that shows your narrator in a situation where they still did not have the knowledge they have now—when they had yet to understand one of the entries to your list.

3. When you're done, put that away and write a second scene closer to the present day, where you *wish* your narrator had the knowledge, but they still didn't.

4. When you're done, put that away and write a third scene *after* your narrator acquires the knowledge, reflecting on the times portrayed in the first two scenes.

5. In revision, work on portraying the scenes so that the reader might discover, as if in real time with your narrator, the knowledge.

5. Integrating Disparate Storylines

We've mentioned "weaving" when talking about previously mentioned works. Another term used for this is "braiding." A braided essay is an essay that takes two or more events, facts, or persons and weaves the "strands" (events, facts, persons) together to form an integrated whole. The key to a successful braided essay is that all the strands come together in some way to form a theme or answer a question.

Sometimes external events or actions or even descriptions of things are braided only with intensely personal reflections. Here's creative nonfiction writer Nicole Walker's explanation of this:

> What is creative nonfiction writing but the shaping and reshaping of self against fact? You take a personal story and give it syntax, grammar, language, punctuation. The simple fact of putting it on paper reshapes it. But now you've got to give it context, associate meaning to it. So next to that personal story, you set a paragraph about apples, or condoms, or chickens, or gun violence. Suddenly, your personal story is reshaped by these new facts, and the facts of your personal story cut into the hard statistics of your paragraph about imported apples or the failure rate of condoms. The facts are the glacier to the soft canyon of your own history. You see the history newly. You see the facts a little more softly.

Walker declares that "the braided essay may be the most effective form for our times."

We're going to include one more example, this one by Pam Houston. Not only does this essay braid the writer's loss of her favorite dog with climate change and themes of friendship, family, and community—it's a brilliant example of the kind of writing that we hope harkens back to the introduction of this book, showing us how a writer managed to find her own style and voice while exploring the subject matter most meaningful to *her*. While reading, look how each strand of the braid informs the others in surprising ways. Also, keep adding to your list of categories.

What Has Irony Done for Us Lately

Pam Houston

1 In 2014 I lost Fenton Johnson the Wolfhound—Mother's Day weekend was his last—which, I know from experience, will make all the Mays from now on a little sadder.

Eleven years is a big number for an Irish Wolfhound, and Fenton had made excellent use of every one. I named him after my dear friend, the writer Fenton Johnson, and as Fenton the dog grew up, he revealed more and more ways the name was apt. Like Fenton the human, he was wise and reticent, the best kind of grandfather even when he was only middle-aged. He wasn't big on asking for affection, wouldn't wiggle up to you like a Black Lab or a Bernese Mountain Dog, wouldn't even very often bump his head up under your resting arm for a pet. He preferred to sit nearby, keeping a loving and watchful and ever so slightly skeptical eye, as if the humans were always potentially on the verge of making a really bad decision, and he would be ready, in that case, to quietly intervene.

When Fenton was a young dog, he would bound through deep snow with an expression of such pure joy on his face it could make even a non-dog person laugh out loud. He would only drink water out of the very edge of a bowl, and only then with his top teeth pressing firmly against the metal rim. When he wanted something he would come over and scratch on the chair or the couch I was sitting on, as if it were the wrong side of a door. When he was happy—for instance, if I rose from a chair with a leash in my hand—he would wag his tail heartily, but when he was ecstatic, like when I came home after a week of working on the road, his tail would make huge happy circles, the scope of his happiness too big to be contained in a movement that only went from side to side.

To say Fenton was intelligent, to say he had a wider range of emotions than anyone I dated in my twenties and thirties is really to only scratch the surface of what a magnificent creature he was. He was the ranch manager, hyper vigilant but not neurotic, keeping his eye on everything—animals, people—making sure no one was out of sorts or out of place. Because of his watchfulness, he had perfected the art of anticipating what would happen next better than any person could have. He knew all of my tastes and my tendencies, and he was always ready to be of service in any undertaking—moving the sheep from one pasture to another, walking the fence line to look for breaks, riding into town to drop off the recycling, cheering me up on a sleepless night by resting his heavy head across one of my ankles, reminding me to get up from the computer after too many hours of writing and go take a walk outside.

This last year, though, the arthritis that first made itself known when he was about eight years old was getting severe. He'd been on Rimadyl—the canine version of Advil—for years. We had had good results from acupuncture, massage, and glucosamine chondroitin. Doc Howard had shelved his country vet skepticism to give a laser gun a try and had been surprisingly impressed with the results, using it on many patients for pain relief, as well as on his wife and himself. Once a week I loaded Fenton in the 4-Runner and we drove to Doc's, donned our Keith Richards goggles (Fenton got some too) and Doc's granddaughter gave Fenton six shots of laser light in his back end. Lately, even the laser gun treatments were reaching the point of diminishing returns.

I'd been away for a few days, in Boston, when I got the call from Kelly, my house-sitter, that Fenton was down and didn't seem to want to get up anymore. A wolfhound isn't meant not to be able to stand and walk around, however comfortable we might be willing to make him.

Months before, I had written on my calendar the following words, "This weekend keep free in case Fenton . . . ," and there was the old boy, as obliging as ever, doing everything, even dying, right on time. I flew to Denver immediately, and invited some of Fenton's closest friends to the ranch for the weekend, knowing that in order to come, they would have to brave the predicted Mother's Day blizzard during the five hour drive from the Front Range to the ranch.

In Boulder, at the Whole Foods, I bought dry-aged organic beefsteaks for everyone I thought might make it, plus a mountain of other groceries. I figured if we were going to be sad—and we were going to be sad—at least we were going to have good food to eat. When I selected the steaks, the Whole Foods butcher, whose name is Jerry (and whose dog's name, I would learn later, is Gristle) took a lot of time and great pleasure describing the dry-aging process, and when I asked for six T-Bones, one for each of the potential guests and another for the old boy himself, Jerry said, "you must be having quite a party." And since he had been so kind and thorough in *his* explanation, I said, "Well, what I am actually doing is having a kind of living wake for one of the best dogs who has ever lived, and I want to buy the very best for him, and for his friends who are making the drive up to my ranch in Creede to be with him." Jerry lifted one of the massive T-bones off the top of the pile sitting on the scale.

"You should have said so to begin with," he said. "In that case Fenton's is on me."

My friend Tami Anderson had a wonderful dog named Taylor who she was as deeply connected to, I believe, as I was to Fenton. I have loved all my dogs, of course, but there is the rare dog—I have had two so far in my life—that asked me to transcend my human limitations and be, at least occasionally, a little more evolved, like them. Fenton was such a dog, and so was Taylor. Taylor and Fenton were puppies together, and they loved each other truly all their lives. When Taylor was coming close to the end, she and Tami would often lie on the bed together and look into one another's eyes. One day, Tami told me, almost in a whisper, they were in such a position, and Tami said, "Maybe next time, I'll be the dog."

But Tami couldn't be there for Fenton's weekend, and neither could my partner, Greg, so it turned out to be me and Kelly, and Linda, who had cared for Fenton so often over the last five years of his life he belonged to her nearly as much as he belonged to me. She had flown in from Reno and met me at the Denver airport and we had driven together. The storm had kept everyone else away.

The weekend was everything all at once. It rained and snowed and blew and eventually howled, and I slept out on the dog porch with Fenton anyway, nose to nose with him for his last three nights. The storm seemed to have been ordered especially for the old boy, who loved the cold and snow most of all, who hated the wood stove and preferred it when we kept the house in the 55-60 degree range, who all his life would literally raise a disapproving eyebrow at me the moment he suspected I was going out to chop kindling.

Linda and I gave him sponge baths and rubbed his face and ears until he didn't want us to rub his face and ears anymore, and then we sat quietly beside him. I will admit to even loving cleaning him up, changing his dog beds, washing and drying him, fine tuning my attention to meet his every need.

When I could stand to tear myself away from him, I cooked—giant pots of soup and pesto and grilled vegetables and salad. I had no appetite but the kitchen was warm and smelled good whenever I walked into it. Fenton ate Jerry's giant dry-aged T-bone in three sittings over two days and enjoyed the bone as much as I've ever seen him enjoy anything in his life, even though he'd mostly lost interest in other food by then. There were times I was sure we were doing exactly the right thing by Fenton, times I thought that if *my* last weekend could be like his, it would be better than pretty much anybody's last weekend I had heard about in the history of the world. Other times, I was in a flat panic. How could I be trusted to make this decision? What on earth gave me the authority or the wisdom to decide when his quality of life had crossed over some determinate line? And all that aside, how would I live in a world without him, without his tender presence beside me, without his increasingly stiff rear end galumphing down the driveway to meet me, without his quiet vigilance as I sat in a chair and did my work?

Fenton was my seventh Irish wolfhound and my tenth dog overall. I was not new to being the decision maker, but no amount of times down this difficult road made it any easier. At one point I got myself so freaked out I thought maybe we would get in the car together—just him and me—and drive and drive and see if we could outrun death.

On Monday morning I saw he was getting the very beginning of tiny sores from sitting still for so long, and I knew Tuesday morning would have to be his last. My friend Kae called from Denver and said she had tried to make it on Sunday, but they had closed highway 285 because of black ice and so far it had not reopened. She asked me if I was okay, and I told her I was. I have always called Kae the moral center of my large and wonderful group of women friends, in part because she was raised by preachers, in part because she has so much backbone, but mostly because she has a remarkable way of orienting toward true north.

Kae and I have the same exact Prius—year and model—and when she pulled in the driveway ten hours later Fenton got more excited than I had seen him all weekend, even though I was sitting right there beside him.

Like there might be two of me, and I might come home all over again and start caring for him as I already was. This was another unexpected gift of the weekend. How many hundreds of times had I seen Fenton at the bottom of the driveway, his tail going in giant crazy circles? But because I was always the one *in* the Prius I had never before witnessed that moment of recognition, the moment he became sure *that* car was my car. Who in your life has ever been that ecstatic over your arrival? Someone, I hope. Some living being.

But of course, it wasn't a second me who got out of the Prius. It was Kae, and when he recognized her, he danced and danced, on his front legs only, because he loves her too, and he knew she had come to see him. As a culture, whenever we want to treat someone or something inhumanely, we declare they don't have emotions, but anyone who thinks dogs don't have emotions should have been on the porch that night in the snow.

Kae had driven ten hours in whiteout conditions, doubling the length of the drive. When I asked her if it was awful, she shrugged and said, "You never *ever* ask for help, so after we talked, I figured I needed to get here."

I said, "I don't think I asked for help this time."

"Maybe not," she said, "But you were close."

We bedded down on the dog porch in sleeping bags under the swirling snow. She said, "You are doing the right thing, Pam. He's not going to get better."

I said, "It feels like a betrayal no matter what I do."

And she said, "I don't think betrayal is a word that belongs on this porch."

I teach sometimes with the Colorado writer Laura Hendrie, and she gives a craft lecture on something she calls the Jaws-Of-Life character, the person who sweeps in and pulls your protagonist from the burning car just when it seems all hope is lost. Kae Penner Howell was my Jaws-Of-Life character that weekend. She came just when all my intrinsic strength and broad-minded philosophy about the cycle of life was about to fail me. She drove ten hours in a Prius on black ice to sleep on a hard wooden porch in a poorly rated sleeping bag with Fenton and me on his last night on earth.

I didn't want to go to sleep because the hours were short now and I didn't want to miss a minute. After we had been quiet a while, a coyote barked and another howled back from a greater distance. Before long and for the last time, Fenton joined their song.

A few hours later, when it was barely getting light, I lay nose to nose with him and petted his perfect ears and said, outloud, "You did such a good job, Fenton. You did such a good job taking care of me." He looked right at me, right into me. He wanted me to know he knew what I was saying. "And I think you already know this," I said, "but you don't have to be afraid." I didn't know where those words came from—if it were me getting the shot in the morning, I sure as hell would be afraid—but I knew when I said them they were the most important ones. In the gathering light he looked in my eyes not with fear exactly, but urgency. He said, *now it's my turn to trust you* and I said, *you can.*

An owl hooted, some geese honked, and Kae stirred in her sleeping bag. One of the lambs started baa-ing, Queeny, probably, the one with the higher voice. I heard Roany nicker softly, heard him walk around on the crunching snow. Somewhere in the distance, the sound of a woodpecker. All the sounds the ranch makes every morning.

Doc Howard came at ten am, through the snow, to give Fenton the shot. Doc is getting older and had told me he would be sending his granddaughter in his place, and I didn't protest, though I know he heard the disappointment and fear in my silence, so I was unsurprised and very grateful to see his small grey head behind the wheel. When I saw he did not have the sedative most vets give initially, before they give the drug that stops the heart, he again heard my unasked question. Doc said, "What's in this syringe is the world's biggest sedative. I don't like to mess around with lots of reactive drugs." Fenton was calm—almost smiling—for the very few minutes it took to put him to sleep forever. I believe he knew what was happening. I believe he was ready to put his head down on my lap one last time.

Everybody cried, even sweet Jay, Doc's brand new vet tech who had only met Fenton a couple of times. When I found my voice again, I told Doc the story about Jerry and the steaks, and he said, "Pam, it turns out there are a lot of really good people in the world."

After we loaded Fenton's body into Doc's truck to be taken to the morgue for cremation, Kae and Linda and I took a pasture walk in his honor. A couple of inches of snow covered the ground, and the Rocky Mountain bluebirds who had returned recently hoping for better weather were almost too beautiful against the freshly whitened pasture to bear. The sun came out, and we fed all the equines apples and carrots from our hands.

Eight hours later I found myself back in the Denver airport which was full of opportunities to do the things I hadn't found the time or the wherewithal to do all weekend: drink water, go to the bathroom, eat food. My plane was delayed two hours, and the corn chowder at Elway's Bar tasted miraculous. I was riding on something I recognized as "having lived through the thing you thought you might not live through" adrenaline. I marveled at all the people around me who weren't grieving, who had had a normal weekend with their families at home. I wasn't sleepy exactly. It was more like the insides of my eyes had been scoured with a Brillo pad.

Fenton the human sent me a text saying Fenton the canine loved and was loved all his life, and there is no condition in all our living and dying that could be more satisfying. Months later he would write Fenton a eulogy that quoted both Thomas Merton (*What we have to be is what we are*) and Whitman (*Life is the little left over from the dying*), and saying, "Fenton the canine, was a teacher . . . he taught through the simple fact of being who he is, who he was. . . . In the losses lie the lessons. . . . if we would only embrace death as another aspect of life—if we would let the animals teach us how to live and how to die—we might just treat each other and our animals better than we do."

As I waited for my plane I found myself thinking back, as I had many times that weekend, to Jerry at the Whole Foods pulling that steak off the top of the pile. He might have thought what he did was a small thing—though the price of those dry-aged steaks make it at least a medium thing, even by the most objective measure—but the relative magnitude of his kindness to me, at that moment, was frankly immeasurable—and I held onto it all weekend, and for the weeks of grief to come.

2   Back in 2000, to help pay for the ranch, I took a teaching job at UC Davis, requiring me to be there for two ten-week quarters each year. I chose spring and fall, because summers are glorious in the high country and miserable in Davis, and because farm animals die most often in winter. I hired a series

of house-sitters to tend the ranch while I was gone, often former students who needed a place to finish a book. Twice yearly I'd trade my down, fleece and Xtra Tuffs for corduroy and linen. Twice yearly, I became a teacher who rode her bright yellow bike to school, who formulated sentences containing phrases like "contemporary fabulism" and "Paul Celoyn-esque," who had regular meetings with the Dean and the Provost, and who usually brushed her hair for them. I read my colleagues' books on *Noir Cinema in a Post Colonial Age* and *Situatedness* and spent a fair amount of time apologizing for my 4-Runner and the percentage of my clothes bearing sports logos.

In Creede, there is no movie theater and no drug store and no one who would ever use a phase like "Paul Ceylon-esque." In Creede I talk to my neighbors about shrinking water tables and bingo at the Elks on Saturday night. When I go to the Monte Vista Co-Op to buy sealant to shoot into the water trough, and mineral licks, and big tubes of Ivermectin horse wormer and Carhartt overalls, I notice how different it is from the Davis Co-Op where I buy organic turmeric and homeopathic allergy medicine, and where people take their groceries home in environmentally friendly macramé nets. To the people in Creede I am intelligent, suspiciously sophisticated, and elitist to the point of being absurd. To the people at UC Davis I am quaint, a little slow on the uptake, and far too earnest to even believe.

In Creede, people believe in hard work, the restorative power of nature, and, in many cases, God. What stands in place of belief within UC Davis English is something you might identify as extreme verbal agility and analytics. God has been replaced by literary theory, of course, which has rolled all the way over, in the seventeen years I have taught there, from Deconstruction to Marxism with brief side trips into Feminism and the Post Colonial. In Creede there is no need for literary theory of any kind because there is such an overabundance of things that are actual. Cold, for instance, sometimes minus fifty degrees of it, and wind and drought, and wildfires that can chew up ten thousand acres in a day.

When I began teaching at UC Davis, it was still the home of the poet Gary Snyder. It was then, and still is, one of the finest environmental literature departments around. But times change, and over the years the talk has changed from riprap and plate tectonics to cyberspace as environment, Prius commercials as representations of nature, the suburban lawn as (and here I quote) "a poetic figure for a space, or spacing, around or under figurality—The lawn therefore a figure for what is excluded in the idea of figure itself—the very substance and/as dimension in which figurality can emerge in itself." [Quote by Timothy Morton, "Wordsworth Digs the Lawn," *European Romantic Review* 15, no.2 (June 2004): 318.]

My colleagues are brilliant, and so is their research, which proves to us, mostly, our own absurdity—tending our lawns, saving the earth with our Prius—the hollow chuckle aimed at ourselves. Departmental lectures focus on global systems and global currencies—the yen and the yuan hot topics in recent years. Last winter, a colleague taught a class in something called "distant reading." Because I have spent half my life teaching *close* reading, when the grad students first told me about it, I thought it was a joke. But distant reading, according to the *New York Times* is "understanding literature not by studying particular texts but by aggregating and analyzing massive amounts of data."

"It's not actually done by people," my student Becca told me. "You take a body of literature, say, all the books set in Paris from 1490 to 1940, plug them into a computer, and the computer can tell you how many mentions of the Pont Neuf there were." It was, I understood, an attempt to repurpose literature. As if all beings are best understood only in terms of their aggregate, as if by making things less particular, one made them more powerful or clear.

I thought about the books that had shaped my sensibility as a young writer: *A Pilgrim at Tinker Creek, Silent Spring, Sand County Almanac, Refuge, A River Runs Through It, In Patagonia* and *Desert Solitaire*. When I asked my classes, as I did each quarter, how many people had ever spent a night sleeping in the wilderness there were diminishing numbers of hands these days, usually only one, or zero. For the first time in my teaching life I was finding myself standing in front of a room full of students for whom the words *elk, granite* and *bristlecone pine* conjured exactly nothing. Was it feasible, or even sane, anymore, to write unironic, non-dystopian books about the natural world?

One answer, of course, was no. My colleagues are realists. They understand as far as the earth is concerned, we are way past game over. In recent years, our government has launched what Robert Redford and others have called the most sweeping legislative attack on our environment ever. The earth is lost, and all that's left is to study the simulacrums, the Man Versus Wild video games and *Survivor*. To write a poem about the loveliness of a newly leafed out aspen grove or a hot August wind sweeping across prairie grass or the smell of the air after a three-day rain in the maple forest might be, at best so unconscionably naive, and at worst so much part of the problem, we might as well drive a Hummer and start voting Republican. If we stand back for just a moment and think about what effort it has actually taken to destroy a whole planet that hadn't even been correctly mapped a couple of hundred years ago, it really staggers the imagination. And now, as we head for the cliff, foot heavy on the throttle, doesn't it seem pointless to write a poem about the essence of a tree? Maybe. But then again, maybe not. Maybe this is the best time there has ever been to write unironic poems about nature.

I have spent most of my life walking in nature, but for the last twelve months, I have been walking five miles a day, minimum, wherever I am, urban or rural, and can attest to the magnitude of the natural beauty that is left. Beauty worth seeing, worth singing, worth saving, whatever that word can mean now. There is beauty in a desert, even one that is expanding. There is beauty in the ocean, even one that is on the rise.

And even if the jig is up, even if it is really game over, what better time to sing about the earth than when it is critically, even fatally wounded at our hands. Aren't we more complex, more interesting, more multifaceted people if we do? What good has the hollow chuckle ever done anyone? Do we really keep ourselves from being hurt when we sneer instead of sob?

If we pretend not to see the tenuous beauty that is still all around us, will it keep our hearts from breaking as we watch another mountain be clear cut, as we watch North Dakota, as beautiful a state as there ever was, be poisoned for all time by fracturing? If we abandon all hope right now, does that in some way protect us from some bigger pain later? If we never go for a walk in the beetle-killed forest, if we don't take a swim the algae-choked ocean, if we lock grandmother in a room for the last ten years of her life so we can practice and somehow accomplish the survival of her loss in advance, in what ways does it make our lives easier? In what ways does it impoverish us?

We are all dying, and because of us, so is the earth. That's the most terrible, the most painful in my entire repertoire of self-torturing thoughts. But it isn't dead yet and neither are we. Are we going to drop the earth off at the vet, say goodbye at the door, and leave her to die in the hands of strangers? We can decide, even now, not to turn our backs on her in her illness, we can still decide not to let her die alone.

3 I have always believed that if I pay strict attention while I am out in the physical world—and for me that often means the natural world—the physical world will give me everything I need to tell my stories. As I move through the world, I wait to feel something I call a glimmer, a vibration, a little charge of resonance that says, "Hey writer, look over here." I feel it deep in my chest, this buzzing that lets me know this thing I am seeing/hearing/smelling/tasting on the outside is going to help me unlock some part of a story I have on the inside. I keep an ongoing record of these glimmers, writing down not my interpretation of them, not my imagined connection to them, not an emotional contextualization of them, but just the thing itself. Get in, get it down, get out and move on to the next glimmer. Then, when I have some time to write, I read through the glimmer files in my computer and try to find a handful that seem like they will stick together, that when placed in proximity with each other will create a kind of electricity.

I try to keep my big analytical brain out of this process as much as possible, because I believe my analytical brain at best only knows part of the story and at worst is a big fat liar. I believe—like religion—that the glimmer, the metaphor, if you will, knows a great deal more than I do. And if I stay out of its way, it will reveal itself to me. I will become not so much its keeper as its conduit, and I will pass its wisdom on to the reader, without actually getting in its way.

In addition to being my method, the way I have written every single thing I have written, it is also the primary way I worship, the way I kneel down and kiss the earth.

4   On Memorial Day weekend, 2015, I drove the dogs back to the ranch after ten weeks in California. They were good sports about our time in Davis but there was no mistaking the smile on their dog faces when we crested the top of Donner Pass and got back over to the leash-less side of the Sierras. We stopped every four hours for walks along forest service roads or multi-use trails all the way across Nevada and Utah, but nothing is better than the first pasture walk back at the ranch.

On Sunday morning, we did what we call the large pasture loop, out to the back of my hundred and twenty acres and then over the style into the national forest, up Red Mountain Creek and across one edge of my neighbor's twelve thousand acres, and then back down alongside the wetland and back over my fence again. It was me, William, Olivia, the pup, and the writer Josh Weil who would be watching the ranch for the next several weeks while I went off teaching in Vermont, Marin County and France.

We were nearly back to my fence line when we heard a high pitched cry, which I first thought was a red tail hawk, until it cried a few more times and I realized William had found himself a baby elk. We ran up the hill, called off William, and watched as the calf took a few sturdy steps and then settled back into the underbrush where she had been hiding. Satisfied she was unhurt, we went another 100 yards down the hill only to find a dead cow elk, the blood in the cavity still wet where the coyotes had pulled the guts out.

I tried to make the hole in the neck look like something other than an entry wound—the tooth of a coyote perhaps or the peck of the little known round-beaked vulture. I did not want to believe one of my neighbors would shoot a cow, illegally, at the peak of calving season, right here at the edge of my property where my horses spend summer nights grazing the edges of the wetland. I didn't want to think anyone would shoot an animal for practice, for pleasure, and then leave the meat to spoil.

"That baby doesn't have a chance," Josh said, as we stared down into the cow's pecked out eye, as we kicked at the wet grass that had been pulled out of her stomach. "It's probably starving already."

We both knew the rule of thumb was to leave abandoned calves alone; we also knew we might be in the presence of an exception. Those unspeakably long legs, those airbrushed spots, the deep brown eyes, and slightly pugged-up nose.

"I wish we hadn't seen the cow," I said, stupidly.

"I do too," Josh said, "but we did."

We were both thinking of the two rejected domestic lambs my previous house-sitter had been feeding, and the mudroom full of milk replacer. We were both looking at the sky, which had begun serving up one of Colorado's famous May blizzards: the temperature was dropping, the snow was sticking, and the wind was starting to howl.

"Let's take the dogs home," I said, "and heat up some milk and bring her a bottle. If she is still here when we get back, if she lets us approach her, maybe you carry her back to the barn."

We took our time getting the bottle. If her mother was still alive we wanted to give her plenty of space to react to the distress cries once we were out of there. We drove the 4-Runner around to the closest road access, so Josh would have to carry her 300 yards instead of 3000. We found her easily, and she blinked up at us sweetly, apparently unafraid. Maybe she was already too weak from hunger to save, I thought, and yet she had jumped right up to get away from William.

I sat down beside her and offered the bottle. She wasn't too keen at first, but when I gave up and drew it back across my chest she stretched herself across my lap to give it another sniff and chew a little on the nipple. She'd only take a little at a time but before long we'd gotten about a cup down her. She put her head in my lap and started to go to sleep. Josh said it might be a good time to try to transport her.

She did not love being carried. She wiggled and squeaked like she had when William had found her, and I prayed a giant elk cow would come crashing through the trees to fight us for her, but the woods were quiet and Josh held on tight and once we got to the 4-Runner she curled up in the dog bed in the back like she had been doing it all her life. Back home, Josh carried her the short distance to the barn, where we made a bed of straw for her, which she rejected in favor of the dirt floor, and I went inside to heat some more milk. That time she drank almost two cups. She shivered in the cold, and I rubbed her warm with my jacket. It was at that point Josh named her Willa.

The Internet said it wasn't uncommon for cow elk to leave their babies for several hours, because the babies could not keep up with the herd at the pace of their daily grazing. It said the calves were scentless, and would not attract predators, and the herd would come back and pick them up around dusk.

"If the dead cow isn't her mother," I said to Josh, "we may have just done a really bad thing." But it was snowing in earnest now, the wind screaming, and mistake or not, Willa was warm and dry in the barn.

I did what I always do in Creede when I don't know what to do and that's call Doc Howard. He said there was a sanctuary near Del Norte that would take her and raise her. He told me to call Brent, the wildlife officer, and that Brent would come get her, take her to the sanctuary, and while he was at it investigate the shooting. He said, "There are several other things you could do Pam, but not without being in violation of all kinds of laws."

I knew everybody had gotten freaked out about elk since chronic wasting disease became a thing in Colorado, but I also knew we had never had a case of it in Mineral County and they checked every elk the hunters took out. Still, I didn't really want to raise an elk baby with a bottle. What I wanted was for some yahoo not to have shot her mother. The website said to feed your orphaned elk four cups every four hours, so I left Brent a message and went out with more warm milk. This time she was interested and drank with less coaxing. She followed me around the stall, and when I would sit down in the straw with her, she would touch her nose to my face and hair.

Josh and I spent another hour with her, watching her walk around on her long long legs, greeting her when she wanted to make contact, feeling what it was like to be in her presence—which had a mystical quality to it, a visitation from some other-worldly being. So calm, she was, so delicate and full of light.

"Now, Pam, I'm going to need you to trust me a little bit," Brent said on the phone, and because of the tone in his voice when he said it, I did. "The sanctuary in Del Norte won't take elk anymore because of chronic wasting. There's a place in Westcliffe I might get to take her, but her best chance at the life she is meant to have is if you put her back out there, exactly where you found her. There's a good chance the herd will come pick her back up."

"Even if the dead one is her mother?"

"Even if," he said. "If the herd has another cow nursing, she'll probably be okay. I'll come up at seven in the morning and if she's still there I'll put her in a kennel and take her to Westcliffe."

It's hard to put a week-old elk calf back in the woods at sunset within a hundred yards of a ripped-open elk carcass the coyotes already know about, but by the time we talked ourselves into it, I had gotten two more cups of milk down her, it had stopped snowing, and the last sun of the day was warming things up a bit. Josh carried her back to the 4-Runner, we drove her around to the back fence and Josh carried her, kicking squeaking, back to the exact tree where William had found her. We didn't know what we were going to do if she followed us, but she didn't. She curled back in right where her mother had put her, and waited, we hoped, for the herd to come at dusk.

"What a story she'll have to tell her friends," I tried, as we turned our backs on her.

"Oh, she just thinks this is what happens to everybody," Josh said. "On the seventh day of being an elk you get to ride in the back of a car."

The next morning, I had to leave for the airport at four-thirty, and the air was clear and full of stars and twenty-nine degrees on my car thermometer. I said another prayer the herd had come back for Willa, that her mother had not been the shot one, and nobody minded she smelled a little like humans and the back of a 4-Runner usually occupied by Irish Wolfhounds. "We might have messed up," I said, to whoever I thought might be listening at that hour—some genderless Druidic earth power, I supposed, perhaps the mountain itself—"but we talked it out every step and tried to make the best decision."

I watched seven come and go as I drove farther away from Creede and closer to the Denver airport. I knew news wouldn't likely come until nine, but every minute after seven was torture. Finding her dead would have been the fastest outcome; loading her into the kennel and sending her off with Brent the next fastest after that. Searching the woods for her would take the longest. It was hard to even know what to hope for.

Finally, when I was sitting at gate B23, Josh called. The cow had been shot; that was certain. They had looked long and hard for Willa and found no sign of her. They had also looked up and down the road for a shell casing to help identify the poacher and had also not found one of those. Brent would go up to Spar City and ask around, but he wasn't hopeful he would find out anything more.

I have decent intuitive skills, which have improved with the onset of menopause, so I tried to quiet my mind to get a sense of Willa. For whatever it is worth, she did not feel dead to me. I know how potentially self-deceiving that sounds. But she was, among other things, a magical being. Josh and I gave her up to the mountain, and I believe the mountain took care of her.

5   It is hard to be ironic about a dying dog. It is hard to be ironic about an elk calf when her nose is touching your face. It is hard to be ironic when the young writer who tends your house and cuddles your dogs and who you know loves the earth with the same passion you do is walking behind you down a dirt trail with thirty-three pounds of baby elk in his arms. It is hard to be ironic when your pasture erupts after an unexpected May blizzard into a blanket of wild iris. It is hard to be ironic when the osprey who returns to your ranch every summer makes his first lazy circle around the peak of your barn.

Last January, I was speaking with an environmental scientist who said he was extremely pessimistic about the future of the earth in the hundred-year frame, but optimistic about it in the five-hundred-year frame. There will be very few people here, he said, earnestly, but the ones who are here will have learned a lot. He also said the carbon driven period will be looked at as the most barbaric, most irresponsible period in the history of the world.

There are times when I understand all too well what my colleagues in Davis are trying to protect themselves from. Times when seeing the world's bright beauty is almost more than I can bear, when my mind is running the grim numbers the scientists have given us right alongside. And it is also true, had I never laid eyes on Willa, I would not have spent five sleep-deprived hours weeping—often sobbing—in the car that morning on the way to DIA. If I hadn't slept those three nights on the porch with Fenton, it would have been three fewer nights of my life spent with an actively breaking heart. But a broken heart—God knows, I have found—doesn't actually kill you. And irony and disinterest are false protections, ones that won't serve us, or the earth, in the end.

For now, I want to sit vigil with the earth the same way I did with Fenton. I want to write unironic odes to her beauty, which is still potent, if not completely intact. The language of the wilderness is the most beautiful language we have and it is our job to sing it, until and even after it is gone, no matter how much it hurts. If we don't, we are left with only a hollow chuckle, and our big brains who made this mess, our big brains that stopped believing a long time ago in beauty, in everything, in anything.

What I want to say to my colleagues is that the earth doesn't know how not to be beautiful. Yes, the destruction, yes, the inevitability, but honestly, Doctor Distant Reader, when was the last time you actually slept on the ground?

How will we sing when Miami goes underwater, when the raft of garbage in the ocean gets as big as Texas, when the only remaining Polar Bear draws his last breath, when fracking, when Keystone, when Inhofe...? I don't know. And I imagine sometimes, often, we will get it wrong. But I'm not celebrating the earth because I am an optimist—though I am an optimist. I am celebrating because this magnificent rock we live on demands celebration. I am celebrating because how in the face of this earth could I not?

Notice how skillfully Houston braids together multiple narrative strands. She has the talent to have written an individual essay on any of the topics she explores: letting go of a beloved pet; the power of friendship; the difficulty of asking for help; the differences between her life in Mineral County, Colorado, as a rancher, versus professor at UC Davis (to name a few).

To add another metaphor to that of the braid, let's talk about bread. The fermentation of yeast in bread dough can produce a rich, nutty, and complex flavor that is very different from its basic ingredients of flour, water, and yeast. Baking it creates an altogether different texture.

In the best of them, something similar happens when the author braids an essay. In this piece, Houston gives her readers something altogether different from a single narrative—different, too, from several narratives stacked back-to-back. Braiding an essay involves the writing equivalent of mixing and baking, so what comes out is an entirely new thing. By combining the threads, she creates something *unlike* any of the parts that make it whole.

The title of her piece clues the reader to her central concern. Houston questions the usefulness (or lack thereof) of irony. Instead of following the subject of the title head-on, she starts the essay with a description of her wolfhound Fenton Johnson at the end of his life. In doing so, the reader forgets about irony. Subtopics are introduced, including the kindness of strangers (the butcher), and the intelligence and companionship offered by nonhuman animals.

As the essay continues, we learn a lot about the writer, her life, her friendships, and her struggles. We barely think about irony. But just as the seemingly tangential thread is stretched so far it's about to break, the essay returns to its main subject.

Vivian Gornick says a great essay has a "situation" and a "story." Perhaps a great braided essay has multiple "situations." If it were visual art, it would be an assemblage or collage rather than a still life of a single object.

Braided essays frequently employ a nonlinear structure, where the different threads are not presented chronologically but are instead interwoven in a way that creates connections and resonances between them. "What Has Irony Done for Us Lately" uses this structure to its advantage, allowing the various narratives to inform and enhance each other.

A well-executed braided essay isn't as simple as portraying several situations. It must maintain cohesion and achieve unity. With her skillful transitions, Houston's essay achieves this consistency through the seemingly inconsistent.

Have you ever had something to tell, but before you get to it, you had to set it up by telling the listener "something else"? And to make that "something else" make sense, you had to talk about a third thing? For example: "I'll tell you about why I'm vegetarian. But first I must tell you about the first time I went to Mallorca, Spain. But before that, I must tell you about enduring the winter every year as a kid, growing up in my hometown of Chicago. Oh yeah. Just before I stopped eating meat, I read a book on dinosaurs. Gotta tell you about the chapter that talked about . . ."

If you have material you care about that comes to you in this way, the braided essay may be a perfect container.

Write Now

1. Choose a very general category. Examples: friendship; the human/non-human animal bond; how war is ultimately as destructive for the so-called winners as the losers; meaningful coincidences.
2. Try to list five widely different times/places/scenes/experiences that would fall under that category. Example: Under the category friendship:

i. My first friend, or friends, a pair of imaginary paternal twins named Dangie and Fonga. Playing with them is my earliest memory.

ii. My dog Joe, a ginger mutt who followed me to school and waited outside my kindergarten classroom, then walked me home.

iii. The food server Rhonda who took me under her wing when I was a twelve-year-old dishwasher. She used to give me rides home in her convertible Mustang. I'd steer from the passenger side as she did her lipliner in the rearview.

iv. My sister-in-law, whom I met at age thirty and who belongs to a religion that regularly discriminates against people like me.

v. My eighty-year-old neighbor, Tom, who invited me to join a two-person book club with him when he was sixty.

6. Write about each of your five times/places/scenes/experiences for two minutes each, in the order in which they're listed. Then do three minutes each, stopping mid-sentence and switching to the next scene as soon as the timer goes off. Then four minutes. Then five.

7. Put away the results of your experiment. Later, reread. See if you can use what you've found to start a braided essay.

Reviewing the Forms of Creative Nonfiction

Now that we've examined why writers might use the container of creative nonfiction for their material, let's look at the various forms the genre itself can take.

Each creative nonfiction subgenre has its own unique characteristics that we can learn from and borrow from.

In this section, we won't do exercises, but keep each of these categories in mind as future containers for the material you've generated in previous experiments.

Also, super important to remember: There are overlaps between these categories, and the same piece of nonfiction may be categorized in a variety of different ways by different readers. What's more, each of us is free to combine, add, subtract, reduce, and push to create new categories or new ways to look at the existing ones.

The following definitions aren't meant to bind you. They're meant to give you a possible direction for when you're ready to use a container to organize your free write material.

This is probably the most popular form that creative nonfiction takes. Memoirs are recollections of the writer's life (or specific parts of the writer's life). There can be a critical central theme, but there doesn't have to be. Most memoirs are book length and can take years to write.

Sometimes the facts in a memoir are so unusual, or even shocking, that they carry the book. The connective tissue is important, of course, but the real draw of the memoir is its storyline.

The Escape Artist, by Helen Fremont, is about a Catholic family that turned out not to be Catholic, but Jewish holocaust survivors. Her story contains extreme behaviors and emotions based on facts that seem shocking. Here's an excerpt.

The Escape Artist (excerpt)
Helen Fremont

Sisters are a setup. Shot from the same cannon, you're sent on a blind date for the rest of your lives.

My sister, Lara, and I had a script we were supposed to follow. My mother and her sister, Zosia, had written it, and they were our role models, which is pretty scary when you consider what they'd been through. During the war, Zosia had saved my mother's life. Or maybe it was the other way around. The stories were twisted and my mother and aunt were bound together in ways that Lara and I didn't begin to understand, but we did our best to follow for most of our lives. Although Zosia lived in Italy and we lived in upstate New York, Mom and Zosia's love was formidable, the stuff of legend, built on a mythic past. One day, they told us, my sister and I would have what they had.

But unlike our mother and aunt, Lara and I didn't have any real wars to test our bond; we had to make up our own. From our earliest years, we liked to go to extremes with each other. We tested our limits, pushed ourselves and each other a little further, a little harder, to see how much we could take. To prove how much we loved each other. Usually these tests of strength took place in the wilderness, far from the comforts and complications of our everyday lives.

In 1990, when I was thirty-three and Lara was thirty-six, we went ski mountaineering in the remote Battle Range of British Columbia. A helicopter dropped us off on a mountain ridge above a wall of ice. The pilot would come back for our group of ten a week later, weather permitting.

Forty feet of snow had fallen in the last three months and they'd had to dig down to find the entrance to the hut we would use as our base. We hustled to get our gear inside and went back out for avalanche practice. We were going to learn how to save each other's lives. After clipping on our skis, Lara and I followed our guide into an unannounced blizzard. The storm had come out of nowhere and we weren't going far—just far enough to feel like an avalanche was possible. Then we began the drill, making an imaginary grid in the snow and finding the buried "victim" using our transceivers. The guide timed us. It was hard to see in the swirling snow, and we struggled against the wind, holding the transceivers in front of us as we walked back and forth in the deep powder trying to locate the signal. We weren't very good at search and rescue, and I could see that the real purpose of the drill was to teach us that we would never survive an avalanche. The guide had come through a few, but despite our years of exercising poor judgment in the mountains, Laura and I had never tripped one.

It was Lara who had talked me into this trip, and I was a little anxious about skinning up a few thousand vertical feet each day. The next morning under clear skies we trekked single file up a steep ravine, skirting a series of heart-stopping crevasses—freakish blue gashes in the snow that dropped hundreds of yards into darkness. Sweat poured from our faces. Not a sound—just the whistle and whip of the wind, the huff of our breathing, and the hushed swish of our skis moving through deep powder, like silencers on our feet.

I liked to follow behind Lara, and imagined that our legs were connected by the same body. When she pushed her right leg forward, mine slid forward automatically, as if invisible strings attached my ski boot to hers. I could sink into her rhythm without losing any of my own energy; I could syphon off her. You can really lose yourself like this. Your *self* actually disappears. Your body is there, a huffing, puffing, pounded machine that slides along with your sister's. But your mind stretches out and your spirit soars, and there is nothing that binds you to the earth. A giddy feeling of floating high above the thousands of miles of mountains around you, and for a moment you feel as if you have touched God, that you dwell in the bodiless land of the spirit, whether it's the wind on your cheek or the blue in the sky or the sharp knives of the peaks in the distance, surrounded by emptiness and snow and the simplest of elements. It's a kind of rapture, a sort of passionate love affair with the universe.

This was the heady bond Lara and I had shared since childhood. You have to climb to the end of the earth because the middle of your life is too weighed down by trinkets of the mundane, the alarm clock with its rigid hands, the same twelve numbers arranged in the same circle, the same wheels that carry you to this street or that; to this desk or that; to this bed or that. I had found my true north. It was the world away from everything. Lara had brought me here, above the trees, above life. It was as cool and creamy and thrilling as death itself.

Back then, there was no doubt that if an avalanche had come for my sister, I'd have leaped in front of it and pushed her to safety. But that was long ago.

Soon enough, readers of *The Escape Artist* will be shown how the narrator and her sister Lara compare to their mother and their aunt Zosia. They'll learn of the circumstances that led to their shifting, often volatile relationship: The events that bonded them (like the opening scene, which you just read) along with their shocking discovery that their parents weren't in fact Catholics, as they'd claimed, but Jewish survivors of the holocaust.

In this small excerpt, you can see how the writer is expertly using all the tools we've been mentioning: particular details and imagery, poetic language, and backstory. But the craft tool that's most inspiring to us is also the hardest one to describe: voice. It starts with the very first paragraph: "Sisters are a setup. Shot from the same cannon, you're sent on a blind date for the rest of your lives."

The idea of voice is as important in memoir as it is in fiction. We suggest that you review our discussion of voice from that chapter, where we quote Mary Karr, a memoirist and author of *The Art of Memoir*, as saying, "Each great memoir lives or dies based 100 percent on voice." Karr emphasizes the importance of authenticity and honesty in memoir writing, encouraging writers to find and embrace what makes them unique.

Readers are skilled at discerning falsehoods. The writer's honesty is crucial even when reporting difficult or painful experiences. Specificity helps in rendering sensory descriptions. Dialogue isn't presented as if "verbatim," but as a way to capture essential truths while paying attention to speech patterns to convey personality and relationships effectively. Writers are encouraged to exhibit emotional honesty when rendering the complex terrain of human emotion. They are cautioned against idealizing themselves (and others) in early drafts, urging them to confront emotionally difficult places for a genuine memoir.

Mieke Eerkens wrote a book titled *All Ships Follow Me*. The subtitle illuminates a hybrid angle: *A Family Memoir of War Across Three Continents*. Here's the jacket copy:

> An engrossing, epic saga of one family's experiences on both sides of WWII, *All Ships Follow Me* questions our common narrative of the conflict and our stark notions of victim and perpetrator, while tracing the lasting effects of war through several generations.
>
> In March 1942, Mieke Eerkens' father was a ten-year-old boy living in the Dutch East Indies. When the Japanese invaded the island he, his family, and one hundred thousand other Dutch civilians were interned in a concentration camp and forced into hard labor for three years. After the Japanese surrendered, Mieke's father and his family were set free in a country that plunged immediately into civil war.
>
> Across the globe in the Netherlands, police carried a crying five-year-old girl out of her home at war's end, abandoned and ostracized as a daughter of Nazi sympathizers. This was Mieke's mother. She would be left on the street in front of her sealed home as her parents were taken away and imprisoned in the same camps where the country's Jews had recently been held. Many years later, Mieke's parents met, got married, and moved to California, where she and her siblings were born. While her parents lived far from the events of their past, the effects of the war would continue to be felt in their daily lives and in the lives of their children.
>
> *All Ships Follow Me* moves from Indonesia to the Netherlands to the United States, and spans generations, as Mieke recounts her parents' lives during and just after the war, and travels with them in the present day to the sites of their childhood in an attempt to understand their experiences and how it formed them. *All Ships Follow Me* is a deeply personal, sweeping saga of the wounds of war, and the way trauma can be passed down through generations.

Finding one's voice in memoir can take time and multiple revisions. We advise writers to be patient with the writing process and to revise and polish their work to refine their voice.

Humor is also important, even with (and perhaps especially with) the most difficult subject matter. Humor and raw honesty add up to rich storytelling, whether the facts are shocking or not. Humor is arguably most needed and effective when earned and authentically used along with what's most painful.

What if nothing shocking has happened to you? Does that exclude you from memoir?

No. In other memoirs, the facts are in themselves ordinary but the creative tissue makes them spectacular. It's the writer's particular interpretation of the facts—accompanied by the writer's voice—that makes us hungry to finish such books.

From Emma Forrest's *Your Voice in My Head*, we get an extraordinarily fresh voice talking about ordinary things and making them extraordinary:

Your Voice in My Head (excerpt)

Emma Forrest

A man hovers over me as I write. Every table in the Los Angeles café is taken.

"Are you leaving?"

My notebook, coffee and Dictaphone are spread out in front of me.

"No," I answer.

"I'll give you a thousand dollars to leave."

"OK," I say, as I pack up my things.

"What?"

"Sure. A thousand dollars. I'm leaving."

He looks at me like I'm mad and beats a hasty retreat. I meant it. He didn't mean it. My radar, after all these years of sanity, is still off when it comes to what people do or don't mean.

My mum calls my cell phone and I go outside to take it.

"How do you pronounce Tóibín," my mother asks me, "as in Colm Tóibín, the novelist?" This is our daily call, me in America, her in England, every day since I moved here at twenty-one. I'm thirty-two now, and she's seventy-one, though she sounds like she's seventeen.

"It's pronounced toe-bean. Like 'toe' and then 'bean'."

"That's what I feared," she says. She lets this marinate a moment. Then, "No. Not acceptable."

"But that's his name! That's how you say it."

"I can't be going around saying 'toe-bean'. It simply will not do."

"Why don't you just not say his name?"

"He's a popular writer."

"Read his books but don't talk about them."

"No,"—I can sense her shaking her head—"some situation will arise that requires me to say his name."

I think my mother has the sense of doom, and guilt about the sense of doom, of Jews her age who weren't directly touched by the Holocaust. When she was growing up in New York, the first bad thing that happened to her was that Irish children moved into the Jewish neighbourhood and stole her kazoo and her sailor hat. She was a fat little girl, guarding the cakes she had hidden in her sock drawer. What was a fat child in 1940s New York, without her kazoo?

The second bad thing was that her dad died and then, soon after, her mother, and she was only a teenager and she didn't know how to make toast. So, she got very thin—deliberately, not through lack of toast—and married a much older man. It didn't last. The best thing that happened was she fell in love with my dad.

Once, when Mum and her first husband had long since lost touch and I was new to mania, I tracked down an address for the man, whom I had only heard about, and sent him a letter asking him whether or not he was dead yet. Not to be mean, just curious.

Mum gets anxious very easily. Something that is a source of calm (she watches her cat as he laps the water bowl: "Good boy, Jojo! What a good boy!") can turn, like the weather (the cat keeps lapping; her smile fades: "Why are you drinking so much water, Jojo? What's the matter, Jojo? Are you sick?").

I talk to myself a lot because I've seen her talk to herself a lot, generally in the kitchen, where she's been overheard saying, with real enthusiasm:

"I'm feeling tremendously optimistic about gluten-free bread!"

And:

"I fear George Clooney's teeth may be his downfall."

I see my mum everywhere. From certain angles, the Brazilian super-model Gisele Bündchen has her face, and from other angles so does the black comedienne Wanda Sykes. I think all white people have a black doppelgänger and vice versa. My dad's black doppelgänger is the father in *The Fresh Prince of Bel-Air*. His Celtic doppelgänger is Sean Connery.

A lady came up to him at a hotel in Jamaica and said, "Last night we thought you were Sean Connery" and Dad said, "Last night I *was* Sean Connery." My dad seems to know everything, so I never use Google. I only use Dad. I email him a query and he figures it out, and then responds in the guise of the billionaire Google founders:

"London to Cardiff: is it expensive? How long is the trip?"

"2–3 hrs by train. Expensive if you don't book in advance.

xx Larry Page and Sergey Brin."

When I was fourteen and wanting to get out of gym class, Dad wrote the teacher a letter in the shape of a perfect triangle:

to

Miss

Jensen, please

do excuse Emma from

gym today as she is feeling

unwell. Kind regards, Jeffrey Forrest

He wrote it like that for nothing but his own delight, meticulous, making me late. When I handed it to her, Miss Jensen ripped it up, threw it on the floor and said she considered it a personal insult from my family.

He once got a credit card saying "Sir Jeffrey Forrest" because American Express was dumb enough to send him an application form with the statement "Print your name as you would wish it to appear."

The last forwarded flight details he sent me were:

Your special requests

SIR LOVELY JEFFREY FORREST   Requested Seat: 12J

MS GRUMPY JUDITH FORREST   Requested Seat: 12K

YOUR SPECIAL REQUESTS SPECIAL MEAL REQUESTED

SEAT

SIR LOVELY JEFFREY FORREST —   12J
MS GRUMPY JUDITH FORREST —   12K

> I asked if it was really wise to ticket himself and my mother like that, and he replied, as if it were out of his hands: "Under the new homeland security rules the ticketed names must be a combination of how they are printed in your passport and your likely appearance at check-in."

Emma Forrest's memoir *Your Voice in My Head* is another memoir that could be described as voice driven. Forrest employs a conversational tone. The book's structure is often fragmented, resembling a series of interconnected vignettes rather than a linear narrative. This fragmented style mirrors the author's state of mind as she grapples with mental health issues and her relationship with her therapist. It also reflects the way memories and experiences can be fragmented in real life.

In *Your Voice in My Head*, Forrest weaves personal reflection, texts from her dad, memories of her mom, and letters she wrote to her therapist. Forrest uses vivid and sensory descriptions to give life to her narrator's experiences and emotions.

In the excerpt we see humor everywhere. Is mental illness funny? No, it is not. Is anxiety? No. Readers come away with a real sense of the narrator's struggle and the struggle her mom endured as well. However, the ways in which serious conditions play out can *also* be funny:

> Mum gets anxious very easily. Something that is a source of calm (she watches her cat as he laps the water bowl: "Good boy, Jojo! What a good boy!") can turn, like the weather (the cat keeps lapping; her smile fades: "Why are you drinking so much water, Jojo? What's the matter, Jojo? Are you sick?").

The use of humor is one of the many ways the author explores complex and often painful emotions. Her willingness to be emotionally vulnerable makes it a powerful exploration of mental health. It's an intimate memoir that delves into her struggles with mental health and the transformative power of therapy. The author's formal choices contribute to the book's emotional resonance and its ability to connect with readers on a deep level.

Personal essays are about personal experiences. They offer the opportunity to create astounding, intimate, raw, and moving pieces based on incidents in real life. Or they can be an intensely personal take on an issue—say a political one—or even an abstract idea. Consider this essay by John Jeremiah Sullivan, originally published in *The Paris Review* and the winner of a Pushcart Prize and a National Magazine Award.

Mister Lytle
John Jeremiah Sullivan

When I was twenty years old, I became a kind of apprentice to a man named Andrew Lytle, whom pretty much no one apart from his negligibly less ancient sister, Polly, had addressed except as Mister Lytle in at least a decade. She called him Brother. Or *Brutha*—I don't suppose either of them had ever voiced a terminal *r*. His two grown daughters did call him Daddy. Certainly I never felt even the most obscure impulse to call him Andrew, or "old man," or any other familiarism, though he frequently gave me to know it would be all right if I were to call him *mon vieux*. He, for his part, called me boy, and beloved, and once, in a letter, "Breath of My Nostrils." He was about to turn ninety-two when I moved into his basement, and he had not yet quite reached ninety-three when they buried him the next winter, in a coffin I had helped to make—a cedar coffin, because it would smell good, he said. I wasn't that helpful. I sat up a couple of nights in a freezing, starkly lit workshop rubbing beeswax into the boards. The other, older men—we were four altogether—absorbedly sawed and planed. They chiseled dovetail joints. My experience in woodworking hadn't gone past feeding planks through a band saw for shop class, and there'd be no time to redo anything I might botch, so I followed instructions and with rags cut from an undershirt worked coats of wax into the cedar until its ashen whorls glowed purple, as if with remembered life.

The man overseeing this vigil was a luthier named Roehm whose house stood back in the woods on the edge of the plateau. He was about six and a half feet tall with floppy bangs and a deep, grizzled mustache. He wore huge glasses. I believe I have never seen a person more tense than Roehm was during those few days. The cedar was "green"—it hadn't been properly cured. He groaned that it wouldn't behave. On some level he must have resented the haste. Lytle had lain dying for weeks; he endured a series of disorienting pin strokes. By the end they were giving him less water than morphine. He kept saying, "Time to go home," which at first meant he wanted us to take him back to his house, his real house, that he was tired of the terrible simulacrum we'd smuggled him to, in his delirium. Later, as those fevers drew together into what seemed an unbearable clarity, like a blue flame behind the eyes, the phrase came to mean what one would assume.

He had a deathbed, in other words. He didn't go suddenly. Yet although his family and friends had known for years about his wish to lie in cedar, which required that a coffin be custom made, no one had so much as played with the question of who in those mountains could do such a thing or how much time the job would take. I don't hold it against them—against us—the avoidance of duty, owing as it did to fundamental incredulity. Lytle's whole existence had for so long been essentially posthumous, he'd never risk seeming so ridiculous as to go actually dying now. My grandfather had told me once that when *he'd* been at Sewanee, in the thirties, people had looked at Lytle as something of an old man, a full sixty years before I met him. And he nursed this impression, with his talk of coming "to live in the sense of eternity," and of the world he grew up in—Middle Tennessee at the crack of the twentieth century—having more in common with Europe in the Middle Ages than with the South he lived to see. All of his peers and enemies were dead. A middle daughter he had buried long before. His only wife had been dead for thirty-four years, and now Mister Lytle was dead, and we had no cedar coffin.

But someone knew Roehm, or knew about him; and it turned out Roehm knew Lytle's books; and when they told Roehm he'd have just a few days to finish the work, he set to, without hesitation and even with a certain impatience, as if he feared to displease some unforgiving master. I see him there in the little space, repeatedly microwaving Tupperware containers full of burnt black coffee and downing them like Coca-Colas. He loomed. He was so large there hardly seemed room for the rest of us, and already the coffin lid lay on sawhorses in the center of the floor, making us sidle along the walls. At least a couple of times a night Roehm, who was used to agonizing for months over tiny, delicate instruments, would suffer a collapse, would hunch on his stool and bury his face in his hands and bellow "It's all wrong!" into the mute of his palms. My friend Sanford and I stared on. But the fourth, smaller man, a person named Hal, who'd been staying upstairs with Lytle toward the end and acting as a nurse, he knew Roehm better—now that I think of it, Hal must have been the one to tell the family about him in the first place—and Hal would put his hands on Roehm's shoulders and whisper to him to be calm, remind him how everyone understood he'd been allowed too little time, that if he wanted we could take a break. Then Roehm would smoke. I remember he gripped each cigarette with two fingertips on top, snapping it in and out of his lips the way toughs in old movies do. Sanford and I sat outside in his truck with the heater on and drank vodka from a flask he'd brought, gazing on the shed with its small bright window, barely saying a word.

Weeks later he told me a story that Hal had told him, that at seven o'clock in the morning on the day of Lytle's funeral—which strangely Roehm did not attend—Hal woke to find Roehm sitting at the foot of his and his wife's bed, repeating the words "It works," apparently to himself. I never saw him again. The coffin was art. Hardly anyone got to see it. All through the service and down the street to the cemetery it wore a pall, and when people lined up at the graveside to take turns shoveling dirt back into the pit, the hexagonal lid—where inexplicably Roehm had found a spare hour to do scrollwork—grew invisible after just a few seconds.

There had been different boys living at Lytle's since not long after he lost his wife, maybe before—in any case it was a recognized if unofficial institution when I entered the college at seventeen. In former days these were mainly students whose writing showed promise, as judged by a certain well-loved, prematurely white-haired literature professor, himself a former protégé and all but a son during Lytle's long widowerhood. As years passed and Lytle declined, the arrangement came to be more about making sure someone was there all the time, someone to drive him and chop wood for him and hear him if he were to break a hip.

There were enough of us who saw it as a privilege, especially among the English majors. We were students at the University of the South, and Lytle was the South, the last Agrarian, the last of the famous "Twelve Southerners" behind *I'll Take My Stand*, a comrade to the Fugitive Poets, a friend since youth of Allen Tate and Robert Penn Warren; a mentor to Flannery O'Connor and James Dickey and Harry Crews and, as the editor of *The Sewanee Review* in the sixties, one of the first to publish Cormac McCarthy's fiction. Bear in mind that by the mid-nineties, when I knew him, the so-called Southern Renascence in letters had mostly dwindled to a tired professional regionalism. That Lytle hung on somehow, in however reduced a condition, represented a flaw in time, to be exploited.

Not everyone felt that way. I remember sitting on the floor one night with my freshman-year suitemate, a ninety-five-pound blond boy from Atlanta called Smitty who'd just spent a miserable four years at some private academy trying to convince the drama teacher to let them do a Beckett play. His best friend had been a boy they called Tweety Bird, whose voice resembled a tiny reed flute. When I met Smitty, I asked what music he liked, and he shot back, "*Trumpets.*" That night he went on about Lytle, what a grotesquerie and a fascist he was. "You know what Andrew Lytle said?" Smitty waggled his cigarette lighter. "Listen to this: 'Life is melodrama. Only art is real.'"

I nodded in anticipation.

"Don't you think that's *horrifying*?"

I didn't, though. Or I did and didn't care. Or I didn't know what I thought. I was under the tragic spell of the South, which you've either felt or haven't. In my case it was acute because, having grown up in Indiana with a Yankee father, a child exile from Kentucky roots of which I was overly proud, I'd long been aware of a nowhereness to my life. Others wouldn't have sensed it, wouldn't have minded. I felt it as a physical ache. Finally I was somewhere, there. The South… I loved it as only one who will always be outside it can. Merely to hear the word *Faulkner* at night brought gusty emotions. A few months after I'd arrived at the school, Shelby Foote came and read from his Civil War history. When he'd finished, a local geezer with long greasy white hair wearing a white suit with a cane stood up in the third row and asked if, in Foote's opinion, the South could have won, had such and such a general done such and such. Foote replied that the North had won "that war" with one hand behind its back. In the crowd there were gasps. It thrilled me that they cared. How could I help wondering about Lytle, out there beyond campus in his ancestral cabin, rocking before the blazing logs, drinking bourbon from heirloom silver cups and brooding on something Eudora Welty had said to him once. Whenever famous writers came to visit the school they'd ask to see him. He was from another world. I tried to read his novels, but my mind just ricocheted; they seemed impenetrably mannered. Even so, I hoped to be taken to meet him. One of my uncles had received such an invitation, in the seventies, and told me how the experience changed him, put him in touch with what's real.

The way it happened was so odd as to suggest either the involvement or the nonexistence of fate. I wasn't even a student at the time. I'd dropped out after my sophomore year, essentially in order to preempt failing out, and was living in Ireland with a friend, working in a restaurant and failing to save money. But before my departure certain things had taken place. I'd become friends with the man called Sanford, a puckish, unregenerate back-to-nature person nearing fifty, who lived alone, off the electric grid, on a nearby communal farm. His house was like something Jefferson could have invented. Spring water flowed down from an old dairy tank in a tower on top; the refrigerator had been retrofitted to work with propane canisters that he salvaged from trailers. He had first-generation solar panels on the roof, a dirt-walled root cellar, a woodstove. He showered in a waterfall. We had many memorable hallucinogenic times that did not help my grades. Sanford needed very little money, but that he made doing therapeutic massage in town, and one of his clients was none other than Andrew Lytle, who drove himself in once a week, in his yacht-sized chocolate Eldorado, sometimes in the right lane, sometimes the left, as he fancied. The cops all knew to follow him but would do so at a distance, purely to ensure he was safe. Often he arrived at Sanford's studio hours early, and anxiously waited in the car. He loved the feeling of human hands on his flesh, he said, and believed it was keeping him alive.

One day, during their session, Lytle mentioned that his current boy was about to be graduated. Sanford, who didn't know yet how badly I'd blown it at the school, or that I was leaving, told Lytle about me and gave him some stories I'd written. Or poems? Doubtless dreadful stuff—but perhaps it "showed promise." Toward the end of summer airmail letters started to flash in under the door of our hilltop apartment in Cork, their envelopes, I remember, still faintly curled from having been rolled through the heavy typewriter. The first one was dated, "Now that I have come to live in the sense of eternity, I rarely know the correct date, and the weather informs me of the day's advance, but I believe it is late August," and went on to say, "I'm presuming you will live with me here."

That's how it happened, he just asked. Actually, he didn't even ask. The fact that he was ignoring the proper channels eventually caused some awkwardness with the school. But at the time, none of that mattered. I felt an exhilaration, the unsettling thrum of a great man's regard, and somewhere behind that the distant onrushing of fame. His letters came once, then twice a week. They were brilliantly senile, moving in and out of coherence and between tenses, between centuries. Often his typos, his poor eyesight, would produce the finest sentences, as when he wrote the affectingly commaless "This is how I protest absolutely futilely." He told me I was a writer but that I had no idea what I was doing. "This is where the older artist comes in." He wrote about the Muse, how she tests us when we're young. As our tone grew more intimate, his grew more urgent too. I must come back soon. Who knew how much longer he'd live? "No man can forestall or evade what lies in wait." There were things he wanted to pass on, things that had taken him, he said, "too long to learn." Now he'd been surprised to discover a burst of intensity left. He said not to worry about the school. "College is perhaps not the best preparation for a writer." I'd live in the basement, a guest. We'd see to our work.

It took me several months to make it back, and he grew annoyed. When I finally let myself in through the front door, he didn't get up from his chair. His form sagged so exaggeratedly into the sofa, it was as if thieves had crept through and stolen his bones and left him there. He gestured at the smoky stone fireplace with its enormous black andirons and said, "Boy, I'm sorry the wood's so poor. I had no idea I'd be alive in November." He watched as though paralyzed while I worked at building back up the fire. He spoke only to critique my form. The heavier logs at the back, to project the heat. Not too much flame. "Young men always make that mistake." He asked me to pour him some whiskey and announced flatly his intention to nap. He lay back and draped across his eyes the velvet bag the bottle had come tied in, and I sat across from him for half an hour, forty minutes. At first he talked in his sleep, then to me—the pivots of his turn to consciousness were undetectably slight, with frequent slippages. His speech was full of mutterings, warnings. The artist's life is strewn with traps. Beware "the machinations of the enemy."

"Mr. Lytle," I whispered, "who is the enemy?"

He sat up. His unfocused eyes were an icy blue. "Why, boy," he said, "the *bourgeoisie*!" Then he peered at me for a second as if he'd forgotten who I was. "Of course," he said. "You're only a baby."

I'd poured myself two bourbons during nap time and felt them somewhat. He lifted his own cup and said, "Confusion to the enemy." We drank.

It was idyllic, where he lived, on the grounds of an old Chautauqua called the Assembly, one of those rustic resorts—deliberately placed up north, or at a higher altitude—which began as escapes from the plagues of yellow fever that used to harrow the mid-Southern states. Lytle could remember coming there as a child. An old judge, they said, had transported the cabin entire up from a cove somewhere in the nineteenth century. You could still see the logs in the walls, although otherwise the house had been made rather elegant over the years. The porch went all the way around. It was usually silent, except for the wind in the pines. Besides guests, you never saw anyone. A summer place, except Lytle didn't leave.

He slept in a wide carved bed in a corner room. His life was an incessant whispery passage on plush beige slippers from bed to sideboard to seat by the fire, tracing that perimeter, marking each line with light plantings of his cane. He'd sing to himself. The Appalachian one that goes, "A haunt can't haunt a haunt, my good old man." Or songs that he'd picked up in Paris at my age or younger—"Sous les Ponts de Paris" and "Les Chevaliers de la Table Ronde." His French was superb, but his accent in English was best— that extinct mid-Southern, land-grant pioneer speech, with its tinges of the abandoned Celtic urban Northeast ("boyned" for burned) and its raw gentility.

From downstairs I could hear him move and knew where he was in the house at all times. My apartment had once been the kitchen—servants went up and down the back steps. The floor was all bare stone, and damp. And never really warm, until overnight it became unbearably humid. Cave crickets popped around as you tried to sleep, touching down with little clicks. Lots of mornings I woke with him standing over me, cane in one hand, coffee in the other, and he'd say, "Well, my lord, shall we rise and entreat Her Ladyship?" Her ladyship was the Muse. He had all manner of greetings.

For half a year we worked steadily, during his window of greatest coherence, late morning to early afternoon. We read Flaubert, Joyce, a little James, the more famous Russians, all the books he'd written about as an essayist. He tried to make me read Jung. He chopped at my stories till nothing was left but the endings, which he claimed to admire. A too-easy eloquence, was his overall diagnosis. I tried to apply his criticisms, but they were sophisticated to a degree my efforts couldn't repay. He was trying to show me how to solve problems I hadn't learned existed.

About once a day he'd say, "I may do a little writing yet, myself, if my mind holds." One morning I even heard from downstairs the slap-slap of the old electric. That day, while he napped, I slid into his room and pulled off the slipcover to see what he'd done, a single sentence of between thirty and forty words. A couple of them were hyphened out, with substitutions written above in ballpoint. The sentence stunned me. I'd come half-expecting to find an incoherent mess, and afraid that this would say something ominous about our whole experiment, my education, but the opposite confronted me. The sentence was perfect. In it, he described a memory from his childhood, of a group of people riding in an early automobile, and the driver lost control, and they veered through an open barn door, but by a glory of chance the barn was completely empty, and the doors on the other side stood wide open, too, so that the car passed straight through the barn and back out into the sunlight, by which time the passengers were already laughing and honking and waving their arms at the miracle of their own survival, and Lytle was somehow able, through his prose, to replicate this swift and almost alchemical transformation from horror to joy. I don't know why I didn't copy out the sentence—embarrassment at my own spying, I guess. He never wrote any more. But for me it was the key to the year I lived with him. What he could still do, in his weakness, I couldn't do. I started listening harder, even when he bored me.

His hair was sparse and mercury-silver. He wore a tweed jacket every day and, around his neck, a gold-handled toothpick hewn from a raccoon's sharpened bone-penis. I put his glasses onto my own face once and my hands, held just at arm's length, became big beige blobs. There was a thing on his forehead—a cyst, I assume, that had gotten out of control—it was about the size and shape of a bisected Ping-Pong ball. His doctor had offered to remove it several times, but Lytle treated it as a conversation piece. "Vanity has no claim on me," he said. He wore a gray fedora with a bluebird's feather in the band. The skin on his face was strangely young-seeming. Tight and translucent. But the rest of his body was extraterrestrial. Once a week I helped him bathe. God alone knew for how long the moles and things on his back had been left to evolve unseen. His skin was doughy. Not saggy or lumpy, not in that sense—he was hale—but fragile-feeling. He had no hair anywhere below. His toenails were of horn. After the bath he lay naked between fresh sheets, needing to feel completely dry before he dressed. All Lytles, he said, had nervous temperaments.

I found him exotic; it's probably accurate to say that I found him beautiful. The manner in which I related to him was essentially anthropological. Taking offense, for instance, to his more or less daily outbursts of racism, chauvinism, anti-Semitism, class snobbery, and what I can only describe as medieval nostalgia, seemed as absurd as debating these things with a caveman. Shut up and ask him what the cave art means. The self-service and even cynicism of that reasoning are not hard to dissect at a distance of years, but I can't pretend to regret it, or that I wish I had walked away.

There was something else, something less contemptible, a voice in my head that warned it would be unfair to lecture a man with faculties so diminished. I could never be sure what he was saying, as in stating, and what he was simply no longer able to keep from slipping out of his id and through his mouth. I used to walk by his wedding picture, which hung next to the cupboard—the high forehead, the square jaw, the jug ears—and think, as I passed it, "If you wanted to contend with him, you'd have to contend with *that* man." Otherwise it was cheating.

I came to love him. Not in the way he wanted, maybe, but not in a way that was stinting. *Mon vieux.* I was twenty and believed that nothing as strange was liable to happen to me again. I *was* a baby. One night we were up drinking late in the kitchen and I asked him if he thought there was any hope. Like that: "Is there any hope?" He answered me quite solemnly. He told me that in the hallways at Versailles, there hung a faint, ever-so-faint smell of human excrement, "because as the chambermaids hurried along a tiny bit would always splash from the pots." Many years later I realized that he was half-remembering a detail from the court of Louis XV, namely that the latrines were so few and so poorly placed at the palace, the marquesses used to steal away and relieve themselves on stairwells and behind the beautiful furniture, but that night I had no idea what he meant, and still don't entirely.

"Have I shown you my incense burner?" he asked.

"Your what?"

He shuffled out into the dining room and opened a locked glass cabinet door. He came back cradling a little three-legged pot and set it down gently on the chopping block between us. It was exquisitely painted and strewn with infinitesimal cracks. A figure of a dog-faced dragon lay coiled on the lid, protecting a green pearl. Lytle spun the object to a particular angle, where the face was darker, slightly orange-tinged. "If you'll look, the glaze is singed," he said. "From the blast, I presume, or the fires." He held it upside down. Its maker's mark was legible on the bottom, or would have been to one who read Japanese. "This pot," he said, "was recovered from the Hiroshima site." A classmate of his from Vanderbilt, one of the Fugitives, had gone on to become an officer in the Marine Corps and gave it to him after the war. "When I'm dead I want you to have it," he said.

I didn't bother refusing, just thanked him, since I knew he wouldn't remember in the morning, or, for that matter, in half an hour. But he did remember. He left it to me.

Ten years later in New York City my adopted stray cat Holly Kitty pushed it off a high shelf I didn't think she could reach, and it shattered. I sat up most of the night gluing the slivers back into place.

Lytle's dementia began to progress more quickly. I hope it's not cruel to note that at times the effects could be funny. He insisted on calling the K-Y Jelly we used to lubricate his colostomy tube *Kye Jelly*. Finally he got confused on what it was for and appeared in my doorway one day with his toothbrush and a squeezed-out tube of this stuff. "Put *Kye* on the list, boy," he said. "We're out."

Evenings he'd mostly sit alone and rehash forty-year-old fights with dead literary enemies, performing both sides as though in a one-man play, at times yelling wildly, pounding his cane. Allen Tate, his brother turned nemesis, was by far the most frequent opponent, but it seemed in these rages that anyone he'd ever known could change into the serpent, fall prey to an obsession with power. Particularly disorienting was when the original version of the mock-battle had been between him and me. Him and the Boy. Several times, in reality, we did clash. Stood face-to-face shouting. I called him a mean old bastard, something like that; he told me I'd betrayed my gift. Later, from downstairs, I heard him say to the Boy, "You think you're not a *slave*?"

There was a day when I came in from somewhere. Polly, his sister, was staying upstairs. I loved Miss Polly's visits—everyone did. She made rum cakes you could eat yourself to death on like a goldfish. There were home-made pickles and biscuits from scratch when she came. A tiny woman with glasses so thick they magnified her eyes, her knuckles were cubed with arthritis. Who knew what she thought, or if she thought, about all the nights she'd shared with her brother and his interesting artist friends. (Once, in a rented house somewhere, she'd been forced by sleeping arrangements to lie awake in bed all night between fat old Ford Madox Ford and his mistress.) She shook her head over how the iron skillet, which their family had been seasoning in slow ovens since the Depression, would suffer at my hands. I had trouble remembering not to put it through the dishwasher. Over meals, under the chandelier with the "saltcellar" and the "salad oil," as Lytle raved about the master I might become, if only I didn't fall into this, that, or the other hubristic snare, she'd simply grin and say, "Oh, Brutha, how *exciting*."

On the afternoon in question I was coming through the security gate, entering "the grounds," as cottagers called the Assembly, and Polly passed me going the opposite way in her minuscule blue car. There was instantly something off about the encounter, because she didn't stop completely— she rolled down the window and yelled at me, but continued to idle past, going at most twenty miles per hour (the speed limit in there was twelve, I think), as if she were waving from a parade float. "I'm on my way to the store," she said. "We need [*mumble*]..."

"What's that?"

"BUTTAH!"

I watched with a bad feeling as she receded in the mirror. Back at the cabin, Lytle was caning around on the front porch in a panic. He waved at me as I turned into the gravel patch where we parked. "She's drunk!" he barked. "Look at this bottle, beloved. Good God, it was full this morning!"

I tried to make him tell me what happened, but he was too antsy. He wore pajamas, black slippers without socks, a gray tweed coat, and the fedora.

"Oh, I've angered her, beloved," he said. "I've angered her."

As we sped toward the gate, he gave me the story. It was as I suspected. The same argument came up every time Polly visited, though I'd never seen it escalate so. They had family in a distant town with whom she remained on decent terms, but Lytle insisted on shunning these people and thought his little sister should, as well. It had to do with an old scandal about land, duplicity involving a will. A greedy uncle had tried to take away his father's farm. But these modern-day cousins, descendants of the rival party, they weren't pretending, as Lytle believed, not to understand why he wouldn't see them—I think they were genuinely confused. There'd been scenes. He'd stood in the doorway and denounced these people, in the highest rhetoric, "Seed of the usurper." They must have thought he was further gone mentally than he was, that when he uttered these curses he had in mind some carpetbagger from olden days, because the relatives just kept coming back, despite never having been allowed past the porch steps. Now Miss Polly had let them into the vestibule, nearly into the Court of the Muse. Lytle viewed this as the wildest betrayal. He'd been beastly toward them, when he rose from his nap, and Polly had fled. He himself seemed shaken to remember the things he'd said.

"Mister Lytle, what did you say?"

"I told the truth," he said passionately. "I recognized the moment, that's what I did." But in the defensive thrust of his jaw there quivered something like embarrassment.

He mentions this land dispute in his "family memoir," *A Wake for the Living*, his most readable and in many ways his best book. That's perhaps an idiosyncratic opinion. There are people who've read a lot more than I have who consider his novels lost classics. But it may be precisely because of the Faustian ego that thundered above his sense of himself as a novelist that he carried a lighter burden into the memoir, and this freedom thawed in his style some of the vivacity and spontaneity that otherwise you find only in the letters. There's a scene in which he describes the morning his grandmother was shot in the throat by a Union soldier in 1863. "Nobody ever knew who he was or why he did it," Lytle writes, "he mounted a horse and galloped out of town." To the end of her long life this woman wore a velvet ribbon at her neck, fastened with a golden pin. That's how close Lytle was to the Civil War. Close enough to reach up as a child, passing into sleep, and fondle the clasp of that pin. The eighteenth century was just another generation back from there, and so on, hand to hand. This happens, I suppose, this collapsing of time, when you make it as far as your nineties. When Lytle was born, the Wright Brothers had not yet achieved a working design. When he died, Voyager II was exiting the solar system. What do you do with the coexistence of those details in a lifetime's view? It weighed on him.

The incident with his grandmother is masterfully handled:

She ran to her nurse. The bullet had barely missed the jugular vein. Blood darkened the apple she still held in her hand, and blood was in her shoe. The enemy in the street now invaded the privacy of the house. The curious entered and stared. They confiscated the air . . . To the child's fevered gaze the long bayonets of the soldiers seemed to reach the ceiling, as they filed past her bed, staring out of boredom and curiosity.

Miss Polly passed us again. Apparently she'd changed her mind about the butter. We made a U-turn and trailed her to the cabin. Back inside they embraced. She buried her face in his coat, laughing and weeping. "Oh, sister," he said, "I'm such an old fool, god*damn* it."

I've wished at times that we had endured some meaningful falling-out. In truth he began to exasperate me in countless petty ways. He needed too much, feeding and washing and shaving and dressing, more than he could admit to and keep his pride. Anyone could sympathize, but I hadn't signed on to be his butler. One day I ran into the white-haired professor, who shared with me that Lytle had been complaining about my cooking.

Mainly, though, I'd fallen in love with a tall, nineteen-year-old half-Cuban girl from North Carolina, with freckles on her face and straight dark hair down her back. She was a class behind mine, or what would have been mine, at the school, and she could talk about books. On our second date she gave me her father's roughed-up copy of *Hunger*, the Knut Hamsun novel. I started to spend more time downstairs. Lytle became pitifully upset. When I invited her in to meet him, he treated her coldly, made some vaguely insulting remark about "Latins," and at one point asked her if she understood a woman's role in an artist's life.

There came a wickedly cold night in deep winter when she and I lay asleep downstairs, wrapped up under a pile of old comforters on twin beds we'd pushed together. By now the whole triangle had grown so unpleasant that Lytle would start drinking earlier than usual on days when he spotted her car out back, and she no longer found him amusing or, for that matter, I suppose, harmless. My position was hideous.

She shook me awake and said, "He's trying to talk to you on the thing." We had this antiquated monitor system, the kind where you depress the big silver button to talk and let it off to hear. The man hadn't mastered an electrical device in his life. At breakfast one morning, when I'd made the mistake of leaving my computer upstairs after an all-nighter, he screamed at me for "bringing the enemy into this home, into a place of work." Yet he'd become a bona fide technician on the monitor system.

"He's calling you," she said. I lay still and listened. There was a crackling.

"*Beloved,*" he said, "*I hate to disturb you, in your slumbers, my lord. But I believe I might freeze to DEATH up here.*"

"Oh, my God," I said.

"*If you could just . . . lie beside me.*"

I looked at her. "What do I do?"

She turned away. "I wish you wouldn't go up there," she said.

"What if he dies?"

"You think he might?"

"I don't know. He's ninety-two, and he says he's freezing to death."

"*Beloved . . . ?*"

She sighed. "You should probably go up there."

He didn't speak as I slipped into his bed. He fell back asleep instantly. The sheets were heavy white linen and expensive. It seemed there were shadowy acres of snowy terrain between his limbs and mine. I floated off.

When I woke at dawn he was nibbling my ear and his right hand was on my genitals.

I sprang out of bed and began to hop around the room like I'd burned my finger, sputtering foul language. Lytle was already moaning in shame, fallen back in bed with his hand across his face like he'd just washed up somewhere, a piece of wrack. I should mention that he wore, as on every chill morning, a Wee Willie Winkie-style nightshirt and cap. "Forgive me, forgive me," he said.

"Jesus Christ, Mister Lytle."

"Oh, beloved…"

His having these desires wasn't the issue. I couldn't be that naïve. His tastes in that area were more or less an open secret. I don't know if he was gay or bisexual or pansexual or what. Those distinctions are clumsy terms in which to address the mysteries of sexuality. But on a few occasions he'd spoken about his wife in a manner that to me was movingly erotic, nothing like any self-identifying gay man I've ever heard talk about women and sex. Certainly Lytle had loved her, because it was clear how he missed her, Edna, his beautiful "squirrel-eyed gal from Memphis," whom he'd married when she was young, who was still young when she died of throat cancer.

Much more often, however, when the subject of sex came up, he would return to the idea of there having been a homoerotic side to the Agrarian movement itself. He told me that Allen Tate propositioned him once, "but I turned him down. I didn't like his smell. You see, smell is so important, beloved. To me he had the stale scent of a man who didn't take any exercise." This may or may not have been true, but it wasn't an isolated example. Later writers—including some with an interest in not playing up the issue—have noticed, for instance, Robert Penn Warren's more-than-platonic interest in Tate, when they were all at Vanderbilt together. One of the other Twelve Southerners, Stark Young—he's rarely mentioned—was openly gay. Lytle professed to have carried on, as a very young man, a happy, sporadic affair with the brother of another Fugitive poet, not a well-known person. At one point the two of them fantasized about living together, on a small farm. The man later disappeared and turned up murdered in Mexico. Warren mentions him in a poem that plays with the image of the closet.

The point—the reason I risk being seen to have "outed" a man who trusted me, and was vulnerable when he did—is that you can't fully understand that movement, which went on to influence American literature for decades, without understanding that certain of the men involved in it loved one another. Most "homosocially," of course, but a few homoerotically, and some homosexually. That's where part of the power originated that made those friendships so intense, and caused the men to stay united almost all their lives, even after spats and changes of opinion, even after their Utopian hopes for the South had died. Together they produced from among them a number of good writers, and even a great one, in Warren, whom they can be seen to have lifted, as if on wing beats, to the heights for which he was destined.

Lytle himself would have beaten me with his cane and thrown me out for saying all of that. To him it was a matter for winking and nodding, frontier sexuality, fraternity brothers falling into bed with each other and not thinking much about it. Or else it was Hellenism, golden lads in the Court of the Muse. William Alexander Percy stuff. Whatever it was, I accepted it. I never showed displeasure when he wanted to sit and watch me chop wood, or when he asked me to quit showering every morning, so that he could smell me better. "I'm pert' near blind, boy," he said. "How will I find you in a fire?" Still, I'd taken for granted an understanding between us. I didn't expect him to grope me like a chambermaid.

I stayed away two nights, and then went back. When I reached the top of the steps and looked through the back-porch window, I saw him on the sofa lying asleep (or dead—I wondered every time). His hands were folded across his belly. One of them rose and hung quivering, an actor's wave; he was talking to himself. It turned out, when I cracked the door, he was talking to me.

"Beloved, now, we must forget this," he said. "I merely wanted to touch it a little. You see, I find it the most *interesting* part of the body."

Then he paused and said, "Yes," seeming to make a mental note that the phrase would do.

"I understand, you have the girl now," he continued. "Woman offers the things a man must have, home and children. And she's a lovely girl. I myself may not have not made the proper choices, in that role…"

I closed the door and crept down to bed.

Not long after that, I moved out, both of us agreeing it was for the best.

I re-enrolled at the school. They found someone else to live with him. It had become more of a medical situation by that point, at-home care. I drove out to see him every week, and I think he welcomed the visits, but things had changed. He knew how to adjust his formality by tenths of a degree, to let you know where you stood.

It may be gratuitous to remark of a ninety-two-year-old man that he began to die, but Lytle had been much alive for most of that year, fiercely so. There were some needless minor surgeries at one point, which set him back. It's funny how the living will help the dying along. One night he fell, right in front of me. He was standing in the middle room on a slippery carpet, and I was moving toward him to take a glass from his hand. The next instant he was flat on his back with a broken elbow that during the night bruised horribly, blackly. His eyes went from glossy to matte. Different people took turns staying over with him, upstairs, including the white-haired professor, whose loyalty had never wavered. I stayed a couple of nights. I wasn't worried he'd try anything again. He was in a place of calm and—you could see it—preparation. His son-in-law told me he'd spoken my name the day before he died.

When the coffin was done, the men from the funeral home picked it up in a hearse. Late the same night someone called to say they'd finished embalming Lytle's body; it was in the chapel, and whenever Roehm was ready, he could come and fasten the lid. All of us who'd worked on it with him went, too. The mortician let us into a glowing side hallway off the cold ambulatory. With us was an old friend of Lytle's named Brush, who worked for the school administration, a low-built bouncy muscular man with boyish dark hair and a perpetual bowtie. He carried, as nonchalantly as he could, a bowling-ball bag, and in the bag an extremely excellent bottle of whiskey.

Brush took a deep breath, reached into the coffin, and jammed the bottle up into the crevice between Lytle's ribcage and his left arm. He quickly turned and said, "That way they won't hear it knocking around when we roll it out of the church."

Roehm had a massive electric drill in his hand. It seemed out of keeping with the artisanal methods that had gone into the rest of the job, but he'd run out of time making the cedar pegs. We stood over Lytle's body. Sanford was the first to kiss him. When everyone had, we lowered the lid onto the box, and Roehm screwed it down. Somebody wished the old man Godspeed. A eulogy that ran in the subsequent number of *The Sewanee Review* said that, with Lytle's death, "the Confederacy at last came to its end."

He appeared to me only once afterward, and that was two and a half years later, in Paris. It's not as if Paris is a city I know or have even visited more than a couple of times. He knew it well. I was coming up the stairs from the metro into the sunshine with the girl, whom I later married, on my left arm, when my senses became intensely alert to his presence about a foot and a half to my right. I couldn't look directly at him; I had to let him hang back in my peripheral vision, else he'd slip away; it was a bargain we made in silence. I could see enough to tell that he wasn't young but was maybe twenty years younger than when I'd known him, wearing the black-framed engineer's glasses he'd worn at just that time in his life, looking up and very serious, climbing the steps to the light, where I lost him.

Every first-person narrator who describes another person, place, or thing is, in varying degrees, also illuminating their own character. You learn a lot about someone from how they describe others. How they see the world. What they choose to include and leave out. In this sense, we start learning *something* about John Jeremiah Sullivan immediately.

At the start, Sullivan paints a vivid and memorable portrait of his mentor, Andrew Nelson Lytle, by showing us the old man's character, quirks, and idiosyncrasies. At first, it reads as biographical. If we were to take two highlighters, one yellow and one green, and use the yellow for what Sullivan says about Lytle and the green for what he says about himself, we'd see a lot more yellow, especially in the essay's first half.

What, beyond what we can glean from how he describes Lytle, makes it *personal*?

Sure, Sullivan reflects on his own experiences living with and learning from Lytle—where he was in his life, his age, his dropping out of college, his friend who introduced the two—and this personal connection adds authenticity and emotional depth to the accuracy with which he portrays the title character.

But where does the essay take its turn? Where does it start to move away from being about Lytle and become *personal*? About the author? The answer to this question is subjective and debatable—with no right or wrong answer. For us, it's here:

> He didn't speak as I slipped into his bed. He fell back asleep instantly. The sheets were heavy white linen and expensive. It seemed there were shadowy acres of snowy terrain between his limbs and mine. I floated off.
>
> When I woke at dawn he was nibbling my ear and his right hand was on my genitals.

Here, Sullivan goes introspective. He gets philosophical about writing, literature, and mentorship. He explores the complexities of the mentor-mentee relationship and its impact on his own development as a writer and as a man. These insights help us see Sullivan as separate from the mentor he's describing.

Sullivan shows us that a personal essay combines personal experiences, introspection, and storytelling. It is characterized by the author's unique perspective, emotional engagement, and exploration of universal themes. Writers connect with readers by reflecting on what they learn, focusing on how they've changed (or their take on a situation has changed) over time. The author's literary craftsmanship, and as Karr insists, voice, are key elements that make it a personal essay.

Literary Journalism

The difference between personal essays and literary journalism is a fine one. We would say that in literary journalism, the emphasis is placed more on the real-life events (on the bones) of creative nonfiction, so the reader walks away with more hard knowledge (about the subject rather than about the author) than in a personal essay. When you read the longer pieces in *The New Yorker* or *The Atlantic*, you find issues and events explored in detail. But that's not always the case. Literary journalists still infuse the facts with their own opinions and can slant the articles to come to decided conclusions. Literary journalism can come in the form of articles or books.

In "Ghost Boat," Eric Reidy combines meticulous research with a definite point of view that separates it from traditional journalism.

Ghost Boat
Eric Reidy

> Her name was Segen. In the early hours of the morning of June 28, 2014, she had boarded a boat in Libya with her youngest daughter, Abigail. Segen was 24, slender; Abi was not quite two years old, a frizz of hair and pudgy

baby cheeks. They weren't alone on the boat: All in, there were at least 243 people on board, crammed together, human cargo.

Segen, like most of the other people on the boat, was a refugee from Eritrea—the "North Korea of Africa," one of the most repressive countries in the world. Everybody was hoping the boat would get them to Italy, away from the hardships back home.

She called her husband, Yafet, the day before the boat left. They hadn't seen each other for four weeks: While she travelled across Libya, smuggled thousands of miles to the coast with her baby, he'd stayed behind in Sudan. When she made it to Europe, he planned to follow.

The smuggler didn't let them speak for long, maybe two minutes. It was OK: Yafet could speak with her once she reached Italy.

He never heard from her again.

✳

Yafet and Segen had met nine years earlier at a neighborhood café in Asmara, the Eritrean capital. He was in 10th grade, she was a year behind him, the coffee shop was a popular hangout for their school friends.

It was frowned on for girls and boys to socialize too much, so larger groups of teenagers would often get together to provide cover for a couple who were dating. That's how Yafet and Segen met: They were accompanying two friends who were seeing each other secretly. And when those friends needed a little privacy, Yafet and Segen would fill the time by chatting with each other. Slowly, he started to fall for her.

"When we started to talk . . . not actually in one day, but after months, I started to like so many things about her: The way she talked; the way she laughed; the way she smiled," Yafet says. "I fell in love, and I asked her to start a relationship."

Yafet was born in 1987. He was the youngest of seven children; his father was a high school physics teacher and his mother taught typing; together they all lived in a four-bedroom house in an upscale district of Asmara. Back then, Eritrea was at the tail end of a 30-year war for independence from Ethiopia, and families like Yafet's—middle class, educated—were poised to form the backbone of the new nation.

Freedom came in 1993, but the optimism didn't last. In 1998, a new conflict with Ethiopia escalated, and within two years 100,000 people were dead. President Isaias Afwerki came under scrutiny for his leadership: He responded by cracking down on dissent, banning the country's privately-owned newspapers, and imprisoning anyone who opposed him. He has ruled ever since.

Today, Eritrea is one of the world's most repressive states: There are extensive reports of torture, forced labor, arbitrary arrests, incommunicado detention, extrajudicial killings, and disappearances. Its primary mechanism of control is national service: Citizens are conscripted for an indefinite period and forced to work in government enterprises for almost no pay. There are restrictions on freedom of expression, assembly, and religion.

Even though he was just a young teen when it happened, the crackdown sticks with Yafet. And once his eyes were open, he couldn't look away.

"I used to ask my mom, 'Mom, why?'" he says. "My mother told me to keep quiet, don't talk like that outside. I'm in my country. I'm just asking what happened. Why can't I say? Later, I saw what happened to the people who asked."

Today, more than 400,000 people—one in every 16 Eritreans—have fled the country.

By September 2007, he and Segen had been dating for two years. Like everyone else in the country, he reported for six months of military training after finishing 11th grade, before returning to high school. After graduating, and just a few days before he was to be officially drafted, he took Segen aside. He was leaving Eritrea, he said.

She wasn't happy. Not because she couldn't see the oppression—she had dropped out of school herself after 10th grade to avoid national service. The fear was that they would never have a chance to build a future together.

But they understood that staying didn't give them that chance either.

"We couldn't imagine having any future there with the government. That's why she accepted it. I promised not to forget her. She told me that she would pray for me ... and that one day we would be together and have kids."

The border between Eritrea and Sudan is a desert of cracked earth where temperatures soar into the 100s. The only distinguishable feature marking the boundary between the two countries is a low mountain ridge that cuts across the horizon.

"Beyond the mountain is Sudan. In front of it is Eritrea," Yafet says. Reaching it meant reaching freedom.

After saying goodbye to Segen and his family, Yafet reported for duty at a military camp in the west of the country. He stayed there for three days while making final arrangements before heading into the desert with eight friends. He was 20 years old, and he knew he'd never be able to go home again.

"I knew where the west was, and I knew if I went to the west [I would reach Sudan]," Yafet said. But it was a two-day walk from the camp to the border, and the government did not treat deserters kindly.

There was no cover—no trees, no bushes—to obscure them from sight, so they travelled mostly at night. But even after dark the moon was so bright that they didn't have much protection. So they devised a system. Each of them would take turns walking several hundred feet in front of the others: That way, if they came across a military patrol, only the scout would be captured, and the rest of the group would have a chance to escape.

It wasn't just the Eritrean patrols that were a threat, though. There was also a chance of running into criminals or security forces on the Sudanese side who would deliver them back to Eritrean authorities in exchange for money.

After walking for two nights and a day in the desert, the group reached the mountain. On the other side, they found it difficult to find their way—nobody in the group spoke Arabic, just the main Eritrean language, Tigrinya, and a little English. Then they came into some luck: A friendly Sudanese man brought them to his house. "He gave us food, water, even milk. We were wearing military clothes. He brought us civilian clothes."

The man pointed the group in the direction of a nearby refugee camp. Yafet had made it. Now he could begin his new life.

"It was the worst place I have seen in my life. There was no food service. There were no houses . . . There were tents that were donated by UNHCR, but it wasn't enough for the people. There was no clean water for the refugees, there were no medical services, there was one nurse and the refugees were maybe 2 or 3,000 at that time. If you had money you could pay for food, but there were people who didn't have money. They were really in trouble."

Yafet was in Wad Sherife, a refugee camp about 10 miles from the border. It was against the law to leave, so three months later, he paid a smuggler $100 to take him to Khartoum, the capital of Sudan, where he could think about going further—to Europe or the U.S.

But Khartoum itself was another horrible shock, an unforgiving and legally precarious place, where Yafet was constantly exposed to danger and abuse. At first he relied on the help of others: One relative in the United States sent him money, another who lived locally gave him shelter. He shared a small room with five other people—it was bare, hot, and didn't even have beds—but still, Yafet was happy. It was the first time he could process being outside of Eritrea.

"It was good for us. We had freedom. We felt that we could relax. We could speak about what we wished . . . things that we wouldn't dare say in Eritrea. We discussed our country. We discussed our futures. They were the things that we hadn't ever expressed."

Things got progressively worse, though. His support network faded, his money ran out. Most nights he scraped together enough to sleep in the underground hotels run out of people's houses; sometimes he slept outside, mingling with other homeless people and keeping away from the police. Eventually, he found a job in a bakery: The owner gave him $3.50 a day in wages and let him sleep in the back of the store at night. It was a tiny bit of stability, but not enough to build a future.

So, when Segen told Yafet that she was coming to Sudan in the summer of 2009, he was not happy.

"I just told her to be a little patient, to wait for me to try something," he says. "I didn't want to bring her and see her be in trouble and I also didn't want to be in more trouble."

Segen decided to come anyway. She didn't have much money, but her cousin—a people smuggler—agreed to help her escape from Eritrea if she could find three friends to come with her who would pay.

Segen finally married Yafet in September 2010—a church service, with about 30 people in attendance.

"I was happy that day because I got my dream girl and it was my wedding day," says Yafet.

Things were looking up. They moved in together, and he had a new job marketing agricultural products online, with his own office, his own computer, and a salary of $500 per month.

Finally being united, however, didn't reduce the insecurity. They argued about whether to stay or try to get out. Segen's family was encouraging her to flee Africa altogether, either to Israel—by crossing the Sinai desert—or to Europe, by boat across the Mediterranean. Both options were dangerous.

"I didn't want to put our lives at risk in order to get a better life," Yafet says. "That's why I wanted to let her know that if we found a better way, a safe way, if we get resettlement or a visa and could leave by plane, that's ok, but, no, we don't have to risk our lives."

Then Yafet's company closed, and he lost his job. Their first daughter, Shalom, was born a month later, on August 16, 2011. He'd work wherever, whatever way he could: cleaning houses, manual labor, restaurants, anything. Then, a few months after she gave birth to Shalom, Segen got pregnant again. Their second daughter, Abigail, was born on October 29, 2012.

Nothing was steady, and Segen was more unsettled than ever. Finding a way to leave became the main topic of discussion. It was too much.

"She wasn't able to get sleep. She wasn't able to eat food. She wasn't able to care for the children . . . She used to cry without any cause. She used to get angry about small things. She was not at peace. I tried to make her feel free, to make her relax. She got worse and worse."

Then, one day, she told him she couldn't wait anymore.

The couple weighed their options. In the end they agreed: Segen would cross the desert to Libya and get on one of the boats smuggling people across the Mediterranean to Italy. Once there, she would head for Norway, which has one of the fastest asylum and family reunification processes in Europe. Yafet would follow. Initially, he wanted both of their daughters to stay with him in Khartoum. But Segen thought that having Abigail with her would help keep them both safe from abuse during the trip and maybe even win some preferential treatment, like receiving extra food and water—things which could make a big difference during the long desert crossing that lay ahead. Yafet conceded.

When you're being secretly carried across international borders, smugglers don't give you an exact date and time for departure. They just call, unannounced, and that's it: You go.

When the smuggler finally told Segen that it was time, Yafet had been preparing himself for a week. But, still, it caught him off guard. He was at work, and she called him to tell him that she was leaving. Yafet couldn't go back home to say goodbye.

✳

The next time Yafet heard from Segen, she had just arrived at her first destination in Libya. It had taken 15 days to cross the Sahara desert—a route without roads, across desolate terrain. She was safe, she explained, but not everyone had been lucky. It was a journey that should have taken them six days, but the truck that was carrying them had broken down, and they had to wait for four days until another one was brought to continue the journey.

Four people died of dehydration while they were waiting.

Segen was crying over the phone.

"I asked her to give me to Abigail . . . to let me hear her voice," Yafet remembers. "She told me that [Abigail] was too tired and sleeping. I was really scared when she said that. I just thought something happened to Abigail."

Yafet doesn't lose his temper often. But he shouted at Segen to let him hear Abi's voice. Segen brought her to the phone.

His fear was not without cause. The desert route she was running is treacherous, and large numbers of refugees and migrants perish without ever reaching the coast, let alone Europe. It is difficult to tell exactly how many die each year in the Sahara because of lack of information and documentation. But with smugglers packing as many as 100 people into old trucks, the number is high.

"All the people had little food and little water. When the water finished they started to drink their urine," Younes Abdi, a 29-year-old Somali refugee who fled to Sicily, told me about his journey across the desert. Twenty people from his group of about 100 died because complications with fuel and the truck they were travelling in slowed down the trip.

Even those who survive face kidnapping, torture, beatings, and sexual violence.

Mohammed Ali, a 28-year-old Somali refugee living in Sicily, told me about being beaten with sticks by smugglers, stabbed, and having his money stolen. Others are kidnapped by smugglers or militias and tortured until their families pay ransom money; women are often raped or sexually abused before they are allowed to proceed.

The situation doesn't improve when refugees reach their first destination inside of Libya. Militias and local police often put refugees in jails, detention centers, and even hold them captive in houses and demand payment. If they can't pay the bribe, refugees are subjected to forced labor and harsh treatment, including torture.

After crossing the desert, Bahousmane, a 33-year-old Senegalese asylum seeker in Sicily, was locked in a house for a year with 150 other people. The group only escaped after two people broke a hole in the wall of the house.

Even outside of prisons and detention centers, refugees face exploitation and abuse as they move through Libya and work to make enough money to afford the journey to Italy.

"They don't like black people. They use black people like a slave," said Osaretin Ugingbe, a 35-year-old Nigerian living in Sicily.

When they eventually make it to the coast and pay for their journey—around $1,500—they are kept in houses run by smugglers for anything from a couple of days up to a number of months, depending on weather conditions and how many people the smuggler has who are ready to make the journey. The human traffickers do not provide much food or water, and violence is common.

The last time Yafet heard from Segen was about a month after she left Sudan. She had arrived on the coast after making the dangerous and trying journey and was in a smuggler's house waiting to leave for Italy.

"I remember the last day I heard her voice was the 27th of June," Yafet says. "She told me she would be leaving the next day, the 28th, or the day after. I just told her to be strong, to take care of herself, take care of our girl."

Yafet called back on the 28th, but no one answered the phone. He kept calling.

It wasn't until the next morning that somebody finally picked up. He asked Yafet who he was looking for. "I told him: Segen," Yafet says. "He asked me if she was the one with the baby girl. I told him yes . . . He just told me that they had left yesterday and ended the call."

In Yafet's mind, the journey across Libya was more dangerous than crossing the sea. Once Segen and Abi made it to the coast they were safe, he figured. All he had to do was wait for their call.

After a week, he began to worry.

"Later I called back the smuggler. I called him on the 4th of July," Yafet says. "He told me that he spoke with them on the phone and they had arrived. He said to me congratulations."

"I just believed him."

The man on the other end of the phone was Measho Tesfamariam, a 30-year-old also from Eritrea. He is currently in an Italian prison, facing charges of conspiracy and aiding illegal immigration, with a trial beginning in December. The claim is that he was part of a smuggling ring that organized at least 23 crossings from Libya to Italy between May and September 2014. Segen's boat was one of those the Italian prosecutor says he helped send into the Mediterranean.

Even though the authorities believe the organization was responsible for what happened to the 243 people, they have no knowledge of their fate. It is entirely possible that the boat sank. But if that happened—a single, tragic incident on the water—experts say there would almost certainly be evidence.

"It's really strange," says Othman Belbeisi, who is the International Organization for Migration's country director for Libya. IOM, which keeps detailed records of activity in the Mediterranean, has no knowledge of rescue operations that match the description of Segen's boat.

"When you talk about more than 200 people, it is hard to hide this number for a whole year. It's really strange that there hasn't been any professional investigation."

Tesfamariam, meanwhile, has said that he was just another refugee, working for a smuggler called Ibrahim: He answered the phone, acting as a go-between only so that he could earn free passage to Europe himself.

In fact, he claims his brother was also on the Ghost Boat. He says he doesn't know what happened to it.

"It's only known by Ibrahim and God," he told an Italian reporter, not long before he was arrested in Germany and extradited.

I met Meron Estefanos for the first time in Tunisia earlier this year. She is a beacon for Eritrea's refugee community—a journalist and activist who has found herself at the middle of the exodus. Like Yafet, she left her home country when she was young, although her departure was legal. Now 40, she lives in Stockholm, Sweden, and uses her platform to help refugees and push back against the Eritrean dictatorship.

At the heart of it all is her weekly radio show, *Voices of Eritrean Refugees*. It's a must-listen for the diaspora. Each week, she covers a range of stories about people escaping the Asmaran regime, and as a result she regularly receives calls when journeys go wrong.

Sometimes it's a panicked voicemail message from a worried cousin or parent or sibling. In cases where people are kidnapped or go missing, she investigates what happened herself. But sometimes it's a distress call from somebody actually stranded on a boat that's sinking beneath them: When that happens, she tries to mobilize authorities to respond. All this has made her a contact for many people fleeing Afwerki's rule. "Everyone has my number," she says.

Estefanos had first heard about the vanishing boat from a group of families who, like Yafet, were lost for answers.

It wasn't clear what was going on, but she knew one thing about the Ghost Boat: What the smuggler had told them was a lie. European authorities had no record of the passengers arriving on their shores, and if they had reached Italy, there would have been a record of the boat's arrival and the people on board would have been able to call their relatives. But none of them ever did.

"There was something fishy about the whole thing," Estefanos told me when we met. "The one thing we know is that there were people in the house of the smuggler after them, so they never returned. Once he took them out to get on the boat, they didn't come back."

Although finding anyone alive seemed a distant possibility, Meron was in Tunisia because of a very specific, very strange clue. The family of one of the people on the boat had received a phone call, in Eritrea, from a Tunisian phone number. The person on the other end of the line claimed to be a prison guard. He said that the people from the boat were being held in his jail in southern Tunisia. Meron had come to investigate.

At this point I had been living and working as a journalist in Tunis for about five months, and a friend of mine who was helping Meron told me about the case. I was curious.

✳

We sat down for coffee at one of the numerous outdoor cafés along the tree-lined Avenue Habib Bourguiba, the main pedestrian thoroughfare that runs through the heart of French colonial era downtown Tunis. Estefanos had just come from the imposing Interior Ministry building across the street, a drab cement construction surrounded by a cordon of razorwire and barricades. They told her that there was no record of the people from the boat having been in the country.

She had spent the previous four days scouring court files and visiting prisons, but her findings were inconclusive.

There were more clues, though. One guard said he had heard about a large group of Africans being detained in the southern city of Sfax around the time of the phone call. Somebody at the court in Sfax said they had heard a similar story, but there was nothing documented.

"It could also be an option. It could be. I don't think I can say absolutely not," Lorena Lando, the International Organization for Migration's director in Tunisia, told me. "I think we can't exclude any option."

Despite the rumors and the breadcrumbs and the stories, Meron didn't have anything concrete to give the families. "It's really sad what the families are going through . . . I wish I could give them closure, but unfortunately I can't," she said. Her voice trailed off.

Today, it's been over a year since the boat went missing. Segen's fate, and that of the other passengers, remains a mystery. Almost nobody has done anything to try to figure out what happened.

"We thought they were in Italy. They weren't," said Yafet. "We thought they were in Libya. Nothing. Also, now, we think that they were in Tunisia, but we don't have any evidence to say that they were in Tunisia."

What we really have now is a string of possibilities, odd occurrences and missing information. Where is the evidence?

Fausto Melluso, an activist and migration expert with the Italian organization Arci in Sicily, told me: "It is inconceivable that a boat with that many people can go missing in 2014 and nobody know about it."

✳

Inconceivable.

For Yafet—and for the families of the other people on the boat—the emptiness is a new kind of torture. Shalom, his other daughter, is now four, and she asks where her mother is, why Mom doesn't call. He tells her Segen is abroad, that they'll meet one day. He doesn't know if he's lying or not.

"Two hundred and forty-three people disappeared. Young people. Women. Children . . . No one cares about it. Even the world doesn't care about it," Yafet said to me over the phone.

He was angry, frustrated.

"If you remember Charlie Hebdo in Paris, 14 or 15 people, they got shot by some terrorists . . . The world stopped for 14 people, but white people, Europeans. The same thing for Malaysia Airlines," Yafet continued.

A passenger jet with 239 people on board goes down and "all the world, all the countries, were trying to find what happened. But, in our case, nothing . . . because we are black? I don't know why. It's really hard. What can I say?"

Yafet sighed.

"We are human."

The author, Eric Reidy, works at *The New Humanitarian*. He is the migration and special coverage editor, reporting on migration, humanitarian aid work, and anti-migrant vigilante groups around the globe. Eric won the 2021 Elizabeth Neuffer Award Gold Medal for his coverage of the COVID-19 pandemic's impact on refugees, asylum seekers, and migrants.

If you read his incredible journalism and know the mission of the outlets where he publishes his work, you'll see a writer who has dedicated his career to human rights. We feel that his work goes beyond informing the reader. His fact-based research and reporting allow us to see the personal effect of the human rights abuses we only hear about in the abstract—or worse, don't hear about at all.

Reidy uses all the same narrative tools that fiction writers, poets, and memoirists use. In "Ghost Boat," for example, he expertly engages with plot to add tension to the narrative and to bring Yafet's and Segen's family story to light. He arranges the order of the scenes so that the reader doesn't know what will happen next. In doing so, the reader becomes invested in whether Yafet will find freedom and stability with Segen and their two daughters. Using Reidy's use of characterization, the reader can glean a lot about Yafet. We see determination and can easily glean some of Yafet's values from the way Reidy portrays him. And then there's setting. The vivid descriptions increase the chance that readers will viscerally respond to the challenges these individuals have faced on their many journeys.

These craft choices personalize the plight of Eritrean refugees. Reidy helps readers understand the lived experience of a family. But let's not forget the bones of nonfiction, which are the facts: that one in every sixteen Eritreans fled the country (at the time of reporting). This is shocking to those who don't know much (or anything) about the East African country of Eritrea and its citizens. And that there's a podcast dedicated to the experiences of Eritrean refugees.

You'll notice that the ratio of self references to facts is the opposite of some of our other examples of creative nonfiction. The point of literary journalism isn't to learn more about the *writer*—but what *the writer deems worthy of reporting*. Here's the only place in "Ghost Boat" where we found any reference to the writer—and even this serves a purpose:

> At this point I had been living and working as a journalist in Tunis for about five months, and a friend of mine who was helping Meron told me about the case. I was curious.
>
> We sat down for coffee at one of the numerous outdoor cafés along the tree-lined Avenue Habib Bourguiba, the main pedestrian thoroughfare that runs through the heart of French colonial era downtown Tunis.

Whether or not the writer intended it this way, we see that the author lives on the same continent, just two countries away from the one he's reporting on. Perhaps, for some readers, this offers him credibility.

If you find the best way to express what's important to you about the world we live in, with little to no focus on yourself (outside of what you deem worthy of your reporting), you may want to use the techniques discussed for creative nonfiction and apply them to literary journalism.

Chapter 9

Hybrid Writing

Fruitful Collisions Between Forms

"Whatever it is
you're seeking
won't come in
the form you're
expecting."
—Haruki Murakami

"Others have seen
what is and asked
why. I have seen
what could be and
asked why not."
—Pablo Picasso

We called this book *The Lab: Experiments in Writing Across Genre* for three reasons:

1. To encourage you to borrow useful techniques from all genres, whether you aim to publish work in that genre or not.
2. To encourage you to mix genres when your vision for the material demands it.
3. To encourage you to create a new genre or subgenre when your vision for the material demands it.

Almost every example of writing we've used in pervious chapters could be categorized in more than one genre. Even if an editor or the writer would be hesitant to label the works "hybrid," each of them, to achieve their impact, successfully and skillfully uses techniques often associated with a kind of writing *in addition to* and *outside* their published genre.

Many of them are hybrid, meaning they mix two or more genres within the piece. As writers seek new ways to express their creativity and engage their readers, the divisions that once defined genres have given way to a rich and dynamic realm of hybrid cross-genre literary writing.

Some newer writers mistake writing hybrids for writing without strategy, without constraint. Don't confuse free writing with hybrid forms.

Even for hybrid writers, constraints are useful. For some artists, the more constraints, the *freer* they feel to express creativity. If the writer chooses the constraint of a single genre or subgenre (for example, a type of poem or one of the existing categories of nonfiction), then all the artist's energies can go into how they will fill that container. Those writers can achieve their vision and maximize their creativity by using the known elements of composition in one existing genre or subgenre. When successful, working within that set of constraints is as effective and as creative as inventing a new genre.

It's not the genre (or mixing of them) that makes the piece original. You make it original. Your voice. Your vision.

Other artists find the process of attempting to use a known form too limiting. Their vision for their material doesn't fit neatly into one existing container, so they must find new ones with new sets of constraints.

Sometimes a writer is just as interested in creating a new container as they are in the material that will fill it. From the first draft, that writer focuses some portion of their creative energy on expanding notions of genre.

Let's use a metaphor to make this less abstract. A vase is the most common container used by floral artists. A floral artist who fills a vase with flowers isn't focused on *creating* the container. Instead, they put their creative energies into the *selection* and *arrangement* of the flowers and how their myriad set of choices leads to visual and olfactory impact.

But what if the florist's vision for their arrangement can't be contained by a vase?

Photo of elevated floral orb. *Used with permission of Master Florist Pirjo Koppi.*

And what if the visual and olfactory impact they're seeking can't be realized by plant materials alone? At left is an image from the 2019 Inferflora World Cup.

Go to a flower show, and you'll see how floral artists use plant materials to create everything from abstract sculptures to giant teddy bears to tiny handbags. When their vision forces them to move outside the confines of the vase, they invent (or borrow from other practices, such as architecture or horticulture) new forms by incorporating foam, wire, adhesives, and on and on. Sometimes, a florist, like Pirjo Koppi, must invent their very own container to realize their vision.

The same is true for the writer. Think of words as flowers, genres as vases. Whether one fits in the other depends entirely on the vision of the artist.

The essence of cross-genre writing lies in its ability to transcend the constraints of conventional literary categories. It defies the notion that writers must conform to a singular genre. Instead, it encourages writers to embrace a fluidity that allows them to draw from multiple genres, styles, and forms to craft narratives that are as unique as the material they contain. In this chapter, we will experiment with techniques and describe how writers have successfully created hybrid pieces.

The Lure of Hybridity

A student of ours, during her pursuit of a bachelor's degree in creative writing, often interrupted craft talks. When she felt things were getting too technical, or binding, she interjected, "If I wanted formulas and rules, I would've studied accounting and math. I want to be a writer, an artist, not a tax adjuster."

Many writers think of themselves as artists. Artists, especially those at the beginning of their careers, can be suspicious or wary of techniques that might seem like rules.

Mature artists see existing techniques as scientists see previous experiments in their field: as gifts, a lineage they inherited when they entered the field. If previous practitioners figured out a technique that allows them to inch closer to realizing their vision, they use it. If not, they modify or discard it for another technique.

Part of the allure of hybrid cross-genre writing is making your own rules, either by inventing techniques or inventing new combinations of existing ones. We believe with our whole heart that experimenting with different narrative strategies and structures is healthy for an artist. Transcending the limitations of a single genre can be thrilling for a writer. And when a writer's choice to expand, invent, or mix genres works to highlight and increase the impact of the piece's thematic concerns, imagery, or story—well, that's when it becomes thrilling for the reader, too.

Experimenting with writing across genre can be exhilarating, but earning a piece's hybrid status is tough. As with all the solo or (so-called) traditional genres, writers must still deliver that "unit of satisfaction" to their audience. To do so, they must grapple with questions of coherence, balance, and thematic unity. How can diverse genres be seamlessly integrated into a single narrative without that narrative feeling disjointed? How do writers strike the delicate balance between exploring different writing styles and maintaining a cohesive voice? These are just a couple of the challenges.

For early drafts, we say forget the idea of an audience, unless that audience is the smartest, most supportive, most permissive one, there to root you on and to encourage you to try everything, no matter how wacky it may seem. Either way, the point is to generate material you care about deeply, honoring the way it wants to be born, before thinking of marketability.

When you really have something of style, substance, depth, and form that you wholeheartedly believe in and are willing to take out into the world, then you can consider questions of marketability. But you may have to ask yourself some questions first: Does your piece ignore genre conventions in a way that allows readers to more deeply inhabit the material? Or will they find themselves disoriented or confused or lost? These questions underscore the need for craft expertise.

Do we believe that a new writer can use rookie luck, talent, artistic vision, and intuition (without craft knowledge) to conjure a brilliant genre-defying piece? Yes. Do we believe that's common? No. In fact, in our fifty years of combined teaching, it hasn't happened . . . yet!

This is why we have encouraged the study of poetry, fiction, and creative non-fiction prior to hybrid forms. It's in understanding the limits and constraints (and the freedoms those constraints offer) that you'll be best prepared to abandon those constraints when your vision for your material demands it.

Rewards

Hybrid narratives have the potential to elicit a wide range of emotions, provoke thought and conversation, and leave a lasting impact on readers. They can offer fresh perspectives, challenge preconceived notions of form, and invite readers to seek out new genres and expand conventional tastes. They can also encourage writers to expand their creative ambition.

In this chapter, we delve into the techniques that enable writers to masterfully merge different genres, examine notable examples that have pushed the boundaries of storytelling, and provide practical guidance for those eager to write across genre.

Let's jump right in.

Borrowing

First let's practice borrowing tools from one form and applying them to another.

Write Now

1. Choose the opening paragraphs from any prose work you've written.
2. Make a poem out of the first two paragraphs. You can take out words and lines, but don't add anything. Focus on breaking your original lines while keeping the words in their original order.
3. See what you learn, then go back to your original genre. Revise according to what you learn.

Once, in a graduate workshop, we asked Darryl White—then an MFA student at San Francisco University—to write a poem using the existing lines of a late draft of one of his stories in progress (later published as "The Arachne Gene"). We challenged him even more by asking him to choose lines that highlighted the story's most important thematic questions.

Here's what he said about doing the exercise:

> In the early drafts of working on "The Arachne Gene," I didn't know my themes, at least not consciously. I'm a speculative fiction fan and had an idea of this guy, a cook, who had not inherited a lot of advantages, but whose struggles left him with a heightened loss of identity. His real name is never mentioned. His frayed experiences leave him feeling small, insect-like, in a much too large world. Only after many drafts did I reread and discover a thematic question. This is what I used to compose the poem: *Can we find purpose and "home" without consistent role models?*

First, read the poem Darryl wrote for the class:

The Arachne Gene
  He was a hungry spiderling
  hunting through garbage,
  an orphan . . .
  He didn't have words like
  help, succor, or home, knew
  no language
  except that of his body.

  He had traveled
  far from those
  origins, but in many ways
  his knotted heart never
  let him forget what he didn't have.

  At near dawn, he
  saw or thought he
  saw the silhouette of an
  old woman, standing by the window.

  Viejita.
  He blinked and she was
  gone. She was the first
  big person to understand the . . .
  language of a stomach
  screaming to be filled.

  She spoke a liquid language, this woman
  akin to sunshine. I chase that
  ghost every time I enter the kitchen.

He wanted to bury
his face in her
apron and breathe beef stock and olive oil.

... within every spider, the
possibility to create its own
home to have something
all his own.

Here's what Darryl said after completing the poetry exercise:

> [Although] I wasn't consciously working with thematic concerns in early
> drafts, by focusing on my characters, especially Spider's desires, fears,
> values, and motivations, a lot of the themes (and metaphors in the story)
> appeared, I guess you'd say, organically.
>
> In other words, I didn't plan them. After doing the [poetry] exercise, I
> didn't change much [in the short story], but I did tighten it. I cut a few repet-
> itive things, where I'd already made the point. I also rearranged the recipes
> and allusions to myth and the insect world to show Spider moving toward
> the ideas of *purpose* and *home*. Getting the piece published was a thrill,
> and validating, but just as thrilling was experimenting with the draft across
> genres.

Now here's the published story that Darryl finished not too long after doing the
poetry exercise.

The Arachne Gene
Darryl White
SHORT STORY

He had a pocketful of possibilities scribbled on napkin backs. The perfect
recipe was like DNA, it held the answer to who he was and where he was
supposed to be. He wasn't found yet, he was on his way, and he'd get there,
wherever there was, if the bus driver didn't kill them first. The Greyhound
bounced down the crowded I-10 spitting exhaust at the cars tailgating

them. The bouncing upset Spider's hand for the two-hundred and seven-teenth time. Again. His pen swerved a blue diagonal line across the napkin sitting on his thigh. Again. Spider would happily give up chicken-scratch imperfection for some relief from the heat.

Summer afternoon penetrated the cabin with hot bayonets while the AC grunted like a constipated nun. Sweat from Spider's nose splashed where pen touched paper. Moisture beaded outward, a blue-bleeding Rorschach muddied up his pambazo recipe. He raised his pen. His lips curled against teeth. Would you please dial down the goddamn sun? Not that Spider expected an answer. The high and mighty sitting in their per-sonal . . . Olympuses? Olympi? Olympiad? Whatever. Those fuckers, they didn't give a shit about flies trapped in a can rolling down concrete. The cloth seats had no give for a man his height and his long limbs were curled against his hunkering body. He massaged his left pec to ease the dull ache trapped under his skin. That damn knot had been kicking up for the past hundred miles. That goddamned barbed knot surrounding his heart mak-ing him feel antsy, making him feel stuck. Spider worked his fingers into his pec-meat, digging until he felt pain. He made hard circles so the outside skin ache out-screamed the under-skin ache.

At times, he imagined his heart as eight arachnid legs clutching a stone egg. His knotted heart pushed him before he knew how to talk. He was a hungry spiderling hunting through garbage, an orphan who never knew where he came from or where he should be. He didn't have words like help, succor, or home, knew no language except that of his body, and feared the pale-skinned giants yelling inside their painted fences. He spent black and naked days, weeks, months with the solitary pattering of rain on concrete, chattering of teeth, and growling of stomach. He had traveled far from those origins, but in many ways his knotted heart never let him forget what he didn't have.

Home. He rented apartments, flats, backhouses, and studios. At least for a while, his knot felt a vague sense of permanence. Home. His real home existed in fantasy. Four walls of peace with a walk-in closet for his best suits, a kitchen with black marble counters, a three-tier stove, twin ovens, a microwave, a dishwasher, an island, and a pantry stocked with onions, toma-toes, garlic, jalapeños, red and green bell peppers.

He lays the bright red cord of skirt steak atop the cutting board and chops halves and then quarters, and then dices. He minces onion, garlic, and jalapeño. He places the carne, onion, garlic, and jalapeños inside a plastic bag to marinate in lime juice, orange juice, cilantro, vinegar, salt, pepper. He seals the bag, lets it sit for an hour, he removes the meat from the bag and shakes off the excess moisture. He lays the carne on a tray and steps into his backyard where the grill is ready.

Outside, he'd have a garden of fresh basil, parsley, lemon grass, and thyme. Warm nights would be reserved for the patio, beer in hand, the red glow of the grill, and the sizzle of carne asada floating fat and salt on the cool breeze. He pictured her arms around him. Dark hair, lost smile, onyx eyes would wrap him in silk until the bright blue-morning evaporated the dew. That day was too far off, but closer than it's ever been.... He only needed the perfect recipe.

He plucked the napkin from his thigh. The blurred ingredients had almost unveiled their coda. A new recipe was like tree climbing. His mental hand stretched for the next ingredient like his hands stretched for the branches on those black oaks he climbed as a kid. Every time a grainy shaft bit into his palm, he felt a brief joy. He could climb for hours, haul himself up, hand over hand, until he was king of the sky.

Climb too fast. Snap goes the branch. You tumble into a circle of waiting fists.

Spider's long black fingers shredded the napkin. He wiped sweat from his face with his hairy forearm, flashed the dark armpit ring staining his white T-shirt to anyone who cared to look, sucked moist heat in open mouthed gulps and was grateful, despite the cramped space, he had a seat to himself.

Everyone in the ass half of the bus pretty much roasted or puddled. Occasionally, somebody spat a heaping wad of yellowish phlegm on the floor to let the dim bus driver know the poor suckers in the ass were still alive. The boy sitting in front of him? Spider listened to that boy's empty stomach for the last four hours. Kid was no older than eighteen, had blue eyes, brown spiked hair, and bright angry zits. His plaid shirt, worn at the joints, revealed ashy elbows. The boy caught the Greyhound at Peridot Station, two hundred miles west from where Spider stole his ticket. A Nigerian man with a Charlotte Hornets cap shading his eyes hadn't moved since

Indio. A couple of green neon backpackers with sunburned faces snored in each other's arms. Across from Spider, a squat brown woman layered in sweat stared at him and his shredded napkin pieces and warded herself with a cross.

Fuck her.

He removed another napkin from his pocket and started a paella. He abandoned his apartment after that last job with Mr. Harvey. *Arborio rice.* Rent paid up to the end of the month. *Shrimp.* Mosquitos could have it all. *Saffron.* He never bothered with the stereo systems, Xboxes, DVD players, or flat screens most grubs wasted their cash on. His cell phone, a prepaid purchasable at any dollar store, was the only thing he couldn't live without because it was close to impossible to find work without one. *Chicken broth, onion, bell pepper.* Blue ink found comfort in the napkin's groves; his knotted heart loosened.

Diced tomatoes, garlic cloves, paprika, lemon juice, parsley. Sauté shrimp and remove from the pan, sauté onions, bell pepper, garlic, add rice, broth, lemon juice, and spices. Stir frequently. Add shrimp, tomatoes, and garnish with parsley.

A green sign with white letters neutral in its welcome read, EXIT 1 MILE. The Greyhound pulled off the interstate. The gray freeway washed into dust covered cracked streets and faded yellow line markers. Banning, California. Population 30,506. A place for those banned or banished from all other civilized life. Plenty of open sky, sidewalks somewhat maintained, and large windowed storefronts with letters in red or gold. The Greyhound pulled into the station and vomited Spider onto the curb, black pitch against the white.

He spent a week learning Banning. Walmart was his first pit stop for fresh underwear, napkins, and blue ink pens. He choked down the cuisine at a few of the local trough-holes. Most of the specials were large chunks of indiscernible meat slathered in a thick—sometimes brown, sometimes red—sauce the consistency of old engine oil. None of the establishments took kindly to his critiques . . . or his inquiries about work. One tattooed cook smelling of stale pork actually took a swing. Spider's five-point rebuttal broke a few teeth.

Spider laid low at the Snooty Fox Motel for the next two nights. Knot pain and cop fear tag-teamed his balls like bat to piñata. Pen and napkin offered little relief, but the recipes wouldn't stop pouring from his head until he had stacks on stacks of theoretical dishes. Food kept him awake until his fuzzed brain couldn't spell and that's when the orphan boys who kicked and pounded him in his youth would come visit. He curled into a ball on the springy bed, whimpered and flinched from their ghost punches. At near dawn, he saw or thought he saw the silhouette of an old woman, standing by the window. *Viejita*. He blinked and she was gone. But so were orphan boys and their ghost punches. Spider was able to sleep.

He never bothered to memorize the date *Viejita* found him digging through the restaurant's garbage. Spider never knew if she owned it or just worked there. He never found out her real name. She came into his life when he was at a loss for words. She was the first big person to understand the unspoken language of a stomach screaming to be filled.

Before that door opened and his life changed, he was still a black and naked spiderling crawling toward four white garbage bags leaning against an alley wall. It was about mid-afternoon, gray clouds cut by glass hung over the drab beige buildings. He nested in a narrow alley between *Viejita*'s restaurant and a beauty supply store. Brown, nappy-headed, toothless old men punched air while the colorful young smoked hand-rolled and passed out bags of green to the cars that stopped. He cared nothing for them as they smelled of death. His knotted heart drove his life. It drove him to feed. He tore into the white plastic with a scavenger's hope, pushed aside papers and wrappings, the foul sour smelling things, the viscous liquids of putrid colors, and searched for something partially whole, partially wrapped, and, if he was lucky, only partially eaten. His hand closed on warm squish wrapped in red, white, and yellow paper. He peeled the paper and saw more white paper, only this paper was chalky. He started to pull that off when he realized it wasn't paper but some kind of thin bread with a few mouth-sized, semi-circles chewed out of it.

The backdoor opened, he flinched and dropped his score. *Ay dios mio*! said a short woman with salt and pepper hair pulled into a bun. She was brown and square, a box in an apron. She spoke a liquid language, *Donde esta tu mama*? Normally he would've run, but there was in this woman akin to sunshine and he couldn't flee the sun. She spoke more of those liquid sounds. *Tienes hambre*? His mouth opened to repeat them but what came out was rain on concrete.

She held a hand palm up and her fingers curled toward her body. He looked at his own hand and mimicked the gesture. Her face curled at the corners, heat radiated from her gaze, she reached out and took a step forward, *Ven conmigo*. He retreated. She stopped, chewed her lower lip, and skittered back inside the restaurant. She left the door open. He stepped closer. She returned with a blue cardboard box filled with something that smelled so good it made him ache.

He saw, for the first time, two tacos steaming with meat. She offered. He shoved a taco into his mouth. Hot juices soaked his tongue, the layers of flavor, an arrangement, a pattern he had to understand. Heat scorched the roof of his mouth and filled his head, he felt euphoric and dizzy. *Viejita* smiled, took him by the hand, and led him into the restaurant. By the time child services arrived, his love of tacos had already built a home in his heart. It had taken two weeks of paperwork, but he was eventually sluiced off to St. Margaret's orphanage.

After a week of scanning the sidewalks outside the Snooty Fox Motel, he realized the cops wouldn't come. He crashed the streets, his mouth dry for a few shots of Patron, he headed north toward a bar he'd spotted before hiding out in his room. It was close to dinner time and the sidewalks were starting to fill. He kept to himself and ignored the looks that came his way. As he rounded the corner, he received hard eyes from three locusts in motorcycle leather talking outside the bar. He recognized these types. They travelled in packs, hid knives in their belts, and rolled anyone stupid enough or different enough to get drunk in their presence—the adult version of the pummeling orphan fists of his youth. Best to find a bar with a better class of bottom feeders. Spider lowered his head, keeping the locusts in view via side-eye, and kept walking. He exhaled when they didn't follow. He turned left and wandered three more blocks.

A red and white HELP WANTED sign in the window of a brick and thatch Mexican restaurant caught his attention along with the tang of overcooked meat. The blue marquee atop the restaurant flashed *Rafael's Eatery* under a sky darkening with diminishing sunlight. After the incident with the other cook, good sense told him to push on. He stared. HELP WANTED. He stepped inside.

The restaurant was bright for about a two-thirds. In the far back, near the unplugged juke box, the lights flickered intermittently. Dirty dishes filled most tables. Wet streaks and sizeable crumbs covered what he guessed were *clean* tables. Two waitresses gossiped with a customer. A third waitress with sandy eyes, blonde ends dyed black, and lips colored by distaste offered to seat him. He asked to see the manager. The waitress pointed to a woman in a blue shirt by the register who was checking her crooked teeth in the flat of a butter knife like she was surprised they were still there. He walked over and introduced himself.

I'm Vanessa, the manager answered. Frowning, she set down the butter knife. Her hands tightened into fists like she was expecting to box over a bill. He raised his hands in surrender. She looked him up and down like she was trying to figure out how much trouble he'd be, licked faded lipstick, and raised the downturned ends of her mouth into a neutral line. What can I do you for?

He let her eyes get used to him. You still got the opening? Spider asked.

Sign's still up, aint it? Vanessa answered.

Manager Vanessa had a Susan B. Anthony sized bruise beneath her chin and a flat upside-down muffin nose of a cheerleader turned prizefighter, a pretty face that had seen rough times and felt rough hands. Spider had no patience for any man who put hands on a woman. He remembered the white orphan boys, their little mallet fists smashing against his black skin, fucking coon, fucking coon, they chanted. The boiling smack of their flesh against his. He curled into a ball to minimize the hurt, legs and arms shielding chest and head. When the boys tired. He spit blood on their scuffed secondhand shoes and climbed to the highest branches of the nearest black oak.

She brushed hair from her face. You aint from around here. Passing through or here to stay?

He shrugged. For now, I'm looking for work.

She chewed her lower lip. Come on back, she said making a motion he should follow. She stepped from behind the register and glanced briefly over her shoulder. Her hips swayed as she walked.

He smiled at the entreaty. She was a full-figured woman, all curves, the kind of body he could grab anywhere and have a handful.

A kitchen in need of a serious cleaning greeted them with a blast of warm air. A mountain of pots and pans filled the sink, grease stains darkened the stainless-steel grill and fryer, and black rubber mats covered a wet floor. Cigarette smoke, fryer oil, and burnt drippings almost masked the rot coming from a box of tomatoes, two days into white and fuzzy, stacked next to a large refrigerator.

Two cooks, smoking under the ceiling fan, glared and followed Spider with their eyes. The younger, whip-thin cook had the same dark hair as Vanessa. The older cook's mustache stretched from ear to ear. He overheard the older cook sneer, another charity case.

Dishes aint washing themselves Zeke, Vanessa said. Zeke, the younger cook, dropped his cigarette to the floor, stamped it out, and headed for the pile of dishes. Spider and Vanessa made a sharp right into a small office more like a closet than anything else. She closed the door and offered a seat.

Somewhere beneath the stacks of crumpled invoices and bills was a metal table better suited for a mechanic's shop. The big butt computer monitor, a holdover from the nineties, filled what was left of the desk's surface. He reached into a cup full of multicolored pens, took out a blue one, and twirled it between his fingers.

Vanessa watched his hands. Got an opening for a busboy. Pay is minimum wage. You can start today if need be.

I cook, he said.

Don't need a cook. I need somebody who can bus tables, wash dishes, and get to work sober and on time, she said.

His knotted heart began to ache. Anybody can bus a table, he said.

I aint asking for a unicorn, she said. You mind me asking where you're from?

Around Texas, he shrugged.

Any city in particular.

Way around Texas.

She held his eyes. Oh, that place. Right next to the penitentiary. We get lots from Way Around. She licked more lipstick off her lips. They don't work out long. Silverware comes up missing.

I aint that kind, he said.

Her eyes seemed to travel up his chest, along his shoulders, and down his arms. She spread her hands and said, You aint here for the peach cobbler, either. I'm sure you've asked for other work. Plenty of polite door slams. This city's been burned by folk from Way Around. Me? I aint particular as long as man's hands gets the job done. I'm not stupid, either. I aint letting a Way Around anywhere near mine until I'm sure.

He could dice onions or pick locks, he'd prefer the former but if he couldn't feed himself he'd do the later. I know what I'm skilled at, he said. I cook. I can have this place filled twenty-four seven.

Most people noticing him either stared, crossed the street, or walked the other way. He recognized best those someone-wanted-to-pound-his-face looks. Vanessa wasn't staring like that; she took him in like he was the Grand Canyon or something, a spectacle she wanted to visit but never had a chance until now.

He pointed at an overdue invoice dated four months ago. This scrap?

She nodded.

The knot tightened. He touched pen to paper. Carnitas mojo de ajo. *Pork shoulder, olive oil, garlic.* His hand moved deftly, smooth confident strokes. *Unsalted butter, pepper flakes, salt, black pepper, lime, cumin, tabasco.*

She watched him. You do that much?

He shrugged. Habit, he said. The knot was squeezing like a sonovabitch and it was all he could do to keep himself in his seat.

Reminds of Charlie, a guy I dated senior year except he made pictures like in comic books. After graduation, he took his pencils and colors off to one of them art schools in Los Angeles. Her expression softened. She touched her chest and curled her fingers over her heart.

Spider blinked. It was like she had a knot too.

He set aside his recipe, reached across the desk, and took her hand. Her fingers were plump, and the skin had the bark-like dryness of someone who washed their hands a lot. Cooks, mechanics, and doctors had hands like that. Let me make you something, he said. Give me fifteen minutes. If you don't like it, I'm gone.

She stared at his hand with an expression he couldn't read except to know she hadn't pulled way.

I aint letting you near my kitchen, she said.

Where then? He glanced at her gold wedding band.

She rubbed the bruise on her chin. Way Around is trouble, she said. I know all about trouble. Sometimes, it seems all I have. Day in. Day out. She pulled back her hand and touched her lips. Where you staying?

The Snooty Fox, he said.

She was trying to be subtle about it, but it damn sure looked like she was smelling her fingers, trying to gauge something of his scent, one breath and then another, inhaling as deep as possible.

She held his eyes. I worked there in high school. Made beds. Washed linens. None of those rooms have kitchens.

I have to show you what I can do, he said.

Vanessa chewed her bottom lip. This don't work out. You need to be on the next bus west. Next bus. You understand?

He nodded.

She glanced at her watch. My shift is over in thirty, but I can head out a little early. I'll take you out back, walk you home so we can avoid trouble.

The job? he asked.

I don't need a cook, she said grabbing her jacket, purse, and keys. But I'm willing to see what you can do.

He followed the gray fingers of smoke wafting around her head. Vanessa took a deep drag and blew smoke out Spider's motel window. She moved like a butterfly with a hurt wing, part grace, part wince. She filled his eyes like a starving boy gorging on tacos, caused the hardness in his chest to soften, and the softness in his crotch to harden. There wasn't nothing wrong with her. Nothing he could see or smell, nothing that hadn't long since been broken and healed.

Recipes littered the room. None quite right. Vanessa had come in, looked around, and said nothing. She'd stripped off her jacket and lit a cigarette. She wasn't shocked by his strangeness, in fact, she'd behaved as if she'd seen far worse.

I told you before. I aint got openings, Vanessa said. I have two serviceable cooks, Gus and Zeke. You can wait tables or sweep up. Best offer.

He took a seat on the bed, frowned at his ceviche recipe on the nightstand next to all the others.

I was a kid, Spider replied, rubbing his chest. Digging through garbage for food. *Viejita* was the first human being who showed me kindness. She fed me. Best tacos I've ever had. I chase that ghost every time I enter the kitchen. I can bring your customers the best food they've ever had.

Onion and *cilantro* sprinkled over *ground beef* mixed with *onions, green bell peppers, garlic, jalapeños, chili powder, cumin,* and something he still couldn't put his finger on. His mouth watered just thinking about it. *Viejita's* tacos were served in a blue cardboard box; grease, the kind you wanted to drink, soaked the corners and he tipped the box to lips and drank. There was a pattern to how *Viejita* assembled a taco—*corn tortilla* first, then steamy *ground beef, onion, cilantro,* and *pico de gallo* sprinkled on top. It was a small home that filled his stomach and made him feel connected.

Vanessa clenched her cigarette between V fingers; her wedding ring reflected the yellowish low watt lamplight. Is that who taught you to cook? she asked.

He shook his head. Sister Athene at St. Margaret, he said. She was a thin woman with an unremarkable face. Not ugly, mind you. Just forgettable. Her choir voice was lost to a three-pack-a-day habit. You couldn't forget her hands, though. Long fingers, constantly moving, like some eight-legged creature. She cut up fruits and veggies like she was playing piano at a concert. I never saw her outside the kitchen, and as far as I was concerned she lived in pots and pans. She taught me everything I know.

She let him hide between the potato and banana crates when the orphan boys with bloody, scuffed, secondhand shoes blockaded the black oaks. Eventually, she coaxed him from the crates with an onion and taught him to dice neat delicate squares. Tears rolled down his cheeks. He wanted to bury his face in her apron and breathe beef stock and olive oil. Spider savored how, during cooking lessons, Sister Athene shared the Greek myths instead of Bible stories. He didn't remember the heroes, but he remembered Arachne and Athena. If possession was a possibility for an orphan, he would've cashed in his beatings to claim her. But she was on loan. By the time he turned seventeen, he was dicing onions alone. Sister Athene dined in Tartarus, or maybe it was heaven. Either way, St. Margaret's stoves grew cold. That was around the time Mr. Harvey, a contractor in name only, was doing some painting and repair work on the church. His eight-dollar smile and wads of cash offered escape.

Vanessa's eyes hardened. Don't mean you can cook, she said. You want to tell me why we're here? Why I'm not on my way home? She looked around for an ashtray and dabbed her ashes into the window sill when she couldn't find one.

Vanessa was a recipe. Find the right ingredients and she'd simmer. He put his arms behind his head and crossed his ankles, the bed creaked and shook before settling. There was a danger to touching her, a danger in claiming what wasn't his, even temporarily. He had made it his life, before, to take things that belonged to other men. He felt the rush of breaking their windows, stealing their safety, and shoving theirs into his pockets. In those days he felt like a king, a confidence so robust, not even the sun dropping on his head could evaporate his mood. And then at night he lay alone, the pattering of rain on windows, grinding of teeth, stilling of stomach.

The summer before I was released into the wild, Spider said. I had the opportunity to make a little cash. There was this guy who came by St. Margaret's. Mr. Harvey was one of those old bloods with forearms of muscle that let you know he worked with his hands his whole life. He had this summer painting service, so he'd hire a few orphans and show us the trade. If we were good, he'd keep us on. I got picked that summer 'cause my height. Hard to reach places and all that.

Spider scratched his chest. Except painting was stealing and the jobs were B and E. Mr. Harvey used his painting company to case potential houses he wanted to rob. How would Vanessa feel knowing that only two weeks ago, he was a thief? He'd given that life up. Realized where that road departed. There was a dead end to Mr. Harvey, a graveyard of locusts and pesticide. It took Spider eight years, but he realized scampering after Mr. Harvey would lead him back to the waiting fists. Only instead of orphan boys, it would be prison guards. There would be no black oaks, no Sister Athene, no Greek myths to save him. Guilty. Case closed. Open-and-shut.

Vanessa slid the window shut, smashed her cigarette against the pane, scooped her jacket off the floor and put it on. Each button snap jerked her shoulders. When she reached the fourth button, her eyes narrowed.

He herky jerked you or you herky jerked him, she said. Same sad song, buddy. I was fifteen when daddy's bestie shoved his hands down my shorts and grabbed a handful of bush. Assholes are the same everywhere.

She finger-combed black hair, stretching to mid-back, away from her face. She had a faded scar along her hairline just above her ear that looked like the Greek eight.

Spider hopped off the bed. Encircled her from behind. Felt his knotted heart snatch her. The back of her head pressed against his sternum. He touched his lips to her neck, spun an invisible thread between them. She hesitated. His mouth wove down her shoulder; his tongue unraveled her recipe. The knot clutched them. He spun her in a slow delicate circle, removed her jacket, shirt, spanks and everything else, and buried his head—when she bellowed the rhythm of bedsprings, it was *Viejita*'s tacos all over again; he drank the grease.

Two sweaty hours later, Vanessa slipped on her panties and lit a cigarette. Between long, closed-eyed drags she said, I'll fire Gustavo next week. But I gotta keep Zeke. My nephew's too stupid to work anywhere else.

A week later, morning heat hung like a thick musky fog. His knotted heart coiled, a familiar compulsion whenever he found a place he wanted to stay a while. He arrived early for his first shift at *Rafael's Eatery* to prep the kitchen. Meat. Chop. Cheese. Chop. Vegetables. Chop. He finished just as the white aproned staff gathered over coffee near the cash register. He occasionally caught words like Gus' replacement or job stealer. He didn't mind. He'd been called worse. Rag in hand, he went around the dining room scrubbing every table from corner to corner and if gum or something else was underneath, he'd scrape it with a spatula. Pretty soon everything in *Rafael's Eatery*, the gum, the grime, the employees, the customers, would be his. He wouldn't be alone anymore. He would be home.

Vanessa exited the kitchen, checking her crooked teeth in a compact. She beamed at what she saw and added more red to already raspberry lips. Her wedding ring was missing and so was the bruise on her chin. Vanessa put away the compact and sashayed to the table he was wiping down. Her citrus tinged perfume turned her normal Marlboro Light's odor into wet cigar scent he didn't find unpleasant—she just smelled different and different was something he could get used to. She leaned against his shoulder, plucked the rag out of his hand, and folded it into a neat deliberate square.

C'mere you, she said, pulling him toward the circle of white aprons' expectant faces.

His heart was loose; it was hard to believe he had been working at *Rafael's* for eight months. It felt longer. His tacos were something of a thing in town. Every lunch hour from eleven to two, grubs piled at the door to order the daily special. He worked fast, *corn tortilla, tender ground beef, onion, cilantro, pico de gallo,* and slapped his masterpieces into blue cardboard boxes. The wait-staff whisked them to their owners and stuffed bountiful tips into their pockets for the trouble. Time got lost, but at the end it was found again. The rush was over; the lunch crowd slimmed to a few satisfied full-bellied caterpillars ready to spin cocoons. It was going to be slow for the next hour. Good. He asked Zeke to cover for him. He could take a fifteen. Even a taco god needed a breather.

Spider wiped sweat from his forehead with a sleeve, stripped off his apron, hung it on a peg, and stepped out back to avoid customers who would surely pat him on the back and try to introduce him to their single daughters. He shook his head. Vanessa more than filled his appetite.

The air was cool against his face and the sun crested the tops of the large pines. Light spilled between the branches leaving patchwork shadows on black concrete. He followed the pattern to a series of water pipes. Beneath the pipes was a bluish-black striped spider crawling neither fast nor slow, twisting its body, until the beginnings of a gossamer home emerged. There was within every spider, the possibility to create its own home to have something all his own. Spider himself would have never thought it a possibility, a small boy, cold and alone, in the alleys of those who don't give a damn to the man he is now. And he did it himself, with his own hands, with his own mind, and skill. He was a goddamned hell of a cook, better than even he himself had hopes to be.

It reminded Spider of a story Sister Athene told him about a beautiful weaver from ancient Greece. There was this weaver who could weave better, faster, and more beautifully than anyone. This woman got so full of herself that she challenged the gods. One day a goddess comes down from Olympus and accepts the challenge. They weave high stakes, winner take all, and when it's all said and done, weaver done kicked goddess ass. The goddess, on some hate, turned the weaver into a spider, dooming the weaver and her descendants to weave webs forever.

> Spider wondered if the story was real and what would happen if that curse were lifted. How would her descendants react if they stopped being spiders and had to be men?
>
> He removed a napkin from his pocket, held the blue pen loosely.

A student read Darryl's poem and story back-to-back and said this:

> I've played around with hybrid material, but never to any serious extent. Seeing what Darryl White did with "The Arachne Gene" opened my eyes to those places where prose and poetry do intersect, and I loved catching those hints of the poem in the published prose piece. It has me thinking of what I could do to make a prose piece out of a poem I've already written, or vice versa.

Writing a prose piece out of a poem is one choice, but you can also infuse prose with the skills poets use. Let's look at examples from writers who, from the very first draft, purposely borrowed from other genres.

This excerpt was published as a stand-alone piece and as the opening of Justin Torres's first novel *We the Animals*. It's fiction. As you read, notice the poetic techniques.

We Wanted More (excerpt from *We the Animals*)
Justin Torres

We wanted more. We knocked the butt ends of our forks against the table, tapped our spoons against our empty bowls; we were hungry. We wanted more volume, more riots. We turned up the knob on the TV until our ears ached with the shouts of angry men. We wanted more music on the radio; we wanted beats; we wanted rock. We wanted muscles on our skinny arms. We had bird bones, hollow and light, and we wanted more density, more weight. We were six snatching hands, six stomping feet; we were brothers, boys, three little kings locked in a feud for more.

When it was cold, we fought over blankets until the cloth tore down the middle. When it was really cold, when our breath came out in frosty clouds, Manny crawled into bed with Joel and me.

"Body heat," he said.

"Body heat," we agreed.

We wanted more flesh, more blood, more warmth.

When we fought, we fought with boots and garage tools, snapping pliers—we grabbed at whatever was nearest and we hurled it through the air; we wanted more broken dishes, more shattered glass. We wanted more crashes.

And when our Paps came home, we got spankings. Our little round butt cheeks were tore up: red, raw, leather-whipped. We knew there was something on the other side of pain, on the other side of the sting. Prickly heat radiated upward from our thighs and backsides, fire consumed our brains, but we knew that there was something more, someplace our Paps was taking us with all this. We knew, because he was meticulous, because he was precise, because he took his time. He was awakening us; he was leading us somewhere beyond burning and ripping, and you couldn't get there in a hurry.

And when our father was gone, we wanted to *be* fathers. We hunted animals. We drudged through the muck of the crick, chasing down bullfrogs and water snakes. We plucked the baby robins from their nest. We liked to feel the beat of tiny hearts, the struggle of tiny wings. We brought their tiny animal faces close to ours.

"Who's your daddy?" we said, then we laughed and tossed them into a shoebox.

Always more, always hungrily scratching for more. But there were times, quiet moments, when our mother was sleeping, when she hadn't slept in two days, and any noise, any stair creak, any shut door, any stifled laugh, any voice at all, might wake her, those still, crystal mornings, when we wanted to protect her, this confused goose of a woman, this stumbler, this gusher, with her backaches and headaches and her tired, tired ways, this uprooted Brooklyn creature, this tough talker, always with tears when she told us she loved us, her mixed-up love, her needy love, her warmth, those mornings when sunlight found the cracks in our blinds and laid itself down in crisp strips on our carpet, those quiet mornings when we'd fix ourselves oatmeal and sprawl onto our stomachs with crayons and paper, with glass marbles that we were careful not to rattle, when our mother was sleeping, when the air did not smell like sweat or breath or mold, when the air was still and light,

> those mornings when silence was our secret game and our gift and our sole
> accomplishment—we wanted less: less weight, less work, less noise, less
> father, less muscles and skin and hair. We wanted nothing, just this, just this.

In dozens of interviews, Torres talked about poetry's influence on his fiction. We can see his use of repetition, compression of language, anaphora, and other elements of poetry all while doing the work of a novel's opening chapter: introducing characters, allowing the reader to enter the world, give us an idea of what's at stake.

In his essay for the *Michigan Quarterly Review* titled "The Poetry of Prose: A Brief Study of Justin Torres's *We the Animals*," Nathan Go writes:

> Lately I've been obsessing about the liminal spaces between prose and poetry, how one can inform the other, and how—stripping bare the artifices for a second—one *is* essentially the other. Prosody (rhyme, rhythm, alliteration, assonance, etc.) can be used in prose as much as it can be for poetry, although the expected intensity and frequency within each tradition differs. Even line, which is perhaps the best marker of poetry, is mostly a virtual artifice, similar to the paragraph for prose. When read out loud and without unnatural attempts to emphasize, lines and paragraphs tend to disappear. . . .
>
> I picked up Justin Torres's *We the Animals* because his style obviously straddles the two genres. It's marketed as fiction, a novel, though his prose has been described as "lyrical" and even "concentrated"—"goes down hot like strong liquor" (says Tayari Jones). On a very superficial level, when reading Torres's prose, one immediately notices the liberal use of word repetition.

In the same essay, Go breaks Torres's prose passages into stanzas with clear line breaks, just like we did in our opening exercise.

Conventional novelists go for smooth transitions. They want an organized and obvious continuity between scenes. Torres's novel uses interrelated vignettes instead of a typical plot, allowing readers to imagine the transitions and fill in the blanks between the vignettes. This choice could be borrowed from poetry. Poets trust readers (and their imaginations and associations) to fill in what the poet purposely omits between the lines, in white space and after ellipses. When successful, the effect can be like a great photo album, or a home film that portrays occasions and notable experiences but leaves the viewer with an idea of an entire life.

Poets also borrow from prose writers' toolboxes to glorious effect. Brilliant poems contain narrative strategies to achieve the author's desired effect, even if, as Go says, the "expected intensity and frequency within each tradition differs."

Let's look at this poem by writer Stewart Shaw.

daddy sings us goodbyes
Stewart Shaw

    1-
    He mixed rhythm
    & blues with his gin.
    Stirred it until
    It was a party

    Caught catfish on Fridays
    swam through ditches
    on his way home.

    Daddy
    through breath, hot
    from Lucky Strikes,
    told his mama when
    he left home the first time—you
    still ma girl. Told mama—when
    he got home, the second time
    baby, you, still ma girl.

    2-
    He is memory
    sepia-toned,
    hands reaching down, out
    of nowhere to
    collect me—he

is ghost haunting
walls and dreams—
an occasional family
picnic.

3-
Daddy wanted to be famous; somebody
thought he was Otis Redding
as he sung with the radio
that was perched on top of the refrigerator.
Wanted to taste the red clay
layered in the music,
wanted to be reminded of home,
the honey cloistered in the soil there.
His dreams
made him forget us for moments
and hours, got him lost in his souring cup,
turned his insides black and rebellious.

4-
And mama, us
kids waited.
Maybe for the real Otis
to slip in behind daddy's singing,
come and lay
hands on
tiny heads napped
like Bible verses,
ease us into light; keep daddy happy
when he wasn't singing, or
maybe when he was.

There's a clear prose writer's narrative strategy at work here in the situation and the story. You can easily imagine this material as memoir. The writer uses expert touches of characterization, details that illuminate a particular setting. And yet, it's inarguably a successful poem. To achieve this poem's mastery, the writer borrows liberally from prose writers' techniques without ever compromising or abandoning the demands of his own genre.

We hope the exercise and examples reinforced our first goal: to get you to borrow from the effective strategies of each genre, even when your material's container starts and remains the same.

Write Now

Borrowing from the previous examples, do one or more of the following exercises:

1. If you have a draft of a short story, reread it. See if you can choose and clearly articulate, like Darryl White did, a thematic question. Once you've done so, create a poem from lines in your story that deepen the exploration of that theme. Revise the story, like Darryl did, according to what you learned.
2. Reread Justin Torres's opening chapter of *We the Animals*. Write (or rewrite) a story opening with a focus on what Nathan Go calls *prosody* (rhyme, rhythm, alliteration, assonance, and so on). Go for *intensity* and *frequency* with a focus on word repetition.
3. Reread Stewart Shaw's "daddy sings us goodbyes." Create a paragraph from each of his stanzas. Imagine yourself into characters, the setting, and dialogue. In other words, turn it (or any other poem, someone else's, or your own) into a story. Work to maintain the mood and tension of the original.

For the experiments we've tried so far, we've used works where the author consciously or unconsciously borrowed tools from a second genre to inform their own. As far as we know, they started and finished their pieces in the same genre.

Sometimes, however, authors attempting one genre experiment with another and decide to switch.

Time for a Change?

Like we've said, sometimes these experiments across genre can help us sharpen the techniques we're using for the material's original container. Other times, writers discover it's time for a change.

You may have just decided after experimenting outside your material's original genre to change genres. This happens all the time.

Cathy Park Hong tried to write about racial consciousness (specifically Asian American consciousness) in satirical poems. When that didn't work, she tried working within the container of a novel. As she continued to grapple, she eventually produced a brilliant book of essays called *Minor Feelings*.

Hong described her experience in an interview with *The Yale Review*. She explained that consciousness of race had been a continual presence in her writing—particularly the consciousness of Asian Americans. What initially inspired her: watching Richard Pryor do a stand-up comedy routine and wondering why the work of Asian Americans lacked the same edginess and honesty that Pryor exuded.

She first tried writing satirical poems. Then a novel. Both ventures failed. Then she started doing stand-up herself. At venues where she was supposed to read her poetry, she did comedy routines instead, "which took a lot of the curators by surprise," she said.

After much experimentation, Hong found a container that worked: creative nonfiction. The careful reader can still see how the writer infused the essays with techniques used by poets and even stand-up comedians as she created "narratives that . . . [are] incendiary and honest and provocative."

Another brilliant writer, T Kira Madden, won a prestigious spot among writers at MacDowell Colony, where she went intending to work on a novel. Instead, she found herself writing what she thought were essays. In the end, it became a memoir. It's called *Long Live the Tribe of Fatherless Girls*. In an interview with Madden, novelist Pik-Shuen Fung commented: "I read . . . you were on your third or fourth attempt at a novel. How did you end up publishing a memoir first?" Madden responded:

> I graduated with my MFA in fiction and I've taught fiction for years. I applied to the MacDowell Colony with a novel and got in off the waitlist, about a month and a half or two months after my father died. I almost didn't want to go, but I decided to give myself that space to try to make art and heal. While I was working on the novel, my dad started showing up as a character in all of my work. At that point, my fiction had always been radically removed from my reality, and it was odd for me to have any real people popping up in my stories. I decided to embrace that, him, and try to wrangle whatever it was that was happening, so I wrote about loving a mannequin who stood in

for a father. It was the first piece of nonfiction I had ever written. While I was grieving, all my other projects felt frivolous. I remember calling Hannah, my fiancée, and I said, *If I were ever a nonfiction writer, which I never will be, this would be an interesting book, and this is what I would call it, and this is how it would look.* She said, *Maybe that's the book you're ready to write.* By the time I left the residency, I had 100 pages of something.

Readers of Madden's memoir can clearly see the influence of her fiction-writing prowess. They feel as if they're experiencing Madden's childhood and adolescence along with her, leading up to the insights she gleans looking back as an adult in the aftermath of her father's death.

While reading the following excerpt, track her expert use of plot, point of view, tone, narrative distance, dialogue, setting, and characterization.

Long Live the Tribe of Fatherless Girls (excerpt)

T Kira Madden

My mother rescued a mannequin from the J. C. Penney dump when I was two years old. He was a full-bodied jewelry mannequin: fancy, distinguished. Those were the words she used. Her father, my grandfather, worked the counter day and night, slinked antique chains and strands of jade across velvet placemats, and felt the mannequin did no work for his numbers; *he's pau*—done. Grandfather said this with both elbows bent, a chopping motion. The mannequin would have to go.

In this part of the story, my mother and I live alone in Coconut Grove, Florida. We're in a canary-yellow apartment damned with beanbag ashtrays, field mice, the guts of flashlights and remote controls (*Where have all the batteries gone? Where do they go?*), and a shag carpet that feels sharp all the way under the shag. She's single, my mother, the crimson-mouthed mistress of my father, a white man, who is back home in downtown Miami with his artist wife, his two handsome boys. Soon, my father will move my mother and me into a porn director's apartment, and then to Boca Raton—*the Rat's Mouth*—to start over, but none of us knows this yet.

My mother, a Chinese, Hawaiian, pocketknife of a woman, shot a man once. She tells me this story all the time. How the strange man tried to crawl through her window, naked, choking out his cock as she slipped into a nightgown. She shot him in the shoulder with a boyfriend's .357 Magnum, his body spat out like a rag doll into the liquid black night. He landed in the street—too far to be trespassing—so she dragged him by the legs back on her lawn for more. The man was paralyzed for the rest of his life; he threatened to sue. My mother never once regretted this incident.

But this is how it was in Coconut Grove in the 1980s and early '90s. Bandits, robbers, glass stems on the sidewalk, bad men doing bad under the bridge. My mother had little to defend in that first apartment of ours—a few gems from her father, frosted Christmas ornaments, her Chinese jade, some cash—but then there was me. We needed a man in our home, a figure bigger than us, she said, to scare off all the other men who would come. All of this to say that the reason she rescued that mannequin, the reason she wrapped her arms wickedly tight around his waist, carrying him to the backseat of our Volvo where the top half of his body slung out the window, his bald head pat-pattering under the rain on our car ride home, all the reasons she did anything—the wrong things, the strange things, the dangerous, the sublime— the reasons she does any of it, still, is to protect me. Remember this.

I name him Uncle Nuke. He has marble eyes, real hair feathering out from his lash line, eyebrows painted with delicate streaks, thin as needles, curved. Little nail moons. He stands six feet tall and smells clean and metallic as the air before a Florida storm. Uncle Nuke wears a tuxedo, and under his clothes, my mother is learning to take advantage of his joints. With a simple twist-pop, she detaches his torso, places him in the passenger seat of our car, buckling him gently like another child. I like staring at the dome of his bald head from the backseat. It's chipped in places—silver, flecked. We're able to drive in the HOV lane with the extra body. *Three makes a family,* says my mother. *At least that.*

My father visits our apartment sometimes, at night, so late that my visions of him are smudged. There's the smell of him: Merit cigarettes, orange juice and vodka, money. The grind of his voice. The word: *father. This here is your father* and *Hello, I'm your father.* He slips up often and calls me *Son.* Mostly, when I conjure him then and remember him now, I think of gold. Gold horse bits on the buckles of his shoes; gold buttons on sailor jackets; a gold pinky ring; the gold chain necklace my grandfather gave him from the fanciest case at J. C. Penney. A trade, he said, for my father to wise up and make a commitment—*a Jew chain for the only Jewish man I've ever met*—to turn my mother into something honorable.

Before my father arrives at our apartment, my mother sits Uncle Nuke in a rocking chair near the front window. My mother likes him like this, in profile, the edges of his regal face chiseled out like a dream. Sometimes his legs lie in the corner of our living room, the trousers pressed, his knees locked into place. My mother and I like to change his socks at least once a week. We pull the bright patterns over his club feet, delicately roll the bands up his calves.

This man doesn't look like he belongs in our home. He looks like he belongs to a different era, someplace far away from here, a life with white dinner gloves, niceties, an engraved cigarette case—*U.N.*—that quietly clicks closed. My father knows all about the mannequin, his practical functions, the way he wards off intruders, but I wonder, still, what his shadow did to my father's heart when he drove up in his white Cadillac—if it stoked something fierce enough inside him to make his temples quake, to whet his desire for my mother and me; if it was Uncle Nuke, not even a real man, who eventually made him unpack and stay.

When my father moves in, I begin crawling out of my bedroom at night to visit Uncle Nuke. We meet at his rocking chair. I coil up at his feet.

Where did you come from? I ask. I grip behind the joints of his ankles, breathing in. *I'm the one who loves you now.*

I press my cheek into the patent leather of his shoes. My mother has my father and I have Uncle Nuke. In the morning, I wear the red indents of his shoelaces across my face like a map.

I can't bear the thought of leaving Uncle Nuke. Not for school, or for walks to Biscayne Bay; I don't even like to leave whichever room he's in. I, too, learn to work his joints. Before school, I twist off one of his hands, hiding it in my lunch box. I hold the hand as much as I can throughout my day, a horseshoe grip around the bulk of fingers.

What's wrong with the kid? I've heard my father ask. *She doesn't get her weird from me.*

She likes to hold him is all, says my mother. *You know kids—you have two others. They like to hold on to things, don't they?*

Here is a memory that still comes to me: I am small, too small, thimble legs in a yellow dress. My parents are getting married tonight. There are steep steps in the lobby of the Omni Hotel, and I am expected to walk down these steps with grace, to flick flowers. My mother wears a Chinese wedding gown, a beaded headpiece like a bird of paradise. She says, *You can do this.* She smiles the biggest smile of her life. My grandfather is wearing his best cuff links, veiny green jade, proud at last. He walks me through the steps I will take, *Count. You can count, right? Everyone will love you.*

They do. I make my way down the stairs with *Ohs* and *Ahs* of delight, the pop of flashbulbs. The bastard child.

My parents seem very much in love. I am old enough to know that. They dance little steps, around in a square. They smear cake and lick it. My father's lips part as he squeezes my mother by her waist, their slow song tickling the water in my glass, and I am jealous of the both of them.

At home, in the half-dark, I tell Uncle Nuke all about it.

I say, *I guess we can keep him. If we have to.*

Readers love Madden's memoir, even when they aren't aware of the writer's use of the fiction techniques she studied. Let's do an experiment based on Madden's process with *Long Live the Tribe of Fatherless Girls.*

Before we do, a final note on substance. Throughout this book, we insist that you care deeply about your material because no amount of switching or experimenting will make shallow work deep. Occasionally, we've seen student writers who attempt switching genres, points of view, narrative timelines, settings, and styles instead of doing the quiet and sometimes emotionally difficult work of finding and digging into meaningful material. Remember: It isn't the container that makes the piece original, it's you.

Write Now

1. Borrowing from what Madden told her fiancée Hannah, finish this sentence: "If I were ever a (name a genre you've never written in) _____ writer, which I never will be, this would be the first line: _____; and _____ is what I would title it; and _____ is how it would look."

2. Write three stanzas, scenes, or pages: one you imagine as a beginning, one

a middle, one from the end in the new form. (In the future, you can abandon the genre and rearrange the order as you see fit.)

So far, we've seen writers who learn and borrow techniques from multiple genres. We've also looked at those who set out to write in one genre and then switched genres, sometimes more than once, to accommodate the unexpected demands of their raw materials. In each case, readers can sense the influence of more than one genre—and in each case, those choices make the pieces stronger. Readers are dazzled by the results. The final forms feel organic and inevitable—just the right vase for its flowers.

But what happens when a single genre just won't do?

Let's study and experiment with forms that combine more than one genre.

The Lyric Essay

The lyric essay is a distinct hybrid form, blending the realms of creative nonfiction and poetry. We're echoing the sentiments of John D'Agata and Deborah Tall by saying that the lyric essay embodies the density and shapeliness of poetry, crafting language with a keen eye for distillation of ideas and a penchant for musicality. Simultaneously, it engages with facts and the actual world, demonstrating a desire to meld the imaginative with the factual.

The form is characterized by its scene-driven narrative, rich description, and incorporation of personal reflections interwoven with research. Its form can be characterized by brevity, fragmentation, and braiding of various narrative threads, as well as the incorporation of poetic techniques and devices.

In the realm of creative nonfiction, the lyric essay challenges traditional notions of objectivity. It prioritizes subjective experiences and emotional resonance over factual accuracy, offering a departure from conventional approaches to storytelling.

Here's an example, titled "Signs," by Kathleen Hellen:

> The likeness of the sun floats pearly, other-worldly on the olive-oil waters of the river. A hazy locus, the ivy trespassing, slouching in and out of rotting fences. Beyond the funeral home, there's carry-out for beer. Amber lots like grasslands dispossessed, where narratives in trails include the lost Manokin, where once the Nanticoke had traded words (about

300)—not used since frail Miss Lydia last spoke—like beaver skins for match coats; where fugitive Acadians once wintered, before their lands were confiscated; where Negro galleries still host a ghostly choir, the old brick founder's church a dutiful memorial. I patronize the yard sales, craft fairs, buy a $50 hat stitched out of colored rags, a cranberry-bran muffin, at the antique shop and bookstore, where a friendly volunteer in cardigan and corduroy guesses that this Dickinson is rare, worth $140 (maybe $2); she can't say for sure because The Internet is "acting up." So I browse the shelves of cookbooks, orphaned by convenience. Huddled in the nooks, biographies of Washington and Franklin, *Treasure Island. Moby Dick.* A threadbare *Rip Van Winkle* snores atop an ailing Keats. Who reads *Evangeline* anymore? I sip mint tea and read the book I bought about the railroad expansion. The bean field where they built the naval base, and over themed displays of guides to popular antiques, limpid watercolors of the Chesapeake. On the way back to the B&B a peel of tape marks "DANGER," surrounds a rusting crane. The public park's gazebo's, for the most part, ornamental. Independence Hall is now a popular café. I stop to take a selfie at the bridge. The water whiffles. The current follows course, escaping down to Tangier Sound, where watermen give way to splashy tour boats, where "Public Auction" trades for new exchanges, the curb a map of annual migrations—yellow arrows flying in the opposite direction.

Hellen used poetic language to tell of her day as a tourist on the Chesapeake Bay. She's curating events to give readers a sense of what has been lost in this region: the true history, traditions of the native people of that land, including the Nanticoke Tribe's language (last spoken by Lydia Clark).

Is her lyric essay scene driven with lots of description? Yes. What's the result? A look at a place once alive with a rich and vibrant history. In it, she herself becomes a consumer, reads about railroad expansion, takes a selfie, returns to a B&B.

Hellen's choice to contrast descriptions of the place both "as is" and how she imagines it "once was" works to create a mood that thrills, shocks, and shifts the meaning.

In his book *Blind Spot*, Teju Cole takes the reader on a journey across the world in 150 photographs and 150 vignette-sized essays. Here are two of his vignettes:

TIVOLI

Spring, even in America, is Japanese. It is not only the leaves that grow. Shadows grow also. Everything grows, both what receives the light, and what is cast by it. There is more in the world, all of it proliferating like neural patterns. Almost all of it: it is also the most melancholy season, for, as Alkman says, there is nothing to eat. Resurrection is far too close to death, and the moment when the sleep begins to leave your eyes is the most fragile, the most porous, for at times in spring, even the emotional granaries are depleted.

I remember the lines from *Sans Soleil*: "Newspapers have been filled recently with the story of a man from Nagoya. The woman he loved died last year and he drowned himself in work—Japanese style—like a madman. It seems he even made an important discovery in electronics. And then in the month of May he killed himself. They say he could not stand hearing the word 'Spring.'"

LAGOS

One sense of sleep is the disappearance of the eyes. The head turns inward, toward darkness. Another is an entry into a state of being carried. Outside a church in Lagos, a man sleeps. The body transitions from carrying itself across the earth into being carried by it, into giving itself up to that. The body of Christ is on the now-lowered cross. A white cloth is draped around him. He is not dead, only sleeping (a sleep of two nights and one long day). Around him at the moment of descent are John the Beloved, Joseph of Arimathea, Nicodemus, Mary Magdalene. Closest to him is his mother, in white. John holds out a larger white cloth with which to receive his body. The earth carries the cross. The cross carries the body. The body on the cross carries the world: in a state of sleep, one common dream is that of superhuman strength.

Tivoli is a small town in upstate New York. The passage begins by evoking the arrival of spring and its connection to Japanese aesthetics, with an emphasis on growth and the play of light and shadow. It introduces a sense of melancholy associated with spring, highlighting the juxtapositions in (human) nature. Alkman's statement and lines from the film *Sans Soleil* add artistic, literary, and historical layers to the text. The passage then references a man from Nagoya who took his own life in May after hearing the word "Spring."

In his second "picture," Cole evokes a man sleeping outside a church in Lagos and connects the act of sleeping to a spiritual or transcendent experience: the closing of one's eyes is a mundane act that also serves as metaphor. The writer suggests it's akin to being carried or surrendering to something larger.

Both passages use poetic and contemplative language to explore themes of nature, seasonality, emotion, and spirituality. They blur the lines between poetry and essay, inviting readers to engage with the text on multiple levels, both intellectually and emotionally. These are characteristic features of lyric essays, which often prioritize lyrical expression and personal reflection over traditional essay structure and argumentation.

Cole's examples bring what might otherwise be unconscious association to the level of consciousness. His pieces unpack the complexity of thought that might happen on a walk through a new place—or by looking at a photograph of that place days or months or years later.

Write Now

1. Reread Hellen's and Cole's pieces, paying particular attention to how they allow flights of fancy without connecting the dots for the reader.
2. Pick a place important to you.
3. List ten "facts" about that place: its history, landmarks, rivers, lakes, and mountains. Perhaps pay particular attention to lesser-known facts.
4. List ten things that place reminds you of: another place (spring in Tivoli, New York, reminds Cole of spring in Japan), another person (Cole, in "Lagos," is reminded of the man sleeping outside the church and of Jesus), another time (Hellen evokes Native land prior to it becoming a place of tourist consumerism), a movie, a book, a quote, and anything else.
5. Write a lyric essay, weaving "facts" about the place with your associations. At all times, prioritize *lyrical expression* and *personal reflection* over traditional essay structure.

Prose poetry has evolved through centuries of literary experimentation. Its origins can be traced back to early examples found in Bible translations and the works of William Wordsworth. But the form we highlight in this book is said to be rooted in nineteenth-century France with symbolist writers such as Aloysius Bertrand and Charles Baudelaire, characterized by the blurring and combining of what were strict boundaries between prose and poetry.

The form has since proliferated worldwide, with notable figures such as Rainer Maria Rilke, Franz Kafka, Jorge Luis Borges, Pablo Neruda, Octavio Paz, William Carlos Williams, and Gertrude Stein. Each writer using the form effectively becomes a co-creator by adding their unique sensibilities, rules, and restrictions.

In recent years, there has been a resurgence of interest in prose poetry, with literary journals dedicating entire issues to the form. While prose poetry lacks the traditional line breaks of verse, it retains the rhythmic qualities and condensed language characteristic of poetry. It offers a reading experience distinct from short stories or flash fiction, inviting readers into a realm where plot, character, and scene take a back seat to gesture, image, and implication.

Cassandra Atherton and Paul Hetherington, authors of *Prose Poetry: An Introduction*, elucidate the unique qualities of prose poetry, highlighting its ability to weave together the voice of the author with other voices—be they characters, intertextual references, or contemporary allusions—creating a tapestry of disparate yet interconnected elements. In prose poems, the limited space exerts pressure on narrative techniques, sometimes resulting in a rupture that blurs the boundaries between prose and poetry, offering readers a glimpse into the complexity of human experience captured within a single form.

Here's an engrossing prose poem by Hala Alyan.

Oklahoma

For a place I hate, I invoke you often. Stockholm's: I am eight years old and the telephone poles are down, the power plant at the edge of town spitting electricity. Before the pickup trucks, the strip malls, dirt beaten by Cherokee feet. *Osiyo, tsilugi.* Rope swung from mule to tent to man, tornadoes came, the wind rearranged the face of the land like a chessboard. This was before the gold rush, the greed of engines, before white men pressing against brown women, nailing crosses by the river, before the slow songs of cotton plantations, the hymns toward God, the murdered dangling like earrings. Under a redwood, two men signed away the land and in history class I don't understand why a boy whispers *sand monkey.* The Mexican girls let me sit with them as long as I braid their hair, my fingers dipping into that wet black silk. I try to imitate them at home— *mírame, mama*—but my mother yells at me, says they didn't come here so I could speak some beggar language. Heaven is a long weekend. Heaven is a tornado siren canceling school. Heaven is pressed in a pleather booth at the Olive Garden, sipping Pepsi between my gapped teeth, listening to my father mispronounce his meal.

This poem succeeds because of the impact it has on the reader. We do not know for sure if the piece is autobiographical. Hala Alyan is a Palestinian American poet and clinical psychologist who grew up in Kuwait, Oklahoma, Texas, Maine, and Lebanon—so it could be.

The piece's opening lines make an immediate impact:

> For a place I hate, I invoke you often. Stockholm's: I am eight years old and the telephone poles are down, the power plant at the edge of town spitting electricity.

The author is a clinical psychologist, and Stockholm syndrome is the psychological condition of a victim who identifies with and empathizes with their captor. In this poem, her speaker hates the place and identifies with it. The author is using the tension to engage readers, a strategy that might be associated with prose. The repetition of "heaven" at the end of the piece and the examples she uses to define heaven allow the reader to glean the complexity of the relationship she has with this place. These tools often come from a poet's toolbox.

Write Now

1. Reread "Oklahoma," by Hala Alyan.
2. Think of a place that brings up contrasting feelings. Are there things about it you see as "heavenly"? Are there things about it that you "hate"?

3. Start with the line "For a place I hate, I invoke you often . . ."
4. Write about how the place "holds you captive."
5. Like Alyan does, end with three examples of "heaven" from that place.
6. Put it away. When you go back to it, shape it into a prose poem.
7. Transform the imitative parts (the first line and the repetition of "Heaven is . . .") into something of your own (as inspired by Hala Alyan).

Flash Fiction

Grant Faulkner, in a LitHub article called "13 Ways of Looking at Flash Fiction," reinforces what the experts say about each of the hybrid genres: Flash fiction resists definition. It's always evolving. For this reason, we thought we'd skip the dictionary definition and include his creative response. In it, he employs the tools and techniques of the form to shine light on it.

1. Dorothy Parker said, "Brevity is the soul of lingerie." A flash story is the lingerie itself: an invitation to come hither, a promise, a hint.
2. Flash fiction is like a tiny island, created from an unknown eruption at the earth's crust, enhanced by the expanse of the sea around it.
3. Flash fiction is like the moment a turtle pokes its head out of its shell.
4. Flash fiction is like an afternoon nap. Short. Dreamy. A respite from a tough day. A strange and intriguing interlude. And when you wake up, you're in a different state.
5. Flash fiction is the moment you hit the brakes.
6. Flash fiction is like a brook flowing through the woods. It's easy to step over, and it's not big enough to be on any map, but then when you pause to observe it, you see life teeming within it.
7. Flash fiction is like the tip of a needle.
8. Flash fiction is like a bonsai tree, compressed, yet sculpted to create movement, proportion, asymmetry, and poignancy. Some trees slant. Some trees cascade. Some are windswept or weeping. "Bonsai art is the display of a landscape—without the landscape," said the bonsai artist Nobu Kajiwara.
9. Flash fiction is like a rare seashell you find on the beach. It's delicate,

yet it's traveled through many waters, only to be mysteriously left on the shore, a found object.

10. Flash fiction is like the faint rustling of a ghost, present, yet absent; alive, yet dead. It has something to tell you, but you have to listen in a different way.

11. Flash fiction is like a submarine, able to go to places beneath the surface of life in a way that other boats can't.

12. Flash fiction is like a pill: small and seemingly harmless, yet full of powerful substances that might heal, might kill—or might just alter your senses.

13. Flash fiction is like the light of a sparkler, spritzing dashes of light into the air for only a minute.

And here's an excerpt from a piece of flash fiction by Tania James.

The South Asian Speakers Series Presents the Archeologist and Adventurer Indiana Jones (excerpt)

Tania James

"But, if you ask me," Indiana Jones said, "it belongs in a museum."

He paused to let that sink in.

He was sitting onstage across from the moderator, an Indian woman whose name he'd failed to catch. Her legs were crossed at the knee. (The legs he'd remember.) He reached for the glass of water on the tiny table between them and sipped.

The moderator uncrossed her legs and shifted to face the audience. "Let's pause here and take some questions."

He followed her gaze to the masses, overflowing into the aisles, lined up along the walls. For the first time that evening, he tried to distinguish faces. Many of them were colored. Faces of color. Not a bad thing. His best friend was Egyptian.

A microphone was passed to the first questioner, a brown-skinned man. "Thank you for your talk, Dr. Jones. I'm wondering about the Indian village, the one that sent you on your quest to retrieve a mystical stone."

"The Sankara stone, correct. The villagers sent me to retrieve it and save their kidnapped children from a demonic cult."

"I was just wondering what the village was called."

"I don't remember."

"You don't remember?"

"I'd just ridden a raft down a waterfall. You'll forgive me if I don't remember the name of the village." Indy grinned in a way that he hoped was charming.

"I believe it was Mayapore?" the moderator filled in, consulting her notes.

"That's it, Mayapore," Indy said. "And the leader of the village was named Shaman."

"Shaman," the questioner said. "Just . . . Shaman."

"Correct."

"So if I went to this Mayapore and went around asking for a guy named Shaman, people would be, like, yeah, Shaman lives over on, I dunno, Cherokee Street."

"Look, pal, I don't know what your problem is—"

"My problem is that all these names sound made up."

"All names are made up. Hey, I was named after my pet dog!"

Some people laughed. Indy prompted the next question.

It came from a pretty woman in a clingy skirt. "Hi, Dr. Jones," she said, and, as she went on, he found himself recalling a student, a girl, from his teaching days. "You mentioned that, at the Maharajah's banquet, you were served a dessert of chilled monkey brains?"

The title of this piece serves double-time as the name of a fictitious academic lecture. This flash examines stereotypes related to Orientalism, racism, and sexism, although it does so in a satirical and subversive manner.

Indiana Jones, a fictional movie character, is recast into James's story. Through Indy's dialogue (he can't remember the names of people or places), she evokes the theme (and threat) of Orientalism, which is the harmful Western tendency to exoticize, stereotype, and misunderstand Eastern cultures and peoples.

The narrative intelligence tells us that Indiana Jones can't remember the name of the Indian moderator but he can remember her legs, underscoring how this film and its genre also reinforce the objectification of women.

Flash fiction will not allow a comprehensive exploration of these important themes, but we see a writer who expertly uses the form, along with satire and humor, to provoke thought about how certain stereotypes and assumptions can shape our perceptions of cultures and gender roles.

Write Now

1. Reread Grant Faulkner's "13 Ways of Looking at Flash Fiction," paying particular attention to this one: "Flash fiction is . . . compressed, yet sculpted to create movement, proportion, asymmetry, and poignancy."
2. Think of a popular character from literature or film that rubs you the wrong way.
3. Invent an interview format inspired by James's academic speakers' series. It could be a TV interview, a red carpet, *Oprah,* a serious news hour, or any other format you can imagine.
4. Use satire and humor so that the recast fictional character exposes, through their dialogue, their own blind spots and shortcomings.

Erasures

Erasure poetry, also referred to as blackout poetry, is a form of "found poetry" characterized by the selective removal or obscuring of existing text to reveal a new composition. As defined by the Academy of American Poets, this process involves the deliberate erasure, blacking out, or obscuring of significant portions of a source text, resulting in the creation of a wholly original work from what remains.

This transformative act of erasure allows poets to engage in various forms of creative exploration. It may serve as a form of collaboration by initiating a dialogue between the original text and the newly created piece.

Erasures can be powerful for many reasons, including choosing the form for confrontation. Writers can challenge the authority or message of the original text by reshaping its content to bring subtext to the surface. Erasure poets play with the intricacies between absence and presence, inviting readers to reconsider familiar or found texts in new ways.

Real-life collaboration can be tricky because people have personalities and opinions and varying aesthetics. Erasure poetry is a different kind of collaboration. Sometimes writers work together with erasures, but it has mostly been a silent collaboration. A writer engages a conversation or dialogue with a text that moves, challenges, excites, or infuriates them. The pieces can be incredibly powerful.

We consider them hybrid because of the reconfiguration of existing text (a writer can use anything, from a previously published poem to ingredients on a cereal box to an entry of an encyclopedia to a chapter in a novel) to offer a new set of revelations that may not have been present in the original. Think of someone who gives new life to found objects. They might buy a painted wooden table at a flea market, strip it of layers of paint, stain it, shorten its legs, add a mirrored surface. It becomes a hybrid of the original object and a new creation in its own right.

Take a look at "The Author Writes the First Draft of His Wedding Vows," a poem by Hanif Abdurraqib from his collection *The Crown Ain't Worth Much*. About the poem, writer Sean Glatch says:

> Each word of this erasure poem is carefully selected, and each word holds a stunning amount of grief, irony, love, and madness. Hanif has preserved the most emotional parts of Woolf's letter while also assembling those parts into something new: a poem that is saved by the madness of love.

Glatch also says:

> Not all blackout poems have a relationship to their source text, but the best blackout poetry often carries a dialogue with its source. As the author Annie

THE AUTHOR WRITES THE FIRST DRAFT OF HIS WEDDING VOWS

(An erasure of Virginia Woolf's suicide letter to her husband, Leonard)

Dearest,

I feel certain I am going mad again.

we will go through   terrible times. And   recover . I
begin to hear your voice, and can't   concentrate. So I am
doing what seems

will give me the greatest possible happiness.

I don't think two people could   have been happier   with
this disease. I know
that without   you   I can't properly feel .

What I want to say is You   have

saved me.

Everything has gone from me

but the certainty of your goodness.

Dillard notes, the meaning of a text "now swings between two poles" in the making of blackout poems, creating a kind of visual dialectic.

> Many blackout poetry examples use literary sources. . . . You might also find inspiration from books, poems, essays, news stories, or letters that deeply impact you.
>
> . . . Be as conventional or esoteric as you'd like: you can blackout recipes, driving manuals, national constitutions, cereal box ingredient lists, toaster oven instructions, Wikipedia pages, etc.

Try it!

As always, we say *care*. Have (or develop) some sort of personal connection and allow the piece to somehow illuminate your worldview (even if you start out doing the experiment for experiment's sake). If you have a strong reaction to the original source—if you think there's something within it that your erasure will expose—keep working it.

We've reviewed but a few of the hybrid containers that writers have chosen frequently enough (and have used effectively enough) so that lovers of the forms have created entire literary magazines and anthologies to showcase them. But what happens when your material begs a form you've never seen?

Create a New Genre or Subgenre When Your Vision for the Material Demands It

Each of the hybrid forms we've reviewed were, at some point, new. Poetry and fiction—even creative nonfiction—were all once new. Literary history shows us that writers, the artists who use words, create new forms when their cultural circumstances and language merge in ways that demand it. An ancient Mesopotamian priestess named Enheduanna is currently thought by scholars to be the author of the earliest poem.

Diane Cole wrote about her for the BBC:

> In conjunction with her status as a religious figure and priestess, Enheduanna wielded political power as the daughter of Sargon the Great—a figure credited by some historians as the founder of the world's first empire. In particular, she played an essential role helping bind together the northern Mesopotamian region of Akkad, where Sargon first rose to power, before

> he went on to capture the Sumerian city-states in the south. She did so by helping meld the beliefs and rituals associated with the Sumerian goddess Inanna with those of the Akkadian goddess Ishtar, and by emphasizing those links in her literary and religious hymns and poems, thereby creating a common system of beliefs throughout the empire. Each of the hymns Enheduanna wrote for 42 temples in the southern half of Mesopotamia highlighted the unique character of the patron goddess to the worshippers in those cities; the hymns were copied by scribes in the temples for hundreds of years after her death.

Perhaps not the most benevolent use of poetry (to convince subjects of a religion to aid the expansion of her father's nascent empire), but quite a few literary motifs originated with Enheduanna.

Advances (or setbacks) in culture and technology evolve how we write. Language, like culture and technology, is a set of codes, and they're constantly changing. We remember when text messaging first started appearing in literature. Now it's rare to read any contemporary piece of prose without text messaging as one means of characterization. A character can present themselves in texts and emails in ways that highlight and contradict how they behave "live." How characters present themselves when writing an anonymous review or sending an email from a stealth account can showcase a set of personality traits that differs entirely from how they'd interact in person or when signing their name.

We now see, in published (and so-called "traditional") poems, the same abbreviations once used primarily in text communication: *LOL*, *WTF*, *IKR*, and *OFC*. Their use, when tethered to important thematic concerns in the piece, can spark life into a poet's stanzas.

So, shifts in culture and technology inspire writers to fill existing containers with new language. Other times, the shifts demand new forms.

We talked to writer, editor, and scholar Jacqueline Doyle about a book project she's in the process of completing. Her vision for the material demanded she come up with several new containers to fulfill her vision. First, let's read the title piece of the project.

The Lunatics' Ball

Jacqueline Doyle

I remember the name "Greystone" from my childhood in the nineteen-fifties and sixties, spoken in a thrilling whisper. It was the local "loony bin" for "nutcases," "fruitcakes," "whackos," "crackpots," "maniacs." At slumber parties, our variants of the "man with the hook" urban legend ended with an escaped lunatic from Greystone, his hook dangling from the car door. And in fact, Greystone did house sex offenders and violent criminals under treatment for mental illness, and there were escapes, though I don't remember any reports of crimes like the ones you see on all the TV shows.

Greystone housed well over seven thousand patients when the singer Woody Guthrie was a patient there in the nineteen-fifties. By the nineteen-nineties, it was largely abandoned, after reports of rampant patient neglect, sexual abuse of patients by staff, patient escapes, and suicides. The buildings were later demolished. "Gravestone," Woody called it. He died—in another psychiatric institution—of Huntington's, a neurodegenerative disease initially misdiagnosed as paranoid schizophrenia.

If she'd survived, would my aunt Maddy have been treated at Greystone Psychiatric Hospital or someplace like it? She could have stayed on the lithium, instead of detoxing on the advice of a quack chiropractor. Or had second thoughts as the carbon monoxide fumes filled the garage. Or been discovered in time to save her life, instead of three days later. She was only forty-seven.

My mother told a story about a lunatics' ball that her mother attended in northern New Jersey in the nineteen-forties—or maybe the thirties. Lunatics' balls for inmates, staff, and visitors were common in late nineteenth-century insane asylums, less common later. It must have been at Greystone Psychiatric Hospital in Morris Plains, not far from Mountain Lakes, where my mother's family lived. Did her mother have a relative there? If so, my mother either didn't know or pretended not to. Maybe attendance was considered entertainment by small-town middle-class housewives. Or a kind of civic duty.

My grandmother danced with a charming, good-looking man who she assumed was a doctor. The punch line to the story was inevitable: he turned out to be a patient. A big laugh from my mother, as if no one in her own family could end up on a mental ward one day. When her younger sister Maddy was diagnosed as bipolar, my mother's main concern was that no one in town learn of it. Maddy's later hospitalization was a secret too. As was mine.

My aunt was only nine years older than me, and I followed her everywhere as a child, besotted. Maddy was the sister I didn't have, the mother I wanted when I was a teenager, generous with her time and gifts. How to describe her? Gorgeous, charismatic, wealthy, fashionable, outgoing, extravagant. High strung. Sleek as a greyhound. My mother was jealous of all the time I spent with her, of her good looks and fancy house and wardrobe.

"She brought it on herself," my mother said after Maddy's suicide, lips pursed, uninterested in statistics about bipolars and suicide. My mother didn't believe in mental illness or "witch doctor" psychiatrists. She believed in moral judgment, particularly of those she saw as unfairly favored by good fortune.

"We're the two crazy ladies in the family," Maddy said to me once. We were drinking red wine at an Italian restaurant, laughing about something. I was in my late twenties then, working on my Ph.D. It was before I got sober, before my own hospitalization and bipolar diagnosis. Only my closest friends, my parents, and my brother knew about my week in the mental ward—by then, Maddy was already gone.

When I look at the sketchy family tree my father started for my mother's family, there are so many names I don't recognize, so much potential for secret afflictions. Who was my mother's Aunt Blossom? Her Aunt Florence? I never met my mother's Uncle Tommy, an alcoholic who died in a hotel fire, probably a Bowery flophouse for drunks, but she mentioned him sometimes. The family said it was the First World War that made him drink. "It's a good man's failing," the Irish say, always ready to find a reason or excuse. When I got sober, my father told me about the funeral of a relative, a great aunt I think, where her daughter took him aside and said, "She was an alcoholic, you know." He didn't know and was surprised to learn it. Shortly before Maddy died, she did a stint in rehab, probably for the painkillers she was taking for her back, though no one knew for sure.

Bipolar family trees invariably include more than two crazies—many relatives suffering from substance abuse disorders, others suffering from depression and anxiety disorders, and from schizophrenia. Scientists don't know why. My mother never acknowledged that sleeping for ten years was a symptom of depression. "I had a lot of colds," she insisted. For a while Maddy stopped speaking to her, after my mother claimed to be the "only normal one" in the family. "Does she think ten years in bed was normal?"

Much later, my mother didn't believe that Lewy body dementia might be the source of her hallucinations. "Thank God we don't have any of that in our family," she said. When she was moved from assisted living to the dementia ward, she believed she was one of the nurses. "We had our hands full today," she'd say when I called her on the phone. "Unbelievable."

Are there other delusional relatives buried in our family past? Alcoholics and addicts who self-medicated for depression and other mental illnesses? Relatives excused as eccentric? Madwomen sequestered in attics? Who might my grandmother have known at the Greystone Lunatics' Ball? There must have been more of us, hidden from sight, or slipping off the family tree like leaves in autumn, unnoticed.

In my dream, they're playing Woody Guthrie's "Cowboy Waltz," two patients sawing away on fiddles, as I dance with Maddy at the Lunatics' Ball. The tables have been cleared away, the Greystone hospital cafeteria festooned with red and green crepe paper. The Hawaiian punch mixed with ginger ale in the large glass punch bowls is strictly non-alcoholic.

"Did you know that Bob Dylan used to visit Woody Guthrie here at Greystone?" I ask Maddy. "Woody said folk songs should comfort disturbed people and disturb comfortable people." Maddy laughs when someone shouts "hee haw!" and the sedate suburban matrons scatter, clutching their Visitor nametags.

Maddy's still forty-seven in the dream, beautiful, but I'm sixty-seven now, showing my age. "You should get a facial, try Botox, honey," Maddy says. "Maybe a brighter hair color. Why not go blonde?" She's always full of outlandish advice. "I love that red dress on you," she adds. "You look like a ripe tomato."

She holds my hand aloft and we execute a perfect turn before whirling across the dance floor. One, two, three, four. One, two, three, four. The other dancers are a blur.

"This is fun," I say. "I should take a dance class. Now that I'm retiring from teaching."

Is that my mother joking with the nurses by the door? Maddy pretends not to see her, but I give her a friendly wave from across the room. I think I see my red-faced great uncles by the punch bowl, Uncle Tommy slipping a flask from the inside pocket of his jacket. And my grandmother! Her companions have their backs to me and I can't see who they are. At home with the lunatics, I feel like I recognize everyone.

"I should have come sooner," I tell Maddy.

How many years has it taken me to join Maddy at the Lunatics' Ball? Fear of our dark kinship held me back. If Maddy and I were the two crazy ladies, and she took her own life, what would my fate be? Could I risk joining her in public? What would happen if my colleagues and students and acquaintances knew I was bipolar too?

"Get a letter from your GP instead," the department secretary whispered to me at my first job. "You don't want a note from a psychiatrist in your permanent file." A department chair in my second job counseled me not to tell. "When people know you're bipolar, that will be your label. They'll think of you as just one thing." I worried too much. Let them think what they want.

Now that I'm finally here, I'm so glad to see Maddy again! The lights blaze, the Christmas decorations glitter, the musicians strike up a new tune on their fiddles. We twirl and spin, dancing, laughing. I'm not sure I ever mastered the box step, but it's all coming back to me. I let Maddy lead.

For us, the essay becomes hybrid with this line, barely noticeable as a shift because of the smoothness of the transition:

In my dream, they're playing Woody Guthrie's "Cowboy Waltz," two patients sawing away on fiddles, as I dance with Maddy at the Lunatics' Ball.

Up until this point, the writer has centered her essay on her mother's denial of family mental illness and her favorite aunt's positive influence as well as her struggle. Once she introduces the dream, the narrator's subconscious desires are laid bare. What else is a dream but the subconscious mind's attempt to bring information to the level of consciousness?

We think the act of writing, when one gets "lost" in it, can mimic a dream state. Writers often say variations of "I didn't know that until I'd reread what I wrote."

Whether or not the writer dreamed (while asleep at night) the sequence she portrays at "The Lunatics' Ball," we, as readers, follow her, take her for her word because of the value of what's revealed.

We interviewed Jacqueline Doyle about her hybrid book in progress. The essays she mentions are all published in a variety of stellar literary journals—all worth researching if you plan to publish hybrid works. Here's what she said:

> "Are there other delusional relatives buried in our family past?" I ask in "The Lunatics' Ball." "Madwomen sequestered in attics?" Soon after publishing my flash "The Lunatics' Ball," I embarked on a full-length collection of disparate "essays" and flash combining research into women locked up in lunatic asylums with memoir about my family's history with bipolar disorder. My quest grew from investigation into my late aunt Maddy and myself and unknown ancestors in our family tree to include essays about scores of spiritual forebears diagnosed with mental illnesses—some well-known, like Zelda Fitzgerald and Sylvia Plath and Nina Simone, others completely unknown, who'd disappeared almost without a trace. "There must have been more of us . . ." It was a challenge: how was I going to write about the silenced, the hidden, the lost, and bring them alive on the page? It seemed obvious that some degree of fictionalization would be necessary if I wanted to push beyond the facts I could unearth. As Virginia Woolf writes when she introduces Shakespeare's sister in *A Room of One's Own*: "Let me imagine, since facts are so hard to come by. . . ." "The Lunatics' Ball" could only be cross-genre and hybrid.
>
> Breaking rules came naturally to me. So did research. I hadn't gone the MFA route. I have a PhD in literature and had been publishing literary scholarship for some twenty years before I started writing and teaching creative nonfiction. By that time I had become impatient with academic writing. I was experimenting. My later articles were segmented, increasingly oblique and poetic, more like lyric essays than conventional scholarship. I looked with longing at the possibilities enjoyed by creative writers and then finally made the leap. I started writing flash—a genre with no set rules that I could see beyond word count—as well as creative nonfiction. Each new piece

posed a different problem and provisional solution. Each new piece presented its own challenges, established its own way of being. I felt like I'd escaped from a straitjacket.

Unschooled as I was in the rules governing creative writing, I sidestepped prescriptive definitions and genre distinctions. From the beginning I was drawn to what Lisa Knopp in a craft essay in *Brevity* calls "perhapsing"—often with no "perhaps" to signal speculative flights in my creative nonfiction. As Robin Hemley and Leila Philip ask in the "Manifesto" for their journal *Speculative Nonfiction*: "Is the truth of an essay sometimes the speculative endeavour itself, a literary engagement not with things or facts but with [what Mary Cappello calls] 'a tidal wave of strange imaginings?' A 'Speculative Essay' concerns itself with the figurative over the literal, ambiguity over knowing, meditation over reportage." Was "Another Mary Doyle," which contains imagined scenes and interludes written from the narrative point of view of my Irish immigrant great-grandmother, an essay at all? Was it fiction or nonfiction? What was I doing with my forays into memoir in "The Dream Lives of Objects," my wandering ekphrastic essay on Joseph Cornell's boxes? With my imagined encounters with personified Death in my pandemic essay "Last Medley"? The boundaries between genres seemed far less important than the borderlands I wanted to explore.

While I have set aside the flash fictions I'd originally intended to include, "The Lunatics' Ball" still features historical vignettes animated by fictionalized speculation and interpolations; lyric riffs based on my subjects' lives and words; memoir essays where I "perhaps" the gaps in my memory; and research-based biographical profiles, often braided with memoir and punctuated by imaginative improvisation. It is a hybrid collection where most of the essays and flash themselves are hybrid.

"Lunatic Impromptu," for example, alternates nonfictional passages culled from a brief account in *The New York Times* of an 1879 fire at Blackwell's asylum and fictional imaginings of the inmates' responses when they were evacuated from their locked rooms. When I read about the tragic outcomes of lobotomies in the mid-twentieth century and how widespread they were, I felt I needed to braid a nonfictional account of the procedure and its history with imagined voices from patients: "Cutting Edge" includes fictional monologues based on facts I was able to uncover about women like Allen Ginsberg's mother, Tennessee Williams' sister, John F. Kennedy's sister. When I combined memoir with longer accounts of forgotten "lunatics" who died in asylums after spending decades there, the facts seemed to invite speculation. In "Cross-Stitching," I had little to work with beyond the fascinating samplers and tapestries that Mary Frances Heaton and Lorina Bulwer left behind. When I wrote about Madeline C. in "Madeline's Trunk," I had the intriguing photographs of her trunk and its contents from Jon Crispin's Willard Suitcases installation, and bits of archival research uncovered by Darby Penney and Peter Stastny for their book on Willard State Hospital. Our lives almost crossed, as Madeline C. died in a board and care under the supervision of the Willard staff the same year that I was finishing my graduate studies, not far away in upstate New York. I felt I needed to summon her shade from the underworld and express all the anger she must have felt after almost fifty years of involuntary incarceration:

I conjure Madeline now, a wizened crone standing in her small bedroom at the board and care. The room is shabby, with a lumpy twin bed covered by a worn pink chenille bedspread, a bath mat serving as a rug next to it. Though her body is hunched and frail, her voice is strong and sure. She raises her arms in invocation. "Come to me now, fellow spirits, you women who died at Salpêtrière, Bellevue, Central Islip, Kings Park, Willard State Hospital. You whose graves in the Willard cemetery are marked with numbers and no names. You who were silenced, locked up, forgotten. You who died unheard. Wail like banshees in the skies, uproot trees, shake buildings, rattle windows, slip through keyholes and under doors. Whisper now to your doctors and keepers, hiss like snakes, raise your voices in their nightmares, shriek in their ears, curse their posterity. I have been robbed of a life, and only you, brave women, have kept my spirit alive."

Is conjuring the same as imagining and is that the same as fiction? It felt more powerful than that. Only a hybrid would let me convey what I was feeling myself.

With the dream in the title flash "The Lunatics' Ball" I step into the make-believe world I would need for much of the remainder of the collection. I love Woody Guthrie's notion that art "should comfort disturbed people and disturb comfortable people," and while I didn't know that I was launching such a large project, certainly it's what I hope I might achieve with my collection as well. By coming out as bipolar and exploring these women's histories I hope to comfort fellow "lunatics" even as I disturb the "sedate suburban matrons" and gatekeepers who have enforced the stigma associated with mental illness.

Maddy leads the way at the close of "The Lunatics' Ball." I had no idea where we were headed. The mad leading the mad, on a journey where there are no rules.

Let's pause here and write a bit, inspired by Doyle's pieces.

Write Now

1. Choose a person for whom you care deeply.
2. Write 300 words that portray the importance of that person to you—the real (as opposed to imagined) history you share—as the narrator does with Maddy in the first part of "The Lunatics' Ball."
3. After 300 words, move into a "dream flash," as inspired by "The Lunatics' Ball," where a slightly different version of each of you (the narrator and the person the narrator cares for deeply) shows up. Write 300 words in dream sequence.
4. Revise it so "the truth" that's revealed about the characters (the narrator and the person the narrator cares for deeply) is "not with things or facts but with [what Mary Cappello calls] 'a tidal wave of strange imaginings.'"

We've shown you how an individual can create new containers for a specific project that demands it. When a group of writers find solidarity in reaction to literary trends or perceived rules about a form, movements are formed.

The Black Arts Movement, for example, emerged symbolically in 1965, following the assassination of Malcolm X. Poet LeRoi Jones, later known as Amiri Baraka, catalyzed the movement by relocating from the integrated Lower East Side of New York City to Harlem, where he established the Black Arts Repertory Theatre. This institution became a hub for workshops in poetry, playwriting, music, and painting, nurturing a burgeoning artistic and cultural renaissance.

According to poet Larry Neal, the Black Arts Movement was intrinsically linked to the ideals of Black Power, advocating for self-determination and cultural autonomy and celebrating the inherent beauty and worthiness of Black identity. Central to the movement was the development of a distinctly Black aesthetic language, drawing inspiration from Black musical genres such as jazz, as well as Black vernacular speech and African folklore.

Poets of the Black Arts Movement evolved the written forms with innovations in sound, spelling, and grammar that asserted Black identity. By using these and other techniques, writers claimed agency and fostered solidarity within the Black community, while challenging established norms and systems of oppression.

New Narrative is another movement. It's also a theory of experimental writing launched in San Francisco in the late 1970s by poets and writers Robert Glück and Bruce Boone. This is how Robert Glück describes New Narrative in his book of essays, *Communal Nude*:

> We were fellow travelers of Language poetry and the innovative feminist poetry of that time: our lives and reading led us toward a hybrid aesthetic, something impure. We (say, Bruce Boone, Camille Roy, Kevin Killian, Dodie Bellamy, Mike Amnasan, Francesca Rosa, myself, and to include the dead, Steve Abbott and Sam D'Allesandro) are still fellow travelers of the poetries that evolved since the late seventies, when writers talked about "nonnarrative." One could untangle that knot forever, or build an aesthetic on the ways language conveys silence, chaos, undifferentiated existence, and erects countless horizons of meaning.
>
> ...We were thinking about autobiography. By autobiography, we meant daydreams, nightdreams, the act of writing, the relationship to the reader, the meeting of flesh and culture; the self as collaboration, the self as disintegration, the gaps, inconsistencies, and distortions of the self; the enjambments of power, family, history, and language.

New Narrative strove to represent subjective experience honestly without pretense that a text can be absolutely objective nor its meaning absolutely fluid. Authenticity is paramount in New Narrative, and is possible with a variety of devices, including fragmentation, meta-text, identity politics, explicit descriptions of sex and undisguised identification with the author's physicality, intentionality, interior emotional life and external life circumstances.

The New Narrative movement includes many gay and lesbian authors, and the works were greatly influenced by the AIDS epidemic in the '80s.

Speaking of frankness and explicit descriptions around sex, we see in this next example how a writer may have (consciously or unconsciously) been inspired by New Narrative (or aspects of the movement) while creating a form all her own.

The following piece is from Carmen Maria Machado's *Her Body and Other Parties*. In this collection of stories, Machado plays in the gray area between realism and science fiction, comedy and horror, fantasy and fabulism.

Inventory
Carmen Maria Machado

One girl. We lay down next to each other on the musty rug in her basement. Her parents were upstairs; we told them we were watching *Jurassic Park*. "I'm the dad, and you're the mom," she said. I pulled up my shirt, she pulled up hers, and we just stared at each other. My heart fluttered below my belly button, but I worried about daddy long legs and her parents finding us. I still have never seen *Jurassic Park*. I suppose I never will, now.

One boy, one girl. My friends. We drank stolen wine coolers in my room, on the vast expanse of my bed. We laughed and talked and passed around the bottles. "What I like about you," she said, "is your reactions. You respond so funny to everything. Like it's all intense." He nodded in agreement. She buried her face in my neck and said "Like this" to my skin. I laughed. I was nervous, excited. I felt like a guitar and someone was twisting the tuning pegs and my strings were getting tighter. They batted their eyelashes against my skin and breathed into my ears. I moaned and writhed, and hovered on the edge of coming for whole minutes, though no one was touching me there, not even me.

Two boys, one girl. One of them my boyfriend. His parents were out of town, so we threw a party at his house. We drank lemonade mixed with vodka and he encouraged me to make out with his friend's girlfriend. We kissed tentatively, then stopped. The boys made out with each other, and we watched them for a long time, bored but too drunk to stand up. We fell asleep in the guest bedroom. When I woke up, my bladder was tight as a fist. I padded down into the foyer, and saw someone had knocked a vodka lemonade onto the floor. I tried to clean it up. The mixture had stripped the marble finish bare. My boyfriend's mother found my underwear behind the bed weeks later, and handed them to him, laundered, without a word. It's weird to me how much I miss that oral, chemical smell of clean clothes. Now, all I can think about is fabric softener.

One man. Slender, tall. So skinny I could see his pelvic bone, which I found strangely sexy. Gray eyes. Wry smile. I had known him for almost a year, since the previous October, when we'd met at a Halloween party. (I didn't wear a costume; he was dressed as Barbarella.) We drank in his apartment. He was nervous and gave me a massage. I was nervous so I let him. He rubbed my back for a long time. He said, "My hands are getting tired." I said, "Oh," and turned toward him. He kissed me, his face rough with stubble. He smelled like yeast and the top notes of expensive cologne. He lay on top of me and we made out for a while. Everything inside of me twinged, pleasurably. He asked if he could touch my breast, and I clamped his hand around it. I took off my shirt, and I felt like a drop of water was sliding up my spine. I realized this was happening, really happening. We both undressed. He rolled the condom down and lumbered on top of me. It hurt worse than anything, ever. He came and I didn't. When he pulled out, the condom was covered in blood. He peeled it off and threw it away. Everything in me pounded. We slept on a too-small bed. He insisted on driving me back to the dorms the next day. In my room, I took off my clothes and wrapped myself in a towel. I still smelled like him, like the two of us together, and I wanted more. I felt good, like an adult who has sex sometimes, and a life. My roommate asked me how it was, hugged me.

One man. A boyfriend. Didn't like condoms, asked me if I was on birth control, pulled out anyway. A terrible mess.

One woman. On-and-off sort-of girlfriend. Classmate from Organization of Computer Systems. Long brown hair down to her butt. She was softer than I expected. I wanted to go down on her, but she was too nervous. We made out and she slipped her tongue into my mouth and after she went home I got off twice in the cool stillness of my apartment. Two years later, we had sex on the gravel rooftop of my office building. Four floors below our bodies, my code was compiling in front of an empty chair. After we were done, I looked up and noticed a man in a suit watching us from the window of the adjacent skyscraper, his hand shuffling around inside his slacks.

One woman. Round glasses, red hair. Don't remember where I met her. We got high and fucked and I accidentally fell asleep with my hand inside of her. We woke up predawn and walked across town to a twenty-four-hour diner. It drizzled and when we got there, our sandaled feet were numb from the chill. We ate pancakes. Our mugs ran dry, and when we looked for the waitress, she was watching the breaking news on the battered TV hanging from the ceiling. She chewed on her lip, and the pot of coffee tipped in her hand, dripping tiny brown dots onto the linoleum. We watched as the newscaster blinked away and was replaced with a list of symptoms of the virus blossoming a state away, in northern California. When he came back, he repeated that planes were grounded, the border of the state had been closed, and the virus appeared to be isolated. When the waitress walked over, she seemed distracted. "Do you have people there?" I asked, and she nodded, her eyes filling with tears. I felt terrible having asked her anything.

One man. I met him at the bar around the corner from my house. We made out on my bed. He smelled like sour wine, though he'd been drinking vodka. We had sex, but he went soft halfway through. We kissed some more. He wanted to go down on me, but I didn't want him to. He got angry and left, slamming the screen door so hard my spice rack jumped from its nail and crashed to the floor. My dog lapped up the nutmeg, and I had to force-feed him salt to make him throw up. Revved from adrenaline, I made a list of animals I have had in my life—seven, including my two betta fish, who died within a week of each other when I was nine—and a list of the spices in phở. Cloves, cinnamon, star anise, coriander, ginger, cardamom pods.

One man. Six inches shorter than me. I explained that the website I worked for was losing business rapidly because no one wanted quirky photography tips during an epidemic, and I had been laid off that morning. He bought me dinner. We had sex in his car because he had roommates and I couldn't be in my house right then, and he slid his hand inside my bra and his hands were perfect, fucking perfect, and we fell into the too-tiny backseat. I came for the first time in two months. I called him the next day, and left him a voicemail, telling him I'd had a good time and I'd like to see him again, but he never called me back.

One man. Did some sort of hard labor for a living, I can't remember what exactly, and he had a tattoo of a boa constrictor on his back with a misspelled Latin phrase below it. He was strong and could pick me up and fuck me against a wall and it was the most thrilling sensation I'd ever felt. We broke a few picture frames that way. He used his hands and I dragged my fingernails down his back, and he asked me if I was going to come for him, and I said, "Yes, yes, I'm going to come for you, yes, I will."

One woman. Blond hair, brash voice, friend of a friend. We married. I'm still not sure if I was with her because I wanted to be or because I was afraid of what the world was catching all around us. Within a year, it soured. We screamed more than we had sex, or even talked. One night, we had a fight that left me in tears. Afterward, she asked me if I wanted to fuck, and undressed before I could answer. I wanted to push her out the window. We had sex and I started crying. When it was over and she was showering, I packed a suitcase and got in my car and drove.

One man. Six months later, in my post divorce haze. I met him at the funeral for the last surviving member of his family. I was grieving, he was grieving. We had sex in the empty house that used to belong to his brother and his brother's wife and their children, all dead. We fucked in every room, including the hallway, where I couldn't bend my pelvis right on the hardwood floors, and I jerked him off in front of the bare linen closet. In the master bedroom, I caught my reflection in the vanity mirror as I rode him, and the lights were off and our skin reflected silver from the moon and when he came in me he said, "Sorry, sorry." He died a week later, by his own hand. I moved out of the city, north.

One man. Gray eyes again. I hadn't seen him in so many years. He asked me how I was doing, and I told him some things and not others. I did not want to cry in front of the man to whom I gave my virginity. It seemed wrong somehow. He asked me how many I'd lost, and I said, "My mother, my roommate from college." I did not mention that I'd found my mother dead, nor the three days afterward I'd spent with anxious doctors checking my eyes for the early symptoms, nor how I'd managed to escape the quarantine zone. "When I met you," he said, "you were so fucking young." His body was familiar, but alien, too. He'd gotten better, and I'd gotten better. When he pulled out of me I almost expected blood, but of course, there was none. He had gotten more beautiful in those intervening years, more thoughtful. I surprised myself by crying over the bathroom sink. I ran the tap so he couldn't hear me.

One woman. Brunette. A former CDC employee. I met her at a community meeting where they taught us how to stockpile food and manage outbreaks in our neighborhoods should the virus hop the firebreak. I had not slept with a woman since my wife, but as she lifted her shirt I realized how much I'd been craving breasts, wetness, soft mouths. She wanted cock and I obliged. Afterward, she traced the indents in my skin from the harness, and confessed to me that no one was having any luck developing a vaccine. "But the fucking thing is only passing through physical contact," she said. "If people would just stay apart—" She grew silent. She curled up next to me and we drifted off. When I woke up, she was working herself over with the dildo, and I pretended I was still sleeping.

One man. He made me dinner in my kitchen. There weren't a lot of vegetables left from my garden, but he did what he could. He tried to feed me with a spoon, but I took the handle from him. The food didn't taste too bad. The power went out for the fourth time that week, so we ate by candlelight. I resented the inadvertent romance. He touched my face when we fucked and said I was beautiful, and I jerked my head a little to dislodge his fingers. When he did it a second time, I put my hand around his chin and told him to shut up. He came immediately. I did not return his calls. When the notice come over the radio that the virus had somehow reached Nebraska, I realized I had to go east, and so I did. I left the garden, the plot where my dog was buried, the pine table where I'd anxiously made so many lists— trees that began with m: maple, mimosa, mahogany, mulberry, magnolia, mountain ash, mangrove, myrtle; states that I had lived in: Iowa, Indiana, Pennsylvania, Virginia, New York—leaving unreadable jumbles of letters imprinted in the soft wood. I took my savings and rented a cottage near the ocean. After a few months, the landlord, based in Kansas, stopped depositing my checks.

Two women. Refugees from the western states who drove and drove until their car broke down a mile from my cottage. They knocked on my door and stayed with me for two weeks while we tried to figure out how to get their vehicle up and running. We had wine one night and talked about the quarantine. The generator needed cranking, and one of them offered to do it. The other one sat down next to me and slid her hand up my leg. We ended up jerking off separately and kissing each other. The generator took and the power came back on. The other woman returned, and we all slept in the same bed. I wanted them to stay, but they said they were heading up into Canada, where it was rumored to be safer. They offered to bring me with them, but I joked that I was holding down the fort for the United States. "What state are we in?" one of them asked, and I said, "Maine." They kissed me on the forehead in turn and dubbed me the protector of Maine. After they left, I only used the generator intermittently, preferring to spend time in the dark, with candles. The former owner of the cottage had a closet full of them.

One man. National Guard. When he first showed up at my doorstep, I assumed he was there to evacuate me, but it turned out he'd abandoned his post. I offered him a place to stay for the night, and he thanked me. I woke up with a knife to my throat and a hand on my breast. I told him I couldn't have sex with him lying down like I was. He let me stand up, and I shoved him into the bookcase, knocking him unconscious. I dragged his body out to the beach and rolled it into the surf. He came to, sputtering sand. I pointed the knife at him and told him to walk and keep walking, and if he even looked back, I would end him. He obliged, and I watched him until he was a spot of darkness on the gray strip of shore, and then nothing. He was the last person I saw for a year.

One woman. A religious leader, with a flock of fifty trailing behind her, all dressed in white. For three days, I made them wait around the edge of the property, and after I checked their eyes, I permitted them to stay. They all camped around the cottage: on the lawn, on the beach. They had their own supplies and only needed a place to lay their heads, the leader said. She wore robes that made her look like a wizard. Night fell. She and I circled the camp in our bare feet, the light from the bonfire carving shadows into her face. We walked to the water's edge and I pointed into the darkness, at the tiny island she could not see. She slipped her hand into mine. I made her a drink—"More or less moonshine," I said as I handed her the tumbler— and we sat at the table. Outside, I could hear people laughing, playing music, children romping in the surf. The woman seemed exhausted. She was younger than she looked, I realized, but her job was aging her. She sipped her drink, made a face at the taste. "We've been walking for so long," she said. "We stopped for a while, somewhere near Pennsylvania, but the virus caught up with us when we crossed paths with another group. Took twelve before we got some distance between us and it." We kissed deeply for a long time, my heart hammering in my cunt. She tasted like smoke and honey. The group stayed for four days, until she woke up from a dream and said she'd had an omen, and they needed to keep going. She asked me to come with them. I tried to imagine myself with her, her flock following behind us like children. I declined. She left a gift on my pillow: a pewter rabbit as big as my thumb.

One man. No more than twenty, floppy brown hair. He'd been on foot for a month. He looked like you'd expect: skittish. No hope. When we had sex, he was reverent and too gentle. After we cleaned up, I fed him canned soup. He told me about how he walked through Chicago, actually through it, and how they had stopped bothering to dispose of the bodies after a while. He had to refill his glass before he talked about it further. "After that," he said, "I went around the cities." I asked him how far behind the virus was, really, and he said he did not know. "It's really quiet here," he said, by way of changing the subject. "No traffic," I explained. "No tourists." He cried and cried and I held him until he fell asleep. The next morning, I woke up and he was gone.

One woman. Much older than me. While she waited for the three days to pass, she meditated on a sand dune. When I checked her eyes, I noticed they were green as sea glass. Her hair grayed at the temples and the way she laughed tripped pleasure down the stairs of my heart. We sat in the half light of the bay window and the buildup was so slow. She straddled me, and when she kissed me the scene beyond the glass pinched and curved. We drank, and walked the length of the beach, the damp sand making pale halos around our feet. She told about her once-children, teenage injuries, having to put her cat to sleep the day after she moved to a new city. I told her about finding my mother, the perilous trek across Vermont and New Hampshire, how the tide was never still, my ex-wife. "What happened?" she asked. "It just didn't work," I said. I told her about the man in the empty house, the way he cried and the way his come shimmered on his stomach and how I could have scooped despair from the air by the handfuls. We remembered commercial jingles from our respective youths, including one for an Italian-ice chain that I went to at the end of long summer days, where I ate gelato, drowsy in the heat. I couldn't remember the last time I'd smiled so much. She stayed. More refugees filtered through the cottage, through us, the last stop before the border, and we fed them and played games with the little ones. We got careless. The day I woke up and the air had changed, I realized it had been a long time coming. She was sitting on the couch. She got up in the night and made some tea. But the cup was tipped and the puddle was cold, and I recognized the symptoms from the television and newspapers, and then the leaflets, and then the radio broadcasts, and then the hushed voices around the bonfire. Her skin was the dark purple of compounded bruises, the whites of her eyes shot through with red, and blood leaking from the misty beds of her fingernails. There was no time to mourn. I checked my own face in the mirror, and my eyes were still clear. I consulted my emergency list and its supplies. I took my bag and tent and I got into the dinghy and I rowed to the island, to this island, where I have been stashing food since I got to the cottage. I drank water and set up my tent and began to make lists. Every teacher beginning with preschool. Every job I've ever had. Every home I've ever lived in. Every person I've ever loved. Every person who has probably loved me. Next week, I will be thirty. The sand is blowing into my mouth, my hair, the center crevice of my notebook, and the sea is choppy and gray. Beyond it, I can see the cottage, a speck on the far shore. I keep thinking I can see the virus blooming on the horizon like a sunrise. I realize the world will continue to turn, even with no people on it. Maybe it will go a little faster.

In a series for *The Atlantic* called "By Heart," writers choose and discuss favorite passages from literature that inspire. In an article from that series entitled "How Surrealism Enriches Storytelling About Women," Joe Fassler interviewed Machado, who chose Shirley Jackson and an excerpt from "The Haunting of Hill House." In that essay/interview, Machado discusses how nonrealism in Shirley Jackson's work emphasizes unique and surreal aspects of women's experiences, helping to reframe and highlight serious topics like sexual violence: "It allows you to defamiliarize certain topics like sexual violence that some people might unfortunately dismiss as 'oh, just another story about rape.'" She notes that nonrealism provides a mythic dimension to female narratives, enriching their inner lives.

Machado also says that being queer offers a different, often surreal perspective, enabling her to see things others might miss. This unique viewpoint, which diverges from the dominant cultural perspective, is a key element she explores in her work.

Perhaps someday we'll evolve enough as a culture that no one would ever be so heartless as to dismiss a work of literature as "Oh, just another story about rape." Machado wanted to write imaginatively by engaging a series of strategies she invented to address the thematic concerns central to her vision. She dazzles and engages readers with her skill. The importance of her vision is realized and shared with an audience without getting dismissed.

Her piece creates its own container in the way it uses speculative aspects (written prior to the emergence of COVID-19, the piece engages a fictitious virus that's now eerily familiar to those of us who witnessed its effects) and how it uses an inventory as a device.

The word "inventory" (which is the piece's title and form) has its roots in the Latin word *inventarium*, derived from *invenire*, which means "to find" or "to discover." It initially referred to a detailed list of items, goods, or possessions, used primarily for recordkeeping or accounting purposes. Over time, the concept of inventories became crucial for managing resources, trade, and wealth in ancient and medieval civilizations. Today, "inventory" encompasses a broad range of meanings related to lists of items, assets, or information in various contexts, such as business management, retail, and logistics.

Gleaning inspiration from Machado's piece, let's write.

Write Now

1. Create a character or use a narrator based on yourself.
2. Borrowing from Machado's lists (or create one of your own), take an inventory of that character's sexual partners, their symptoms, their animals, the spices in a dish they make, or their emergency supplies.
3. Write a paragraph for each, making sure that the item and how it's described reveal things about your character or narrator.
4. When you get to the third item on your list, add a surreal element: a post-apocalyptic setting or a horror element (Zombies? Vampires? Possession?).
5. In revisions, see if you can seamlessly merge the forms to say something

about your character or narrator that could not have been said using "traditional" storytelling techniques.

Before we conclude this section on hybrids, we'll give you a few more of our favorite examples.

Two of our hybrid favorites are *Lincoln in the Bardo*, by George Saunders, which won the Booker Prize, and Sigrid Nunez's *The Friend*, winner of the National Book Award for Fiction.

The Booker Prize website says this of Saunders's debut novel:

> The novel, based on a factual incident, describes one night in the life of Abraham Lincoln as he visits the body of his dead 11-year-old son Willie in a Georgetown cemetery. The night the grieving father spends there is populated by both the quick and the dead—by Lincoln and by innumerable souls caught in limbo who can communicate with each other but not with him and who have much to say since they are not yet ready to be dead. The death of one small boy and the pain it engenders is a microcosm of the death of thousands in the American Civil War. What Saunders does in the novel is explore not just death but life, too—its possibilities, its meaning, its missed opportunities.

As Lola (Baroness) Young, one of the Booker Prize judges, pointed out, "To create this multiplicity of voices, Saunders invented a new format, a hybrid narrative in which there are sections that read like a play as the dead yammer to one another, with passages of monologue, and sections that introduce real historical facts"—such as how full the moon was on that particular night. There's no denying that it is a deeply serious novel, but Saunders wraps playfulness around the idea of history too.

Lincoln in the Bardo is a book about craft as much as imagination. Nunez's personal website describes *The Friend* this way:

> When a woman unexpectedly loses her lifelong best friend and mentor, she finds herself burdened with the unwanted dog he has left behind. Her own battle against grief is intensified by the mute suffering of the dog, a huge Great Dane traumatized by the inexplicable disappearance of its master, and by the threat of eviction: dogs are prohibited in her apartment building.

> While others worry that grief has made her a victim of magical thinking, the woman refuses to be separated from the dog except for brief periods of time. Isolated from the rest of the world, increasingly obsessed with the dog's care, determined to read its mind and fathom its heart, she comes dangerously close to unraveling. But while troubles abound, rich and surprising rewards lie in store for both of them.
>
> Elegiac and searching, *The Friend* is both a meditation on loss and a celebration of human-canine devotion.

Writer and translator Monika Zaleska, in an interview for Lithub, shared the following thoughts and posed a question to Nunez:

> *The Friend* is partly written in direct address to a "you" that is sometimes her mentor who passed away, sometimes the dog Apollo, and sometimes perhaps an unidentified someone. How did you arrive at this style—the address of someone no longer there? The novel feels like an epistolary project, or like a diary or journal that's been tucked away.

Sigrid Nunez answered:

> It's not something I worked at, or thought a lot about. I started the book and then realized that I was addressing this person. But I also knew that I didn't want that to be consistent; I wanted it to come in and out. There are long sections of the book where the "you" drops out—where I'm not addressing him anymore. I didn't think of it as a diary, but it's interesting that you bring up the epistolary form because I did want it to have the feeling of a letter. I wanted that intimate, urgent tone—the idea of speaking to someone in a hushed voice—but not necessarily always to him. Sometimes I'm addressing the dog, and sometimes I'm just addressing the air, but I wanted that tone of a letter, a love letter, not necessarily in content, but with that same intensity and intimacy.

We paired these stories together because they are each, in a certain way, a new take on ghost stories. Both Nunez and Saunders allowed, unlocked, and gave way to what each of their projects demanded: conversations with dead people.

To be a writer is to be a reader. The best pieces seem to resist initial analysis. Even seasoned writers forget they're reading. Instead, they find themselves transfixed in an experience the writer has created—simultaneously looking at and forgetting the fact that it's words on a page. This is an especially useful distinction when choosing others' works as inspiration points. It may be tempting to turn to pieces in which the writer's strategies are easy to decipher. We beg to differ.

Blackouts, by Justin Torres, is another wonder of form and content. The book jacket describes the hybrid novel this way:

> Out in the desert in a place called the Palace, a young man tends to a dying soul, someone he once knew briefly but who has haunted the edges of his life: Juan Gay. Playful raconteur, child lost and found and lost, guardian of the institutionalized, Juan has a project to pass along, one built around a true artifact of a book—*Sex Variants: A Study of Homosexual Patterns*—and its devastating history. This book contains accounts collected in the early twentieth century from queer subjects by a queer researcher, Jan Gay, whose groundbreaking work was then co-opted by a committee, her name buried. The voices of these subjects have been filtered, muted, but it is possible to hear them from within and beyond the text, which, in Juan's tattered volumes, has been redacted with black marker on nearly every page. As Juan waits for his end, he and the narrator recount for each other moments of joy and oblivion; they resurrect loves, lives, mothers, fathers, minor heroes. In telling their own stories and the story of the book, they resist the ravages of memory and time. The past is with us, beside us, ahead of us; what are we to create from its gaps and erasures?
>
> A book about storytelling—its legacies, dangers, delights, and potential for change—and a bold exploration of form, art, and love, Justin Torres's *Blackouts* uses fiction to see through the inventions of history and narrative. A marvel of creative imagination, it draws on testimony, photographs, illustrations, and a range of influences as it insists that we look long and steadily at what we have inherited and what we have made—a world full of ghostly shadows and flashing moments of truth. A reclamation of ransacked history, a celebration of defiance, and a transformative encounter, *Blackouts* mines the stories that have been kept from us and brings them into the light.

Nathan Go, when talking about Justin Torres's work, used the word "prosody," which at first glance, especially in the context of this chapter, may look like a compound word for prose + poetry. In fact, the etymology (according to Oxford Languages Dictionary) is late fifteenth century, from the Latin *prosodia*, "accent of a syllable," from the Greek *prosōidia*, "song sung to music, tone of a syllable," from *pros*, "towards" + *ōidē*, "song."

"Toward song." If the project you're working on is moving toward achieving its unique set of rhythm and tone and lyrics—so it can sing—you're well on your way.

In Jenny Boully's *The Body: An Essay*, the author employs a list of footnotes to a book that doesn't exist (at least not in a way that is available to Boully's readers). It has been excerpted in both *The Next American Essay* and *The Best American Poetry*, illustrating the fluid nature of the piece. *The Body* upends all sorts of conventions about creative nonfiction by playing with plot and narrative, form, and story fragments.

The Body: An Essay (excerpt)
Jenny Boully

8 July 8, 1976

9 The fact that she named her imaginary child Zeno should be considered along with the following excerpts. The last time she saw X, they met in New York on her birthday. She wrote on a series of postcards to Andy, and these are given in the order in which they arrived in his mailbox:

(POSTCARD 4): "Therefore, place does not exist." But he was mistaken, Andy, terribly mistaken. Moving through these streets, flying away from E. time and time again, measuring "out my life with coffee spoons," I harbor a sure sense always of always existing in the plane of "here" while E. is always "there," always "elsewhere." I miss you. I wish I were not here. I Remain, as ever, yours, etc., JB

(POSTCARD 2): of hotel sheets. I am already envying them their placement of ornaments on Christmas trees and their china and silver sets. At my age, a woman should be wary of having children. Zeno of Elea is known to have said, "If place exists, where is it? For everything that exists is in a place. Therefore, place is in a place."

(POSTCARD 1): My dearest Andy, today, I turned 36 and summertime in NY is no longer pink candlelight. My eyes carry the crumbling veins of autumn leaves, and E., who is 40, has just confessed to asking a 20 yr old to marry him, to which she replied yes and that this must be the last of our time together as lovers who can share no secrets anyhow under cover

(POSTCARD 3): "This goes on to infinity."

10 John 20:9 "For as yet they knew not the scripture, that he must rise again from the dead." 20:11.6.10.99 "But (insert name here: _____) stood without at the sepulchre weeping: and as she wept, she stooped down, and *looked* into the sepulchre," **a** 20:13 "And they say unto her, Woman, why weepest thou? She saith unto them, Because they have taken away my Lord, and I know not where they have laid him." 20:14.21401 "And when she had thus said, she turned herself back, and saw _____ standing, and knew not that it was _____ . 20:15.33333 . . . " _____ saith unto her, Woman, why weepest thou? whom seekest thou?"

> **a** Not a sepulchre, but an envelope; not an envelope, but a door; not a door, but a fire escape. *
>
>> * The inclusion of this note was deemed necessary by the editor, lest false surmisesÝ lead to injuries.
>>
>> Ý"And there is a third nature, which is space and is eternal, and admits not of destruction and provides a home for all created things, and is apprehended, when all sense is absent, by a kind of spurious reason, and is hardly real— which we, beholding as in a dream, say of all existence that it must of necessity be in some place and occupy a space, but that what is neither in heaven nor in earth has no existence. Of these and other things of the same kind, relating to the true and waking reality of nature, we have only this dreamlike sense, and we are unable to cast off sleep and determine the truth about them." (52*b-c*)

11 thought about it late and then early again this morning, why it is that we put down the book in the middle of reading it (or else clutch it to us) and stare off as if to assimilate the beauty found *there* and integrate it within the *here*–to keep it *here*–to make it, so to say, real.

12 Actually, he would never read her letters that way. Dated her 25th year:

".& yet why do I keep rereading what I have written, attempting to surmise what you might be inferring, wondering if you will understand me, hoping that you will fall in love with *something* I've written here & thus fall in love with me? If I were to turn this life into a movie, we'd all be under bridges, then under tables, then under water, then in the belly of a sperm whale, all the while speaking of sky; moreover, we'd wear mourning veils, heavy coats, silk gloves & communicate solely through quill pens and carrier pigeons. If I were to turn these love letters into a book, the inscription would be by Barthes, & it would say: *To know that one does not write for the other, to know that these things I am going to write will never cause me to be loved by the one I love (the other), to know that writing compensates for nothing, sublimates nothing, that it is precisely* there where you are not-*this is the beginning of writing.* If this were a cartoon, you would be a giraffe & I'd be a mouse & we'd live in sycamore-leaf shaped house & we'd fight all the time, that is, when you could hear me, your head being so high up, so far off; I'd sleep in your little alarm clock, sing a morning song for you, chew holes in your favorite socks, hide my best straw and bits of yarn in your breast pockets, let you use my tail to mark your places in books."

Maggie Nelson's *Bluets* is another unclassifiable creative nonfiction book because its author invented both container and contents. Written in numbered prose segments, the subject matter shifts from theme to theme, grounded by historical research, and all centered on the color blue. *Bookforum* named it one of the ten best books of the past two decades.

Bluets (excerpt)
Maggie Nelson

1. Suppose I were to begin by saying I had fallen in love with a color. Suppose I were to speak this as though it were a confession; suppose I shredded my

napkin as we spoke. *It began slowly. An appreciation, an affinity. Then, one day, it became more serious. Then* (looking into an empty teacup, its bottom stained with thin brown excrement coiled into the shape of a sea horse) *it became somehow* personal.

2. And so I fell in love with a color—in this case, the color blue—as if falling under a spell, a spell I fought to stay under and get from under, in turns.

3. Well, and what of it? A voluntary delusion, you might say. That each blue object could be a kind of burning bush, a secret code meant for a single agent, an X on a map too diffuse ever to be unfolded in entirety but that contains the knowable universe. How could all the shreds of blue garbage bags stuck in brambles, or the bright blue tarps flapping over every shanty and fish stand in the world, be, in essence, the fingerprints of God? *I will try to explain this.*

4. I admit that I may have been lonely. I know that loneliness can produce bolts of hot pain, a pain which, if it stays hot enough for long enough, can begin to simulate, or to provoke—take your pick—an apprehension of the divine. *(This ought to arouse our suspicions.)*

5. But first, let us consider a sort of case in reverse. In 1867, after a long bout of solitude, the French poet Stéphane Mallarmé wrote to his friend Henri Cazalis: "These last months have been terrifying. My Thought has thought itself through and reached a Pure Idea. What the rest of me has suffered during that long agony, is indescribable." Mallarmé described this agony as a battle that took place on God's "boney wing." "I struggled with that creature of ancient and evil plumage—God—whom I fortunately defeated and threw to earth," he told Cazalis with exhausted satisfaction. Eventually Mallarmé began replacing "le ciel" with "l'Azur" in his poems, in an effort to rinse references to the sky of religious connotations. "Fortunately," he wrote Cazalis, "I am quite dead now."

6. The half-circle of blinding turquoise ocean is this love's primal scene. That this blue exists makes my life a remarkable one, just to have seen it. To have seen such beautiful things. To find oneself placed in their midst. Choiceless. I returned there yesterday and stood again upon the mountain.

7. But what kind of love is it, really? Don't fool yourself and call it sublimity. Admit that you have stood in front of the little pile of powdered ultramarine pigment in a glass cup at a museum and felt a stinging desire. But to do what? Liberate it? Purchase it? Ingest it?

Multigenre writers Brenda Miller and Suzanne Paola, in their textbook *Tell It Slant: Creating, Refining, and Publishing Creative Nonfiction*, describe using "found" forms as writing "hermit crab" essays. Hermit crabs are born without a shell. They look for the empty shells of other species and make them their homes. In hermit crab essays, writers use an existing "container" as a constraint, writing in the form of, for example, a Dear John letter or a shopping list. The idea is that having the constraint of the form frees up the writer to do more creative things with their material.

"We Regret to Inform You," originally published in *The Sun*, is one of Miller's own hermit crab essays, based on the form of rejection letters. Note the progression from light-hearted to quite serious.

We Regret to Inform You (excerpt)
Brenda Miller

The following letters, though never written, are based on real events. Any resemblance to the author's life and the people she has known is purely intentional.

April 12, 1970
Dear Young Artist:
Thank you for your attempt to draw a tree. We appreciate your efforts, especially the way you sat patiently on the sidewalk, gazing at that tree for an hour before setting pen to paper, and the many quick strokes of charcoal you executed with enthusiasm. But your smudges look nothing like a tree. In fact, they look like nothing at all, and the pleasure and pride you take in the work are not enough to redeem it. We are pleased to offer you remedial training in the arts, but we cannot accept your "drawing" for display.
　　With regret and best wishes,
　　The Art Class
　　Andasol Avenue Elementary School

October 13, 1973

Dear Tenth-Grader:

Thank you for your application to be the girlfriend of one of our star basketball players. As you can imagine, we have received hundreds of similar requests and so cannot possibly respond personally to every one. This letter is to inform you that you have not been chosen for one of the coveted positions, but we do invite you to continue hanging around the lockers as if you belong there. This selfless act will help the team members learn the art of ignoring lovesick girls.

Sincerely,

The Granada Hills Highlanders

P.S.: Though your brother is one of the star players, we could not take this familial relationship into account. Sorry to say no! Please do try out for one of the rebound-girlfriend positions in the future.

December 10, 1978

Dear College Dropout:

Thank you for the short time you spent with us. We understand that you have decided to terminate your stay, a decision that seems completely reasonable, given the circumstances. After all, who knew that the semester you decided to enroll at UC Berkeley would be so tumultuous. That unsavory business with Jim Jones and his Bay Area followers left us all reeling. And then Harvey Milk was shot, a blast that reverberated across the bay. It truly did feel as if the world were falling apart—we know that. We understand why you took refuge in the music of the Grateful Dead, dancing until you felt yourself leave your body, caught up in their brand of enlightenment. But you do realize that's a delusion, right?

And given that you were a drama major, struggling on a campus well-known for histrionics and unrest—well, it's only understandable that you'd need some time to "find yourself." You're really too young to be in such a big city on your own. When you had your exit interview with the dean of students, you were completely inarticulate about your reasons for leaving, perhaps because you still have no idea what they are. You know there is a boy you might love in Santa Cruz. You fed him peanuts at a Dead show. You imagine playing house with him, living there in the shadows of tall trees.

But of course you couldn't say that to the dean, as he swiveled in his chair, looking so official in his gray suit. He clasped his hands on the oak desk and waited for you to explain yourself. His office looked out on the quad, where you'd heard the Talking Heads play just a week earlier, and beyond that the dorm where the gentleman you know only as "Pink Cloud" provided you with LSD, which you took in order to experience more fully the secrets the Dead whispered in your ear. You told the dean none of this, but simply shrugged your shoulders and began to cry, at which point he cleared his throat and wished you luck.

We regret to inform you that it will be quite a while before you grow up, and it will take some cataclysmic events in your life before you really begin to find the role that suits you. In any case, we wish you the best in all your future educational endeavors.

Sincerely,

UC Berkeley Registrar

October 26, 1979

Dear Potential Mom:

Thank you for providing a host home for each of us during the few weeks we stayed in residence. It was lovely but, in the end, didn't quite work out. Though we tried to be unobtrusive in our exit, the narrowness of your fallopian tubes made some damage unavoidable. Sorry about that. You know you were too young to have children anyway, right? And you know it wasn't your fault, not really. (Though you could have been a *tad* more careful in your carnal acts. But no matter. Water under the bridge.)

We enjoyed our brief stay in your body and wish you the best of luck in conceiving children in the future.

With gratitude,

Ira and Isabelle

November 3, 1979

Dear Patient:

We regret to inform you that, due to reproductive abnormalities, you will not be able to conceive children. *Barren* is not a word we use these days, but you may use it if you so choose. Your two miscarriages were merely symptoms of these abnormalities, which we surmise were acquired in utero. It's not your fault, but you may choose to take this misfortune as a sign of God's displeasure and torture yourself with guilt and self-loathing for many years to come.

All the best,
Student Health Center
Humboldt State University

April 14, 1994
Dear Potential Wife:
Thank you for your application to be my spouse. While I see much to admire here, I regret to inform you that you do not meet my needs at this time.

I do want to commend you for your efforts over the past five years. You did your best, but your anxiety made it difficult to proceed. Even so, we did love our coffee in the morning, our home-cooked meals in the evening, and our travels through the Middle East. (Let's just forget the argument we had while walking the walls of the Old City in Jerusalem. Water under the bridge.) You laughed at my jokes; thanks for that. And of course it was fun being fledgling writers together, before reality intervened.

Try to remember that we loved the only way we could: not perfectly, nor entirely well, but genuinely. I adored your lisp and the little mole above your lip. I touched your scars, and you touched mine. We tried. But at some point in a relationship you shouldn't have to try so hard, right?

It may just be bad timing. Best wishes in your future matrimonial endeavors. I'm sure your talents will be put to good use elsewhere. I hope we can remain friends.

Your Grad-School Boyfriend

Write Now

It's your turn: invent your own container for your material, one you haven't yet seen or read or experimented with. Try any of these: recipe, map, diary entries, text messages, court transcripts, a choose your own adventure, social media posts, scientific report, interview transcripts, music playlist, timeline, obituary, user manual, magazine articles, postcards, tarot cards, dream journal.

As is always the case when discussing any subgenre, the possibilities are endless. We hope this chapter gave you permission. We hope it enables you to recognize when an existing container needs to be used, adjusted, or abandoned, so that your vision as an artist shines.

Once you find a container, you can start forming your materials into it. After, you can start rearranging for maximum impact.

Our final chapter will be on doing just that: revising.

PART III

Developing

Finding Your Own Form and Moving a Project Toward Completion

Chapter 10

Controlling Chaos in the Re-Visioning of Your Initial Drafts

The biggest *behavioral* difference between those who end up publishing and those who don't is the willingness to draft. An initial sketch, formed in a moment of inspiration, is usually taken through quite a process prior to it becoming something (others would agree is) worthy of an audience. The author must be mature enough to know, in advance, that in early drafts, the very qualities that will eventually prove to be most compelling about the piece are dormant. In fact, "dormant" is an advantage. More often, those qualities are born out of drafting and redrafting. Then authors must have the patience and determination to see, shape, resee, and reshape the drafts until the piece is able to deliver those "units of satisfaction."

But how do writers transform raw materials into literary pieces that leave a lasting impact on their readers? How do writers navigate the delicate balance between control and creativity, process and product? When does a writer keep at it? Let go?

In these final pages, we'll introduce the idea of "controlled chaos," a revision strategy that asks you to honor your "nonconforming oddities" and then put them to the test. We'll also explore a second revision strategy that uses the scientific notions of expansion and contraction. Our goal is to provide you with a set of adaptable practices and options to get to the point where you are satisfied enough to let go.

Keep in mind: *perfection is the enemy*. This book is structured to get you to experiment, to mine the topics most important to you. Any desire to turn those experiments into great art right from the first draft can easily backfire. Weird thing about perfectionism? It significantly raises the odds of failure. As artist Jean DuBuffet remarked:

> A girl belting out a song while sweeping the stairs moves me more than a complex cantata. I love the little. I also love the embryonic, the badly made, the imperfect, the mixed up. I love best diamonds in the rough, in their rock. And with flaws.

This quote reminds us that "perfect" doesn't mean "better." We acknowledge that the concept of "good art" is subjective, a matter of taste. While DuBuffet prefers a girl simultaneously belting out a song while working, others prefer a well-rehearsed performance of a complex cantata. As an artist, you work to understand what it is you want your audience to hear, then work to get it there.

Wanting your piece to contain everything and not being satisfied until it meets certain artistic and aesthetic criteria is part of being an artist. Feeling that you haven't gotten there yet is also part. As is, eventually, letting go.

The draft process isn't just about final polish and line editing (although writers *do* engage in deep revision with a particular focus on the line). That final-final edit is the (relatively) easy (and fun) part that takes place after an involved set of steps. Those previous steps require persistence, dedication, and patience.

Since most writers report that their works are not assembled according to a plan, but captured through the threefold process of experimentation, discovery, and development—and that each individual piece is written according to a unique and mysterious set of inspirations and demands—we couldn't possibly offer a one-size-fits-all guide to creative revision. While we hope that each chapter in this book engages all three processes, the first six chapters are meant to focus primarily on experimentation, the genre chapters on the discovery (or review) of strategies. Now it's time to talk about development.

Developing Work Using Expansion and Contraction

Vital practices in science laboratories involve expansion and contraction. These practices can also serve the writer during revision.

In the experimentation chapters, the aim was to help quiet that mean editor (or at least politely request that they take a back seat). The point was to engage the right half of your brain, get it into the realm of the subconscious, and see if our experiments could help you discover something you'd be excited to revise.

In the genre chapters, you were introduced to or reminded of elements of composition, or strategies—not only in your chosen genre, but in several. The focus was on tools other writers have used to transform an impulse, or an obsession, or an initial idea through the draft process, eventually molding it into a readable form with the power to transmit those units of satisfaction.

In this final chapter, you're encouraged to combine those strategies in a manner custom made for your project with a more intentional way to work with what your subconscious provided. We aim to bring that left side of the brain back online to help you organize what you've gathered so that it earns the attention of an audience.

We want to share a few strategies so you can transform what you've gotten down in moments of inspiration into something you are excited to share.

To do so, we'll talk about ways to expand your piece and ways to contract it.

Defining Revision

Literary revision is the artful and meticulous process of reevaluating, refining, and reshaping a written work, with a keen focus on enhancing its thematic depth, narrative coherence, stylistic precision, and emotional resonance. It involves a delicate interplay between deconstruction and reconstruction, where the writer skillfully dissects their original creation, stripping away excesses and inconsistencies, while concurrently infusing fresh insights, nuances, and layers of meaning.

This transformative endeavor demands engagement with any number of elements of composition in the literary form, including (not always, nor limited to) language, syntax, and symbolism, resulting in a work that transcends its initial form to become as close to the piece the author visioned (and re-visioned) it to be.

To illuminate our approach, we insert a hyphen after the first two letters of "revision." Vision = how we see. Re = to do something again. In a way, the process of re-vision is to go back to a piece and see it again.

Or to be more precise: again and again and again.

Beginner writers often think that a first draft is "step 1" of a two-step process, revision being the second. It's not. Some writers report hundreds of micro-revisions to arrive at their very first beginning-to-end draft. Others spit out a first draft, no matter how unorganized, and then spend months deciding what stays, what gets expanded, what goes.

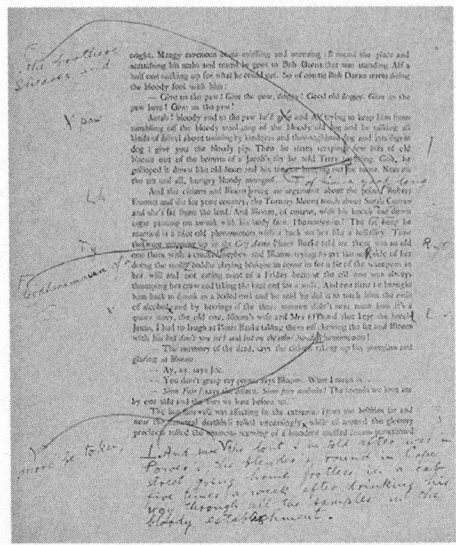

Detail of Placard for the Cyclops episode in James Joyce's novel *Ulysses*. [Dijon: Maurice Darantiere, October 1921] *Houghton Library, Harvard University, part gift of Marian Willard Johnson in memory of Sylvia Beach, and part purchase with funds from the Amy Lowell Fund, 1969; Ms Eng 160.4 (83).*

Look at James Joyce's galley proof of *Ulysses*. Page proofs are the final pages before a book is published. The text has been written, edited, proofed, typeset, and laid out into pages and is ready to be printed. Before getting to this stage, the book has passed back and forth between writer and editors—multiple editors—numerous times. Many, many eyes have already scrutinized it. By this stage, only the most egregious errors should be flagged as needing fixing. Yet look at all the changes Joyce suggested at this very final point!

When published writers give readings, it can be disconcerting for them when someone in the audience follows along with a copy of the book. Why? Because writers almost always revise as they read. Yes, this is after (sometimes years after) a book has been published, reviewed, and purchased by readers. They see things that they wish they could change—so they spontaneously edit as they speak, presenting the "new" version rather than what's in print.

Entering Expansion Mode

What do writers do when entering expansion mode? They take an early draft and ask themselves (and their writing partner or group if they have one) what's interesting, surprising, worthy of exploration. They pursue each of those moments and fill them in like a painter might a sketch. And they *read*.

As writers we:

1. Read.
2. Pay attention to what stirs emotion/wakes us up from complacency/breaks our hearts/infuriates us.

3. Go back to those lines or scenes and formulate questions about strategies we imagine the writer used to achieve step 2.
4. Experiment with personalized versions of that strategy in our own work.

This may sound basic, but it's not. The deeper you go, the more it'll serve you. In expansion mode, when a piece may still be in the early- and mid-draft stages, a writer may find it helpful to read the works of others, seeking solutions to their own project's problems. If you've ever sat down to finish a subsequent draft and just can't, pick up a book you love—any genre, no matter how different from your own, so long as the writer's work moves you.

A (good) critic analyzes a writer's work based on whether it lives up to the promises set forth by the piece itself. When in search of inspiration, you can do this, too, but you must also ask what processes the writer engaged in to get this work from an idea to published piece.

In 1998, when Oprah Winfrey announced that Toni Morrison would be her guest on *Oprah's Book Club*, a friend of ours was almost aggressively eager to be a part of the event. He'd been at work on a manuscript. He wanted his novel to have the same level of impact on his future readers as Morrison's had on him—all while resisting the pressure to pander to trends.

In his view, Morrison wrote books that reached a mainstream audience without compromising her vision one iota. Most of all, our friend loved Morrison's artistry, her control of the sensory-evoking power of language. He also admired how Morrison's work centered Black characters while opening the minds and hearts of readers of all identities.

His curiosity bordered on compulsion. He wanted to personally quiz Morrison on her draft process, how she came to discover the character Beloved's voice, and how she'd decided to portray the ghost. He wanted to ask her whose writing, if anyone's, she turned to for inspiration.

So, he spent an entire day writing a letter to Ms. Winfrey asking if he could participate in her show.

Alas, Ms. Winfrey's book club didn't choose him. He watched the program on television. But the process of formulating the questions for Morrison and imagining her answers helped him with the expansion and revision of his own novel.

Here's how he did it. He wrote down all the questions he wanted to ask. He imagined what Morrison might say in response. Then, he came up with writing prompts for his own novel based on his speculations about her processes.

An example:

> Did you choose to embody the ghost of Beloved from the get-go? It doesn't seem to fit the classic ghost story, so I imagine you didn't, but that the story itself demanded it.
>
> [Prompt: Even though you're not writing a classic ghost story, attempt to have Claire's dad show up as a ghost. A ghost that can be seen and heard, one that engages with her, talks back. See if you can earn it without being cheesy.]
>
> Did you ever attempt to have Beloved haunt Sethe's memory (instead of show up embodied)? I imagine this because everything else in your novel seems to borrow from the tradition of realism. The ghost is the one surreal element.
>
> [Prompt: Rework the scene where Claire's dad shows up as a ghost—as if it's a dream—make sure it's not cheesy. When she wakes up, make it clear to the reader that her dad is haunting her subconscious, but is not embodied in real life.]
>
> Did you turn to other genres or traditions for inspiration, like horror or ghost stories? I can't imagine where you got the idea, and wondered if there were another literary example you used as a jumping off point.
>
> [Prompt: Reread the "creation of the monster scene" from *Frankenstein, or, The Modern Prometheus* by Mary Shelley, study the moment Frankenstein's monster is born. Imitate what you admire. Reread "Ligeia," by Poe, study the scene where the titular character returns from the dead through the power of the narrator's drug-induced obsession. Then, in your work, focus less on portraying Claire's dad as an embodied ghost. Instead, focus on Claire's psychological state. Like Poe, experiment with blurring the line between reality and hallucination. Compare the two, see which is better.]

Often, when in creative mode, what captivates us about another person's work is the set of solutions sewn inside—even if another writer's strategies would require modification for our own work. In other words, the piece's magnetism to our psyche may offer hitherto-unseen insight into the piece the artist-reader is working on. We just need to turn on the lights.

Writers seek these solutions across genre. Some novelists find it impossible to go to other novels when revising. Some poets find it impossible to go to poetry. There are a range of reasons. They may rightly fear copying the writer they admire (which is different from observing their techniques and attempting an application of their own). They may be too intimidated by the work's mastery in its final draft. So, they go outside their genre or art form for direction. To illustrate how this can work, let's turn to architecture for a moment.

A friend of ours is a commercial architect. She's always looking at buildings for inspiration, but when needing solutions to her own projects in process, she "sees" in a different way. She recently pitched an office space to a client. Before making her bid, she found nothing useful to sketch after an exhausting study of other architects' office spaces. Then, one afternoon, close to her bid deadline, walking in the park, she studied how the landscape architects achieved "solutions." Although she was sitting alone and able to have "privacy," she also felt a part of her surroundings. Acoustically, she noticed she was close enough to the hustle and bustle of the city—so there was "white noise"—but she also sat far enough away that she could relax. Able to see others around her, she felt a sense of community without feeling disturbed because the white noise made it impossible to hear the nearby group's conversation. She scrutinized the compositional choices that led to these "gathering" and "solo," "public" and "private," and acoustic opportunities within the space and left with a plan.

She asked herself, "What's the office-version of this park? What can I learn from the landscape architect's choices?" She said, "No one needs another bunch of cubicles." With that in mind, she designed the office space, the bid was accepted, and the office design, inspired by a park, is currently in progress.

Matthew Frederick, in his illustrated book *101 Things I Learned in Architecture School*, wrote:

> The design process is often structured and methodical, but it is not a mechanical process. Mechanical processes have predetermined outcomes, but the creative process strives to produce something that has not existed before. Being genuinely creative means that you don't know where you are

going, even though you are responsible for shepherding the process. This requires something different from conventional, authoritarian control; a loose velvet tether is more likely to help.

Engage the design process with patience. Don't imitate popular portrayals of the creative process as depending on a singular, pell-mell rush of inspiration. Don't try to solve a complex building in one sitting or one week. Accept uncertainty. Recognize as normal the feeling of lostness that attends to much of the process. Don't seek to relieve your anxiety by marrying yourself prematurely to a design solution; design divorces are never pretty.

Let's turn back to writing.

Write now

1. Read this Ellen Bass poem two or three times. Make notes as to which lines you find most moving.

   Any Common Desolation
   Ellen Bass

   > can be enough to make you look up
   > at the yellowed leaves of the apple tree, the few
   > that survived the rains and frost, shot
   > with late afternoon sun. They glow a deep
   > orange-gold against a blue so sheer, a single bird
   > would rip it like silk. You may have to break
   > your heart, but it isn't nothing
   > to know even one moment alive. The sound
   > of an oar in an oarlock or a ruminant
   > animal tearing grass. The smell of grated ginger.
   > The ruby neon of the liquor store sign.
   > Warm socks. You remember your mother,
   > her precision a ceremony, as she gathered
   > the white cotton, slipped it over your toes,

drew up the heel, turned the cuff. A breath
can uncoil as you walk across your own muddy yard,
the big dipper pouring night down over you, and everything
you dread, all you can't bear, dissolves
and, like a needle slipped into your vein—
that sudden rush of the world.

2. Choose a piece you've written. If you haven't yet written anything, come back to this exercise later once you have something. If you have several pieces to choose from, take your time in choosing. Land on a piece that most fits these two conditions: You feel passionate about it in some palpable way. *And* it's a mess—hopefully because there's *too* much going on.

3. Look at it as objectively as possible, then write yourself a kind letter from your inner editor.

For an example, we've included portions of a real-life rejection letter to a writer friend from the editor of a major magazine who had kind things to say about a creative nonfiction piece she had sent out.

> **Dear Writer,**
> I finally had a chance to read through the whole piece and really enjoyed it. It doesn't quite fit the parameters . . . —I can only publish [pieces] that articulate some kind of argument or opinion. If the piece is more of a personal essay, it has to dovetail with some kind of contemporary issue. . . . That being said, many parts of your beautiful essay could be zoomed in on to create a more compact piece, if you're interested in that. I see a lot of potential stories to focus on: childhood friendship as amelioration of violence [or issues concerning] . . . mixed-race and nationalities . . . Or even stories like the one about your friend who moved from San Francisco to Oakland. . . .
>
> Let me know if developing any of these . . . sounds exciting to you and I'll definitely take a look again. You're a fantastic writer.

The editor's feedback is clear. It says: *This is good. This is a mess.* That's exactly why she would be wise to choose this piece for this part of the exercise.

4. Reread your piece carefully. See if you can note any themes that came up in the letter from your kind editor: topics as important to you *now* as when you first wrote it. Choose one.

Here is our writer friend's answer, which she based on the feedback in the letter she had received from the editor: "My most prevalent theme: How friendship can (and cannot) help a victim endure or recover from violence."

5. Focusing on one thematic concern, answer this Bass-inspired questionnaire from the POV of the speaker of your piece (or a character or narrator). Do not use logic or rationale. Just associate, see what happens. Keep it short. Let it get weird. We'll help you make sense of this before the chapter is over.

    i.   What desolation has occurred in your (character's) life?
    ii. What kind of tree do you (or does your character) always see?
    iii. Describe the time of day you (or your character) last saw it and describe the leaves.
    iv. Finish this sentence: "You may have to break your heart, but it isn't nothing to know . . ."
    v.   Describe a sound you heard last time you felt grateful to be alive.
    vi. Describe a smell that you smell frequently but always surprises you.
    vii. Describe something you see on your walk or in your car every day that others might see as mundane but that you think is beautiful.
    viii. Name an article of clothing you appreciate for its texture and/or form and/or function. For example, warm socks.
    ix. Finish this sentence: "I remember my (enter a person most important to you/your character during childhood) and their . . . (enter seemingly small but meaningful action)."

Example:
What desolation has occurred in your (character's) life?
Moving from a place I had friends to one I didn't.
What kind of tree do you (or does your character) always see?
I always smell honeysuckle, even blocks away.
Describe the time of day you (or your character) last saw it and describe the leaves.

*Morning time, getting off the bus at 23rd and Noe; the tender pink flesh of
the flower emerging from all those green leaves.*

Finish this sentence: "You may have to break your heart, but it isn't nothing to
know ..."

*You may have to break your heart, but it isn't nothing to know the heat and
shelter of another's body.* ·

Describe a sound you heard last time you felt grateful to be alive.

*It's not last time I felt grateful, but remembering Colleen's caustic laugh—
amid all the bullshit—certainly is a balm.*

Describe a smell that you smell frequently but always surprises you.

Coffee.

Describe something you see on your walk or in your car every day that others
might see as mundane but that you think is beautiful.

Wild fennel.

Name an article of clothing you appreciate for its texture and/or form and/or
function. For example, warm socks.

My father's Navy cap.

Finish this sentence: "I remember my (enter a person most important to
you/your character during childhood) and their (enter seemingly small but
meaningful action)."

*I remember Colleen and her looking away, pretending at that moment she
hadn't heard what the boys called me.*

Put that aside for now; we'll come back to it later.

Ellen Bass said about her poem:

> A friend once told me that the beauty of two colors—the right two colors—
> next to each other was as wonderful to her as an orgasm. During a rough
> time in my life—prolonged family illness—I was sitting in the yard and when I
> saw a yellow leaf glowing in the blue sky like a little lantern, I thought of her.
> And I felt how the vivid life of the physical world can amaze us even when
> we feel inconsolable.

Ellen Bass's lecture on "Controlled Chaos" for Hugo House is worth watching
in its entirety and then watching again. Here's an excerpt from her talk, given in

September 2016. While reading, it may be useful to think of the "chaos" as the right-brain expansive part and the "control" as the left-brain contraction part.

> **Controlled Chaos**
>
> A certain kind of poem has a long arm and sweeps disparate, unexpected things into its net. It scoops in a great deal of material that is more or less obviously related. It doesn't hug the shore. It doesn't walk a narrow line. It retains a kind of wildness. It can seem untamed. And yet all the elements have enough magnetic or gravitational attraction, enough resonance, that the poem or essay or story feels organically whole.
>
> I'll be talking mostly about poems tonight, but this all applies to other genres as well.
>
> To write this kind of long-armed poem, to allow the excitement, tension, and passion of chaos into our writing, we have to open the doors. We have to be willing to be surprised, even startled, even shocked. We have to be willing to experience the most essential state of creativity—the state of not knowing. Of being open, of being willing to be changed.

In his poem "Song of a Man Who Has Come Through," D. H. Lawrence summons the strange angels. Toward the end of the poem, he writes:

> What is the knocking?
> What is the knocking at the door in the night?
> It is somebody wants to do us harm.
>
> No, no, it is the three strange angels.
> Admit them, admit them.

So, we want to be open to all the strange angels who might want to enter the poem.

Let it all in. Your earliest drafts may not hold the complexity you're seeking and may seem "messy" for one of two main reasons. They may lack focus and *seem* to be about "too much." This can be an excellent problem to have, like a chef with tons of ingredients. Another could be that you're trying too hard and too soon to control the chaos, limiting yourself.

To expand, look at your current draft. Is there something you discovered in the answers of the questionnaire that isn't yet in the current draft but that contains "enough magnetic or gravitational attraction, enough resonance" that you want to work it in there?

And from Ellen Bass: "Before Ezra Pound said, 'Make it new,' Tolstoy said, 'Make it strange.' Here's a poem by Frank O'Hara that meets both poets' demands."

Today

Frank O'Hara

    Oh! kangaroos, sequins, chocolate sodas!
    You really are beautiful! Pearls,
    harmonicas, jujubes, aspirins! all
    the stuff they've always talked about

    still makes a poem a surprise!
    These things are with us every day
    even on beachheads and biers. They
    do have meaning. They're strong as rocks.

Frank O'Hara allows everything into his poem. And he says that all these things have meaning even on beachheads and biers, even in the face of war and death. In this way, he includes what delights us, as well as our suffering, and shows us how they are inextricably joined. It's a short poem, not difficult to grasp even on a first reading. And yet it has scooped the chaos, the complexity, the paradox of our lives into its eight lines.

Is there, in what you chose to revise, an opportunity to explore a "paradox of our lives"? If your piece includes "what delights us," is there also an opportunity to show "our suffering" (or vice versa)? If so, expand your piece.

Doing Ourselves a Favor by Letting the Strange Angels In

How to let them in:

1. Care. The idea may seem odd. You might be thinking, "Of course I care, why else would I take time out of my life to sit and write?" But we want to challenge you to dig deep. As a thought experiment, imagine that the piece

you're holding is missing what you care about most deeply. Perhaps there's an anecdote that hints at what you care most about. Perhaps there's an emotion underneath the emotion you're portraying. Perhaps you're performing what you think your reader wants from you instead of saying what you *really* want to say.

2. Give yourself permission to get wild. Even if you envision your finished draft published in the most academic and/or conservative journal, is there a "strange angel" you're not letting in?

3. Be authentic. Are you hiding behind abstractions? Artificiality of some kind? Inauthentic use of language? Relying too heavily upon tropes? Even if it's about challenging subject matter, could you expand your piece by putting in more of everything you love? If your narrator or character is based on yourself, is it only the flattering parts you want others to see?

4. Trust the piece itself more than your logical mind's reaction to it. It may be telling you what it needs.

Talking about the poet Frank X. Gaspar, Ellen Bass said:

I am a great admirer of Frank Gaspar's poetry. In his work we are privileged to see intimately into the workings of the poet's mind. That sense that he opens the window of his mind and lets us look in, is so compelling. Allen Ginsberg said, "Write your mind." And I think this is what Frank's poems do.

His poetry inspired me to coin a new poetic term, the long-armed poem, because he reaches out a long arm and scoops so much disparate, seemingly unrelated matter into his poems and yet there's always a sense of inevitability that these things do belong together—a strong magnetic or gravitational attraction.

His poems combine a keen quality of observation with a deep vulnerability. They plumb despair, but there is always a song of praise in them as well. I asked him about this in an interview that I did with him for *American Poetry Review*—this joining of despair and praise, and he said: "... the despair and praise are not so much a call and a deliberated response, but the rising of two wings that beat together."

It's this kind of thinking in what, for me, is unforgettable imagery, that makes me return again and again to his poetry.

"A keen quality of observation" plus "a deep vulnerability." We see this idea again and again in our favorite writers of all genres. We also hear about it in what they admire about others. Here is a poem by Frank X. Gaspar, followed by a conversation with Gaspar that Bass included in her talk at Hugo House.

June/July—Eleven Black Notebooks at the Desert Queen Motel
Frank X. Gaspar

Then night again. The dry lightning like artillery over the far reefs
of stone and the thunder-god shearing the air—all the gods in foment
and calamity, but it is not enough. The rumble and rupture, the shattering.
Out there in the wilderness. Isaiah, Ezra, their lamentations, insufficient
in the madness, and me with my tall can of iced beer leaning
at the railing outside my door, like at the taffrail of a ship, but instead
of the big turbines thrumming on blackoil, now only the small throats
of the air conditioners gagging and moaning. The cold aluminum sweats
in my hand, and I'm pleased for this small miracle, water out of the
cracked desert air, but it is not enough. My happiness now, with the
work coming forth in fits and then gouts, is not enough, for it saves
nothing, yet it is a happiness after all, and therefore inexplicable.
The stars crowd one another out of their familiar lines. The arm
of the galaxy, its bright muscle against the belly of the sky. Not enough.
My heart full or empty, not enough. Now, to set something down in
the midst of folly, one true word, one simple cry out of the black arroyos
and dangerous washes, the canyons, the granite redoubts, but the lone sob
of the desert hen is not enough, the television's mangled voices creeping
through the drywall and stucco are not enough, and I am running out of
time and money, always time and money. And love, I don't forget love,
but it's not enough either, it doesn't save anything, the graves open for all
the beloved to lie down in and all the despised as well, and it is still not enough.
Stepping back into the cramped room I think of that ship again. How a ship will
fit into the poem at this juncture. Perhaps my own ship from that other time.
One hundred thousand tons of death and empire. Grand under my feet. Rolling
with the long ocean swells. Sky like desert sky, shot with the unutterable trillions.
And the engines banging forward blindly. Into that darkness. Under that blaze.

BASS: In that . . . poem, you have a wide wide sweep from Isaiah and Ezra in the wilderness to the iced beer to the arroyos and canyons and desert hen, and back into the cramped room and the ship (and again, inviting the writing in—"How a ship will fit into the poem at this juncture") which becomes your old ship—"One hundred thousand tons of death and empire." And then onto that gorgeous and dangerous way we are all living as we bang forward "into that darkness. Under that blaze." Can you say a little about this gathering into the poem with such long arms, how you sweep it all in onto one small page?

GASPAR: Oh, I like that, Ellen: Gathering into the poem with long arms. It's so visual. Okay, I'll accept that, the long arms, it's talking about embracing, hugging, pulling in. Of course it's all in there anyway. I do often type very long drafts. I might have six pages of lines, most of them bad, without sound or shape, but circling around, looking for the currents to rise on. Then—and this is important for me—at some point I turn the poem over to the poem. Poems are smarter than I am. They know what they want to be. I stop and take a breath. Or a lot of breaths over many days. And I see what I have given myself. Where does this poem want to go? What is hidden, occulted in here that is the deep thing that wants to be expressed? The thing that does not take direction from my feeble conscious mind? Sometimes there is just a debris field of seemingly random words and phrases. So you have to find out if there is a secret logic to them. If there is, then you must subsume your will to it. Aid it in its coming out. Stay out of the way with your crummy language and listen to how it has to sound on its own terms. Because the mind writing itself doesn't sound like you writing. We are full of dead language. The mind makes its own logic. Like in dreams. So you have to bend. Then you have to bend the poem! It's hard to explain. Oh, it's a tango. Two parts wrestling for control, both being essential. So a cold beer can condensing water out of the desert air can appear to fit perfectly with a ship of war coursing through the seas. You might even say, in terms of the poem, they need each other. This isn't magic. It's a lot of work. But it's a certain kind of work, moving through registers and tones of language, through levels of consciousness. I do not explain it well. It is very pleasing to do, though.

Gaspar says he doesn't explain it well, but we disagree. He pinpoints exactly what we're encouraging you to do. Uncovering what is "hidden," "occulted." Possessing the humility to recognize the limitations of the "feeble conscious mind." Looking for "a secret logic." A willingness to "bend"; to "work."

Before we move to the compression part of revision, where we zoom out and become as objective as possible while inviting the logical mind—which has been waiting in the wings—back in, let's do a bit of expansion, some more writing.

Write Now

1. Take any piece you'd like to continue to work on, or write something new that hints at or addresses a thematic concern important to you.
2. Use "the long arm and sweep disparate and unexpected things into its net." Allow "chaos" to enter. Go maximalist. Go highly highly associative. Borrow from your warm-up. Borrow from the invented Bass strategy. Forget about what you're trying to say. Let it go insular. Let it get highly particular. Attempt to braid at least two of the seemingly disparate answers from the warm-up (or anything else you've thought of since) into a rough draft.

We'll come back to it in a bit.

Editing in Contraction Mode

Remember, we're not trying to turn our creations into one-size-fits-all. We're seeking to elevate our creations and share them when they reach their full potential. Learning to skillfully discern what to trim or cut takes practice. Here are a few things to look out for.

Repetition: A poet's tool, repetition can be effective when applied to any genre. To earn it, make sure it has the impact you intend. Redundancy of ideas or the portrayal of scenes usually can be cut. When a point has been adeptly made or a tableau vividly depicted earlier, further reiteration can become distracting, superfluous, or boring.

Unneeded Particulars: We keep saying it's all in the details! Get them all in there! But once you reach the revision stage, put each detail to the test. Does it provide sonic resonance or enrich character depth or propel plot intricacies or expound upon thematic undercurrents? If not, cut it. Choose the best one or two details, cut the rest, and see how it sounds and feels.

Vividness and Conciseness: What are you going for? Lush? Spare? Minimal? Baroque? And how does that stylistic choice serve the piece's themes? Once you land on the right style, go for evocative descriptions and narrative economy. Even maximalist poems, books, and memoirs had many lines, images, and scenes that didn't serve the piece and were cut prior to the final iteration. Conciseness isn't about making something smaller. It's not about the number of lines or pages. It's about impact.

Tangents, Strange Angels, Mosquitoes: Subplots and secondary narratives must earn their place. It's up to you to decide whether these artistic diversions significantly contribute or hinder what's most alive in your piece. Had Herman Melville listened to a sensible editor, we wouldn't have *Moby-Dick*. Many great works achieve their brilliance by portraying lines, scenes, even entire chapters that an average reader might find tangential.

Excessiveness: Related to repetition, unneeded particulars, and tangents is excessiveness. But don't forget: excessiveness as a stylistic choice can be, like wonderful tangents, a great thing! But does your excessiveness in any form add to or disrupt the flow? Is the reader to discover essential information in each sentence? If so, give us the excess! If not, cut the lines, paragraphs, and pages where disruptions hinder rather than serve your greater vision.

What Did You Just Say to Me? We talked about dialogue in the fiction chapter, but dialogue is best when put to the test in all types of creative nonfiction and hybrid forms, too. When speech represents something spoken (or thought, in the case of internal dialogue), it should be more impactful than if rendered in straight prose. Conversations that merely meander, that fail to propel the plot or illuminate character intricacies or cultivate tension, fall under scrutiny. People say weird and random-seeming stuff all the time. So can your characters and narrators. As in life, random-seeming words mostly distract. Occasionally, they're enlightening. You decide which is which. Cut what doesn't work.

Focus: Sometimes, in the draft process, writers portray ten things to find the one thing that fits, but then forget to cut the other nine. We encourage you to question lines, scenes, and paragraphs that lack a clear trajectory or relevance or those that regurgitate information without adding depth. If you find them, cut them.

Do You Need all the Backstory? While backstory can deepen characterization, authors need to determine whether extensive flashbacks or intricate histories warrant their length by maximizing impact. A great question to ask: Does interrupting the present-day scene for history or flashback add to the overall tension? If not, consider cutting.

Pacing Is Paramount: Authors vigilantly identify lines in their poetry or passages in their prose that impede narrative momentum, refining prose to perpetuate reader engagement. Think of your piece as a runner gliding toward a destination. Cut anything that trips.

Is the Subtext Too "Sub"? Not "Sub" Enough? Subtext tends to fall flat and subtract from a reader's engagement when excessively veiled or overtly glaring. Look for both and consider cutting. Sometimes what's on the surface is more powerful than the subtext. Readers are smart. They will glean more from your work if you trust them to do so.

Keep Your Darlings (At Least for Now)

"Kill your darlings" is a popular phrase tossed around haphazardly in workshops. (More on workshops in a moment.) The phrase has since been attributed as the advice given by many great writers, but we want to present a warning.

There's wisdom here: if, *in final drafts*, a section of a piece isn't working and you stubbornly keep it in just because it took months to write or it contains a compelling image, that will do your work a disservice. The section may not be enough to "earn its keep," and it might weaken rather than strengthen your piece.

When turning your writing in early drafts over to others for *criticism*, the situation is different: that person is *looking for* things to tell you to change. A skilled reader will see the difference between a "darling" and a "strange angel." But far too often the feedback giver conflates these two and tells the writer in early stages to cut something wonderful prior to its earning its keep.

Don't do it!

If something about your draft seems utterly odd or strange and you have a gut feeling it belongs, work to earn it. Don't get rid of it.

Monique Jenkinson is a multifaceted artist who describes her first book, *Faux Queen*, as "a collection of essays in drag as a memoir." She performs on stage as a drag queen and made *herstory* when she was the first cis woman to win a major drag pageant. When asked about her revision process, she said this:

> Since this was my first long-form writing project, I had to write through all the big feelings. I produced thousands more words than I used—literal excess. I have a very bitchy inner *editrix* who made that first just-get-it-out draft difficult, but I did it. Then I invited her (and others) back in to impose the constraint of the drag filter. I hope there is still the right amount of excess spilling over in the places that want it. I . . . like work that evokes feelings.
>
> The tension between excess and constraint is crucial both to my performance-making and writing process. The real genesis of the book's material was a choreographic constraint. In early solo shows, I started telling stories to buy myself time onstage while changing costumes. These became monologues, which seeded some of the chapters of the book. So, this literal constraint was extremely productive—as it often is.
>
> Also, I felt a huge responsibility toward the people I was representing in the book, so I tried to do right by them.

Jenkinson's description is pitch perfect for this two-fold process. After letting the "long arm" sweep everything in, she developed constraints. Jenkinson is a professional dancer, a choreographer, and a teacher. She could've written about her experiences in any of those fields—and she did—but *eventually* cut all that didn't shine light on her experience in the drag scene. The book is incredible and lets in so many strange angels, but eventually they all tie back into the piece's main thematic concerns about art, identity, femininity, humor, and friendship. A voracious reader, Jenkinson studied numerous books for form, content, and style and experimented until she found the voice of the book.

Perhaps all works of art are, in some way, love songs to something outside the self: nature, another writer, a community, an individual. So long as we're on the subject of love songs, let's bring up the writing groups.

Before we close this chapter, let's talk briefly about giving your drafts to readers and writing workshops for critical feedback. As with everything else, the usefulness of this process depends on two things: your expectations and who's giving you feedback.

Again and again in this book and chapter, we encourage you to gauge these two things when inviting, limiting, implementing, or rejecting others' reactions to your work. Embrace the probability of confusion and disappointment. Enjoy the high that might come from the first draft and expect an eventual crash.

If you're in a creative writing program, you're likely to workshop in one way or another. Entering a program implies that you want to receive feedback. Some participants also want to give feedback. Others do it as the price of admission. In every case, the quality varies.

If you're not in a writing program, you get to choose. Some of us use readers and groups, others don't. Some writers have a group of tight friends (not all of them writers) that they trust to give honest and—more importantly—useful insights into late drafts.

Others have *very*-rough-draft groups or writing partners, trusting the group will not squelch any strange angels but instead shine a light on them and encourage more to knock on the writer's door.

The workshop is like the real world in one sense: once you let a project go out into the world, you cannot control who will see it or how they will respond. There are usually people in that group who will not, for a variety of reasons, be able to pick up what you're trying to lay down, no matter how effective the draft. That can be okay, even useful, if the workshop is respectful, has strong community agreements, and has paths forward should it accidently veer off. Some workshops devolve into battles of will, where individuals insist on edits based on their own biases. This is, at the very least, irritating; at worst, harmful.

Workshops can be facilitated in a variety of ways that can increase the chance of making them useful. Here are three books that can help facilitators maximize the participants' chances of enabling a creative project in process: Felicia Rose Chavez's *The Anti-Racist Writing Workshop: How to Decolonize the Creative Classroom*; Matthew Salesses's *Craft in the Real World: Rethinking Fiction Writing and Workshopping*; and Charlie Jane Anders's *Never Say You Can't Survive: How to Get Through Hard Times by Making Up Stories*. Each offers a multitude of possibilities, directly and indirectly, for facilitators and participants, in how to prepare or approach a manuscript and provide feedback. There are many other books and articles on the subject. We hope you'll explore some of them.

We believe the important opportunity offered by writing groups is the practice of honestly and respectfully critiquing others' work. In the same way that reading published work is useful, this practice leads to an improvement *in your own work*, whether the person receiving your critique likes it or not. Often, it's more useful to use the critiques you give to others as guidelines for how to improve your work.

To some, this might sound strange, but we believe a critique should be something of a love song, even if part of what's lovingly conveyed is difficult to hear.

The critique giver must believe, in advance, that the draft *can* reach its potential, and they work to infuse their feedback with that belief. The satisfaction comes from helping the writer who may be stuck; not from being the one to point out obvious (or even not-so-obvious) flaws. Most importantly, a critique should focus on what the piece is attempting to convey (versus what the critique giver is "used to" or is "comfortable with" or "prefers to read"). And it should be done with cultural humility: not making assumptions about the subject matter or style without considering how many subject matters and styles may fall outside one's own experience.

Also, a warning: Telling someone else what they're allowed to write about or what words they can or cannot use is always oppressive. Work to make your arguments about what's "effective" or "ineffective" from within the goals of the piece, without attempting to censor. Words and works meant to carelessly harm others are rarely interesting enough to reach publication. If a writer has a blind spot, attempt to point out how that blind spot is limiting the piece. If you do not want to do that labor, step aside. The writer can figure it out. Just do not become an arbiter of what someone else can or cannot do. Censorship is the opposite of liberation, the opposite of art. If someone is portraying a character or asserting a worldview that's contrary to yours, do not try to change the writer. Instead, put that energy into your own art, and with it change the world.

If you decide to workshop, we suggest, at the very least, making and keeping an evolving list of community agreements with your group and checking in on a regular basis to maximize the group's usefulness.

All ninety minutes of Ellen Bass's Hugo House talk feels like a love song to poets whose work she admires. She articulated something she found distilled in Frank X.

Gaspar's work—this idea of a long-armed poem—and has succeeded in writing such poems herself, but in a manner that greatly differs from the poems she mentions. And Bass also offers us a "how": how to put the "controlled" into the "chaos."

Stephen Dunn, in his book *Walking Light*, talks about the good versus the not-so-good poem:

> The good poet "lets in" the unruly, the difficult, the unformed—in a sense, the unmanageable—and is able to make a livable environment for them. The more the imagination can accommodate, the more chaos the poet is equal to, obviously the richer the poem.
>
> The not-so-good poet may try to let in the very same elements, but is overwhelmed by them. The poem, then, is too much like one's unreconstructed life; we can learn little or nothing from it.

This is where we make selections.

And again from Ellen Bass:

> Everything must be serving a purpose, earning its keep. Even elements that are intrinsically interesting in themselves must be asked to leave the poem if they do not contribute to the effect of the poem.
>
> So, although we want to open the door to those strange angels, we can't let the whole population of heaven in. Everything there must be aware that it's in conversation with everything else. In every poem we want the parts to be talking to each other.

In his book *Poetry as Survival*, Gregory Orr writes about the balance of order and chaos:

> In the ceaseless interplay of disorder and order in our daily lives, it is possible (and important) to imagine that there are certain situations where this unstable interaction can be held for a moment in a steady state. One such suspended moment is the poem....
>
> Robert Frost once characterized poetry as "a momentary stay against confusion," and his phrase articulates with eloquent simplicity a poem's

power to lift moments of clarified drama out of the ceaseless, discombobulating flow of experience and, by doing so, to restabilize the self. . . .

Some readers have a higher threshold for disorder and need more disordering in the poems they read. Others have a lower threshold and need a larger proportion of order to disorder in the poems that give them pleasure or that resonate meaningfully with their own experiences. The essential point is that for a poem to move us it must bring us near our own threshold. We must feel genuinely threatened or destabilized by the poem's vision of disordering, even as we are simultaneously reassured and convinced by its orderings.

Often arguments about taste, about whether a particular poem is "great" or not, simply have to do with differences in readers' thresholds. To say that we find a poet or a poem "boring" might be another way of saying it does not bring us close enough to any threshold. Or to say a poem seems to us "meaningless chaos" might be another way of saying that it throws us way past our threshold.

Here's an early draft of Bass's poem "Waiting for Rain." You'll also see the finished poem and notes of how she took her own advice.

Waiting for Rain (early draft)
Ellen Bass

Finally morning. This loneliness feels more familiar
in the light, more like my face in the mirror.
[No one will understand you.
You might as well get that straight.] I read Lucretius
when I couldn't sleep. He said the world goes on
making and unmaking.
So maybe it's not getting better or worse. [In spite of
the immigrant dream, my grandmothers schlepping
me here packed tight in their ovary purses, hidden better
than diamonds in the cavities through which
my parents would be born. And my life is better—
well, easier, surely—after all I'm sitting here at 10 am

in my backyard writing on pale blue lines listening to birdsong and a plane
on the flight pattern to San Jose rather than hawking
newspapers on the street corner, rather than standing
11 hours a day, selling beer and half pints of peach brandy.]
The rain they say is coming, hasn't gotten here yet.
It's still working its way over the Pacific. It's got a long
way to travel, sailing in those purplish nimbus clouds.
And that could get me started on climate change
which would be a pretty good argument
for the world getting worse. But Lucretius
says it's all just creation and destruction
and neither ever gets the upper hand. [I had what they call
"a good cry" on the sofa last night. Maybe it's
like a correction in the stock market. Things had just been going too well.]
My daughter in the ER again.
Something she ate? Something she breathed?
They want to kill me, she sometimes says,
as though it's a joke. And I try to imagine for a minute
what it would feel like to never know what's going to
stop your breath or merely knock you out of commission.
[Mostly I try not to think about it. Or I repeat the words,
other people feel this too. How could I be lonely
when most of the world is worrying over a sick child
or mourning a dead one? Now I can hear the wind
rattling the high scarlet leaves still clinging
to the maple. The wind comes, passes through
and goes on its way.] All night I plastered my body
to Janet's body breathing when she breathed.
Usually that helps. But her skin, warm as it is, does
after all, keep me out. [The finches are calling out
so loud in the bamboo, you can almost feel them forcing
little lungfulls of air out into the gray morning.]
How temporary it all is. My daughter's coming home
next week. She'll bring the pink plaid suitcase

we bought at Ross that's so easy to spot on the carousel
when she points it out to the person pushing her wheelchair.
[I'll double wash her bedding and open the windows
so no trace of scent remains.] I just want to touch her.

Now compare it with the final version.

Waiting for Rain (final)
Ellen Bass

Finally morning. This loneliness
feels more ordinary in the light, more like my face
in the mirror. My daughter in the ER again.
Something she ate? Some freshener

someone spritzed in the air?
They're trying to kill me, she says,
as though it's a joke. Lucretius
got me through the night. He told me the world goes on

making and unmaking. Maybe it's wrong
to think of better and worse.
There's no one who can carry my fear
for a child who walks out the door

not knowing what will stop her breath.
The rain they say is coming
sails now over the Pacific in purplish nimbus clouds.
But it isn't enough. Last year I watched

elephants encircle their young, shuffling
their massive legs without hurry, flaring
their great dusty ears. Once they drank
from the snowmelt of Kilimanjaro.

Now the mountain is bald. Lucretius knows

we're just atoms combining and recombining:
stardust, flesh, grass. All night
I plastered my body to Janet,

breathing when she breathed. But her skin,
warm as it is, does after all, keep me out.
How tenuous it all is.
My daughter's coming home next week.

She'll bring the pink plaid suitcase we bought at Ross.
When she points it out to the escort
pushing her wheelchair, it will be easy
to spot on the carousel. I just want to touch her.

Bass said that she didn't know that "my grandmother's ovary purses" didn't belong for a long time. It's one of many moments from the first draft that "had to go." She also says that Lucretius doesn't "quite get enough airtime in this first draft. We need more of Lucretius. We need to let the world in more." More elephants, too, so as to evoke themes of climate change.

We want you to think about why she may have made other changes, expansions, and contractions. Study the differences. Also, notice the first draft form and the final, in just eight quatrains. Ask why. How do these choices help the author deliver units of satisfaction to us, her readers?

You may have a different "threshold" than someone else. Just like some people derive meaning and catharsis from seeing horror films, others can't. Likewise with historical documentaries. What a lover of a great historical documentary looks for in film may be different from someone who prefers action.

When passionately expressed, all genres offer something crucial about what it means to be human. That's why we encourage you to write for yourself, to imagine your audience as smart people who are ready, willing, and open to receiving what you're giving. You care about them and want to give them the very best you've got.

Suggestions on condensing:

- *Is it earning its keep? If not, cut it.*
- *Search for moments you deem as "overwhelming" your piece. Cut them.*

- *Search for vague details that do not direct your reader. Clarify or cut.*
- *Search for details that may be interesting in themselves but do little or nothing to serve the larger concerns of your piece. Cut them.*
- *Search for moments of confusion. See if they contain a positive destabilization of the world. If not, consider clarifying or cutting.*

Read your piece aloud after making such cuts. If any or all of the cuts make the piece seem further away from (rather than closer to) your goals, "undo." Let's take another look at Frank O'Hara's poem.

Today
Frank O'Hara

> Oh! kangaroos, sequins, chocolate sodas!
> You really are beautiful! Pearls,
> harmonicas, jujubes, aspirins! all
> the stuff they've always talked about
>
> still makes a poem a surprise!
> These things are with us every day
> even on beachheads and biers. They
> do have meaning. They're strong as rocks.

Ellen Bass, in her talk at Hugo House, said:

> He wrote this, of course, after WWII...we start off with kangaroos and sequins and we wind up on beachheads and biers. It's the beauty of actual things, the chaos of them, he tosses them all in here like a salad, and he affirms them even in the face of death and war. It's a kind of manifesto for surprise and surprise is one of the most essential elements of writing. We want to be surprised when we read, and we want to surprise ourselves when we write.
>
> We can't control chaos unless we have some chaos in the first place.
> Allow the mosquitos in. See what happens as it accumulates.
> We learn to trust what arrives and give it a chance.
> Frank O'Hara is a poet open to these strange angels.

In O'Hara's poem, the kangaroos, sequins, chocolate sodas, pearls, harmonicas, jujubes are all images that bring to mind celebration. The poem turns on aspirins, and then we see how these objects juxtaposed and coexist simultaneously with the destruction of war, tethering what the poet may find frivolous to some bigger, more universal concern.

Revision tool: allow "the world" in. Perhaps "the world" is the ancient Roman poet Lucretius, like it was for Bass. If you're writing a scene or a poem and it feels too insular, only personal, too much like the musings in a diary, perhaps turn to the newspaper. If you're writing a realistic scene set in history, what else happened on that day? A quick web search might reveal details.

Go back to any of your previous pieces.

Is there something on the list you made of thematic concerns that most rises to the top? That helps you control the chaos? Perhaps in this draft you'll focus on one of those thematic concerns. Or two.

Our student writer focused in on this question: *how friendship can (and cannot) help a victim endure/recover from violence.* He hopes to borrow examples and imagery from the remaining thematic concerns, but those might be separate essays. He'll try to get it all in, but only if he can control the chaos. If not, he'll have to, as Ellen Bass says, "let it go."

Now continue writing your scene or poem. This time, keep an eye on what's universal: what reaches out from the particular/insular to the rest of us, and from the rest of us to the rest of the world.

See if you can keep going until you have a draft where you've succeeded in controlling the chaos.

Remember the piece for which our student received the very encouraging rejection? Here's the beginning of a revision for that. Here we're showing you just the first page, but for your own work, go for a full beginning-to-end draft.

SEPTEMBER 1985

Madonna pulled her torso across the floor on MTV like no virgin I'd ever seen, and a girl named Colleen slid across the hallways of our high school on the wooden soles of her scuffed oxfords, carrying her binder and books on her chest, her arms X'd in front of her like a shield.

"You like Depeche Mode, too?" she said, looking at the band's crude symbol that I'd taped to the inside of my locker door, and like that, we were the school's least likely friends.

> I was a freshman and she was a junior. She was in German Club. I was in band. She wore her hair natural. Mine was gelled and sprayed into elaborate spikes. I was a boy; she, a girl, and neither of us wanted what came with those labels.
>
> Colleen and I both occupied the space at the bottom of the high school's social status ladder. Each of us must have known something of the other as a target, and I'd guess that we each had reasons to suspect (and hope?) the other existed on a lower rung.
>
> Perhaps fearful that one could bring the other down, we developed what I now see as sophisticated navigational strategies to simultaneously acknowledge and deny our own and the other's place on that ladder, so our friendship would unfold in secret places: on the stairs behind the curtain dividing the cafeteria/auditorium from the stage. In the woods behind the school; on the train from our suburb to Boston and Cambridge's Harvard Square. And on the telephone. Hours and hours and hours on the telephone. When we met at school, we did so briefly, and usually right in front of that locker door.

Once you have your draft, title your piece. Go back again and concentrate on getting something of the "subject" in the first few lines.

As a final step of this writing practice—now that you have some chaos to control—you'll condense what you've written to its very essence. As poet Jane Hirshfield says, "you are selecting which one of those directions is most fertile and meaningful." And here, again, is Ellen Bass:

> After a subject has been established in the title or the first few lines the writer can move away from it. While the farther he or she gets, the greater becomes the tension unless the bond is actually broken. Again: the writer is playing what we know against what we don't know. What is necessary is that the writer occasionally connects with the subject and of course eventually returns to it or so changes the terms of the poem that the original subject becomes irrelevant.

Now that you've moved "far away from the subject," use the hints on revision to condense.

We'll leave you with this, an essay our students have found useful for years. Chris Offutt shares his process of becoming a writer and then discovering a draft process that works for him. "Fat one, thin one" is a distilled prose writer's individual version of the expansion/contraction concept.

The Eleventh Draft

Chris Offutt

I didn't set out to be a writer. In chronological order, I wanted to be a baseball player, an explorer, a race car driver, a detective, a movie actor, an artist, and a forest ranger. I was a voracious reader as a child, consuming several books a week. At age ten, I asked the town librarian for a book about baseball and she gave me *Catcher in the Rye*. What I recall most is the shock that writing could be that way—personal, told in an intimate way, about family issues of supreme importance. I never read another book for juveniles.

In grade school, I kept diaries that detailed problems I had with Billy, a neighbor who lived across the creek and was a consummate bully. In Spelling class I wrote stories about battles between two knights—Sir Christophoro and Sir Billyano. Billy beat me in real life, but in the world of fiction, Sir Christophoro always won.

After leaving my native Kentucky, I spent nearly a decade working part-time jobs around the country. My writing was confined to a journal, in which I wrote an average of 30 pages a day. I usually wrote in public—on benches, in buses and trains, in restaurants and bars. It was important that people saw me writing. The perception of strangers granted a feeling of self-worth, an identity as a struggling young writer.

I began collecting photographs of my favorite writers, which I studied carefully. My greatest admiration was reserved for those writers whose faces reflected the most suffering. In my early twenties I felt that I didn't deserve to be a writer due to a lack of genuine experience, and I became grateful for the acne pocks on my jaws and the scar between my eyes. These marks of life lent the illusion of being a writer. I bought a typewriter for two hundred dollars, the most money I'd spent on an item. One day, I removed the mirror from the bathroom and fastened it to the wall above my typewriter. Around the mirror I taped the photographs of my favorite writers. When I sat at the typewriter, my face joined theirs.

If I wasn't writing, I wasn't visible.

Writing is the most difficult task I've ever undertaken, which is perhaps why I do it. For much of my life, I cared about little except the act of writing. Writing taught me to trust myself, which enabled me to trust others. This resulted in marriage, and within a year my wife convinced me to apply to an MFA program. I did so reluctantly, and with no alternative. We'd moved back to Kentucky, where we were living without benefit of plumbing, heat, or jobs. The summer I turned thirty, we borrowed a thousand dollars and headed for Iowa. This decision literally changed my life.

We rented a condemned building near the jail. Daylight showed between the wall and the floor, and the landlord's solution was stapling sheets of plastic to the exterior wall. Our house looked like a giant bread sack. The bedroom ceiling eventually fell in, but Rita and I were happy. The new place had water and a furnace. We'd moved up.

Several years before, while living in Salem, Massachusetts, I enrolled in a Dostoyevsky class through Harvard's continuing education. The class was small. A student assured me that the instructor was a genius. We sat for two hours discussing the first chapter of *Crime and Punishment*, a hundred-page section, which I'd read twice in preparation. I was excited as only a naive country boy can be who had fought his way out of the Appalachian Mountains and into a Harvard extension program. At the end of class I left without a word to anyone. I was ashamed and embarrassed. Though I had listened carefully, I had no idea what anyone was talking about.

At Iowa, I was fearful of undergoing the same experience. The majority of my classmates held degrees in English, and possessed a unique vocabulary for the analysis and discussion of writing. Many of them were graduates of private schools. Having never taken a writing class, I was intimidated, envious, and terrified. My brain and my interests had always made me feel like an outsider, and slowly I realized that the other students felt the same way. For the first time in my life I was around people like me—devoted to the twin acts of reading and writing. Class, race, and education didn't matter. I'd spent a lifetime learning to conceal my intellect, reign in my vocabulary, and guard my personality. In Iowa I was allowed to be smart. For many years I had taken writing very seriously, but now I took myself seriously as a writer.

A first draft was like a wonderful drug that made me feel good. Revision was the horrible crash. For years I avoided the crash by refusing to revise. In order to generate a first draft, I staked everything on the act of writing. My identity and emotional well-being went into each page, paragraph, sentence, and word. Making a single change was like a surgeon performing a complex procedure on his own heart. I found it impossible.

At Iowa, I overcame this problem by simply starting a new story. Once I was emotionally involved with a fresh piece of writing, I could return to the first one with the necessary distance. It became important to have several stories underway, because work on one was always going badly. I then turned to another until becoming overwhelmed, at which time I worked on a third, and so on. The only rule I had was to complete a first draft before revising. When I switched my focus to another story, I gave the entire manuscript a full revision. To my utter surprise, I began to accumulate story manuscripts. They were never completed, merely abandoned, a practice I still maintain.

Being among a community of writers granted me permission to write what scared me most—stories about people in Appalachia. These were essentially stories of myself, seen through the magnifying veil of my own experience in the world beyond the hills. After years of wanting to be someone else—an actor, a painter, a ranger—I suddenly realized that people are what they do, not what they want to be. And what I did was confront existence through language. I was no longer someone who wanted desperately to be. I had become someone who simply was—a writer.

The notion of submitting anything to a magazine filled me with terror. A stranger would read my precious words, judge them deficient, and reject them, which meant I was worthless. A poet friend was so astonished by my inaction that he shamed me into sending my stories out. My goal, however, was not publication, which was still too scary a thought. My goal was a hundred rejections in a year.

I mailed my stories in multiple submissions and waited eagerly for their return, which they promptly did. Each rejection brought me that much closer to my goal—a cause for celebration, rather than depression.

Eventually disaster struck. *The Coe Review* published my first story in spring 1990. The magazine was in the small industrial town of Cedar Rapids, Iowa, with a circulation that barely surpassed the city limits. The payment was one copy of the magazine, and the editor spelled my name wrong. Nevertheless, I felt valid in every way—I was no longer a hillbilly with a pencil full of dreams. I was a real live writer.

The second year of school, I doubled my efforts—more discipline, more work, digging more deeply into my own life. We moved into a tiny house with a basement that was only accessible through a tornado hatch outside. I installed a plywood floor and a wall. Each morning I went outside, lifted the heavy door that was flat to the ground, and descended into my imagination. The light was dim, the walls were close, and the ceiling low. At day's end I emerged from the earth, squinting like a mole.

My process of writing had developed until I preferred the act of revision to first draft. I printed a story and made all my changes on paper. I then inserted those changes into the computer and printed it. My files were meticulous. Each draft was numbered and dated, and I kept them in chronological order. Often I went back to previous drafts, seeking a remembered line that I'd cut along with a paragraph. Occasionally I resurrected entire scenes that I'd trimmed.

The move to revision became so complete that I no longer cared about the story as product. What mattered was the evolution of the act of creation. I spent many joyful hours simply shifting material from one narrative to another, gauging the success of the integration, attempting greater risks on the page. Plot was a loose form I could rely on in the same way that poets might utilize a sonnet or villanelle.

The more I worked, the more I understood that a writer never really stops writing. Leaving my basement didn't end the process. I continued to write in my head. My relationship with the world was one of narrative, and I engaged life eagerly while simultaneously keeping a segment of my mind detached to notice sensory detail. My pockets filled with scraps of paper that held description of light and land, snippets of conversation, and observation of character. In my basement I organized the notes, typed them under various headings, and kept them close at hand.

My first drafts are very long. The second one is a rapid chop job of all the junk I threw in during the delirium of a first draft. The third revision is workable. I pare the story down and then fatten it up. Subsequent drafts are the same—fat one, thin one, fat one, thin one. The pattern is similar to the action of a bellows expanding and contracting, forcing oxygen to the fire of narrative. The stories get shorter in length, but thicker in detail. I add and cut, trying to let the story dictate what it wants. My mind jumps from a ruthless objectivity to an intensely personal interaction with the story and then back to the emotional distance necessary to revision.

An average short story is a result of ten or eleven drafts over a two year period. The longest is thirty-five versions written during eight years. It's an intensely autobiographical story, both in event and emotional content, with only the ending being written from scratch. The story was originally about my father and me. During the writing, I became a father, and the story shifted gears as my identity changed. The problem was simple—trying to control the actions of the characters. After I let them do what they wanted to do, the story quickly completed itself. I felt as if I had been on a train stalled in a rail yard that suddenly shot down the tracks with no warning. Instead of writing the story, I was a passenger.

As long as I am sitting at my desk with my imagination plugged into the world of my characters, I consider myself engaged in the act of writing. On a rare day, I'll write several pages, while other days only a page. There are times that require four hours to squeeze out a mere paragraph. The toughest writing sessions are those when not a word spills forth.

I regard all of these times as equal to one another and valid to the act of writing. Two words are the same as two pages. I am writing simply by virtue of allowing my mind to enter the world of my characters. If I go three days without writing a word, I know that the eventual sentences will be that much stronger for the time spent in the company of my characters.

The only way I can create anything worthwhile is to concern myself solely with the moment, to maintain as much freedom as possible during the interaction between my mind and narrative. This has led me to write what I need to write, instead of what I want to write. My work, both fiction and nonfiction, is about my current emotional state, my past behavior, and my recent thoughts. The years of revision enable me to understand myself. The irony is that by the time I learn from my work, it's too late to do anything, because those difficulties are over and I'm in the midst of a whole new batch of problems.

Five years after moving to Iowa I was a father of two boys, and an author of two books. My sense of self had changed so drastically that I was at a loss of who I was anymore. My response was to write a novel about a man who leaves Kentucky, moves to Montana, and changes his identity right down to his name and Social Security number. To write it, I had a thousand-dollar yard sale and moved to Montana.

Today, ten years after Iowa, I have returned to Kentucky, where I am polishing galleys for *Out of the Woods*. It is a book of stories written over the past decade. Each story concerns someone from eastern Kentucky who has left and misses it. Some return and some don't. At this point I utterly despise the manuscript. It is the final stage before publication, and I'm reduced to changing commas to conjunctions and back to commas. I am perpetually dismayed by what the book says about me, although I cannot pinpoint any particular insight. Perhaps I can in the future. Until then, I am planning the next book.

In order to let this book go, I need to hate it, because I'll miss it so badly. Publication means snatching its life away. A part of me goes with it. Nothing will fill the absence but another project, another imaginary world. Nothing will save me but the act of writing.

Acknowledgments

Acknowledgments from Matthew Clark Davison:

Dedicated to the memory of the late greats Janice Mirikitani and June Jordan, my first writing teachers, who found me in a community outreach program in the basement of Glide Church in San Francisco's Tenderloin District. They taught me and countless others to see ourselves as writers.

This book is for every single "Labber" who created and shared on Douglass or Hyde Streets, in the basement of the church on Bush Street, at the historic Swedenborgian, and at SFSU. Thanks to all the hosts, including Mark Rubnitz, who, for years, allowed me to teach "The Lab" in his gorgeous home.

1,000 thanks:

To all the artists and thinkers who inspired the writing prompts that fill our syllabi and these pages.

To Anne Galjour and Junse Kim, writers/teachers/heroes of mine, whose endless encouragement helped me keep on track with this project while navigating a full-time lecturer faculty position.

To Jewelle Gomez, Brighde Mullins, Michelle Carter, and Robert Glück, who all illuminated possibilities for me as a queer first-generation college student.

To Michael Mullen—brilliant writer, musician, and cherished friend—whose unyielding and constant support and mentorship gave me the courage to start "The Lab" in 2007.

To Jill Bialosky, who first envisioned "The Lab" as a book, and for the team at Norton, including Laura Mucha, for helping us bring it into the world.

To this book's fabulous agent, Victoria Skurnick, and the whole team at LGR.

To my coauthor. This book could not have been written without the intelligence, experience, and knowledge of my dear friend Alice LaPlante, whose fiction and textbook on fiction have inspired and enabled me and hundreds of my students. For decades, she has cheered me on and shared her resources. Alice, you're also the world's best big sister, and I cannot imagine a better or more fruitful collaboration (and you know I have a pretty good imagination).

Finally, thanks to my family, both logical and bio, and my husband, Philip

Ansumana Munda Hull. Each offers support and humor, but Ansu holds the record for showing up front row and acting as helper and cameraperson to the dozens of The Lab's public readings over the years.

I'm deeply appreciative of you all.

Acknowledgments from Alice LaPlante:

I wish to profusely thank all my family and friends who supported me during the writing and production of *The Lab*, especially (but not in the least limited to) David Milnes Renton and Sarah Seidner. Much gratitude to our superstar editor, Jill Bialosky, the team at Norton, and our amazing agent Victoria Skurnick, of the Levine Greenberg Rostan Literary Agency. I owe an enormous debt to all the students who passed through my classes over the decades, at Stanford, San Francisco State, and, most recently, the Tramontana Writers' Group in Mallorca. I learned so much from them. And, finally, to my collaborator and friend, Matthew Clark Davison, who has been the very best of the best partners to work with, and whose talent, generosity, and wisdom so inform the book.

Glossary

Abstract, abstraction: Words or phrases that convey concepts, qualities, and ideas that are not tied to specific, tangible objects or experiences.

Aesthetic force: As defined by author Sarah Lewis, a trait of writing that is "animating" and which leaves us "changed—stunned, dazzled, knocked out."

Ambiguity: A situation or description with two or more possible meanings.

Braided essay: A type of essay in which two or more events, facts, or persons are woven together to form an integrated whole. The key to a successful braided essay is that all the "strands" must come together in some way to suggest a theme or answer a question.

Cadence: The rhythmic flow and pattern of sounds in a piece of text. Cadence encompasses the tempo, intonation, and modulation of words and sentences, contributing to the overall musicality and readability of a piece of writing.

Characterization: Defined most simply, the set of techniques writers use to create characters, with characters (human or otherwise) being the "who" in a piece of writing.

Complexity: An overall effect of writing that has multiple layers of meaning, intricate structures, and sophisticated ideas or themes, which challenges the reader to think deeply and engage more fully with the text.

Concrete: Perceivable by one or more of the five senses (readers are left with a feeling they can see it, hear it, taste it, touch it, or smell it).

Constraints: Limits on what writers can do with language, theme, structure, or any other element of writing. The word "constraint" can have certain negative connotations. Despite this, constraints are immensely useful to artists (so much so that W. W. Norton published a book by Alice devoted to constraint-based exercises). In this book, we prefer to think of them as "friendly" constraints.

Direct address: A literary technique where the narrator or a character speaks directly to the reader. This technique creates a sense of intimacy, breaking the conventional "fourth wall" and making the reader feel more involved. It can be used to convey important information, provide commentary, or engage readers on a personal level.

Erasure poetry: Also referred to as blackout poetry, erasure is a form of "found poetry" characterized by the selective removal or obscuring of existing text to reveal a new composition.

Fiction: Traditionally, a form of narrative writing that involves events and characters made up (or exaggerated, expanded upon, or modified) by the author. As one of the primary genres of literature, it is typically distinguished from nonfiction, which is based on factual events and real people.

Figurative language: A word or phrase that is not meant to reflect reality but to skew, interpret, distort, or compare something to something else. The goal of this "distortion" is to give readers insight into a situation, character, theme, or emotion.

First language: The vocabulary, phrases, grammar, and syntax that come naturally to a writer. Poet June Jordan encouraged her students to write in their first languages, leaving it up to them how they defined those languages. Her students have named numerous languages they felt most comfortable with, including "Black English," "Spanglish," "mixed Mandarin," and "gay English."

Form: The overarching structure or pattern of a piece of writing. Certain forms of poetry—for example, sonnets, villanelles, limericks—must stick to very specific rules about length, rhythm, and rhyme that act as constraints, or limits, on what writers can do with language.

Free write: The process of spontaneously generating a piece of writing that doesn't conform to any preconceived ideas, themes, outlines, or plan.

Generative: Referring to prompts or exercises designed specifically to stimulate creativity and generate new pieces of writing. Generative prompts and exercises help writers overcome writer's block, explore new themes, and develop craft skills.

Genres: Categories of writing based on traditional, shared conventions, styles, themes, and forms. They can help readers—and writers—understand and categorize different types of writing. But as this book stresses, cross-genre writing is increasingly common and is ripe territory for innovation and creativity. Numerous genres exist under the fiction umbrella alone. Lengthwise, you can write everything from micro fiction (short-short fiction) to short stories, to novellas, to novels, to multibook serial novels. Other genres are based on subject matter and style. These include speculative stories, science fiction, fantasies, mysteries, romances, thrillers, and what's called literary fiction. And finally, there are audience-based categories: children, preteens, young adult (YA), or adult, among others.

Haiku: A succinct form of poetry originating from Japan, characterized by its adherence to strict syllabic and structural constraints. In English, it typically comprises three lines, with a total syllable count of seventeen, distributed in a 5-7-5 pattern.

Hermit crab essay: An essay for which writers use an existing "container" as a constraint, writing in the form of, for example, a Dear John letter or a shopping list. This was named a "hermit crab" essay by multigenre writers Brenda Miller and Suzanne Paola, because hermit crabs are born without shells and look for the empty shells of other species in which to make their homes.

Hybrid writing: Writing that blends elements from multiple genres, styles, or forms to create a unique type of "container." This approach allows writers to break conventional boundaries and explore new ways of storytelling, expression, and structure. Hybrid writing can be found in fiction, nonfiction, and poetry and often incorporates features such as prose, poetry, essays, memoir, and more. Some newer writers mistake writing hybrids for writing without strategy or constraint, but that is not the case. Don't confuse free writes with hybrid writing.

Image: A vivid and descriptive representation that appeals to the senses, helping readers to visualize scenes, objects, or concepts. A critical writing device, images are used to create sensory experiences and evoke emotions, making writing more impactful, and should engage as many of the five senses as appropriate, not just sight (visual imagery).

Imagination: In poetry, imagination is one of the four "temperaments" of the writer, according to poet Gregory Orr. It delivers a seamless flow of images that connect in ways that are not always obvious.

Internal rhyme: A rhyme that occurs in the middle, instead of at the end, of a line of poetry or prose. A single line of poetry or prose can contain internal rhyme (with multiple words in the same line rhyming), or the rhyming words can occur across multiple lines.

Line breaks: A typographic element used in writing to signify the end of a line of text and the beginning of a new one. Line breaks are important in both poetry and prose, as they heavily impact the flow, rhythm, and visual presentation of the writing. Also be aware that line breaks are about pauses—short breaks between the last word of the previous line and the first word of the next line. The pause will be even longer if a stanza or paragraph break is involved.

Literal language: Language (a word or phrase) that means exactly what it says. For example, when Michael Ondaatje describes the "thin tight hips" of the title character in his novel *The English Patient*, we are meant to take that literally, as a reflection of the reality of the novel when it comes to his appearance.

Lyric essay: A distinct form of hybrid writing, blending creative nonfiction and poetry. The form is characterized by its scene-driven narrative, rich description, and incorporation of personal reflections interwoven with research. It can also involve brevity, fragmentation, and braiding of various narrative threads, as well as the incorporation of other poetic techniques and devices. In the realm of creative nonfiction, the lyric essay challenges traditional notions of objectivity. It prioritizes subjective experiences and emotional resonance over factual accuracy, offering a departure from conventional approaches to storytelling.

Memoir: A form of autobiographical (nonfiction) writing that typically focuses on specific experiences, events, or time periods in the author's life. A personal narrative that provides insight into the author's thoughts, feelings, and reflections on those experiences, memoirs are one of the most popular types of nonfiction being published today.

Metaphor: A subset of imagery that compares two unlike things.

Meter: The rhythm of a poem, determined by the pattern of stressed and unstressed syllables in each line. Meter is what gives poetry its musical quality and helps convey the poem's emotion and meaning.

Music: In poetry, rhythm and sound, with the poet controlling the poem's pitch, duration, and stress (think meter and rhyme). Poet Gregory Orr talks about poetry in terms of the temperaments of the poet, the varying inclinations for story, structure, music, or imagination.

Narrator: The voice or character that tells a story or presents a poem to readers. The narrator's perspective, style, and reliability significantly influence how the piece is conveyed and perceived.

New narrative: A literary movement and theory of experimental writing launched in San Francisco in the late 1970s by poets and writers Robert Glück and Bruce Boone that blends narrative and poetry on (largely) autobiographical and sexual themes.

Nonconforming oddity: Any unexpected or off-topic detail, theme, or thread. It can be that section that a traditional writing workshop tells you to "cut" out of adherence to static ideas of form and consistency. But this book encourages you to identify those moments as possible gold among the straw—and then see if your piece, in its final draft, earns it.

Nonfiction: Writing that is based on factual events, real people, and true information. Unlike fiction, which is rooted in the imagination, nonfiction aims to inform, explain, document, or convey factual information and truth, albeit through the personal lens of the writer's individual perspective.

Novel: When used as an adjective and applied to science or (in the case of this book) to the arts, "new and not resembling something formerly known or used" (as per Merriam-Webster).

Pacing: The speed at which a piece of writing unfolds. It controls how quickly events progress, and influences readers' experiences of tension, suspense, and emotional engagement with the writing.

Paradox: The effect when authors play with words or concepts that appear contradictory at first glance. As readers delve deeper, they can discover complexities that challenge their perspective, encouraging them to explore hidden layers of meaning within a text.

Persona: The voice or character adopted by a writer to narrate a piece. This persona can be distinct from the writer's own voice and can embody a variety of perspectives, emotions, or experiences. The use of personas allows writers to explore different identities, viewpoints, and imaginative scenarios, providing a richer and more complex narrative.

Plot: The sequence of events, placed in a certain order, that drives the emotional impact and theme in a piece of narrative.

Poetry: Language, composed in strategically arranged lines on a page using compressed imagery, with attention paid to its rhythm and sound, which transports readers to a new, surprising space. Poetry can use a structured arrangement of words, line breaks, and stanzas, or it can be completely unstructured. When poet Gregory Orr talks about poetry, he does so not in terms of craft or the aforementioned characteristics, but as the temperaments of the poet: story, structure, music, or imagination.

Prose poetry: A type of poetry that has evolved through centuries of literary experimentation. Its origins can be traced back to early examples found in Bible translations and in the works of William Wordsworth, but the prose poetry highlighted in this book is said to be rooted in nineteenth-century France with the symbolist writers such as Aloysius Bertrand and Charles Baudelaire. It is characterized by the blurring and combining of what were once strict boundaries between prose and poetry.

Protagonist: The main character around whom a piece of narrative writing revolves. This character is often the central focus of the narrative. The protagonist's actions, thoughts, decisions, and development are critical to the plot and overall theme of the story.

Revision: The process of reviewing, rethinking, refining—and, particularly, re-envisioning—a piece of writing to improve its clarity, coherence, structure, effectiveness, and overall emotional impact. It can involve making major changes to the language, structure, and style of the writing to better convey the intended theme or story.

Rhyme: A poetic device where words or lines of poetry have matching (or similar) sounds. There are several types of rhymes, including: end rhymes, the most common type of rhyme, where the final words of two or more lines match; internal rhymes, where rhyming occurs within a single line or between the middle of one line and the end of another; and slant rhymes, where words have similar but not identical sounds.

Setting: The time and place in which the story unfolds, and which is an integral part of how characters interact and plot develops, as setting can influence the story's mood, atmosphere, and overall meaning.

Short-short story: Also known as flash fiction, a very brief piece of narrative prose that typically ranges from a few words to around 1,000 words. Despite its brevity, a short-short story aims to tell a complete story, often focusing on a single event, character, or idea. The length constraints challenge writers to be extremely selective about language and details.

Simile: A metaphorical (comparative) statement in a piece of writing that uses "like" or "as."

Slant rhyme: A type of rhyme in which words have similar, but not identical, sounds. Most slant rhymes are formed by words with identical consonants and different vowels (called consonance), or vice versa (called assonance).

Speculative essay: A type of nonfiction that concerns itself with the figurative over the literal, ambiguity over knowing, and emotional observations over reporting.

Story: A narrative that describes a sequence of events, often but not always involving characters, a setting, and a plot. It can be based on fact or made up, like fiction. A successful, finished story is hard to define, but generally involves delivering a "unit of satisfaction" to the reader even if it doesn't follow traditional craft or structural conventions.

Structure: The organization and arrangement of ideas and elements within a piece of writing. It encompasses how a text is built and the way its parts are connected to create a coherent and effective whole. Structure offers readers the pleasure of finding patterns in language and delivers a sense of balance and even beauty.

Subtext: The underlying or implicit meaning beneath the surface level of a piece of writing. It involves subtle, unspoken messages or themes that are not explicitly stated but can be inferred by readers.

Synesthesia: A way to make a metaphor by describing something from one sensory realm through a different sensory realm. This often creates a fresh experience of something familiar. For example, you might describe the taste of your coffee as "loud."

Syntax: The word order of a piece of writing and the way in which it works with grammatical structures (as per the Poetry Foundation). Writers use syntax to produce a variety of sound devices to make their verses "sing" in such a way that the meaning is enhanced by the sound of the text—whether read aloud or heard in one's own head when reading to oneself.

Termite art: As coined by art critic Manny Farber, art committed to detailed observation, deep attention, and "nibbling" around the edges of a subject in seemingly random order—as opposed to works of art made by artists who are thinking too big and with grandiosity.

Unit of satisfaction: This book's way of describing a piece of writing that "works" for the reader, not necessarily by resolving conflicts or tying up plot points, but by providing emotionally resonant experiences that lead to a sense of wholeness, or completion, upon reading it.

Voice: An aspect of a piece of writing that presents a persona or point of view. The voice can be that of the author, the piece, or the character(s) or narrator(s) within the piece. Each is distinct.

Bibliography

Abdurraqib, Hanif. "The Author Writes the First Draft of His Wedding Vows." In *The Crown Ain't Worth Much*. Button Publishing, 2016.

"About Syntax." Poetry Archive Glossary.

Adams, Douglas. *The Meaning of Liff*. Pan MacMillan, 1983.

Alexander, Elizabeth. "Ars Poetica #100: I Believe." In *Crave Radiance: New and Selected Poems 1990–2010*. Graywolf Press, 2012.

Als, Hilton. "Toni Morrison's Profound and Unrelenting Vision." *New Yorker*, January 2020.

Alyan, Hala. "Oklahoma." *Poetry Magazine*, July/August 2017.

Baker, Will. "Grace Period." In *Flash Fiction: 72 Very Short Stories*, edited by James Thomas, Denise Thomas, and Tom Hazuka. W. W. Norton, 1992.

Bass, Ellen. "Any Common Desolation." In *Indigo*. Copper Canyon Press, 2020.

———. "Controlled Chaos." In *Living Room Craft Talks*. ellenbass.com.

———. "The Thing Is." In *Mules of Love*. BOA Editions, 2002.

Bialosky, Jill. "LV. Snow of Childhood." In *Asylum: A Personal, Historical, Natural Inquiry in 103 Lyric Sections*. Alfred A. Knopf, 2020.

Bishop, Stephanie. "In Praise of Destruction: How Embracing Elimination Can Make Our Writing Better." Literary Hub, July 2023.

Boully, Jenny. *The Body: An Essay*. Essay Press, 2007.

Brodsky, Joseph. "1 January 1965." In *Nativity Poems*, translated by George L. Kline. Farrar, Straus and Giroux, 2001.

Burke, Katie L. "First Person: Mona Hanna-Attisha." *American Scientist*, September/October 2019.

Burroway, Janet, and Elizabeth Stuckey-French. *Writing Fiction: A Guide to Narrative Craft*, 7th edition. Longman, 2006.

Carson, Ciaran. "The Fetch." In *For All We Know*. Wake Forest University Press, 2008.

Charters, Ann. *The Story and Its Writer: An Introduction to Short Fiction*, 7th edition. Bedford Books, 2006.

Cole, Teju. "Tivoli." In *Blind Spot*. Random House, 2017.

Cron, Lisa. *Story or Die: How to Use Brain Science to Engage, Persuade, and Change Minds in Business and in Life*. Ten Speed Press, 2021.

cummings, e. e. "[anyone lived in a pretty how town]." In *Complete Poems 1904–1962*, rev. ed. Liveright, 2016.

———. "dim / i / nu / tiv // e." In *Seven Poems*. Liveright, 1950, 1978, 1991.

D'Ambrosio, Charles. "The Dead Fish Museum." In *The Dead Fish Museum: Stories*. Alfred A. Knopf, 2006.

Davis, Lydia. "Fear." In *The Collected Stories of Lydia Davis*. Farrar, Straus and Giroux, 2009.

de Botton, Alain. *The Course of Love*. Hamish Hamilton, 2016.

Derricotte, Toi. "The Peaches of August." In *"I": New and Selected Poems*. University of Pittsburgh Press, 2021.

Dickinson, Emily. "Not Any Higher Stands the Grave." Amherst, Massachusetts, autograph manuscript poem, 1873.

Didion, Joan. "On Keeping a Notebook." In *Slouching Towards Bethlehem*. Farrar, Straus and Giroux, 1968.

di Prima, Diane. "To a Student." In *The Poetry Deal*. City Lights Books, 2014.

Doty, Mark. "Esta Noche." In *My Alexandria: Poems*. University of Illinois Press, 1993.

———. *The Art of Description: World into Word*. Graywolf Press, 2010.

Doyle, Jacqueline. "The Lunatics' Ball." *F(r)iction* 14, Summer 2019.

DuBuffet, Jean. "Make Way for Incivism." *Art & Text* 27 (December 1987–February 1988).

Dunn, Stephen. *Walking Light: Memoirs & Essays on Poetry*. BOA Editions, 2014.

Eerkens, Mieke. *All Ships Follow Me: A Family Memoir of War Across Three Continents*. Picador, 2020.

Erdrich, Louise. *The Night Watchman*. HarperCollins, 2020.

———. *The Painted Drum*. HarperCollins, 2005.

Evaristo, Bernardine. *Girl, Woman, Other*. Black Cat/Grove Atlantic, 2019.

Faulkner, Grant. *The Art of Brevity: Crafting the Very Short Story*. University of New Mexico Press, 2023.

Fay, Sarah. "Kay Ryan, The Art of Poetry No. 94." *The Paris Review*, Winter 2008.

Forrest, Emma. *Your Voice in My Head*. Other Press, 2011.

Frederick, Matthew. *101 Things I Learned in Architecture School*. MIT Press, 2007.

Fremont, Helen. *The Escape Artist*. Gallery Books, 2020.

Gaspar, Frank X. "June/July—Eleven Black Notebooks at the Desert Queen Motel." *American Poetry Review* 43, no. 1 (January/February 2014).

Geary, Valerie. "The Stories We'll Tell: Getting Ready for a Total Eclipse of the Sun." Literary Hub, 2017.

Glatch, Sean. "What Is Blackout Poetry? Examples and Inspiration." Writers.com, October 2023.

Glück, Robert. Definition of "New Narrative." In *Communal Nude: Collected Essays*. Semiotext(e), 2016.

Go, Nathan. "The Poetry of Prose: A Brief Study of Justin Torres's 'We the Animals.'" *Michigan Quarterly Review* (March 2015).

Groff, Lauren. *Matrix*. Riverhead Books, 2021.

Gross, Terry, and Maurice Sendak. Interview with Maurice Sendak. NPR, *Fresh Air* with Terry Gross, 2011.

Harvey, Yona. "Hurricane." In *Hemming the Water*. Four Way Books, 2013.

Hazelton, Rebecca. "Learning the Poetic Line: How Line Breaks Shape Meaning." Poetry Foundation, September 2014.

Hellen, Kathleen. "Signs." *Eastern Iowa Review*, 2016.

Hewitt, Nicole M. "How Much Is Too Much? Sometimes Life Is Stranger Than Fiction. Let's Discuss." Feed Your Fiction Addiction, March 23, 2019.

Hicok, Bob. "Getting By." In *Frequencies*. YesYes Books, 2013.

Holiday, Harmony. "Dear Babylon." *Poetry*, October 2017.

Hong, Cathy Park. "Cathy Park Hong on Minor Feelings." *Yale Review*, June 2020.

Houston, Pam. "What Has Irony Done for Us Lately." *About Place Journal*, October 2007.

Hugo, Richard. *The Triggering Town: Lectures and Essays on Poetry and Writing*. W. W. Norton, 1992.

James, Tania. "The South Asian Speakers Series Presents the Archeologist and Adventurer Indiana Jones." *New Yorker*, August 2020.

Jamison, Leslie. "Instead of Sobbing, You Write Sentences: An Interview with Charles D'Ambrosio." *New Yorker*, November 2014.

Kingsolver, Barbara. *Demon Copperhead*. HarperCollins, 2022.

———. *Flight Behavior*. HarperCollins, 2012.

———. *High Tide in Tucson: Essays from Now or Never*. HarperCollins, 1995.

———. Interview by Flora Lichtman (host), "Climate Change Takes Flight in New Novel." NPR, *Talk of the Nation*, November 9, 2012.

Kurlansky, Mark. *Salt: A World History*. Bloomsbury, 2003.

Larkin, Philip. "The Pleasure Principle." In *Required Writing: Miscellaneous Pieces 1955–1982*. Farrar, Straus and Giroux, 1982, 1983.

Laurentiis, Rickey, and Sara Slaughter. "Rickey Laurentiis Interviewed Before Headlining New Orleans New Writers Literary Festival," *Room 220*, March 14, 2016.

Levertov, Denise. *Poems 1972–1982*. New Directions, 2001.

Lewis, Sarah. *The Rise: Creativity, the Gift of Failure, and the Search for Mastery*. Simon & Schuster, 2014.

Machado, Carmen Maria. "Inventory." In *Her Body and Other Parties: Stories*. Graywolf Press, 2017.

Madden, T Kira. *Long Live the Tribe of Fatherless Girls: A Memoir*. Bloomsbury USA, 2019.

Madden, T Kira, and Pik-Shuen Fung. "Discovering the Illusion: An Interview with T Kira Madden." *The Margins*, March 2019.

Mann, Randall, and Tobias Wray. "The *Duende* of Poetry: A Conversation Between Randall Mann and Tobias Wray." *The Adroit Journal* 36, January 2021.

Mann, Randall. "Straight Razor." In *Straight Razor: Poems*. Persea Books, 2013.

Miller, Brenda. "We Regret to Inform You." In *An Earlier Life*. Ovenbird Books, 2016.

Moore, Lorrie. "People Like That Are the Only People Here: Canonical Babbling in Peed Onc." In *Birds of America*. Picador, 1998.

Mouritz, Adrian P. *Introduction to Aerospace Materials*. Woodhead Publishing, 2012.

Mullen, Harryette. "[Kills bugs dead.]" In *Recyclopedia: Trimmings, S*PeRM**K*T, and Muse & Drudge*. Graywolf Press, 2006.

Nelson, Maggie. *Bluets*. Wave Books, 2009.

Nunez, Sigrid. *The Friend*. Riverhead Books, 2018.

Nunez, Sigrid, and Monika Zaleska. "You Can't Explain Death to An Animal: An Interview with Sigrid Nunez," Literary Hub, 2018.

O'Brien, Tim. *The Things They Carried*. Houghton Mifflin, 1990.

Offutt, Chris. "The Eleventh Draft." In *The Eleventh Draft: Craft and the Writing Life from the Iowa Writers' Workshop*, edited by Frank Conroy. William Morrow, 1999.

O'Hara, Frank. *The Collected Poems of Frank O'Hara*. Alfred A. Knopf, 1971.

Oliver, Mary. "At Black River." *Poetry*, August 2003.

Ondaatje, Michael. *The English Patient*. Alfred A. Knopf, 1992.

Orner, Peter. "Writing About What Haunts Us." In *Am I Alone Here?: Notes on Living to Read and Reading to Live*. Catapult Books, 2016.

Orr, Gregory. *Poetry as Survival*. University of Georgia Press, 2002.

Orwell, George. *1984*. Harcourt, 1949.

Peelle, Lydia. "Reasons for and Advantages of Breathing." In *Reasons for and Advantages of Breathing: Stories*. HarperCollins, 2009.

Peters, Sara. "Mercury." In *I Become a Delight to My Enemies*. Strange Light Books, 2019.

Pevear, Richard. "Introduction." In Fyodor Dostoevsky, *The Brothers Karamazov*. North Point Press, 1990.

Pound, Ezra. "A Few Don'ts by an Imagiste." *Poetry*, 1913.

Reidy, Eric. "Ghost Boat: Episode 1: How do you find a boat that vanished without a trace?" *Medium*, October 2015.

Rich, Adrienne. "For This." In *Fox: Poems 1998–2000*. W. W. Norton, 2001.

Ryan, Kay. "Turtle." In *Flamingo Watching: Poems*. Copper Beech Press, 1994.

Sendak, Maurice. "You Have to Take the Dive." TateShots (Tate Modern, December 2011).

Shaw, Stewart. "daddy sings us goodbyes." *African American Review* 50, no. 3 (Fall 2017): 326–27.

Shepherd, Reginald. *Orpheus in the Bronx: Essays on Identity, Politics, and the Freedom of Poetry*. University of Michigan Press, 2008.

Smith, Danez. "summer, somewhere." In *Don't Call Us Dead: Poems*. Graywolf Press, 2017.

Strayed, Cheryl. "Write Like a Motherfucker." In *Tiny Beautiful Things: Advice on Love and Life from Dear Sugar*. Vintage Books, 2012.

Sullivan, John Jeremiah. "Mister Lytle." *The Paris Review*, Fall 2010.

Taylor, Jill Bolte. "My Stroke of Insight." TED Talk transcript, 2008.

Temple, Emily. "Jamaica Kincaid on How to Live and How to Write." Literary Hub, 2017.

Torres, Justin. *Blackouts*. Farrar, Straus and Giroux, 2023.

———. "We Wanted More." In *We the Animals*. Houghton Mifflin Harcourt, 2011.

Walker, Nicole. "The Braided Essay as Social Justice Action." *Creative Nonfiction* 64 (Summer 2017).

Welty, Eudora. "Must the Novelist Crusade?" *The Atlantic*, October 1965.

White, Darryl. "The Arachne Gene." *The Write Launch* 18 (October 2018).

Winterson, Jeanette. *The Passion*. Bloomsbury, 1987.

Yakich, Mark. *Poetry: A Survivor's Guide*. Bloomsbury Academic, 2015.

Yuknavitch, Lidia. "Woven." *Guernica*, August 2015.

Credits

Hanif Abdurraqib, "The Author Writes the First Draft of His Wedding Vows," by Hanif Abdurraqib, from *The Crown Ain't Worth Much*. Copyright © 2016 by Hanif Aburraqib. Courtesy of Button Publishing Inc.

Elizabeth Alexander, "Ars Poetica #100: I Believe," from *Crave Radiance: New and Selected Poems 1990–2010*. Copyright © 2005 by Elizabeth Alexander. Reprinted with the permission of The Permissions Company LLC on behalf of Graywolf Press, Minneapolis, Minnesota, graywolfpress.org.

Hilton Als, "Toni Morrison's Profound and Unrelenting Vision," by Hilton Als, *New Yorker* © Condé Nast.

Hala Alyan, "Oklahoma," from *Poetry* magazine (July/August 2017). Used with permission of the author.

Will Baker, "Grace Period," story from *Flash Fiction: 72 Very Short Stories* (W. W. Norton), 1992. Used with permission of the Baker family.

Ellen Bass, "Any Common Desolation," from *Indigo*. Originally published in Poem-a-Day on November 18, 2016, by the Academy of American Poets. Copyright © 2016, 2020 by Ellen Bass. Reprinted with the permission of The Permissions Company LLC on behalf of Copper Canyon Press, coppercanyonpress.org.

Ellen Bass, "Controlled Chaos" excerpts are taken from Ellen Bass's "Living Room Craft Talks," available online at ellenbass.com. Used with permission of the author.

Ellen Bass, "The Thing Is," from *Mules of Love*. Copyright © 2002 by Ellen Bass. Reprinted with the permission of The Permissions Company LLC on behalf of BOA Editions Ltd., boaeditions.org.

Jill Bialosky, "LV. Snow of Childhood," from *Asylum: A Personal, Historical, Natural Inquiry in 103 Lyric Sections*, by Jill Bialosky, copyright © 2020 by Jill Bialosky. Used by permission of Alfred A. Knopf, an imprint of the Knopf Doubleday Publishing Group, a division of Penguin Random House LLC. All rights reserved.

Stephanie Bishop, "In Praise of Destruction: How Embracing Elimination Can Make Our Writing Better," Literary Hub, July 2023. Used with permission of the author.

Jenny Boully, *The Body: An Essay* (March 1, 2007), used with permission of the author, Jenny Boully.

Joseph Brodsky, excerpt from "1 January 1965," from *Joseph Brodsky: Selected Poems*, by Joseph Brodsky, translated by George Kline. English translation copyright © 1973 by George L. Kline. Reprinted by permission of Farrar, Straus and Giroux. All rights reserved.

Katie L. Burke, "First Person: Mona Hanna-Attisha" (2019), reprinted with the permission of *American Scientist*, magazine of Sigma Xi, Scientific Research Honor Society.

Ciaran Carson, excerpt from "The Fetch," by Ciaran Carson, from *For All We Know* (2008), Wake Forest University Press, and *Collected Poems: Volume One* (2023), published by The Gallery Press. www.gallerypress.com.

Ann Charters, from *The Story and Its Writer: An Introduction to Short Fiction*, by Ann Charters, © 2006 by Bedford Books.

Teju Cole, excerpts from "Tivoli," from *Blind Spot*, by Teju Cole, copyright © 2016, 2017 by Teju Cole. Used by permission of Random House, an imprint and division of Penguin Random House LLC. All rights reserved.

Peter Orner, "Writing About What Haunts Us," from *Am I Alone Here: Notes on Living to Read and Reading to Live*. Originally appeared in the *The New York Times* (January 12, 2013). Copyright © 2013, 2016 by Peter Orner. Reprinted with the permission of The Permissions Company LLC on behalf of Counterpoint Press, counterpointpress.com.

Gregory Orr, from *Poetry as Survival*, by Gregory Orr, copyright © 2002 by University of Georgia Press.

George Orwell, from *1984*, by George Orwell. Copyright © 1949 by Harcourt Inc. and renewed 1977 by Sonia Brownell Orwell. Used by permission of HarperCollins Publishers.

Lydia Peelle, "Reasons for and Advantages of Breathing," from *Reasons for and Advantages of Breathing: Stories*, by Lydia Peelle. Copyright © 2009 by Lydia Peelle. Used by permission of HarperCollins Publishers. Reprinted by permission of Georges Borchardt Inc. on behalf of the author.

Sara Peters, "Mercury," from *I Become a Delight to My Enemies*, © Strange Light Books, 2019.

Richard Pevear, excerpt from "Introduction" by Richard Pevear, from *The Brothers Karamazov*, by Fyodor Dostoevsky, translated by Richard Pevear and Larissa Volokhonsky. Copyright © 1990 by Richard Pevear and Larissa Volokhonsky. Reprinted by permission of North Point Press, a division of Farrar, Straus and Giroux. All rights reserved.

Ryan Pittington, exercise example contributor. Used with permission of the author, Ryan Pittington.

Ezra Pound, "A Few Don'ts by an Imagiste," by Ezra Pound, *Poetry* magazine, March 1913.

Eric Reidy, "Ghost Boat." Used with permission of the author.

Adrienne Rich, "For This," by Adrienne Rich. Copyright © 2001 by Adrienne Rich. Used by permission of W. W. Norton & Company Inc.

Zac Russi, exercise example contributor, used with permission of the author, Zac Russi.

Jeanette Russo, exercise example contributor, used with permission of the author, Jeanette Russo.

Kay Ryan, "Turtle," from *Flamingo Watching: Poems*, by Kay Ryan. Originally published by Copper Beech Press. Used with permission of the author.

Maurice Sendak (interviewee), from the transcript/interview "You Have to Take the Dive" from TateShots for Tate Modern.

Stewart Shaw, "daddy sings us goodbyes," published in *African American Review*, vol. 50, no. 3, Fall 2017, and republished in the collection *The House of Men: Poems*, Glass Lyre Press, 2019. Used with permission of the author.

Reginald Shepherd, from *Orpheus in the Bronx: Essays on Identity, Politics, and the Freedom of Poetry*, by Reginald Shepherd. Used with permission of the University of Michigan Press.

Danez Smith, excerpt from "summer, somewhere," from *Don't Call Us Dead*. Copyright © 2017 by Danez Smith. Reprinted with permission of The Permissions Company LLC on behalf of Graywolf Press, graywolfpress.org.

Cheryl Strayed, excerpt from Cheryl Strayed's Facebook page. Used with permission of the author.

Cheryl Strayed, "Write Like a Motherfucker," from *Tiny Beautiful Things: Advice on Love and Life from Dear Sugar*, by Cheryl Strayed, copyright © 2012 by Cheryl Strayed. Used by permission of Vintage Books, an imprint of the Knopf Doubleday Publishing Group, a division of Penguin Random House LLC. All rights reserved.

John Jeremiah Sullivan, "Mister Lytle," originally published in *The Paris Review*. Copyright © 2010 by John Jeremiah Sullivan, used by permission of The Wylie Agency LLC.

Terese Svoboda, original interview, used with permission of Terese Svoboda, author of 21 books of poetry, fiction, biography, memoir, and translation.

Syntax, information about, used with permission of Poetry Archive Glossary, poetryarchive.org/glossary.

Jill Bolte Taylor, from "My Stroke of Insight" (TED Talk transcript). Excerpts used with permission of the author.

Index